FRENCH CULTURAL POLITICS & MUSIC

FRENCH CULTURAL POLITICS & MUSIC

From the Dreyfus Affair
to the First World War

JANE F. FULCHER

New York   Oxford

Oxford University Press

1999

Oxford University Press

Oxford   New York
Athens   Auckland   Bangkok   Bogotá   Buenos Aires   Calcutta
Cape Town   Chennai   Dar es Salaam   Delhi   Florence   Hong Kong   Istanbul
Karachi   Kuala Lumpur   Madrid   Melbourne   Mexico City   Mumbai
Nairobi   Paris   São Paulo   Singapore   Taipei   Tokyo   Toronto   Warsaw

and associated companies in
Berlin   Ibadan

Copyright © 1999 by Oxford University Press, Inc.

Published by Oxford University Press, Inc.
198 Madison Avenue, New York, New York 10016

Oxford is a registered trademark of Oxford University Press.

Library of Congress Cataloging-in-Publication Data
Fulcher, Jane F.
French cultural politics and music : from the Dreyfus affair to
the first world war / Jane F. Fulcher.
p.   cm.
Includes bibliographical references and index.
ISBN 0-19-512021-3
1. Music—France—20th century—History and criticism.
2. Music—France—19th century—History and criticism.
3. Music and society—France—History—20th century.
4. Music and society—France—History—19th century.
5. Music—Philosophy and aesthetics.
I. Title.
ML270.5.F85   1998
780'.944'0904—dc21   98-12193

1 3 5 7 9 8 6 4 2

Printed in the United States of America
on acid-free paper

To My Mother and
the Memory of My Father

ACKNOWLEDGMENTS

I am deeply grateful to many friends and colleagues in musicology, history, sociology, art history, and literary studies in both the United States and Europe who helped me so generously with this project. The historians Roger Chartier and Jacques Revel of the Ecole des Hautes Etudes en Sciences Sociales in Paris provided me with not only ideas and advice but also the valuable opportunity to present material from my study in their seminars at the Ecole as "Directeur d'Etudes Associé" in 1996. I have profited greatly from conversations with the sociologist Pierre Bourdieu, of the Collège de France, who graciously read much of my work and invited me to present aspects of it in his seminar, from which I gained a great deal. Christophe Charle, of the Department of History at Université de Paris I, was always ready to discuss my ideas and to provide references and rare material to which he had access; he also gave me the valuable opportunity to present parts of my work to his seminar. The historian Maurice Agulhon of the Collège de France generously took time to talk with me and to provide further references and advice.

I am grateful to the composer-philosopher Hugues Dufourt and to the musicologist Joël-Marie Fauquet for their interest and their help and for welcoming me to their seminar on music history at the Centre National de la Récherche Scientifique in Paris while I was a visiting "Directeur de Récherche" there in the fall of 1991. While a fellow at the Wissenschaftskolleg zu Berlin in 1986–87, I profited from the help and the perspective of the historian Maurice Garden, the sociologist (and director of the Institute) Wolf Lepenies, and the musicologist Herbert Schneider, who graciously came to and commented on the lecture I presented there on my material.

Colleagues at Indiana University have been of invaluable assistance throughout the research and writing of this book, providing me with help, encouragement, and advice from the perspectives of their various fields. William Cohen, of the History Department, was always ready to share his expertise on France in this period and to give me information, advice, encouragement, and a steady stream of valuable bibliographic references. Gilbert Chaitin, of the French Department and Comparative Literature, generously shared his knowledge of the period and its sources, as well as of relevant theoretical texts, and read part of the manuscript, offering very helpful suggestions. Rosemary Lloyd, chair of the French Department, provided constant encouragement, as well as a valuable literary perspective on the late nineteenth century. Ingeborg Hoesterey, of the Department of Germanic Studies and Comparative Literature, was a continual source of advice concerning both theoretical works and comparative studies on literature and the visual arts. Marc Weiner, of the Department of Germanic Studies, was a stimulating source of conversation and information concerning both Wagner and anti-Semitism. I also profited from conversations with Richard Bauman, of the Folklore Department, concerning the field of "performance studies" and the relevant anthropological literature. I am particularly grateful to Brian Hart, who was writing his dissertation on the related subject of the French symphony under my direction during the period while I was at work on this book. Both he and his study were a continual source of references and information, as may be seen by the many citations from his excellent work throughout this volume.

I am also indebted to American, Canadian, British, French, and German colleagues in musicology, who provided me with stimulating conversation, comments, references, encouragement, and sources. These include Richard Leppert, Sabina Ratner, Richard Taruskin, Philip Gossett, David Grayson, Annegret Fauser, Manuela Schwartz, Hermann Danuser, Jan Pasler, Martin Marks, Leslie Wright, Elizabeth Bartlet, Roger Parker, Ruth Solie, Elinor Olin, Miriam Chimènes, Michael Strasser, Pamela Potter, Steven Huebner, Marion Green, Jean Gribenski, François Lesure, and the late Patrick Gillis. Both European and American colleagues in history, art history, and sociology were valuable sources of information, advice, references, and conversation about my material. These include the historians Peter Jelavich, William Weber, Robert Wohl, Michael Steinberg, Joel Blatt, Avner Ben-Amos, Marie-Claude Gênet-Delacroix, Patrice Veit, Donna Evleth, Christophe Prochasson, Christian Jouhaud, Jean Hébrard, and Etienne François and the sociologists Antoine Hennion, Pierre Birnbaum, and Pierre-Michel Menger. I am grateful to the art historian Melissa McQuillan, who invited me to present part of my material in a session she organized at the national meeting of the British Association of Art Historians in 1989 and from which I gained a great deal.

I am especially grateful to the historian Carl E. Schorske, who has not only inspired me to pursue cultural history (as a musicologist) but generously encouraged and helped to guide my work over the past twenty years. I am also very grateful to the musicologist Edward Lippman, whose excellent training in musical aesthetics and encouragement of a broad perspective have been so central to my endeavor. Finally, I wish to thank the four anonymous readers of my manuscript for their suggestions.

In addition to support from the Centre National de la Recherche Scientifique, the Ecole des Hautes Etudes en Sciences Sociales in Paris, and the Wissenschaftskolleg zu Berlin, I received a fellowship for individual research from the National Endowment for the Humanities and grants from the program in West European Studies and the Office of Research and Graduate Development at Indiana University.

CONTENTS

FRENCH CULTURAL
POLITICS & MUSIC

INTRODUCTION

This book is about a phenomenon of central importance to cultural studies and, as such, to current attempts to situate musical culture within a historical landscape. Its subject is the "invasion" of one cultural area or field by another—in this case the *occupation* of French musical culture by political culture at the turn of the century.

As this volume demonstrats, the impact of the phenomenon was both broad and profound: it affected all aspects of French musical culture, which reacted back on political culture itself. Hence, as opposed to existing music histories, it argues not only that this political penetration occurred but also that perceiving it opens new perspectives on contemporary French musical semiotics and values; meanings and priorities we have previously construed as "purely aesthetic," autonomous, or related to the inner dynamics of the art and the field were, rather, freighted with ideological significance. Underlying this conviction lies the premise that in order to comprehend this fact we must reexamine the transformation of French political culture during and after the Dreyfus Affair.

Historians of France have long established the ideological roots of the Dreyfus Affair, or the enduring conflicts it articulated and that helped to imbue it with the power of myth. Extending back to the French Revolution, they lay specifically in what Timothy Tackett has referred to aptly as the "tragic flaw at the core of the first revolutionary settlement" (p. 313). Although Enlightenment ideals had triumphed, they were not founded on complete consensus, especially concerning models of government or the relation between Church and State: the counterrevolution implacably kept both of these sensitive issues alive—conflicts henceforth embedded in postrevolutionary France, ready to explode in the right political compound. This occurred once again in the late nineteenth century, when the Boulanger and the Panama scandals helped incite antiparliamentary and anti-Semitic sentiments, formulating the chemistry that the affair would ignite.

Myriad histories have narrated the events that constituted the Dreyfus Affair and established their role in helping to transform contemporary political culture in France. Succinctly, in 1894 a Jewish captain in the army, Alfred Dreyfus, was summarily convicted in a court-martial of selling French military secrets to the Germans. Public opinion was at first solidly in support of the army's conclusions, but in 1896 the chief of intelligence, Colonel Picquart, discovered exculpatory evidence: it implicated not Alfred Dreyfus but rather a Major Esterhazy, who was subsequently tried but ultimately acquitted by French army authorities.

At this point, Dreyfus's brother, Mathieu, contacted Emile Zola, the prominent novelist, whose interest in Republican politics was, by now, widely known; Zola, perceiving a miscarriage of justice replete with far greater implications, determined, with the temerity of a renowned public figure, to bring the scandalous "affair" to light. In 1898, with shrewd effrontery, he published an open letter to the president of the Republic, consisting of a litany of charges, all beginning with the words "J'accuse" (I accuse). It resulted in an indictment for libel. Zola's subsequent publicized trial and conviction, while compelling him to flee for England, expanded the arena of the "Dreyfus Affair."

Now in the public sphere, it seized the attention and spurred the engagement of not only major political but intellectual and literary figures on both sides of the question. They, like Zola, recast the issues as a referendum on those that had bifurcated France since the Revolution, and particularly since the birth of the Third Republic in 1870: Did "tradition" and the rights of the State take precedence over those of the individual citizen? Did those of the army outweigh civil authority, even if the former were found in error? Two conceptions of France baldly confronted each other once more, as they had in 1789 and have periodically ever since. One maintained the incontrovertible authority of the army, the Church, and the nation, while the other implacably asserted the judicial and egalitarian ideals of the French Revolution. New tactics of political organization and direct intervention immediately spawned to mobilize individuals and groups for alignment on each side of the incendiary ideological questions: political leagues, demonstrations, and petitions now thrust their way into French public life, politicizing new social groups and rending most sectors of society in France.[1]

Strenuous ideological combat did not subside with the "closure" of the Dreyfus Affair—the presidential pardon of Dreyfus in 1899, followed by his exoneration in 1906. Defeated French nationalists refused to concede and pertinaciously continued the fight through two of the leagues that survived by refocusing their aims—the Ligue de la Patrie Française and the Action Française.[2] These leagues did share certain features with others (of the Right) that were born of the Dreyfus Affair and the preceding political scandals, such as the Ligue des Patriotes and

the Ligue anti-Sémitique: as opposed to political parties, which proposed a
"global" program, or an ideological blueprint for society, leagues were distinguished by their strictly limited political aims. They wished to "destabilize" the
government, believing the parliament to protect special interests, thus to be
guilty of corruption as well as irresponsibly negligent of the French electorate. In
search of a more unified society, they rejected political parties as too divisive and
embraced anti-Semitism, perceiving Jews as yet another factor in the loss of community. And, finally, unlike parties, which they held were incapable of articulating public opinion or aspirations, the leagues advocated "direct action"—mobi-
lization of the "masses," both metaphorically and in the streets.[3]

What distinguished the Ligue de la Patrie Française was, first, a more specific
ideological goal, despite an absence of the doctrinal coherence that would appear
with the Action Française.[4] The other distinguishing factors of the league (as well
as of the Action Française) were its membership, the nature of its "program," and
the kind of impact it would have. Both leagues were conceived by an intellectual
elite and, despite their more limited membership, acted as "zones of high ideological pressure," influential in the circulation of French nationalist ideology.[5]
But most significant here is that both now turned to the domain of culture in
order, legally, to prolong the war over contestatory conceptions of essential
French values. Cultural criticism thus became for them a form of political intervention and action, a means to articulate and indirectly diffuse their conceptions
of the "authentic essence" of France. The Patrie Française, moreover, sought to
prove that the Left had no monopoly on "intelligence" and hence recruited those
brilliant intellectual personalities who seemed sympathetic to its point of view.[6]

Prominent in both leagues were writers, or those whose major concern was
the arts, particularly Maurice Barrès (in the Patrie Française) and Charles Maurras (in the Action Française).[7] Political and literary historians have amply established the conceptual connection that these thinkers and their followers helped
to forge between French nationalist ideology and artistic values.[8] Most recently,
David Carroll has emphasized the central and seminal nationalist conception of
the culturally unified nation as the cognate of a great work of art. For Barrès and
Maurras, politics and art were to be imbued with the same "national spirit," from
which each was originally born, and which inherently endowed them with an
identical nature.[9] As Carroll observes, for Maurras the strength of the nation, its
fundamental unifying principle, was determined by history and supported by tradition in a manner analogous to great art. Hence, literature, for the far Right,
would become "the principal model and support of politics," expressive of "the
ideal form and fundamental nature of the national community and the people."[10]

Maurice Barrès placed consistent emphasis on the tight imbrication of nationalist politics and art, stressing in particular the role of art in "the mythologiz-
ing" of the nation. For Barrès as well as for Maurras, revolution in culture (including the arts) was no less than essential—a prerequisite for the return to an
endemic state, organically at one with the nation. Both authors were henceforth
to be central in what Carroll has termed the fascist "aestheticizing of politics,"
which would concomitantly contribute to the further politicizing of art in
France.[11]

FRENCH NATIONALIST LEAGUES AND MUSIC

The impact of such nationalist theories was by no means limited to politics and literature in France: the two leagues strove to implement them throughout French culture, with ramifications we have not yet fully appreciated. This they were able to do through various new networks of communication and "sociability," such as journals, publishing houses, and several prestigious Parisian salons. These all facilitated the circulation of nationalist doctrine throughout the arts, as well as its common vocabulary and its distinctive set of metaphors and historical references.[12] Historians of art have recently begun to address the intriguing question of how this nationalist "campaign" helped to transform the criteria of aesthetic legitimacy and thus critical standards. As they have shown, well before World War I art critics and nationalist writers were applying such politicized conceptions, and thus subtly shaping aesthetic direction in art: throughout the decade preceding the war, the conceptual and aesthetic terrain was being prepared for a return to tradition and an elevation of classicism as the French "national style."[13]

Analysis of the impact of nationalist cultural initiatives on music is only beginning, and it is the goal of this book to reveal how profoundly the field was, in fact, affected.[14] As I shall demonstrate, not only was the musical world "invaded" as a part of the cultural aggression of these two leagues after the Dreyfus Affair—the Republic "had" to respond. In this manner the field of music was penetrated by political ideology so overtly and directly that it indeed recalls the politicization of music during the French Revolution.[15]

Distinctive in music was the institutional dimension. To a greater extent than in other cultural fields, professional training and thus "consecration" in music was dominated by a state institution. The Conservatoire National de Musique controlled "legitimate" education in music, but it now found itself confronted by a nationalist challenger in the form of the Schola Cantorum. The latter's eventual director, Vincent d'Indy, was a prominent member of the Ligue de la Patrie Française, and through the school he set about establishing a musical culture in systematic opposition: he marshaled the prestige and resources of the league and took advantage of the widespread perception of the pedagogical limitations of the Conservatoire in order to legitimize his own school of music. The resulting institutional opposition was eventually to generate a structural opposition, at once both professional and ideological, that would gradually pervade the French musical world; each side would produce its own conmpositional groupings and find supporters not only in the press and salons but through the official, academic world or through the cognate nationalist "institutes."

The Schola Cantorum did not just define a specific range of musical values that it considered to be "national"; it established a "code" that associated these values with genres, styles, repertoires, and techniques. Hence, while literature diffused nationalist "ideas," as embodied creatively in fictional form, and the visual arts engaged with politically charged images, music opened up another powerful realm:[16] it "manifested" nationalist values through a potent symbolism that was inherently bivocal—that is, simultaneously resonant in invoking the fields of both French politics and art.

Music was valuable as a symbol, for these nationalist leagues were well aware of all it could evoke when framed by a discourse that imbued it with ideological meaning: it could engage the realm of what Freud refers to as "primary process thought," or what is associated with "projection, fantasy, and the incorporation of disparate ideas."[17] Hence, it was particularly useful for the French nationalist Right in this period because, as such, it was inherently immune to conventional rational Republican critique. The Republic, which to this point had largely neglected to imprint its values through music, now responded in kind, making it an agent in the battle over political-symbolic domination.[18] The "war" would bifurcate French music, which, far from being monolothic and dominated by "impressionism," was sundered by aesthetic-ideological disputes, a phenomenon that our histories have too often dismissed.

CONTENT AND ORGANIZATION

Part I of this study analyzes the process through which French music was pulled into the cultural war launched by these nationalist leagues as a response to their defeat in the Dreyfus Affair. Temporally, it concerns the period between 1899 and 1905, under the anticlerical ministry of Waldeck-Rousseau, a coalition of Radical-Socialists, Socialists, and Moderates.[19] Its central concern is the institutional opposition, how it developed and spread throughout the French musical world, and how this structure of confrontation and the stylistic codes it created affected the music taught, supported, performed, and composed.

Chapter 1 examines the Schola, and particularly the resonant new discourse it developed, one that transcended political abstractions and evocatively conflated political, religious, and aesthetic dimensions. It reveals, in particular, not only how closely d'Indy's ideas mirrored those of Barrès but also how they generated the code that associated them with genres, styles, repertoires, and techniques. The chapter then turns to how the Republic first responded through the intermediary of the Dreyfusard composer Alfred Bruneau, who forged a Republican discourse for the musical programs of the 1900 Exposition; it traces how opposing political values thus articulated with aesthetic oppositions and analyzes the symbolic structure of this ideological confrontation, or the stylistic and formal qualities that encoded it. From here it examines the networks through which supporters on both sides of the battle disseminated the doctrines and codes of the warring institutions, affecting the musical culture at large.

Concomitantly, chapter 1 reveals that arguments over canonicity were central in these disputes, involving partisan scholars and critics in addition to institutions that were henceforth locked in battle. Moreover, in contrast to the Conservatoire, the Schola created a canon that was not just used for pedagogical study but publicly performed, framed by a discourse that explained its political significance. As this chapter demonstrates, the French university system soon responded to the Schola's challenge in music history and the canon, leading to the flourishing of musicology in France.

Chapter 2 concerns those composers who responded most prominently and directly to the battle or to the growing politicization they experienced throughout French musical culture. It reveals the impact of the Dreyfus Affair on the way in which French musicians conceived their role—as engaged intellectuals—joining political parties or participating in associated projects and journals. As it further demonstrates, some reacted by consciously employing new politicized meanings; others found that their works, conceived outside these codes, were nevertheless construed within their framework.

D'Indy, in the first case, responded not only through his pedagogy at the Schola Cantorum, but also through specific compositions that were intended to encode an anti-Dreyfusard ideological message. But such was not the case with the politically active composer Gustave Charpentier, who found that the message he had intended in his earlier naturalist opera *Louise* was misconstrued in this context. Chapter 2 analyzes the gulf between his attempt in this work at a multi-layered projection of his own psychosocial condition and its interpretation as Dreyfusard, on the basis of subject and style. As it demonstrates, the work's inherent polyvalence was temporarily and unfortunately fixed and, thus, its message distorted within this framework of signification; for naturalism in opera had become associated with a Dreyfusard stance because of the operatic collaboration of Emile Zola and Alfred Bruneau.

By focusing on stylistic codes of meaning as understood within the period, this study seeks to avoid imputing political meanings on the basis of our current perceptions of political homologies or metaphors. Such an "essentialist" approach (which posits an absolute connection between style and ideology, ignoring the political valences of styles in different contexts) must be replaced by the historical and anthropological study of meaning.[20] We must attempt to excavate the systems of meaning in which specific works were both conceived by composers and then understood by audiences of the time—which were not necessarily identical. In the case of *Louise,* we shall find that the two were indeed substantially different; moreover, the context of performance played a central role in determining how the contemporary public and critics "read" the work. Presented with the support of the Republic, at one of its theaters shortly after the Affair, the highly personal message of *Louise* was submerged by the context, which skewed it ideologically. As this book demonstrates, although politics was not always present in the messages or modes of communication of the music, it affected conditions of both presentation and reception.

Chapter 2 further demonstrates (as does chapter 4) that the relation between music and ideological meaning was mutable—transformable through the political, intellectual context, as well as through the dynamics of performance. Not only could different systems of meaning be applied in interpretation, but the manner, venue, and political context of presentation could play a politically semantic role. This was true of contemporary French music, but also of the canon or the "classics," particularly those of Rameau and Beethoven, as we see in chapters 1 and 3. Traditional "reception history," centered on the "horizons of expectation" of a given audience, cannot account for such factors in a performing art such as music. A central goal of this book is to establish that, in interpreting the meaning of a work historically, we must, like anthropologists, examine how significance was constructed, on all its levels, by contemporaries. Certainly, we cannot ignore the inherent qualities of the work or text, but we must strive to understand what could credibly be done with it by different groups under certain circumstances.[21]

Chapter 2 goes on to explore the case of other composers, like Albéric Magnard, who were equally victimized by a politicized culture that misread or refused to register their message. Magnard emphatically declined to accept the dominant codes of meaning and attempted to articulate a Dreyfusard message, using what was considered an "anti-Dreyfusard style." Finally, chapter 2 examines responses to the pervasive politicization in other aspects and venues of the musical world, including repertoire choices, official subventions, and musical journalism. As it shows, the same codes of meaning were at work throughout these domains: no aspect of French musical culture was spared from the battle waged by the two nationalist leagues.

Part II concerns the escalation and the further ramifications of this battle as new groupings publicly entered the political-cultural arena between 1905 and the advent of the war. Temporally it begins with the dissolution of Emile Combes's ministry and its anticlerical program, which was followed by a more conservative collaboration of Radicals and Moderates in the new government. Within this changed political context, chapter 3 explores how the existing aesthetic-political discourses were addressed by others that were tied to new French ideological positions; specifically, it examines the new musical programs that emerged with the unification of the "internationalist" French Socialist Party, as well as the points of emphasis that it introduced into the political-cultural dialogue. Just as important, it considers the response of those who were dissatisfied with both Right and Left and who joined together briefly as "National-Socialists," with their own distinct aesthetic ideals. Prominent here, too, was the Action Française, which implacably intensified its battle not only on official culture in general but specifically on the educational system, which included the Conservatoire.

Chapter 3 also examines how the government responded to this damaging assault on its legitimacy through a thorough reform of its own national conservatory of music. As we shall see, the Republic, in spite of the Conservatoire's institutional inertia, finally brought about badly needed changes because of the symbolic challenge of the Schola and its many advocates; however, its new director, Gabriel Fauré, had to balance these reforms (largely drawn, if modified, from the Schola) with values that resonated symbolically with the Republic's own political ideas. Again, the translation from political concepts to musical principles is not transparent, for it had to do with opposition to the Schola, as well as with the Conservatoire's social role and traditions.

Important here were journalists and writers on music, who entered the battle of the two institutions and their associated compositional factions, now called "chapelles." As this chapter demonstrates, they perceptively analyzed the interests that lay beneath each, drawing an explicit connection, as they perceived it, between musical taste and French political ideologies; moreover, they astutely pointed out the difficult position into which French composers were thrust, often for professional reasons being forced into an alliance with one of the camps. Professional and political stakes were inseparable: aesthetic groupings were instinct with ideological dimensions, drawing their support from the government or its opponents, which even partisan critics could see.

Finally, as this chapter illuminates, the symbolic battle was being fought through various controversies or skirmishes between the warring compositional schools or "chapelles." These disputes, again, no longer transparent or consistent in their logic today, refracted ideological oppositions through the prism of French musical and aesthetic issues. Here it is also important to note that such altercations were closely related to, and in some cases generated by, those already rending other French cultural fields. Hence, it is within this context that disputes we have not perceived as ideologically charged emerge as fraught with value-tensions that were inseparably bound to the political world. As this study thus consistently argues, it is impossible fully to grasp this musical culture—its practices, codes, comportment, and discourses—apart from the political culture that impinged upon it.[22]

Chapter 4 returns to the responses of composers, here focusing on those most prominently implicated in cultural conflicts during the period of mounting nationalist hegemony before World War I. Of central concern to this chapter is how those composers most frequently used as symbols or exemplars by the warring schools responded to the battle, and then to nationalist dominance. It examines how they lived and worked in this culture, within its codes of meaning, its professional practices, its contentiousness, and its centralized, bellicose institutions. Here the goal is to reveal how this context helped to shape not only their careers and the reception of their works but also their professional and, in the end, certain creative decisions. It returns to the complex issue, raised in chapter 2, of how composers attempted to inscribe ideology or comment on the warring factions through their style. For they could evince an awareness of the dominant ideological and stylistic orthodoxies by employing current codes creatively, in order to define their own particular stance. One goal here is thus to establish that the semiotics of French music in this period is inseparable from this context and that understanding it helps to uncover new layers to certain works.

No French composer during this period could escape awareness of these structures of meaning or of the battles and tensions that continually subtended the litigious French musical factions. Most did not or could not retreat from politics, now such an integral part of their experience: many engaged it subtly, commenting on the situation in a variety of ways. Some did so more prominently than others during the period under scrutiny here; the latter, such as Ravel and Saint-Saëns, although important, are thus examined only in passing.[23] And since some did indeed participate publicly throughout the entire period under study, and in several different contexts, they are discussed as their roles become relevant, in several of the chapters. Again, because the subject of this study is the interaction of French musical and political cultures and its many effects, now lesser-known composers (such as Magnard, Roussel, and Ropartz) are discussed at some length.

However, of particular importance are the compositional "commentaries" of two major composers—Debussy and Satie—whose works reveal what artists can do creatively with political symbols. While Debussy, here a central figure, grew overtly sympathetic to French nationalist ideology, he refused to adopt its aesthetic orthodoxies, instead forging a unique response. Significantly, his written and verbal discourses were not transcribed through current codes in his music, although the ascription of political meaning to musical styles did influence certain of his choices. Chapter 4 stresses, in particular, the original way in which Debussy, in his later works, related symbolically to the ideas of Barrès, but in a manner far different from that of d'Indy: such ideas—and especially those of the self in relation to the collective—were for him not doctrine to be translated but, rather, an impetus to his creative use of the past.

This volume thus seeks to establish that awareness of Debussy's relation to the ascribed meanings of his period can enrich our understanding of these complex, multivalent works. Clearly, not only minor works were affected by the ideological context of this musical culture fraught with bivocal political-aesthetic disputes: great works responded to these tensions, with a degree of aesthetic integrity that both relates them to and helps them transcend the politicized culture in which they were born.

Another implicit argument in this chapter is that political tensions were here not simply those of class: ideology in this period transcended class divisions, particularly with the advent of a new populist Right. This book thus participates in the more recent turn within French history from a stress on class to cultural representation and language in social formation and identity.[24] Debussy, as Chapter 4 reveals, indeed grew confused in his class identity and, like so many others, found refuge in a nationalist ideological stance.

Erik Satie took the political path opposite to that chosen by his friend Debussy, but he also responded originally with games about current meanings in order to say something "other." This is not to claim that Satie was necessarily supported by those with the same ideological sympathies that he often ironically professed to hold: like Debussy, he consciously sought to confound those politicized critics who would impute a factional position to him on the basis of his musical style. Hence, his polyvalent compositions were used not only by the Radical-Socialist Party (which he joined) but also, in the eve of the war, by the nationalist Right he opposed. Each group "constructed" the composer by emphasizing elements in his style that it perceived plausibly to accord with its own aesthetic-ideological stance. Satie's style was malleable enough to be used by even politically contestatory groups, including those whose positions he protested and that appropriated it in ideologically different ways.

Not all composers responded so creatively. D'Indy and Charpentier became obsessed with political issues and musical-political programs, if from opposite sides of the French political spectrum. Others remained caught in the middle, the victims of increasingly shrill and intolerant camps that were dismayed by the seeming disjunction between their political sympathies and musical style. Chapter 4 concludes by analyzing how the ideological battle continued to rage; the last skirmish before the traditionalist victory was fought over Stravinsky's *Le Sacre du printemps*. It relates the final shift in hegemony to the loss of autonomy in French musical culture, or the inability of the professional world or field to enforce autonomous aesthetic criteria.[25] In this way it seeks to explain the otherwise inexplicable, and often overlooked, return to tradition in music in France well before the First World War.

As this book seeks to establish, throughout these years French music was inextricably bound to the political culture within which it was a symbol and that affected it in multifarious ways. As a result of the initiatives of two French nationalist leagues, other political groupings in France, including the parties in power, came to recognize music's potential ideological agency. Hence, music played a significant role in the ideological and symbolic battle in France before the war, one integrally important to the political combat for French nationalist hegemony.

Cultural divisions between music and politics in this period in France are not easily made; the demarcations were much less clear than today, and the boundaries were continually blurred. To cite the words of Johan Huizinga, the task of a cultural history is to "penetrate" the historical landscape, identifying areas that touched, in an historically unique terrain. This book attempts such a task, but its concern is, ultimately, the results for "meaning" within the two spheres that touched in this period for discernible reasons—those of politics and music. For the goal of cultural history, most fundamentally, is to decipher meanings, to grasp the significations invested in symbolic forms, and it is this intent that has shaped this book.[26]

I

THE BATTLE IS ESTABLISHED
Musicians Enter, 1898–1905

1

THE NEW CULTURAL "WAR" AND
THE FRENCH MUSICAL WORLD

Few historians of France would dispute that the political landscape experienced seismic shifts in the traumatic, tumultuous period during and after the Dreyfus Affair; a new range of political tactics, comportments, practices, and actors made their debut in—to switch to an equally apt metaphor—the new "theater" of French politics. Now making their dramatic appearance on the national stage in this seminal period were political leagues and parties, new social groups, and new forms of propaganda.[1] It is one particular variety of the latter that demands our special attention here because its impact on the musical world in France was to be direct and profound: born in the wake of the Affair, its nexus was the milieu of those defeated—those who refused to capitulate in the struggle for the principles they had defined in the course of the conflict. With the triumphant Third Republic stolidly in control of political discourse, the cynosure of their propagandistic effort henceforth was culture and, above all, the arts.

In the wake of the Affair, French nationalists turned to culture as an effective but indirect means through which to articulate and subtly insinuate the political values they still hoped to diffuse.[2] For the debate over Dreyfus had engaged the central question of French identity, or the fundamental political and moral values for which the nation stood: Did the authority and tradition of the state, the army,

15

the aristocracy, and the Church take precedence over those principles and rights that had been defined so emphatically by the French Revolution? With the closure of the Affair, the question of "What is France?," legally at least, was resolved conclusively in favor of the defenders of the Revolution and of Captain Dreyfus;[3] but the cunning rejoinder of two Rightest leagues that were born of the Affair and that were now redefining their tactics and role was the cognate question "What cultural values are French?"

Originally conceived to act outside the established political channels, the leagues had forged new modes of political activity and enlarged the area of political action;[4] once defeated, two leagues in particular defined the new realm of ideological debate in which they could propagate their conception of French cultural identity—and thus of France as the arts. Actively co-opting prominent critics or writers on the arts, they were also forming critics from within their own networks or producing and infiltrating influential publications. Here, in numerous articles, such writers ascribed political associations or values to styles and concomitantly made aesthetic or artistic legitimacy a political question.

Although the league called the Action Française was soon to be central in this domain, another, initially more influential, was already presciently preparing the way; created directly as a result of the Dreyfus Affair, the nationalist Ligue de la Patrie Française helped shift the political grounds of debate to authentic French culture and art.[5] Indeed, this was implicit in its origins, for the founders of the league had aimed at recruiting not only the political and intellectual elite but also those prominent in the artistic world; significantly, its opening declaration enjoined adherents to work within their professions "à maintenir, en les conciliant avec le progrès des idées et des moeurs, les traditions de la Patrie Française" (to maintain, while conciliating with the progress of ideas and morals, the tradition of the French homeland). Important artists responded, and the directive committee itself included the writers Lemaître, Brunetière, and Barrès, and the composer Vincent d'Indy.

The presence of the musician d'Indy, while often overlooked, should not be minimized, for nowhere was the League de la Patrie Française more successful in its cultural politics than in music. Through d'Indy, it began the process of impregnating French musical discourse with terminology, conceptions, and values that were derived from the political realm. It thus played a pivotal role in making French music a stake in the symbolic battle now being waged by the Republic's critics and in assigning political meaning to style.

Chapter 1 examines the way in which music was drawn into the cultural war that was launched by this French nationalist league in the immediate aftermath of the Dreyfus Affair. It demonstrates how musical programs became, in effect, political initiatives, means to attach ideological meanings to music that could thus symbolically manifest the league's creed. In the course of this chapter we trace the structure of the ideological and institutional opposition established between the Republic's Conservatoire and d'Indy's nationalist cognate, the Schola Cantorum. By analyzing the Schola's program and discourse, we may reveal its close ties to the basic concepts of the Ligue de la Patrie Française, which helped support the school as a vehicle to disseminate its doctrine. We also discover that the Schola, although marginal, developed a wide base of support because of its moral emphasis (interpreted differently by Right and Left) and its badly needed pedagogical reforms.

Just as important within this temporal framework—from the closure of the Affair until 1905, or when the backlash against the leagues was strongest—is the Third Republic's response to the Schola. The latter now ostensibly perceived that French music could be used ideologically as a means to articulate a Republican conception of inherently French cultural values. It responded in stages, beginning with the musical programs of the Universal Exposition of 1900, which defined a Republican canon, framed by the discourse of the Dreyfusard Alfred Bruneau. In this chapter we thus trace the construction of rival models of French musical identity and examine how each side thus availed itself of music to propagate its cultural conception of "France."

In this context, we also see the Republic's simultaneous riposte to the nationalists' attempted appropriation of music history as it promoted it itself through the university system. It was indeed as a result of this cultural war and its battle to define the "quintessentially French" that the discipline of music history began at last to flourish in France. Ideological exchanges were to proliferate in the context of articles and lectures on music in new institutions like the Ecole des Hautes Etudes Sociales, further attaching political meanings to style. This affected almost all aspects of musical culture in France, as it was ineluctably pulled into the combat over competing French political myths.

Our point of departure to understand this phenomenon must necessarily be the Affair itself, and the way in which the political divisions it engendered implicated music, along with other professions. It was, indeed, to the initial engagement of the Dreyfusard composer Alfred Bruneau that d'Indy would eventually respond, if on a deeper, ideological level. Hence, although the Affair itself had little immediate effect on the musical world in France, its long-term effects were to be both profound and tenacious.

The Engagement of French Musicians

The Dreyfus Affair and the divisions that it inevitably engendered spared few of the professions in France; this impact by no means excluded French musicians, particularly those in Paris. They too were approached by leagues and political groups on both sides of the issues and asked to lend their signatures and thus their prestige to the petitions and protests circulated by each side. Why they were sought out and responded publicly becomes less of an enigma if we examine the circumstances, beginning with their changing self-conceptions or professional self-images in the 1890s. This was not only the period when Wagner's works were dominating the operatic stage but also a time when his theoretical writings were widely known and actively read in France. In large part because of his impact, it was not only acceptable but indeed expected that a composer would take an interest in or espouse larger philosophical and social ideas.[6]

In addition, as Christophe Charle has shown, during the period immediately preceding the Affair, social categories and the conceptions of different professions were shifting in France. Even before, intellectuals (although not always referred to specifically as such) were beginning to claim both a special political role and a distinctive power. This was particularly true of artists, who were beginning to conceive of themselves and to be perceived as intellectuals, or as serving as "educators of a new truth." Already by the early 1890s, journals like *Entretiens politiques et littéraires* were equating the two, or grouping French poets together with other intellectuals; devices such as the survey and "protest" were also confounding these categories by approaching writers, journalists, and men of letters alike, and without distinction.[7]

By the decade of the 1890s, French musicians were manifesting awareness of new conceptions of the artist in order to protect their professional interests and, concomitantly, those of French music: concerned that French operas were being abandoned in favor of foreign operatic works, they did not hesitate to lobby the Chamber of Deputies or the relevant ministries on their own behalf. Moreover, they were learning to use the press to identify their specific professional concerns with larger national interests, and thus to win the support of sympathetic politicians.[8] And so it is not surprising that many French musicians aligned themselves politically during the Affair, believing it their responsibility to sign the various polemical documents. Although it is difficult to generalize concerning the mechanisms through which they arrived at their decisions, we may gain some insight by examining several of the important cases.

As is well known, the Dreyfusard "Manifest des Intellectuels" was headed by prominent literary figures, most notably, Emile Zola, Anatole France, and Marcel Proust; but among its myriad other signatories were well-known and now-forgotten French composers, musicians, musical scholars and historians, and critics of music. Most prominent were the composer Charles Koechlin, the music historian Henry Prunières, the composer Alfred Bruneau, and the musical scholar Lionel Dauriac. Signing the opposing petition circulated by the nationalist Ligue de la Patrie Française was the composer Vincent d'Indy, the composer Augusta Holmès, the director of the Opéra Comique Albert Carré, the critic Henri Gauthier-Villars (or "Willy"), the composer Pierre de Bréville, and the professor of music history at the Paris Conservatoire, Louis Bourgault-Ducoudray.

Others hesitated to choose a side but signed the public petition circulated by the Comité de l'Appel à l'Union in favor of reconciliation and first published in *Le Temps* on January 17, 1899. Among those subsequently lending it their signature were the composers Claude Debussy and Gustave Charpentier, the music historian and critic Julien Tiersot, and the conductor Edouard Colonne.[9] The latter case provides special insight since Colonne, who himself was Jewish, expressed his reprehension not of anti-Semitism but of militarism to Saint-Saëns; the latter, although in fact a believer in the innocence of Dreyfus, was deeply disturbed by this remark, pointing out that there had been three generals in his family. Hence, Saint-Saëns refused a request to set a Dreyfusard chanson to music and did not sign petitions, but he did agree to join the Dreyfusard Ligue des Droits de l'Homme.[10]

Yet the leading musical figures in the Affair, those who would go on to make the connection between the political and the artistic principles, were Alfred

Bruneau and Vincent d'Indy. In both cases, the generalization that historians have made concerning the basis for the choice of side among other French artists and intellectuals appear to hold true. Those who wished to uphold positions of dominance in society or their professions and, concomitantly, "tradition," tended to be anti-Dreyfusards. In the world of arts and letters, this prominently included members of the Académie, those who had attained an official consecration, as well as recognized "official" artists.[11] In contrast, those who were outside the established society or "system" and who were not interested in preserving its traditions often tended to be in favor of Dreyfus, as was the case of Alfred Bruneau. But in Bruneau's case there was another compelling reason for his choice: his friendship and professional collaboration with the Dreyfusard leader Emile Zola.

Bruneau had met the writer Zola through a mutual friend, Frantz Jourdain, in 1888, two years after Bruneau had won the Second Grand Prix de Rome. Jourdain, an architect and novelist, was also the founder of the Salon d'Autonome, for which Bruneau was entrusted with organizing a "Section Musicale."[12] The son of a music publisher, Bruneau, although he attended the Paris Conservatoire, was not dependent upon the official system, and he could afford to explore alternatives; this also encouraged his stylistic independence, which grew from his dissatisfaction with the dominant operatic conventions, and led him into the fold of those young composers who were seeking dramatic reform. The latter had grown dissatisfied with what they considered to be the superficial and "Italianate" style associated with French composers of the preceding generation.[13] Although Vincent d'Indy as well would eventually come to share this disdain, Bruneau's solution was distinctive and very different from d'Indy's. For his goal was "logical construction," one that was simultaneously "human" and moving, one that combined poetry with realism by employing contemporary situations to express modern feelings. Like so many other young French composers (including d'Indy), Bruneau, inspired by Wagner, sought to adapt the master's innovations to his own dramatic ends.

Bruneau's meeting with Emile Zola occurred at a propitious moment, when the novelist was becoming increasingly interested in writing for the theater, including the opera. This was the period when Zola was attempting the transcription of his novels for theater and when, from an attempt at greater thematic unity, his style was becoming increasingly symbolic. And perhaps because of his failures in the theater, Zola was now reflecting on theoretical issues and becoming deeply interested in the writings and the ideas of Richard Wagner.[14] Hence, Zola, with Bruneau, immediately embarked on a series of operatic collaborations, beginning with the adaptation of the most appropriate or lyrical of Zola's novels, Le Rêve, in 1891. Other works were soon to follow: L'Attaque du moulin (1892–93), Messidor (1894–96), and L'Ouragan (1897–1900).[15]

The style of these works is important to note, since, when Zola became embroiled in the Dreyfus Affair, they became immediate targets, as well as symbols of a "Dreyfusard style"; as critics quickly perceived, in an attempt to remain as "truthful" as possible to Zola's texts, Bruneau sought to mirror their inflections and accents in the music. Thus the two styles, the literary and the musical, were eventually to be confounded and attacked by critics hostile to both Dreyfus and

Zola and branded with the label "Dreyfusard." It is, then, significant to note that before *Messidor,* Zola's operatic texts were neither in prose nor in informal diction, despite their proletarian subjects: already critics were charging that his texts were pretentious and "inflated" (*gonflée*), and thus unlikely declamation for the characters depicted, as well as monotonous in rhythm. Zola was discovering a basic dilemma for those seeking operatic reform—how to be dramatically realistic in a genre that was inherently so unreal. Such disparity in aesthetic distance, or the problem of operatic verisimilitude, was to lead Zola and Bruneau to both an impasse, and eventually to politicized attacks. In chapter 2 we examine their style in detail in the context of the more successful solution that was discovered by a younger and more gifted French composer, Gustave Charpentier.

Most important here is the critical reception of their operatic works, particularly at the moment when the Dreyfus Affair was reaching its peak of intensity. For the appearance of Zola's devastating article, "J'Accuse," in January 1898, in Clemenceau's *Aurore,* marked a turning point in public responses to the work of both artists. Despite the novelty of his works, Bruneau had become a popular French composer, which had led to his being awarded the Légion d'honneur in 1895; after the appearance of Zola's "J'Accuse," however, Bruneau's musical style, along with Zola's texts, became a target when their operatic works were attacked. For hostility toward Zola was immediately focused on his operas: the popular anti-Dreyfusard press declared them to be as "criminal" as the bomb of the anarchist Ravachol and thus worthy of pursuit as a national "peril." Hence, *Messidor* provided a focus for violent public anti-Dreyfusard demonstrations, first in Nantes and then in other cities, that led to the cancellation of its performances by worried theater directors.[16]

Critics in anti-Dreyfusard journals were quick to add their voices by attacking Zola's libretto on a simultaneously political and stylistic basis. 'O'Divy' (or Jean Drault), the music critic for *La Libre parole,* castigated Zola's use of prose and his mixture of "'correct'" and colloquial usage and of realistic and fantastic elements. Zola, who had assaulted the forces of "tradition" on a political level, was now doing so in opera by ignoring the rules of both propriety and convention.[17] But the critic for the Dreyfusard *Petite République* defended Zola's texts on grounds that were similarly an inextricable conflation of aesthetic and political concepts. According to Alfred Dubarry, Zola's libretti were meritorious not only because of their naturalness and life but above all because of their artistic "truth." Indeed, "truth," together with "justice" and the rights of the individual, was the primary concept or term that had become characteristic of Dreyfusard discourse.[18] Critics on both political sides of the issue soon transferred this same criterion to the attack on or defense of Bruneau's setting of Zola's texts. Later in this chapter we see how Bruneau responded to his critics by developing an even more complete Dreyfusard or Republican musical aesthetic and history. Another reason he would do so was the challenge that was posed by his nemesis, the even more engaged, ardently anti-Dreyfusard composer Vincent d'Indy. For d'Indy's obsession with what he termed "artistic Dreyfusism" was to have a decisive influence not just on his career and music but on the school of music he helped found.

D'Indy and the Dreyfus Affair

To understand d'Indy's engagement and why the Affair was a directive force in his life, we must, of course, examine the composer's background, professional position, and social identity; these help to explain why d'Indy eventually did not distinguish his professional from his political interests, or his aesthetic from his ideological beliefs. Hence, it is important to analyze the political and the musical background together as they simultaneously helped to shape the composer's responses at the time of the Affair. It is also important to note that d'Indy fits into the typical paradigm of the anti-Dreyfusard, or the profile of the dominant membership of the Ligue de la Patrie Française; for, again, the first adherents of the league came from positions of social or professional authority—the aristocracy, the Institut de France, the Collège de France, and the Académie Française.[19] By the time of the Affair, d'Indy was at the peak of his professional reputation, firmly ensconced in the musical establishment and considered a leading French composer. A believer in collective authority, the army, the Church, and the greatness of ancestors, he was also a prominent member of the paternalistic French nobility.[20]

Born into an aristocratic family from the upper Vivarais region (in the department of the Ardèche, in southern France), he was raised in the traditions and values of the old French aristocracy; but just as significant is that, since his mother had died while giving birth to him, he was raised by his paternal grandmother, whose background was different from that of the rest of the family. Unlike them, she was both instilled with the utopian ideals of the Saint-Simonian movement and had a great admiration for Napoleon. She passed both of these beliefs on to her grandson, to the family's consternation.[21] Her belief in the ideals of utopian socialism, which she bequeathed to d'Indy, may well have influenced his late ideological attraction to the Ligue de la Patrie Française. For, in distinction to both Marxism and Anarchism, its model, according to Brunetière (in 1899) was rather what he considered to be "le vrai socialisme française" (true French socialism); like the Saint-Simonians, the league believed in the social responsibility and the directive force of the intellectual and financial leaders of society, maintaining that such a hierarchy guaranteed order.[22] D'Indy's attraction to the ideology of the Ligue de la Patrie Française—as opposed to that of other nationalist leagues—was already well prepared.

Another important inheritance from his grandmother was d'Indy's love and knowledge of music, for she was an accomplished musician, having studied piano with Pixis, Adam Père, and Kalkbrenner. In addition, d'Indy's uncle Wilfred was an amateur composer of operettas and other light works, and when the family moved to Paris he introduced the boy to the world of concerts and theater. As a child, d'Indy was given piano lessons by his rigorous grandmother, who forced him to submit regularly to "examinations," with the family as the jury.[23] This was probably one of the factors that determined his later pedagogic approach, which abjured such systems of examination, modeled ultimately on those of the Conservatoire. Not content with her own instruction, when d'Indy was thirteen (in 1864) his grandmother selected a private teacher of harmony and orchestration for him; this was the young Albert Lavignac, a recent graduate of the

Conservatoire and later to become one of its noted professors, and a teacher of Claude Debussy. Hence, it is not surprising that, as an adolescent, d'Indy's compositional models resembled those of Conservatoire students—Meyerbeer, Gluck, Mendelssohn, Schumann, and Wagner.[24]

D'Indy's life was to change abruptly when, in 1870, with the advent of the Franco-Prussian War, he entered the 105th Battalion of the National Guard. Although he served in the army only six months, in the course of his brief experience his idealistic, aristocratic image of a military career was inexorably shattered; so marked was d'Indy by the real horrors of war that he felt compelled to record his impressions in a "soldier's journal," which he published in 1872.[25] It was at this point that, despite his family's expectations, and to their considerable consternation, he decided resolutely against pursuing a career in the French military. But, as we shall see, d'Indy, in fact, transferred his brief experience of military discipline and camaraderie to his pedagogical ideal.

After the war, the Commune, and the advent of the Third Republic—to which the aristocracy was generally opposed—d'Indy, who was no exception, professed to have an interest in nothing but music. This was also the period when his taste in music was being transformed, a process that had begun just before the war, when he met Henri Duparc, a student of César Franck. During the war d'Indy had been introduced to Franck himself, an event that was to have a momentous impact on both his life and his career:[26] he now began to associate closely with the coterie of students that coalesced around Franck, a group whose aesthetic their contemporaries described as aristocratic, conservative, and "bien pensant" (right-thinking). It was indeed this circle that would later become the central core of reactionary, anti-Dreyfusard musicians, promoting aristocratic social traditions. Already, they considered the music of Rossini, Mendelssohn, and Meyerbeer to be not only too sensual but also meretriciously calculated to achieve immediate financial success. Hence, these composers, in contrast, stressed the qualities of "'intelligence'" and the "ideal," which they associated with truly great works or, as they put it, "la grande musique."[27]

Although Franck was a professor at the Conservatoire, he was isolated from most of his colleagues , by his idealistic approach, as well as by the musical models he taught. Probably because of his Wagnerian proclivities, at a time when Wagner was suspect in France, he was given not a class in composition but one in organ, although he surreptitiously taught composition in it. And so it is not surprising that Franck's circle began to criticize the Conservatoire as an institution, and to condemn all "enseignement officiel."[28] This was now to become a constant theme for Vincent d'Indy and to take on an even greater significance at the time of the Dreyfus Affair.

After the war, d'Indy's father expected him to enter the Faculty of Law, since the traditions of his family and the aristocracy were against his becoming a professional musician.[29] But the young man was implacable, spurred on by his friendship with the group around Franck, as well as by his rapid rise within the professional musical world in Paris. This was a world in the process of rapid change in the aftermath of the Franco-Prussian War, with the older dominant generation now dying or having fled during the fighting; moreover, it was a world in which taste was changing. Because of the devastation caused by the war and the subsequent political turmoil, the strangle-hold of opera was temporarily broken.[30] French musicians turned to the development of both chamber and symphonic music and to the goal of bettering the victorious Germans in their own abstract musical forms.

This was precisely the aim of the Société Nationale de Musique Française, a new concert society that d'Indy helped indefatigably to found in 1871. Its other members included Lalo, Franck, Saint-Saëns, Massenet, Bizet, Bussine, Duparc, and Widor—all dedicated to the rebirth of a new and more "serious" French music. Most had suffered under the dominance of grand opera during the Second Empire, when music was controlled by a small group of selected successful composers, to the exclusion of younger French artists. Sensitive to German charges that French "frivolity" had helped to bring its defeat, they now sought to define and affirm the basic qualities of "la génie française." They were thus convinced that abstract musical forms, to this point largely belittled in France in favor of lyric theater, could be filled with what they believed to be "French content," emphasizing clarity, formal ingenuity, and grace. The Société was thus to provide an important new venue, one that was badly needed in Paris, for the cultivation of contemporary French instrumental music. But this group would be rent by dissension well before the Dreyfus Affair over the issue of what to perform and of what indeed was authentically French. The divisive issue was the question of foreign musical influences, particularly that of Wagner, whom d'Indy admired so ardently. The bifurcation of the French musical world, already present in embryo, would reach its full maturity when the leagues introduced the ideological dimension. When the initial split occurred, in 1886, it was d'Indy's faction that was to win and, in effect, to take over the society with him as its new president, replacing Saint-Saëns.

Initially, as a member of the new society, d'Indy was eager to have his own music performed, and when Franck rejected two of his works, he formally became Franck's composition pupil.[31] Since that event coincided with the death of d'Indy's grandmother, the dominant force in his life to this point, the role of his new "father" and creed seem clear: "Franckisme," a doctrine conceived by d'Indy and his circle of friends around the "master," was to provide the guiding principles for the rest of his life and career. Moreover, with the death of his grandmother, d'Indy now came into his full inheritance, which allowed him considerable latitude with regard to his future path. In 1873, despite his ire over France's recent defeat, he went to Germany and was able to meet Liszt and Brahms, both of whom he greatly admired. He even managed to meet, if briefly, his true musical idol, Richard Wagner, and was present at the opening of the Bayreuth Festival in 1876.[32] At a time when many French composers saw ardent nationalism and Wagnerism as incompatible, d'Indy chose to ignore the contradiction, and he would later find a way to reconcile it ideologically.

The following decade was one of increasing professional prominence for d'Indy: he became the secretary of the Société Nationale, and both the Pasdeloup and the Colonne concert societies sought his works. His status rose precipitously when his *La Mort de Wallenstein* was warmly received at the popular Pasdeloup concerts in 1880. In 1886 his success was confirmed when he won the prestigious competition that was sponsored by the city of Paris (and brought three official performances) with his "dramatic legend," *Le Chant de la cloche*. But, despite this success, Franck was still not satisfied with d'Indy's work, believing he needed a clearer and more "robust" conception, and he thus urged him to write an opera.[33] In order to prepare himself for the task, d'Indy read the writings of Wagner, which were permanently to influence his thought and to prepare for his engagement in the Affair.

By the late 1880s d'Indy was firmly ensconced in both French high society and the musical world, and in 1890 he was elected president of the Société Nationale. This was also the period when he began the construction of a grand chateau on the family property near Combray, which he named "Les Faugs." D'Indy's status in the official world was so high that in 1888 he was selected as a member of the Commission des Auditions Musicales for the Universal Exposition of 1889 and also named secretary of the Troisième Section de Musique. But the culmination of his recognition came in 1892, when d'Indy received the distinction of being named Chevalier de la Légion d'Honneur. Given that, like so many French aristocrats, he opposed the Republic in principle, it would seem to be another contradiction that he would accept its honorific awards; yet it is important to remember that this was the period of "Ralliement," when Pope Leo XVIII urged French Catholics to embrace the Republic and its institutions, or to meet the Republican "Opportunists" half way. D'Indy, devoutly Catholic, did not hesitate to follow the Church's directives, either now or later, during the period of the Dreyfus Affair.[34]

In 1892, also, the Director of the Beaux-Arts, Henri Roujon, with whom d'Indy had friendly relations, named him to an important official commission: it was a body of experts named to propose a reform of the program of studies at the state Conservatoire, which even its director, Ambroise Thomas, acknowledged it needed.[35] The commission produced a detailed report that called for far-reaching changes, including the introduction of a class on the symphony, which traditionally had not been taught at the Conservatoire. Such "Franckiste" ideas were shocking to some, given the relatively low status of symphonic, as opposed to vocal, music, as reflected in the Conservatoire's instruction. But the commission's work came to naught, for in 1893 the funds to implement its many recommendations were peremptorily denied. As d'Indy later bitterly recalled, its report was recognized only to the extent that it was printed at state expense, only to be promptly "buried."[36]

D'INDY, ANTI-DREYFUSISM, AND THE SCHOLA

D'Indy's bitterness toward the Republic escalated with the advent of the Dreyfus Affair, which, like the Revolution in Dresden for Wagner, led him to merge his hopes for political and artistic reform. Like other French aristocrats no longer actively involved in Republican politics, he now stepped forward to defend the "nation" and the army that he maintained protected it. For French aristocrats harbored a keen sense of their responsibility as an elite that was welded to the nation and thus to the army, as opposed to the political state.[37] From this point on, d'Indy approached his political and professional goals as one, throwing himself into the development of a musical culture in systematic opposition to that of the Republic. This he was to do through his involvement in a school of music, the Schola Cantorum, which he would use to launch his challenge to state control over "legitimate" education in music. Later, when referring indirectly to his role in the Ligue de la Patrie Française, d'Indy employed the following revealing analogy between the school and the league: he spoke of the inherent relation between what he termed "l'institution intégralement nationale" and the Schola, which he considered "l'institution intégralement musicale."[38] D'Indy's involvement in both institutions was tangled, since for him the question of what French music should be and how to attain this was politically charged.

From his inchoate "Franckiste" ethos, d'Indy was now to develop an aesthetic system, a pedagogical approach, and a musical philosophy that was inseparable from his belief in the league: his musical and political ideals shared a system of concepts, meanings, references, vocabulary, and values that derived ultimately from the league's distinctive nationalist creed. The theoretical patterns of his political ideology thus informed his basic assumptions concerning not only musical value but also music history and its implications for the present. But d'Indy, in addition, would be an integral figure in a network of intellectual influences that would encourage receptive musicians to equate their own interests with the goals of the league. And he helped spread a perception that Republican hegemony in the musical world represented both a cultural power and a moral authority that had to be contested. Moreover, by assigning political meanings to styles and to musical forms and genres, he would help make aesthetic legitimacy in music a political question. Finally, through his teachings, d'Indy would make the history of French music an integral part of French national history, and thus of the league's public pedagogy and propaganda. More than any other institution, then, it was to be the Schola Cantorum that would pull French music into the cultural war that had been aggressively launched by the nationalist leagues. And d'Indy would employ the mobilizing themes of the league in a way that would serve both the professional aims of the Schola and those of the league.

To understand the relative success of the Schola, the status and power that it was to accrue, and thus the threat that it would pose to the Republic, there are two facts of which we must be aware: one is the poor state of religious music as Republican anticlericalism grew, and the other is the parlous state of the pedagogy at the now discredited state-funded Conservatoire. Indeed, the Schola filled a gap in the teaching of religious music in France and helped to raise public consciousness about the quality of the music being performed in churches. Despite periodic attempts at the reform of plainchant in the nineteenth century, it was generally performed in a harmonized version, with rhythm imposed, and accompanied by a "sepent," low strings, or organ. "Maîtrises," or choir schools, existed, and from the Second Empire on so did Louis Niedermeyer's school of "classic" and religious music, intended to train choir masters and organists. But funds for the "maîtrises" were severely reduced in the anticlerical 1880s, with only six receiving any money at all from the French state.

As founded in 1894, the Schola Cantorum was originally a society for the promotion and teaching of religious music, especially Gregorian chant. Its immediate inspiration was a performing group, Les Chanteurs de Saint-Gervais, founded in 1892 by Charles Bordes, the choir-master of Saint-Gervais.[39] The Schola itself was Bordes's idea, but he soon enlisted the collaboration of his sympathetic friends and colleagues Alexandre Guilmant and Vincent d'Indy. The latter eagerly embraced the idea, seeing it as an opportunity to implement the reforms in education that he had proposed for the state Conservatoire. It was indeed a bold project since it had no financial base of support (apart from donations and fees from its students) and, at first, no established cultural legitimacy; before we discuss how it defined itself both professionally and politically, we must first examine the institutional identity and pedagogical limitations of the state Conservatoire.

The Conservatoire and Its Traditions

Since its founding in the revolutionary period, the Conservatoire National de Musique et de Declamation had a monopoly on "legitimate" or "authorized" musical education in France. Nowhere among French institutions was the academic system stronger or more central and domineering than it was in the field of music. Although this is evident only on close examination, the Conservatoire was one of the academic institutions whose identity, sense of function, and "memory" were linked most closely to the Republican mentality: established by Gossec and Sarrette in 1792 as a school for military music, it consciously defined itself against the former Ecole Royale de Chant. The following year it joined together with the Institut National de Musique in order to prepare musicians to participate in the massive celebrations of national *fêtes*.[40]

From its inception, the Conservatoire was conceived as a functional institution to train "professionals" who would serve the state's various musical institutions and theatrical needs. The Conservatoire was also imprinted with several fundamental values or traits of Republican thought that were to continue to inform its "memory," as well as its logic. The first was an inherent suspicion of all previous authorities and traditions—the only tradition it recognized being that which could be altered to meet new social needs;[41] second, it rigorously institutionalized the Republican principle of meritocracy, founding advancement within its system upon the basis of regular and successive competitions. In principle, anyone could succeed in the system by mastering the requisite technical skills—a case in point being the director between 1896 and 1905, Théodore Dubois. Dubois could not have come from a background more different from that of Vincent d'Indy, a fact that became increasingly important as the political-cultural tensions between the schools intensified. Thus it is important here briefly to review Dubois's social origins, which helped determine his bellicose commitment to the Conservatoire's ideals during the Affair.

Not atypically for a Conservatoire student, Dubois's early life was difficult, for his origins as the son of a basket-maker and the grandson of a primary school teacher were humble.[42] Nevertheless, he received piano lessons and soon attracted the attention and protection of the Vicomte Eugène de Boreuil, who introduced him to professors at the Paris Conservatoire. The Vicomte then moved to Paris, allowing the boy to live in the garret of one of his buildings, where he shared his meals with the house's servants. Because of his penurious condition, Dubois lived a life that was austere and focused on his work, as did many others who would be students at the Conservatoire during his tenure as director. He soon attracted the attention of Franck, eventually becoming his assistant organist, and later was one of the founding members of the Société Nationale de Musique. But Dubois was to distance himself from the society in 1886, when the ideological schism that resulted in d'Indy's dominance finally took place; already employing a political analogy, Dubois referred to the parties of the Right and the Left, and specifically to the increasingly "exclusive" spirit of the former faction.[43]

Dubois was a firm believer in the merits of the Conservatoire's education, one based on a practical and systematic approach to what were considered the professional fundamentals. These centered on solfège and harmony, with a particular emphasis on the latter, especially for students who wished eventually to gain entry into a class in composition. Once in such a class, they were taught the techniques of counterpoint and fugue, although most analysis done in such classes was approached from the perspective of the progression of chords.[44] This emphasis was by no means ideologically innocent, for harmony still carried a strongly scientific connotation, dating back to the Enlightenment and Rameau. Counterpoint, on the other hand, carried clerical associations that were considered threatening in a Republican institution and was thus systematically deemphasized.

Because of its practical emphasis, the Conservatoire was oriented toward the needs of the lyric theaters, the principal ones of which were the national or officially subventioned stages; because the repertoire of these theaters centered on the nineteenth century, the Conservatoire placed little value on music history or the performance of works from the distant past. As we shall later see when we examine Gabriel Fauré's reforms, although a class on music history was offered, it was not required and was ill attended; the repertoire of the students reflected this, being largely centered on standard virtuoso compositions, as well as on more recent well-known operatic works.

A "canon," as such, thus did not exist as a component of the institution's instruction, although the Société des Concerts du Conservatoire, which performed in the Conservatoire's hall, had introduced the German canonic repertoire in France. As William Weber has shown, these concerts were the province of an exclusive, elite public, for whom they filled a gap in the classical French tradition that had been associated with the Bourbon monarchy. Significantly, these concerts soon established ties to the state bureaucracy, which not only legitimated them symbolically but helped in turn to legitimate the Orleanist monarchy on an elite level imbuing it with a patina of high culture. Although the Third Republic did continue to provide subventions for the concerts, it did not recognize the symbolic value of promoting the French classical heritage (now safely removed in time from monarchical associations), together with the German canon, through the Conservatoire itself.

This would eventually change, but only in response to the Schola's challenge

and to the escalating assaults on the institution in the next decade by the nationalist Right. In chapter 3 we shall examine the recurrence and intensification of attacks on its pedagogy, particularly its neglect of the French and German classical
canons. But finally, here, when considering the Conservatoire's dominant position, it is important to note that its pedagogy was not limited to Paris: it extended
throughout the entire country.[45] Branches of the Conservatoire, as well as municipal schools and those choir schools (maîtrises) that received subventions,
had to conform to the program outlined by the Conseil Supérieur des Etudes du
Conservatoire National.[46]

The Schola's Counteridentity

It was in opposition to this power, this spirit, and this program that the Schola
defined itself, and with greater explicitness, as the Affair reached its peak; hence,
the school was now characterized by a fusion of ideological and musical goals, as
is clear from both its programs and the written discourse it produced. Indeed, the
Schola's published discourse and pedagogical practices were inseparable, for
every professional goal was explained at length on both a practical and an ideological level; this was done not only in classes but also in the school's many publications, as well as through the public lectures and the "pedagogical concerts" it
offered. In the diffusion of this musical ideology to the public at large, the Ligue
de la Patrie Française, and then the Action Française, would be crucial.

D'Indy was well aware that this battle against the state could not be waged
alone—that he needed both legitimization and support from outside Republican
institutions. As we have noted, the league was powerful within the "cultivated"
world, which included the academy along with the diplomatic and the political
corps; this was facilitated, in part, through the prestigious Parisian salon of the
Comtesse de Loynes, a major patron and force behind the league.[47] Hence, the
league offered a substantial audience that was inclined to be receptive to art, as
well as to the Schola's ideas, and could provide it with a base of support. Moreover, the league had considerable influence within the Parisian press, including
Le Gaulois, La Libre parole, L'Intransigeant, L'Eclair, La Presse, and L'Echo de Paris.
Through this press, which amounted to two-thirds of the Parisian dailies, the
league could reach more than two million readers each day, which gave it a pronounced advantage.[48]

As we have noted, the Schola's "project" coincided felicitously with the ideals
of the league, and we may witness this consanguinity in its journal, Les Annales
de la Patrie Française. Begun in 1900, and vaunting prominent writers on its editorial board, the journal articulated as one of its goals the promotion of nationalism in literature and thus the mounting of attacks on "intellectuals" and their
conception of "progress." The league associated such conceptions with abstract
ideas, or with what it considered to be mere "formulae," and which it maintained
issued from "cosmopolitan" or Jewish elements.

Here the league's anti-Semitism went beyond the Affair itself, being linked to
its philosophical analysis of the foundations of France's decline. As Barrès articulated it, the Jews were inherently a "foreign" element, incapable of true assimila-

tion into French culture and, emblematically, French taste. The Affair, for Barrès (and for d'Indy) only proved that the Jews were exacerbating the decline of the "common idea," or the tradition that purportedly once linked the French.[49] These same conceptions appear repeatedly in the Schola's discourse, for d'Indy made a connection between such traits and specific musical characteristics. The mobilizing themes of the league, especially anti-Masonism and attacks on "cosmopolites" and "métèques" (half-breeds), filled d'Indy's writings and public lectures.

Hence, the league had every reason to support the Schola Cantorum, for the school fit perfectly into its program of diffusing what it termed an "education nationale" through cultural projects. These included different cultural levels and embraced public lectures, as well as popular libraries, all of which it helped to finance through the substantial treasury that it was amassing; for adherents of the league solicited new members and funds not just from those in the business world inclined to support their cause, but in elegant salons in which they themselves participated.[50]

D'Indy became part of this recruitment effort through his own professional network, using the office of his editor, Durand, as a base from which to accept subscriptions for the league. At the height of the Affair, in 1898 and 1899, he was proudly writing to the league to announce his successful recruitment of Ernest Chausson and Pierre de Bréville. By 1902, when the Schola was in serious financial difficulties, d'Indy was writing letters of thanks to the league, which would seem to indicate that it had contributed funds to the school. The league apparently realized the value of such an association, the way it could use the symbolic power and cultural prestige of music as a mobilizing force: d'Indy's discourse could help it transcend mere dry uninspiring political abstractions, for it cogently conflated the political, religious, and aesthetic dimensions. After internal dissension in the league in 1901 over the use of violence in the streets, its focus was henceforth on education and propaganda. The Schola was useful within this context, particularly when the league hoped, through subtle means, to influence the legislative elections of 1902 (which were indeed successful for the nationalists in Paris, as opposed to the rest of the country).[51]

The conflation of the political and aesthetic emerged in almost every aspect of the Schola's teaching, which, as we shall see later in this chapter, was to find a considerable network of intellectual influence; in chapter 3 we discuss how the symbiotic relationship between the Ligue de la Patrie Française and the Schola was to be followed by that between the Schola and the Action Française. For the ideological basis of both leagues as well as of the Schola was "Tradition"—a word that d'Indy, to manifest his profound respect, was always careful to capitalize. The tradition that he taught was one that was based on authority of the "masters," one that, while primarily French, he construed as part of a more comprehensive universal tradition; it was one that he believed ultimately grew out of religious music and, hence, one whose works were imbued with spirituality and an implicit or explicit moral message.[52] D'Indy's conception of such "grande musique" was thus not a socially sequestered high art, above social purpose, isolated from life, or elevating humanity in an abstract manner; yet for d'Indy, this did not mean that its message should be either direct or explicit, for he saw art as an idealization, a "magnified impression" arising from the soul of the artist.[53] His conception of art was elitist, but this did not exclude the lower classes; rather, he believed that art was a means of social reform through spiritual elevation.

If d'Indy thus defined the Schola's purpose against the Conservatoire's, he did so as well with regard to its student body or general clientele. For unlike the Conservatoire, virtually anyone could enter, and at any age; hence, the Schola filled a notable gap in musical education in France. More than one observer noted the heterogeneity of the Schola's student body, but perhaps the most incisive observer of all was Claude Debussy, in 1903: writing in *Gil Blas* (on February 2), he remarked, "It is a strange thing, but at the Schola, side by side, you will find the aristocracy, the most left-wing of the bourgeoisie, refined artists, and coarse artisans." But many also remarked about the Schola's aristocratic conception of art, one that stressed the "disinterested," or the disdain of any facile success;[54] to this, however, we might further add another aspect of its instruction that set it apart from the Conservatoire: its students' avoidance of all competition, for traditionally the French nobility disdained the spirit of "concours" and the kind of professionalization characteristic of the official educational system.[55] Indeed, Proust evokes the tone of the school in *Le Côté des Guermantes,* when he describes aristocratic women who attended to learn counterpoint and fugue, and the rigid opinions imbibed there by aristocratic young men.[56]

The Schola's Curriculum

The curriculum of the Schola, as instituted in 1897, included a five-year course in music history, analysis, and aesthetics begun in the second year. Again, unlike the Conservatoire, this was preceded by a one-year study of the fundamentals of music, or what d'Indy generally referred to laconically as "le métier." Whereas this was the one and only concern of the pedagogy at the Conservatoire, for d'Indy it was merely the starting point from which one could eventually rise to the level of "art." Moreover, the training in "le métier" did not start with harmony or solfège as at the Conservatoire but simultaneously exposed the students to harmony, counterpoint, and Gregorian chant. This premininary study also required that students participate in a choral ensemble, where they learned sacred polyphony, from simple organum up through the works of Palestrina. For one tenet of the Schola was that music be studied simultaneously from several points of view—those of practical performance, analysis, and the history of musical aesthetics. Again, the ideological dimension that informed d'Indy's aesthetics was never far from his actual pedagogy and helped to focus his reforms.

The next phase of study, as we have noted, was that which d'Indy referred to as "art," which led students through the study of music up to the Baroque and to the history of harmonic and tonal theory. Holding a quasi-Hegelian view of the stages of the evolution of art toward the "higher" or more perfect, d'Indy implicitly applied this in his program of study: the "chain of tradition," he believed, began with the "decorative" art of plainchant and was followed historically by the "architectural" art of Renaissance polyphony; this, in turn, was succeeded by the "expressive" art of the early seventeenth-century Italian masters of vocal music, and particularly Monteverdi.[57] D'Indy was, in effect, attempting to illustrate the historical logic of those values he, as opposed to those at the Conservatoire, emphasized in his teaching. Students then went on to study music for solo instruments, including canon, fugue, suite, sonata, and variation forms; they subsequently advanced to ensemble instrumental forms (including chamber music), with a particular stress on the concerto, the symphony, and the symphonic poem.

The inclusion of the symphony was indeed unprecedented in musical education in France, since it was considered by the Conservatoire to be an inherently "lower" genre. But its position was reversed in d'Indy curriculum precisely because he did not conceive it as tied to the functional, mundane needs of the Third Republic. In his teaching of the symphony, d'Indy emphasized, above all, the Viennese classics, perceiving Beethoven's symphonies, in particular, as the most elevated examples of "musique pure"; hence, his model was based on Beethoven, although in the distinctive manner in which d'Indy construed the composer and thus the historical implications of his art. For d'Indy, as for Franck, the symphony's status derived from his resolute belief that it was the most expressive genre of all—able to communicate both feelings and ideas; as we shall shortly see, these were of a moral and political nature, which made the symphony a hortatory genre through which ultimately to "improve" society. For, once more, at the Schola "Tradition" was conceived as a canon of great works imbued with the capacity to "teach" through the moralizing and elevating messages they were thought to convey. Finally, in accordance with the early ideals of the Société Nationale, d'Indy perceived the symphony as a genre through which to better the Germans on their own ground.[58]

The Schola versus "Dreyfusism artistique"

Predictably, by 1902, d'Indy was perceiving opposition to his elevation of the symphony on the part of those musicians associated with the so-called Dreyfusard Republic. In a letter to Guy Ropartz, of October 10, 1902, he points out and complains of the low esteem in which Conservatoire students still held the symphony: seeing it as a false or "bastardized" genre, they demean it, he claims, to the greater glory of what he disdainfully terms, invoking Bruneau, "le vérisme boulevardier." Here d'Indy once again contraposes positivistic realism with a larger, intuited "truth" that intellect or the senses can never grasp. He then explicitly attributes this denigration of the symphony to "Dreyfusisme artistique," adding that the results are no better here than in "Dreyfusisme politique."[59] This obsession with "artistic Dreyfusism," or with supposed Dreyfusard plots against the Schola Cantorum, long remained prominent in d'Indy's correspondence.

Since d'Indy believed that a knowledge of elevating "musique pure" was fundamental to the study of "musique appliquée aux paroles," the latter was studied only at the end of the program; it was when nearing completion of the Schola's syllabus that students finally arrived at the genres considered central to the Conservatoire—opera, oratorio, and cantata.[60] Here, too, the works studied were substantially different from those at the Paris Conservatoire, which was centered, as we have seen, on the nineteenth-century repertoire. D'Indy's emphasis was on the French pre-revolutionary and classic composers, beginning with Lully, whom he considered "the creator of French dramatic music"; it also included Gluck and Rameau, the latter having already caught the attention of the Société Nationale de Musique Française, which had hoped to renew interest in his work.

In his teaching of nineteenth-century opera, d'Indy was strongly influenced by Wagner who, as we have noted, was his idol, as well as his model for operatic composition. Like Wagner, he considered most of the operas written in nineteenth-century France to be "decadent"—servile and meretricious imitations of successful Italian composers; like Wagner as well, he considered this the inevitable and unfortunate result of the insidious Jewish influence that had harmed so many aspects of different national cultures. Clearly, d'Indy's musical anti-Semitism was the result not only of his nationalist politics but also of both his Catholicism and his careful reading of Wagner's writings. It was a powerful amalgam that went beyond the Dreyfus Affair itself and remained prominent in his writings until his death three decades later.[61]

D'Indy was as unrelenting as Wagner in his attack on Jewish composers too heavily influenced by what he considered the meretrious Italian style of the day; in his lectures at the Schola, he echoed Wagner's rhetoric by tracing the so-called "style mélodique judaïque," leading up to its culmination in Meyerbeer. For d'Indy, however, such a label could also be applied to non-Jewish composers who had the bad taste, greed, or simple misfortune to come under this pernicious influence. And so, in the present, Massenet was ultimately the product of this "école Judaïque," but, since "real Jews," he claimed, had only material desires, he allowed Massenet more "sensual feeling." In short, for d'Indy, all Jewish composers were inherently not only superficial but derivative, as well as mercenary in their art—in search only of financial gain.[62]

Wagner was clearly d'Indy's model for true operatic writing, for in his works d'Indy saw the same "elevation' or moral message that he sought in the symphony. And, given his admiration for the German symphonic school, it is not surprising that he equally admired its application to opera, as embodied in Wagner.[63] But, again, it was not only the application of motivic or thematic and formal techniques from the symphony to the opera that he admired—it was also the communication of a larger social message.

D'Indy, unlike many other French nationalists, particularly those in the Action Française, perceived no contradiction between his ardent nationalism and his love of the German Wagner. But we must remember that his nationalism was not only one that promoted the strength of France; it was also one that represented a specific notion of French identity: in this conception, France represented one aspect of a universal tradition, one that was lofty and pure, untainted by less noble elements. Hence, d'Indy believed that the entry of another strain of this great tradition, even from outside France, could have a salutary influence upon French culture. Indeed it was Wagner himself who had urged him to help renew his own national theater by restoring its tradition and thus by purging it of the "contaminated" Jewish style.[64]

Wagner's example, d'Indy believed, could help bring about this purgation, and in this belief he was seconded by a fellow member of the league, Maurice Barrès. Both d'Indy and Barrès perceived that Wagner's stress on the nation, on the instincts over reason, and on the power and directive force of myth complemented the ideals of the league; for it, too, stressed irrational attachment to the traditions of the nation, to the primacy of feeling and instinct over abstract and logical reasoning. Hence, both believed that the return to a purified national tradition in opera could be achieved in part through the cleansing force of Wagnerian innovations.[65] For Barrès, Wagner's rejection of the formulae that encumbered civilization was a prelude to the rebirth that could now occur on national soil; d'Indy shared this perception, but he added another dimension: Wagner's music had more in common with Gregorian chant than with the tainted "Italo-judaïque" style. Both, according to d'Indy, represented a "discours libre," or a quality of infinite and subtle variation, a freely unfolding musical phrase, as opposed to the Jewish and Conservatoire styles. D'Indy believed, with Barrès, that "authenticity" in art could come about only after "purgation" and the individual's realization of the necessity of unity with an organic past.[66]

But this was not the only theme that d'Indy shared with other members of the Ligue de la Patrie Française and that penetrated the discourse of the Schola Cantorum: we find the league's characteristic emphasis on moral reform, as well as on collective authority, both based fundamentally on tradition; we see continual articulation of the league's other mobilizing themes designed to incite the passions of those who either adhered to or were sympathetic to it. These prominently included anti-Masonism, as well as the attack on "cosmopolites" or "métèques," which meant generally "half-breeds" but often, in this discourse, specifically Jews. "Métèques," in the rhetoric of the league, were constantly being accused of undermining France from within, or of both corrupting and manipulating its political life. The league, as well as the Schola, opposed this manipulation to "French solidarity" and to the spirit of generosity, or "bonhomie," and brotherhood.[67]

This spirit, for d'Indy, was bivocal, for it not only carried an ideological message but helped to define the school against the professional competitiveness of the Conservatoire. Students at the Schola, he asserted (with clear anti-Semitic implications) were pursuing lofty goals and would never be content to seek profit from their art. As he put it, "laissons ce négoce aux trop nombreux sémites qui encombrent la musique depuis que celle-ci est susceptible de devenir une affaire" (let us leave this commerce to the too numerous semites who have encumbered music since it has been susceptible to becoming a business). The role of art was rather to teach, to elevate the spirit of humanity or, as he phrased it, by quoting Kundry at the end of *Parsifal,* "dienen," or to serve.[68] Hence, his goal was to produce not "professionals" but "artists"—those with a "calling"—which led him to abolish any formal competitions and to emphasize working collegially. D'Indy's pedagogical paradigm derived from his conception of the Middle Ages, in which art was collaborative and master and pupil were bound by mutual respect and faith. Yet, as contemporaries noted, when d'Indy took over the school completely himself, in 1903, he imposed a spirit of "camaraderie" and lofty "disinterestedness" along with military discipline.[69]

Other mobilizing themes of the league that run through d'Indy's rhetoric prominently include the attack on anticlericalism and hence the defense of the Catholic Church. During the Affair many members of the religious orders, as well as prominent Catholics like d'Indy, had declared themselves to be anti-Dreyfusards; hence, under the government of Waldeck-Rousseau the reprisal against the Church began, together with that against the Republic's other "enemies," the army and the Rightest leagues. The Republic now did not just subordinate the military to civilian authority; by 1901 it had placed the religious orders under the purview of the Chamber of Deputies.[70] Thus the league was deeply concerned with the defense of the Catholic Church and, simultaneously, with "l'enseignement libre," or religious as opposed to state education.

As we might expect, this theme appears abundantly in d'Indy's discourse, which had all the more significance since the Schola, as of 1900, was housed in a former convent on the Rue St.-Jacques. (Conveniently, moreover, this was located within the realm of the student quarter, or the "Quartier Latin," which had become the center of rightest political agitation.) D'Indy's lecture to inaugurate the new location outlined the Schola's major concerns, in both a specifically artistic and a larger ideological sense: entitled "Une École d'art répondant aux besoins modernes," its subtext was the anachronism of the state Conservatoire from the perspective of nationalist conceptions. Here d'Indy stressed not "progress" but, rather, his conception of "progression," or the "natural" transformations that the art of music has undergone in time; he stressed the fact that even unconsciously we proceed from the work of our predecessors, and observed that recent French history confirmed that "Tradition" cannot be ignored with impunity.[71]

D'Indy thus here identified his specific musical goals with a larger nationalist perspective or position concerning the political history of France. This identification reemerged when he spoke of his comprehensive goals of leaving the Schola's graduates "better armed for the modern combat."[72] For d'Indy this meant imbuing students with a sense of "natural" evolution, which, in his conception, applied simultaneously and inextricably to both politics and art.

But the nationalism in d'Indy's address was explicit as well as implicit, for he went on to "declare war" on what he termed "particularism": by this he meant those forces that undermined French solidarity, like the league, and in his speech he referred to it specifically as "that unhealthy fruit of the Protestant deviation."[73] Implied here, undoubtedly, is the Protestant stress on the individual conscience as opposed to the instinctive adherence to tradition that French nationalists valued so highly. And associating Protestants and Jews, from here he went on again to attack Jewish art, which he asserted refuses to recognize the "logical chain of the past":

Cette tendance paraît être encore un dernier avatar de l'école judaïque, qui retarde la marche de l'art pendant une grande partie du XIXe siècle . . ."[74]

(This tendency would seem to be yet a last metamorphosis of the Jewish school that retarded the progression of art during a large part of the nineteenth century . . .)

D'Indy continued to play subtly on the dual political and artistic resonance of his terms and concepts to the very end of this inaugural speech; for he concluded by thanking those who had been "brave militants" and then went on to promise that the work of the Schola would be to the glory of both the country and of art.

THE REPUBLIC'S FIRST RIPOSTE:
THE 1900 EXPOSITION AND MUSIC

D'Indy's perception of a "war" with both the "Dreyfusard Republic" and with its national Conservatoire was expressed even more vehemently in his letters, as we have seen. By 1900, convinced that the Schola was under attack from the Republic via the state institution, his sense of paranoia was rapidly reaching its peak. In a letter of November 20, 1900, to his friend Guy Ropartz, he expressed his alarm over what he termed "le nouveau Conservatoire Dreyfusard." By this he meant a project to found what was apparently to be called the "Collège d'esthétique sincère" that Alfred Bruneau, Gustave Charpentier, and Alfred Bachelier were planning in Montmartre. As d'Indy put it, "Leur programme est sincèrement co-casse et il me semble que cette manifestation doit être soutenue et encouragée par Théodore [Dubois] afin de faire piège à la Schola. (Ils veulent la guerre, ils l'au-ront.)"[75] (Their program is sincerely comical and it seems to me that this demon-stration must be supported and encouraged by Théodore [Dubois] in order to set a trap for the Schola. [If they want war, they will have it.]) D'Indy's sense of being surrounded by politico-aesthetic plots is reflected in another letter to Guy Ropartz, who was about to go to Lyon: on August 2, 1901, he warned Ropartz about musical circles there, especially the alliance of Jews and Socialists around Dreyfus, and urged them to "take precautions."[76]

D'Indy was correct in his perception that the Republic, in the wake of the Dreyfus Affair, was not about to let the Schola's challenge go without a riposte. Yet it was to respond in stages, beginning with the development of a musical dis-course that was similarly bivocal, or simultaneously of political and artistic sig-nificance. Indeed, the challenge of the Right had made the new government more aware of the important role that French music could play in national education, but according to its own conception. This first becomes clear in the context of the musical programs that were an integral part of the Universal Exposition that was held in Paris in 1900. They, too, were surrounded by discourse, but one that was intended to affirm Republican power and in order to do so also assigned political significance to composers, to genres, and to styles. Both these musical programs and their concomitant exegetical texts were attempts to ensure that French taste developed in accordance with Republican priorities, values, and ideals; for this was the moment when, in the light of the challenge being posed by the political Right, the Republic was determined to assume control of all aspects of French culture.[77] Hence, as we shall see, official policies in culture from this point on were not conceived solely from Republican doctrine but emerged through a dia-logue with the political opposition.

In order to understand the way in which French music was presented at the Universal Exposition, we must, of course, also understand the latter's ideological goals. Certainly, one of its aims was to promote an image of stability and progress that was to be projected to the world in the aftermath of the traumatic Dreyfus Affair. As opposed to the picture of a decaying and unjust nation that was diffused in the domestic and foreign press, the Exposition was to present the country as devoted to "art, industry, pleasure, and peace." Indeed, Zola condemned the event for attempting to divert and to tranquilize, since the Republic promptly dropped the issue of the Affair, thus "strangling truth and justice."[78] From this perspective the Exposition could be seen as both a celebration of modernity and, in the words of the President, Emile Loubet, "a symbol of harmony and peace." And with special resonance, in light of the Affair, the Socialist Minister of Industry, Alexandre Millerand, who was officially in charge of the Exposition, stressed the role of science in triumphing over ignorance and misery. It thus seems plausible to interpret the Exposition as a quest for consolidation, as well as for stability on the part of the new Republican government now legally in place.[79]

It is also important to see the Exposition and its musical programs in terms of its attempt to justify and promulgate specifically Republican values and ideals, for, in the wake of the Dreyfus Affair, the Republic did have a pressing symbolic need—to project a positive purpose or vision that differentiated it from both its predecessors and its enemies. As Maurice Agulhon has shown, the Republic had been in search of a repertoire of themes, symbolic figures, and rituals that would rival those of the monarchist camp; but, since its political principles were based on ideas and not on a living incarnation in a monarch, it faced the problem of translating intellectual abstractions into symbolic terms. One response was to develop the cult of the "great man," in particular great literary and scientific figures of the past as incarnations of the symbolic authority on which the Republic was founded.[80] It is important to realize, however, that, although a Pantheon of great literary figures was already established—if interpreted in different ways from different political perspectives—this was not true of music: not yet being part of a generally shared culture, the musical Pantheon and canon was by no means defined and thus, in the context of the "cultural war," was at stake.

The Schola had already shown how music could be used integrally in this battle, as well as in the conflict over public pedagogy, or within a Nationalist educational scheme. The Third Republic itself had long developed an interest in education as a means of producing good French citizens, patriots in the proper Republican mold. Now, after the Affair, "science and vérité," or knowledge and truth, with their Dreyfusard connotations, were intended to enlighten and thus protect the nation: henceforth the Republic emphasized a socialist approach to education, as seen in the "Universités Populaires" and other avenues for extending education and culture to French workers.[81] With the challenge of the Schola, as we shall see, the Republic would attempt to incorporate music into its educational scheme through different venues, and on several levels. Education was thus one of the themes that would emerge in the musical discourse surrounding the programs of French music presented at the 1900 Universal Exposition.

Another point of emphasis now, one that the Exposition could be used to reaffirm, particularly in light of the Schola, was the growing anticlericalism of the Republic. As we have noted, the government of Waldeck-Rousseau was determined to exact revenge, "to affirm the Republic and cow its enemies in the church, the army, the leagues, and the street." In 1900 Waldeck-Rousseau announced that the nation was now on the eve of "a decisive battle to snatch the favorite weapons of the reaction."[82] He began immediately to diminish the powers of those who had been the worst offenders within the church at the time of the Dreyfus Affair—the Assumptionist order; for reasons of political timing, as soon as the Exposition closed, a far more massive and intensive anticlerical campaign was to ensue.

The other cultural theme of the Republic after the Affair that was to color the Exposition and its musical discourse was the role of the revolutionary heritage in national identity, for if the Affair had been "an epic struggle between Right and Left for the political soul of France," for the Left, at the core of that soul lay the French Revolution.[83] Since the Revolution remained a point of reference for Republican identity in France, the Republic had turned the memory of it into a myth, as well as a cult. Indeed, one of the themes that we have already noted in the Conservatoire was the primacy of the "individual" and the negation of subservience to any established tradition.[84] This was an idea that was to become even more important and to gain a new emphasis in light of the growing competition with the Schola Cantorum. So, too, would the central Republican tenet of social progress, or the necessity of change—the refusal to consider an established order as indefinitely satisfactory. And finally, from the Revolution came the approach to culture as a secular, moralizing force, a means of establishing a Republican morality that was distinct from religious tradition.[85]

All of these goals and themes are pertinent to our understanding of the ideological aims of the cultural and specifically musical programs of the Universal Exposition of 1900, and they are especially significant for our comprehension not only of the decisions made but also of the character of the official discourse that surrounded and explained them. In this discourse we may glean a conception of what constituted the "soul" of the nation, or an attempt, in answer to the Schola, to define the "true" French identity in music.

The Role of French Composers

The inclusion of programs of French music at the Exposition was not automatic, however: it was the result of a number of simultaneous pressures placed on Republican officials. Here, typically, professional interests, Republican ideology, bureaucratic structures, and political conjunctures were all to interact in an inextricable manner. Initially, it appeared to the Exposition's officials that French, as opposed to "exotic" foreign music, had very little to contribute to its larger political goals; this was probably, in part, the result of the considerable success of the programs of foreign and non-Western music in the Expositions of 1878 and 1889.[86] Official plans were gradually revealed, and by 1898 musicians became alarmed over the lack of provisions being made for the performance of French music. This concern was by no means new, for we have noted the pressure that musicians were putting on legislators in the 1890s for the performance of their works. The so-called "groupe de la musique" included the composers Xavier Leroux, Alfred Bruneau, Camille Erlanger, Gabriel Pierné, and Georges Hüe.[87]

In response to such pressures, in the mid-1890s the Paris Opéra began to present a series of concerts devoted to the performance of new works by French composers: these concerts were intended to help found a distinctive sense of the "École Française," or, as it was put at the time, of "une specificité musicale nationale." Such efforts won the enthusiastic praise of the president of the Republic, as well as the slightly more reserved or guarded approbation of Vincent d'Indy.[88] By 1899 the agitation for further actions was mounting, but now because of the pressure of nationalist agitation on the Left, as well as on the Right; although their conceptions of what to perform were substantially different, both sides were alarmed by the dominance of foreign works, particularly Wagner's, at the Opéra. The "rapporteur" of the budget of the Beaux-Arts, while recognizing the significance of Wagner, nevertheless advised, "Il faut se garder cependant de se laisser entraîner au-delà de ce qu'il convient par une race qui a ses conceptions personelles étrangères aux nôtres"[89] (It is necessary to prevent ourselves from being pulled beyond what is appropriate by a race with its own personal conceptions foreign to ours). He also went on to warn that French music indeed had powerful adversaries and that, at the forthcoming Exposition, productions from all over the world would be competing with the French: hence, in order for the French to establish their artistic vitality, he urged the Opéra's director to demonstrate the important place held by France in the art of music.[90]

In addition to this rhetoric, which encouraged the activism of French composers, another factor, as we have noted, was one stimulated by the Dreyfus Affair. At the very moment when French musicians were persuaded to sign the petitions being circulated by both sides, they chose to engage in this form of pressure themselves. In 1898, the year of the Dreyfusard "Manifest des Intellectuels," they submitted a petition requesting that a concert hall be reserved for the performance of French music; since their request was not granted, they proceeded, under the aggressive leadership of the composer Léon Gastinel, to take other, more forceful measures. On August 2, 1898, Gastinel addressed a letter on the subject to the head of the Commission générale of the Universal Exposition, Picard; in it, he complained that the question of music was clearly unimportant to the Commission, for it was being treated with far less concern than the other fine arts.[91]

His letter did not go unanswered: in response, an open letter appeared in the important newspaper Le Temps, which served as an official reply to the plaints of French composers. Picard here abruptly changed his position, now proposing the organization of "giant festivals" that would include the participation of choral masses, as well as diverse grandiose ensembles. This was not a novel conception; for the commemoration of Bastille Day in 1889, two thousand musicians had been assembled to perform on the Champ de Mars.[92] But the change of heart was significant, and it indeed did have an explanation: a bureaucratic restructuring that redefined the jurisdiction over the musical programs at the Exposition.

Now, all the decisions concerning musical performances at the Exposition passed into the domain of the Ministère de l'Instruction Publique et des Beaux-Arts. The implications of this were important: the placing of an art within the jurisdiction of the bureaucracy concerned with teaching and the encouragement of "letters" was an implicit acknowledgement of its role. For an art merited the protection of this ministry not because of the delectation it afforded the few but because it met a comprehensive need—the development of the aesthetic sense in the Nation. The Republic maintained that the love of beauty was directly connected with the progress of civilization and thus, by logical extension, with French national glory.

Already, shortly after the founding of the Third Republic, the fine or visual arts were entrusted to this ministerial authority. This meant that they were now administered by the same bureaucracy that was in charge of the social sciences and the humanities, which would influence the way they were approached. Almost from the start of the Republic, Gambetta was concerned with the problem of symbolism: of how to incarnate "l'âme française" in a coherent system of representation. It was through the use of symbols that he and the Third Republic's founders hoped to sacralize, immortalize, and unify "the memory of the nation."[93] The value of the art was thus historical, for it could be used to manifest the "progress" that French culture had undergone in time, to the greater glory of the nation itself. As we have seen, the leagues were ultimately to respond to such cultural tactics with a counterdiscourse concerning artistic "tradition"—as opposed to "progress."

As early as 1871, a chair in the Archeology and History of Art was founded at the Sorbonne—testimony to the belief in the role of the discipline in forging national memory. The foundation of such a chair was thus considered a means of implementing the Republic's goal of creating a system of national values as articulated through the symbolism of art; moreover, Republicans believed the discipline would instruct the nation in its essence or identity by promulgating a sense of the fundamental unity and power of French art. And the 1880s saw an even greater emphasis on the social function of the arts, now as opposed to their associations with the privileges of a sociocultural elite. One of the Republic's recurrent themes became the citizen's "right to culture," and thus the importance of implementing and ensuring this right through administrative means.[94] In the Republic, art was to serve a moral and a pedagogic end, as it had in the revolutionary period, by promoting the love of nature, of man, and of progress; by the 1890s the emphasis was on the social and historical aspects of art as a symbolic representation of the cultural legitimacy of the regime.[95] Again, this would be the basis on which the leagues were to launch their attack on the Republic and on its political legitimacy in the wake of the Dreyfus Affair; this, as we have seen, was the point at which they introduced a powerful new cultural stake—one not yet employed for these purposes by the Republic—the art of music.

Planning the Musical Programs

Much was to change in the Exposition's plans with the redefinition of the status of music as it came under the aegis of the Ministère de l'Instruction Publique. By 1898 a preponderant reason for these changes might well have been the growing status of the Schola and the example that it set of propaganda through music. Now, committees multiplied and special distinguished commissions were formed;

supporting staff was enlarged and a larger budget was both requested and ob-
tained. In addition, and as a consequence, music was assigned an ideological program, one that we may construe in a dialogic relation with that of the Schola.

On December 4, 1899, the Minister of Public Instruction assembled an elite
committee of musicians—those with the most professional prestige in French
music. This meant that he was forced to include individuals who were hostile to
the Republic, but, since they were clearly in the minority, it was probably assumed that their voice would, in fact, be small. Such an inclusion might also have
been an attempt to palliate or mollify and thus co-opt the "enemy" camp by offering it official recognition and a voice. The committee thus consisted of the major
figures of the Republican musical institutions; but, given the Schola's visible prestige and success, it also included d'Indy.

The commission comprised (among others) the professor of music history at
the Conservatoire (and former anti-Dreyfusard) Bourgault-Ducoudray; the director of the Conservatoire, Théodore Dubois; and the composers Bruneau, Fauré,
Gigout, Guilmant, de Jonciére, Marty, Massenet, Paladilhe, Pierné, Pugno, Réty,
Reyer, Rousseau, Deschapelle, Bernheim, and (J.) Bizet. The critic for Le Temps,
Pierre Lalo, was quick to note its domination by members of the Institut and by
officials of the Conservatoire, as well as of the Parisian theaters.[96] In an eloquent
discourse, the Minister charged this varied but distinguished group with an ambitious and, given the political conjuncture, particularly daunting task: they were,
through the selection of examples to be performed, to provide, in effect, a history
of French music from its origins to the present day.

This had broad implications, one being the construction of an official canon,
based on a sense of filiation and affinity of those great works in the so-called
French school. Certainly the existence of the new Scholiste or nationalist canon
was a factor in the nature of the Minister's charge to the predominantly loyalist
Republican commission. The group set to work immediately, beginning with the
election of its officers: Saint-Saëns as president, Dubois and Massenet as vice
presidents, Bruneau as "rapporteur," and Bizet as secretary. It was a formidable
task imposed on such a motley group—to arrive at the canon of great French
works and to define the criteria that identified and linked them. The commission
therefore adopted a method that seemed democratic as well as logical: Dubois
would propose a list of celebrated composers from different epochs, on which
each member was to vote, and to which each was free to add further suggestions.

Given the preponderant academic and official presence on the commission,
the results of the voting process, to contemporary observers, were indeed predictable. But the logic or the reasoning behind these preferences becomes clearer
when we examine the document produced by the "rapporteur" to explain their
choices. The largest number of votes (nineteen) went to Gluck, Berlioz, Delibes,
Lalo, Bizet, Lefebvre, and Messager; the next largest block (thirteen) was for
Thomas, David, Gounod, and Hillemacher; these were followed (with twelve
votes) by Jannequin, Lully, and Leroux and (with eleven votes) by Franck,
Guiraud, Godard, Chabrier, and Charpentier.[97] As we might expect given the inclusion of some dissidents from outside the official musical world, not all members of the group were pleased with the outcome; this was clearly the case with

d'Indy, who later wrote of his frustration in a letter of March 30, 1900, to Paul-Marie Masson. Here he refers to his combat, together with Garbiel Fauré, against the bad intentions and obstructionist tactics of the "légumes officiels." Since this was well after the commission met, it may well have referred not only to the voting but also to the subsequent concerts, in some of which d'Indy himself participated: he directed a number of programs performed by the Chanteurs de Saint-Gervais in the historical reconstruction of a "petite église du Vieux Paris." As we shall see, the musical programs, much to d'Indy's consternation, included little symphonic music and consisted largely of operatic excerpts.[98] Yet, as we may surmise, to do otherwise at this particular point would have been to negate the principles of the Conservatoire in favor of the renegade Schola Cantorum.

Alfred Bruneau's 'Report'

The results of the committee's voting required an ideological explanation, one that was to be made explicit in a formal discourse and then to be printed at the expense of the state. This was the task of the rapporteur, who, as we have noted, was Alfred Bruneau, a figure by now identified closely with the ideals of the triumphant "Dreyfusard Republic." Because of his role in the Dreyfus Affair, Bruneau enjoyed a high level of prestige, a fact from which his career would continue for many years to reap the benefit. Having been made a Chevalier de la Légion d'Honneur in 1895, he was subsequently promoted to the prestigious rank of Officier in 1904; in 1911, as he explains in his Memoires, it was due to his connection with Clemenceau, at the time of the Dreyfus Affair, that he was made Inspecteur Général des Beaux-Arts. This would be followed by still more honors, all ultimately deriving from the Dreyfus Affair: in 1919 Bruneau became Commandeur de la Légion d'Honneur, and in 1925 he was elected to the Académie des Beaux-Arts. Such honors also facilitated his entry as a major music critic for such important journals as *Gil Blas, Le Figaro,* and *Le Matin.*

Bruneau's report on the musical programs performed at the Exposition in 1900 undoubtedly solidified his position as a spokesman for the Republican musical aesthetic. For he clearly understood his charge to arrive at a musical discourse that would do for the Republic what d'Indy had done so effectively for its political adversaries. This meant employing concepts, references, vocabulary, and values that would have a similar resonance, making reference simultaneously to both political and musical realms; moreover, an implicit expectation was that he would further develop those Republican themes already ensconced by the 1880s concerning the pedagogical and social role of art. In short, Bruneau was faced with the task of refracting the government's goals and themes through the prism of a musical discourse concerning the historical evolution of French musical taste: he would have to generate musical symbols and meanings as powerful as those of Vincent d'Indy and to relate the "master fictions" of Republican ideology to music history and values.[99] This meant not only defining his position against that of the adversary within but simultaneously defining French musical values against those of Germany, or the threat from without.

Although conceived as a book on French music and intended for a wide distribution, the report is presented in the guise of a formal statement to the Minister on French musical taste. Bruneau begins by acknowledging both the nobility and difficulty of his task and credits the Minister with being the first to place music on a level equal to the other arts, for it was he who wished to demonstrate to the "multitude, which is less indifferent to beauty than is generally thought," the route that this illustrious art has followed from age to age. Bruneau also credits the Minister not only with seeking to illuminate the past, but also with wishing to clarify the path that will lead French music forward towards a promising future.[100] The official context established, he proceeds to give an outline of French music history that is, in every way, as selective and ideologically charged as that of d'Indy.

Several themes run through Bruneau's sketch and determine his interpretation—themes that are patently drawn from Republican tradition, as well as from recent Dreyfusard discourse. One is anticlericalism, which, in implicit contrast to Scholiste ideology, implies that the history of music in France is completely independent of the Roman Catholic Church. Hence, Bruneau's history pointedly begins not with the Church and Gregorian chant but, rather, with a composer he presents as consciously and independently ignoring it—the Trouvère Adam de la Halle. For Bruneau, de la Halle is indeed the veritable founder of the "French School," one that is characterized by independence, especially from any kind of clerical constraints; moreover, his *Le Jeu de Robin et Marion* is, Bruneau boldly claims, the point of departure for that quintessentially French dramatic genre, Opéra Comique. De la Halle, he argues, was already seeking the union of melody and text, a goal he accomplished by deriving inspiration from popular sources—from the "people" themselves. Thus, whenever his music becomes "difficult" or mannered, it is because it has been subjected to the rigid rules of the "official tonality" established by Pope Gregory. Gradually, Bruneau continues, the composer freed himself from the constraint of these rules and was able to create with complete and glorious independence of spirit and soul.[101] The theme of independence as a fundamental French artistic trait is one that was long to endure in Republican musical discourse.

The other theme, of the "popular" as a source of inspiration for music—one of a similar longevity—recurs in his discussion of Josquin's *Missa l'homme armé.* (Josquin, who was born and died on the present Franco-Belgian border and who spent a large part of his career in France, becomes, for Bruneau, a French composer.) Here Bruneau delights in describing how the composer embroiders skillfully on a popular theme that, he claims, Josquin incorporated in order to echo the "real" world outside.[102] For Bruneau, this technique represents not the interpenetration of the sacred and the secular but the fundamentally French propensity for the incorporation of nature and life in music. Already, we may perceive the teleology in the report that would eventually culminate in what was considered the Dreyfusard genre "par excellence," Naturalist opera. In addition, taking aim at the Schola, Bruneau asserts that in this work Josquin transformed the "cold" and "dry" technique of counterpoint into a medium of sincere expression. Like d'Indy, he argues for the principles of honesty and sincerity in art, but, as we can see, their conceptions of the nature and manifestations of these qualities were distant.

Bruneau's bias towards secular music becomes even more evident and egregious in his discussion of the secular chansons of Jannequin. Here the focus is on Jannequin's adroit incorporation of Parisian street cries, which Bruneau presents as a "tableau des moeurs" and hence an incipient Naturalism. He then proceeds to argue that this is a constant in French music history—the inspiration from the "popular" and the streets, from real life and even mundane events.

Bruneau's French tradition proceeds, like d'Indy's, to Lully, Rameau, and Gluck but then centers on composers of the revolutionary period, who d'Indy's survey studiously ignored. After crediting Grétry with the invention of the leitmotif, he proceeds to praise Méhul, Gossec, Cherubini, and Lesueur and, in the nineteenth century, Boieldieu and Berlioz. Unlike d'Indy, Bruneau places Berlioz centrally within the tradition, claiming that it was he, not Wagner, who "rescued" French music from its decadent "Italianism."[103] After praising Félicien David, Charles Gounod, and Ambroise Thomas, Bruneau recognizes the other composers who received votes—Bizet, Delibes, Lalo, Chabrier, Chausson, and Franck. He presents Saint-Saëns's symphonic poems as incarnations of French independence, since, formally, they refuse to be "slaves" of tradition or placidly to follow routes already traced; French values, for Bruneau, as seen in Saint-Saëns, include not only measure and clarity (ideals that date back to the Société Nationale) but also the more Romantic characteristics of frankness, "heart," and audacity.[104]

When discussing contemporary music Bruneau, like d'Indy, could hardly avoid the increasingly crucial question of German influence, particularly that of Wagner; as a composer heavily influenced by Wagner, Bruneau had the difficult task of defining not only the significance of Wagner's innovations but also that which did not accord with French art. Like Zola, he stresses the independence of musical form that Wagner brought, the perfect union of melody and text, the fusion of voices and orchestra, and his "noblesse," "ampleur," and "eloquence."[105] In his *Musiques d'hier er de demain,* which was published in 1900, Bruneau credits Wagner with inaugurating a new musical theater of greater reason, rigor, and logic; in the "drame lyrique," as developed by Wagner, the music, so closely united with the word, imparts life, movement, and passional interest to human actions. This, of course, relates to Bruneau's own conception of authentic musical theater as an art of movement, of life, of expression, and in consequence of "truth." As we have noted, Bruneau's rhetoric, in the context, was undoubtedly meant to be and, as we shall see, immediately was, construed as invoking Republican values.

In this book, as in the *Rapport,* Bruneau is compelled to point out those fundamentally "Germanic" elements in Wagner's art that inherently distinguish it from the French: this includes the length of his works, his abstract philosophy, and his "idealistic" myths, as well as the symbols he employs which, for Bruneau, are purely German. Yet Wagner, he asseverates, like d'Indy, has revealed the path for "true" French art, although the explanation of what this implies differs substantially between the two. According to Bruneau (and d'Indy), Wagner showed that the spirit of a people and the love of the soil inspire the noble and the grand, and therefore the French must be true to "themselves." In contrast to d'Indy, who believed in the importance of instinct as a primordial force that binds the French people, Bruneau stresses the French propensity for "action" and not for "dreams."

The theme of the necessary proximity of art to life, to reality, and to action, a theme that would be central to the aesthetics of the Left in France, runs through Bruneau's *Rapport*. Bruneau argues that this is true in the present, since it provides the justification for his placing French Naturalist opera at the point of culmination of the teleology he has traced; hence, it is in an opera performed in the context of the Exposition, that of his friend, Gustave Charpentier, in which he identifies the purest French traits. For Bruneau, *Louise* represents the latest and most progressive incarnation of all those values he has associated with the Republican or "authentic" French tradition. We shall see in chapter 2 the extent to which Bruneau's interpretation and the influence it exerted was to affect the immediate responses to Charpentier's opera; we shall also see not only how fundamentally wrong his construal was, but how this misreading affected the responses to the opera by his political adversaries.

In Charpentier, Bruneau perceives not only a highly original composer, but, even more important, a "passioné de la vérité et de l'idéal."[106] Again, "vérité," a word still charged by the discourse of the Dreyfusards, becomes here, as elsewhere, Bruneau's highest term of artistic approbation. As he then elaborates, since a composer feels emotion only from that which he has experienced, Charpentier chooses his artistic subjects from contemporary life; according to Bruneau, the composer does not stop here—he proceeds to "elevate" his subjects or to make them "musical," through the use of appropriate symbols. Hence, for Bruneau, *Louise* represents the culmination of the true French tradition, not just because of the values it incarnates, but because it employs Parisian street cries; this conveniently allows him to trace a line of development directly from the secular and "popular" tradition of Jannequin up to Charpentier.[107]

Because of the musical values he espouses, those rooted in his conception of essential French traits, Bruneau is clearly confronted with a problem when he turns to Claude Debussy. For, like so many others whom we shall examine, he could construe Debussy's innovations only within the narrow framework of his own aesthetic-political discourse. Although Bruneau observes that the composer's musical talent is now beyond question, he finds such works as *L'Après-midi d'un faune* alarming in its implications for the future; for, he opines, in it Debussy is heading in a dangerous direction—the work is ruined by harmonic overrefinement, or continual modulation, and a "mollesse de facteur." Such qualities, of course, are fundamentally contrary to his essential aesthetic criteria that a work be "virile" and "human" in order to instill a durable emotion in the listener.[108] Debussy's music was indeed to continue to perplex and alarm the aesthetic spokesman not only for the Republic but also for many of its political adversaries. It would not be until shortly before the First World War, when the Action Française developed a coherent commentary on his works, that they would be recognized, within its discourse, as "French."

Responses to Bruneau's 'Report'

As we might expect, the contestation of Bruneau's report was both immediate and emphatic, in view of its importance in the battle over competing politico-aesthetic conceptions. For again, this was the period of the nationalist assault on the Republic's aesthetic ideals, perceived as symbolic incarnations of the values that now informed its fundamental political creed. Bruneau's adversaries thus acutely grasped and directly addressed his political subtext and, just as he, employed an ideological discourse that had emerged from the Dreyfus Affair. Although their responses carried a political charge, perhaps the most damaging and scathing review was one that professed to attack the report on purely professional or musical terms. Shortly after the report was published in the format of a book, a lengthy examination of it appeared in the important *Revue d'histoire et de critique musicale*.[109] This one was particularly damning since its author identified himself only as "X," further qualified by the phrase "Ancien membre de la Commission"; moreover, he accuses Bruneau not only of venturing beyond the scope of his talents but of inaccuracy, error, and even consciously distorting the deliberations of the commission.

The critic begins by professing deep embarrassment over his task, claiming to have great esteem for Bruneau's sincerity as an artist and for his "vaillance artistique"; he distinguishes Bruneau the composer, whom he considers as worthy of praise, from Bruneau the "critique-rapporteur," who merits only condemnation.[110] He then explains his inability to remain silent on this important issue, given the function and authority of the report, as an official document on French musical taste; for, as we have noted, its implications in the context were considerable since it represented an "authorized" conception of French cultural and thus political identity.

In order properly to evaluate the report as a statement on behalf of the commission, the critic explains that he decided to review the "procès-verbaux," or minutes, of the various meetings. Here he emphasizes the degree of dissension that actually existed among the members, as well as particular cases in which specific individuals (especially d'Indy) disagreed with the majority. One case in point, he claims, is the session of June 5, in which d'Indy expressed his regret at the absence of the works of Ropartz, Magnard, Dukas, and Rabaud in the symphonic programs;[111] given such clues, the general style, and the nature of the argument that follows, it is highly probable that d'Indy himself was the author of the review.

As we might expect, a particular concern of the review is what the critic sees as the inaccuracies and distortions in its view of French music history. He begins with the discussion of Adam de la Halle and points out how ridiculous it is to consider *Le Jeu de Robin et Marion* as lying at the origins of Opéra Comique. After noting other historical errors, he then takes particular exception to the claim that de la Halle's music written in the Gregorian modes was mannered, distorted, and "difficult"; he further disqualifies Bruneau's interpretation by observing that it was on the basis of a modernized version of the work (one published in 1888, with a piano accompaniment by Weckerlin) that Bruneau refers to the composer as a "trouvère harmoniste et mélodiste."[112] The author also ridicules Bruneau for all the periods his sketch of French music history ignores, such as the fifteenth century and thus, by extension, the development of religious polyphony; moreover, in the sixteenth century, the critic goes on to complain, the author primarily considers only Jannequin, Josquin, and Goudimel. As he puts it, in high dudgeon:

> Nous ne pouvons pas comprendre qu'un compositeur éminent, ancien élève de Con-
> servatoire de Paris, ancien Prix de Rome, investi d'un rôle officiel et écrivant pour le
> Ministre de l'Instruction Publique un rapport destiné à l'Imprimerie Nationale, parle
> de notre XVIe siècle musicale aussi légèrement.[113]

> (We cannot understand that an eminent composer, former student at the Paris Con-
> servatoire, former Prix de Rome, invested with an official role and writing for the
> Minister of Public Instruction a report destined for the national press, speaks so
> lightly of our sixteenth century.)

The tactic here is subtle but trenchant and would recur among the critics of Republican cultural institutions and their spokesmen much later in the 1930s: the
critic openly accuses an official spokesman for the state of distorting the nation's
great cultural patrimony or heritage through the grave sin of omission.

Given the probable identity of the author, it is not at all surprising that he is
particularly distressed by the patent anticlerical bias of the text; he attacks
Bruneau's classification of Jannequin as a "pantheist" in several chansons simply
because the word "berger" appears at the beginning of the collection. Here he
pointedly clarifies that in the context of the sixteenth century, this, in fact, signified nothing more than a "receuil de morceau choisis"[114] (a collection of selected
pieces). Bruneau, he astutely perceives, is simply attempting to identify historical
antecedents for Realism in French music in order to justify it aesthetically in the
present; he incisively adds that the idea of employing realistic street cries, which
Bruneau presents as an essential French trait, was eclipsed for almost four hundred years.

The critic then enumerates the important figures and subjects that Bruneau
ignores, with a particular emphasis on counterpoint and the growth of harmony
"from it." This, as we have seen, was one of d'Indy's peculiar conceptions, one
that, in order to disqualify the emphasis on harmony at the Conservatoire, he re-
iterated at the Schola. But the critic notes other lacunae, almost all of which were
subjects ignored at the Conservatoire while being important areas of study in the
contestatory program of the Schola Cantorum. He asks rhetorically, "what place
does the motet occupy in French music history? And what of the madrigal, dance
music, the cantata, and the symphony?[115] Given the meanings that d'Indy had attributed to these forms in his historical conception, these "disqualifications," in
such a context, were indeed ideologically pregnant. He also notes Bruneau's apparent preference for the nineteenth century, a period that, as we have noted, was
stressed at the Conservatoire as opposed to the Schola.

Finally, singling in on the reality of Bruneau's political engagement, he notes
the composer's reference to the current "battle," but without directly implicating
himself; he then indirectly accuses Bruneau of cowardly hypocrisy, claiming that
by his indiscriminate praise of all in the present, he is no longer a "militant" but
rather an arbitrator.[116] The review concludes with a discussion of the commission's decisions concerning the repertoire to be performed by the "orphéons, harmonies," and "fanfares"; here the author complains that the "orphéons," or large
choruses of male workers, were, aside from one work by Rameau, not given an
historical repertoire.[117] D'Indy, who had long taken an interest in these societies,

as a paternalistic aristocrat, often vocally expressed his belief that the level of their repertoire should be raised. Perhaps reflecting the utopian social beliefs of his formidable grandmother, d'Indy held that the different classes could be united through a shared body of culture.[118] Hence, he points out the need for an appropriate historical anthology for these groups, one that includes the masters of vocal composition from its origin to the present, but his ideological interest (as a member of the league) emerges when he explains the goal: to develop a taste for the history of French music—and, implicitly, tradition—among this group.[119]

Such an attack on Bruneau was not isolated. Another anti-Dreyfusard militant—the powerful critic Henri Gauthier-Villars, or "Willy"—ridiculed the *Rapport* from a more explicitly political perspective. In the same journal, two years later, Willy raised identical issues in an article pointedly and provocatively entitled, "Qu'est ce que la musique française?"[120] As we have noted, Willy supported the Ligue de la Patrie Française in its condemnation of Dreyfus and signed the petition that was circulated against him; during the Affair, when he perceived that many Dreyfusards were also Wagnerians, he smugly recalled Wagner's anti-Semitic remarks concerning Mendelssohn and Meyerbeer.[121]

Here, with obvious reference to the Affair, still an obsession for the Right, he begins by referring to the view of French music history that is held by intellectuals or, as he puts it facetiously, "gendelettres" [sic]. He claims that for this group, French music history consists primarily of Adam, Auber, Gounoud, and Thomas, implying by these names that they are Jewish, "popular," or official composers. In the present, he continues, this "history" centers on Bruneau, Charpentier, Dubois, Huë, Massenet, and Saint-Saëns—in other words, the official Republican musical establishment. Willy then points out the combative nature of such "men of letters," as well as their rapid reversal of position concerning the influence of Richard Wagner. This was probably intended to refer specifically to Bruneau who, as we have seen, was in the process of qualifying his earlier Wagnerian enthusiasm.[122]

But the attack on what Willy considers to be a Dreyfusard aesthetic becomes more blatant when he proceeds to parody what he refers to as the Republicans' "Style parlementaire"; for example, when addressing the issue of "le génie français," they would claim to attempt to "verser quelques lumières sur le débat et porter la question sur son véritable terrain"[123] (shed some light on the debate and put the question on its true ground). Again, the implication is that to this sensitive issue, one that is inherently intuitive and emotional, the parliamentary Republic brings only pretentious and abstract logic. He then makes his point even further by observing how officials at state ceremonies invariably praise the same specific set of aesthetic qualities as being "truly French": for this group, the essential "cachet" of "le génie français" consists of moderation, balance, and reason, and, as he implies, nothing more.

Willy then turns to works he considers to be "authentically French," praising, in particular, Vincent d'Indy and his early Wagnerian opera *Fervaal*; the critic, an ardent Wagnerian, notes not only its "robust" nature but the clarity of its themes, its logic, and its orchestration along with the variety and suppleness of its rhythms. While agreeing with certain Republican conceptions of what is distinctively French (those articulated at the founding of the Société Nationale), he emphasizes rhythmic fluidity, as at the Schola. Then, like d'Indy, he goes on to deplore the gradual disappearance of the influence of Richard Wagner; Willy thus considers anti-Wagnerian currents to be destructive, believing, similarly, that Wagner, although German, had a "cleansing effect" on French music. Not surprisingly, then, he concludes that the current and rightful leader of the so-called "French School" in music is undoubtedly Vincent d'Indy.

SOURCES OF SUPPORT FOR THE SCHOLA

Willy, in a sense, was right, since, to the Republic's great consternation, the Schola was perceptibly gaining in status, and specifically to the detriment of the state Conservatoire. For some of its growing group of supporters the reasons were primarily ideological, while for others, who attempted to minimize its ideology, the reasons were fundamentally professional. As we shall see later in this chapter, this separation was eventually to become impossible as the battle between the institutions escalated and was fought on ideological terrain; but in the years immediately following the turn of the century, the Schola Cantorum developed a wide network of supporters and of journals to disseminate and explain its aesthetic ideals. These included political, literary, and musical journals, and, in several cases, the same writers were active simultaneously in all three categories. But of central importance here is not only the intertextual references in all three types of journals but the way they broadly disseminated the meanings that the Schola applied to forms and to styles. Such a press provided an effective network of intellectual influence and a circuit for establishing musical significations in both the musical and the larger culture.

Despite its marginality, the Schola Cantorum was to have an enormous impact, for it attracted a wide range of supporters from the far Left to the Nationalist Right. This was increasingly the case as the so-called Dreyfusard Republic waxed more pragmatic and politically centrist, thus disappointing its former supporters. It was at this point that the two political extreme positions on the Left and the Right joined together in the pursuit of an ethical or "moral" conception of art; music became a key subject for both, and hence intellectuals associated with each position drew attention to this aspect of the Schola, in contrast to the Conservatoire. Both sides were drawn to the Schola's coherent and convincing aesthetic rhetoric, one that was unprecedented in educational institutions of music in France and which contained elements that could be selectively used.

Not surprisingly, the artistic journal in which d'Indy participated, L'Occident, played a central role in diffusing both his political and artistic beliefs. The Schola, of course, did have publications aimed specifically at the French musical world, the *Tribune de Saint-Gervais* and the *Tablettes de la Schola,* but L'Occident brought these journals to the attention of a larger public by frequently making reference to them or by publishing excerpts of articles from them. Significantly, L'Occident proudly and unequivocally identified itself as the organ of Nationalist artists, or "artistes vrais, et pas Dreyfusard." These included the adamantly anti-Dreyfusard writer Maurice Barrès (a dominant influence), as well as the equally committed Edgar Degas and Maurice Denis.[124] The latter became one of the Schola's strongest artistic supporters and indeed articulated its political premises more lucidly than even d'Indy himself. Later to collaborate with d'Indy on the production of his "anti-Dreyfusard opera" La Légende de Saint Christophe, he was integral in explaining and diffusing knowledge of the Schola's nature and goals. In his prewar lectures and writings on the need for the renewal of religious art, Denis used the Schola as a model for the kind of institution he would conceive for artists; for his ideal, like d'Indy's, was the Middle Ages, when art was an "enseignement," serving simultaneously to express and to further the ineffable "foi collective."[125]

According to Denis, as well as d'Indy, the Renaissance brought about an aesthetic decline, for artists full of "pride" and "rhetoric" then embraced individualism and abstraction. The Renaissance thus initiated the decay of "craft," encouraging the mere manipulation of materials, or an excess of virtuosity devoid of sincerity and cut off from tradition. Denis thus decried the reappearance of what he termed "pagan," platonic tendencies in art, and the kind of "oriental" abstraction that the Occident had abandoned during the Middle Ages. Certainly, there had been a vogue for the Orient, promoted by, among others, Symbolist circles, which associated it with the "exotic" or mysterious. Yet "oriental" here, in the specific context of Right-wing discourse, had become a frequent code word for "Jewish," implying that it belonged to a different cultural world. For a massive immigration of Jews began in 1905, and, as Paula Hyman has shown, the majority, from Russia and Romania, chose to settle in Paris. Hence, while non-Jewish immigrants generally remained on the Mediterranean coast or in the industrialized north and east, Paris felt the strong presence of "exotic" immigrant Jews. The Eastern Europeans, unlike the Sephardic Jews from the Levant or North Africa, did not speak French and were not familiar with French culture or customs. Predominantly working class and impoverished, they were often singled out by the prewar Right-wing press as "importers of inferior moral standards and squalid living conditions." But the "Orient" also signified the "barbaric," in the broadest sense, which embraced not just the Jews but equally Protestants and Germans. (Significantly, the Masonic order was called the "Grand Orient de France.") In short, the "Orient," for nationalists, was the "constructed" antithesis to the West, or "Occident," and the French, the vehicle through which the latter attempted to define what it was not.[126]

Denis thus considered the Schola to be a salutary artistic institution that would help to reverse the noxious "oriental" trends of the day. But another important supporter of d'Indy who helped to spread his reputation, not only in the musical world but beyond it, was Lionel de la Laurencie. Later to become the first president of the Société Française de Musicologie, La Laurencie was a frequent contributor to nonmusical journals, including L'Occident. In an article tellingly entitled "Un Musicien de chez nous," he relates d'Indy's principles concerning form and technique to the social metaphors the journal's readers would surely appreciate.[127] Undoubtedly attempting to evoke the promilitary sentiments of the anti-Dreyfusards, La Laurencie explains d'Indy's concern with form by employing explicitly martial imagery:

Véritable général d'armée, il règle les mouvements des masses sonores . . . et signe des ordres de marche. . . . Sous sa direction, chacun trouve la place qui convient à ses aptitudes, et son esprit méthodique s'en va trier les gens et les choses, séparant l'ivraie du bon grain.[128]

(Veritable army general, he regulates the movements of the sonorous masses . . . and signs the marching orders. . . . Under his direction, each finds the place that suits its aptitudes, and his methodical spirit goes on to sort out men and things, separating the rye grass from the wheat.)

Through this metaphor, La Laurencie confers d'Indy's approach with an intellectual authority or legitimacy that would have been recognized or registered by the journal's readers.

La Laurencie then goes on to develop the idea of the "occidental"—again as opposed to the insidious "oriental"—but here applied specifically to the art of music. After referring to d'Indy's doctrine as quintessentially "occidental," he explains that it was in the occident that the principle of "association," the backbone of the social body, was born: such a principle, he continues, extends to occidental music, especially to polyphony, since vocal counterpoint is, in essence, an "association" of melodies. Why, he asks rhetorically, doesn't a voice, instead of following its "liturgical shepherd" in a disciplined troupe, not leave it in distinct and organized corporations? It is because, he then explains, all are working together toward the same ultimate end, although proceeding towards it by following distinctively different paths.[129] As we shall see in chapter 3, the social theory that La Laurencie is invoking here closely approximates one that the Ligue d'Action Française would soon be propagating; for one of its goals was to reconcile the authentic regional interests of France with those of the centralizing monarchy that it still wished to restore. Hence the league would be quick to perceive this propinquity of idea and technique and to adopt this and other Scholist metaphors for its ideological end.

Switching to a religious metaphor equally resonant for L'Occident's readers, La Laurencie proceeds to discuss the Schola's concept of "la libre musique." "Libre," or free, in this context refers to that which is outside the control of the state, specifically to the Catholic Church, then under persecution by the Third Republic. According to La Laurencie, the "libre musique" that d'Indy recommends is one that employs supple rhythms as it aims at the "emancipation" of the individual melody within the musical "body." Hence it is different from that of the official Conservatoire as it proudly remains free of the stylistic standards imposed by the state institution. Finally, explicating or rationalizing the foreign influences in d'Indy's works, particularly that of Germany, La Laurencie explains the occidental "synthesis" to his readers: once a foreign influence enters French culture it is immediately synthesized into an intellectual amalgam that is characteristic of the occidental world.[130] Presumably, however, this does not apply to the Jewish influence, which, according to d'Indy's dogma and that of the league, could never become a part of this compound.

La Laurencie helped diffuse d'Indy's influence not only in artistic journals of the Right but also in the Catholic press, similarly predisposed to his cultural doctrine. The historical conjuncture was particularly felicitous in 1903 and 1904, when Pope Pius X published his "Motu proprio" concerning religious music. The rules he then imposed on Catholics—Gregorian chant and polyphony—corresponded perfectly with the ideals that were promulgated at the Schola Cantorum. Indeed, in the 1890s the Church had been developing an antimodern discourse and concomitantly encouraging a return to the study of the Middle Ages. Given these points of consonance with the Schola, it is thus by no means surprising that the school itself collaborated in the Vatican's edition of Gregorian chant.[131]

D'Indy was thus now actively disseminating his ideas in Catholic circles, particularly since they apparently had been receptive to his anti-Semitic attacks; as his contemporaries reported, such tirades were especially well received in the impassioned lectures that he delivered at the Institut Catholique. La Laurencie faithfully communicated this rhetoric in an article he published in the Catholic journal of art and literature *Durendal,* entitled "L'Oeuvre de Vincent d'Indy."[132] La Laurencie begins by noting (falsely) the elevated tastes of d'Indy's family, as well as their intimate familiarity with the works of the classical masters; hence, d'Indy, he asserts, frequented only the "temple" of great art and ignored the "byzantine constructions" and flashy brilliance that attracted the public of his time. Ignoring d'Indy's taste before he encountered the Franckiste circle, he claims that the composer escaped the musical "contagion" of the Rossinian-Meyerbeerian school.[133] As the reader will recall, for d'Indy this became the "Italo-judaïque" school, a conception that La Laurencie was now attempting sagaciously to ensconce in Catholic circles; like d'Indy, he was seeking to instill a belief in a fundamental dichotomy between the morally instructive power of great art and the mere "pleasure" that the more base imparts.

Against this background, La Laurencie then explains d'Indy's disdain for the Renaissance, with its stress on technique and the "materialization" of art as the result; instead, he continues, d'Indy's artistic sympathies lie with pre-Renaissance artists, or "les primitifs," who created the sculpted saints that ornament the great cathedrals.[134] Then, after recounting the birth of the Schola and detailing its accomplishments, La Laurencie proceeds to educate his public on the evils of the state Conservatoire: here, he points out, music is taught in "bastardized manuals" that are filled with "exemples d'école," thus teaching the students a style that is at once both conventional and false. He also notes the poor attendance at the Conservatoire's class in music history, explaining that only on the basis of history can one find a truly "scientific" doctrine. He ends with d'Indy's image of the spiral, always rising from that which came before: it is thus, he concludes, that true progress builds fundamentally upon tradition.[135]

It was not only among anti-Dreyfusard and Catholic circles that La Laurencie attempted to propagate the teachings of d'Indy and the Schola but also among advanced artistic circles: for in the important Belgian journal *L'Art moderne,* he elaborated on the place of "d'Indysme" within the larger concerns and proclivities of contemporary French society. Here his aesthetic and social propaganda, which was based on the Schola's, was aimed not at educating the already converted but rather at winning over a wider group. Hence, his goal in such a journal was to relate the Schola's teaching to the growing preoccupation of the Republic and the

Left with defining a responsible "social" art. We shall shortly see how effective this intellectual tactic actually was—how even committed Socialists at first interpreted the institution's goals as primarily "moral."

La Laurencie begins by noting the propensity in contemporary French society for the proliferation of "dogmatic" or ideologically founded "schools" in all the arts; among these he includes as examples not only of "Nationalist" and "Christian" literature, in which, as we have seen, he himself participated, but also Socialist literature.[136] As La Laurencie observes, each bases itself on a different kind of authority, but one common concern is art's contribution to the cause of "progress." As we have noted, this could be construed in many different ways, on the basis of varying fundamental conceptions of the social order. La Laurencie here comments that of these various social ideologies one indeed is no longer tenable in light of the tendencies that characterize the present: this ideology is Liberalism, which La Laurencie here implicitly argues is as outdated in politics as it is in art. For the current of contemporary French society is rather toward "strong" opinions—a tendency, of course, into which the teaching of the Schola perfectly fit; moreover, he continues, art is "liberating itself" through religious feeling and thus increasingly its ultimate goal is pedagogical—in d'Indy's words, to "teach." Here La Laurencie, like d'Indy's friend and biographer Léon Vallas, compares d'Indy's teaching with that of the art historian who influenced him, Emile Mâle, and he notes that Mâle's argument in his *L'Art religieux au XIIIe siècle* is identical to d'Indy's: the goal of religious art is basically to "teach." He then goes on to relate this to the theme now so widely heard in France—the social role of art in educating the masses, hence the importance of exposing them to "beauty." D'Indy, he concludes is thus by no means positioned on the cultural margins, but is participating, in his own way, in the ineluctable current of the present day.[137] We shall see in chapter 2, however, how fundamentally different d'Indy's conception of this education of the people was from that of the Third Republic. But La Laurencie's desire here was to place d'Indy and the Schola in the mainstream, thus obfuscating the anti-Republican character of his social thought.

The Schola and the Socialist Left

La Laurencie's argument concerning d'Indy's participation in true "social" art was not unique but indeed was echoed by a major figure on the Socialist left. Again, the criticism of Republican institutions was growing not only on the Right but on the far Left, as the Dreyfusard "mystique" was transformed into a banal "politique." Critics of the Republic on the Left included not only prominent former Dreyfusard writers such as Charles Péguy and Georges Sorel but a host of others as well:[138] one such figure was Camille Mauclair, whose writings continually crossed several fields, thus further helping to obscure the boundaries that separated politics, literature, and the arts. Having passed through an anarchist stage at the time of his engagement with Symbolism, Mauclair then moved into Dreyfusism and Socialism at the time of the Dreyfus Affair.[139]

In 1901 Mauclair published an article on the Schola in *La Revue,* in which he makes the reasons for his support of the musical institution immediately clear:

the Schola Cantorum, for him, is first of all a "phénomène morale," for subtending it is no less than a new way of thinking about human emotions. According to Mauclair, the younger generation of artists is in search of a moral education and, as a result, is now unequivocally rejecting "l'enseignement officiel"; the Schola is thus an expression of the desire for a moral renovation in the musical world: it heralds the advent of "l'ère nouvelle du spiritualisme musicale." This ideal accorded perfectly with Mauclair's professed philosophy of art—that at the core of its mysterious power ultimately lies the moral component.[140]

Such a connection is not surprising, given Mauclair's former background in Anarchism, for it is just this position that was articulated in Anarchist journals such as *Le Libertaire*. Here we encounter an overriding concern with how, given modern aspirations and needs, one might define a new morality that is appropriate to current society.[141] Once defined, the journal's authors argue, this new morality must then be spread, and the vehicle that they identify to do so most effectively is the art of music: for music, together with words, possesses a power of penetration that allows it to contribute integrally to the birth and development of a "new humanity." As we shall see in chapter 3, this position did not disappear with the Anarchist movement but was rather later taken over and developed, if slightly altered, by syndicalist circles. Here, probably because of the intrepretation of Wagner by the French Left, the journal presents music as thus capable of providing a detailed "analysis" of moral problems that is "hautement libertaire." Hence, opera was believed to propagate the social ideals that were central to Anarchism—the fundamental and essential feelings of independence and human dignity. Already we may see that although this movement, like the Schola, espoused the moral power of music, it was with a very different conception of what constitutes the "moral." Other articles in the journal further clarify its perspective, as well as the reasons opera was to play such an important role in the Anarchist social program. One of April 4–11, 1896, for example, points out that "le spectacle" is one of the most important means through which to disseminate an ideological message, for it exerts an overwhelming influence not only on the ideals of a epoch but also and simultaneously on its feelings, thus making it all the more effective.

Mauclair was clearly influenced by these currents in his panegyric of the Schola, which he here attempts to present in the most favorable possible light. Ignoring d'Indy's combative rhetoric and incontrovertible dogma, Mauclair argues that the institution innocently neither imposes nor opposes a thing.[142] Rather, he speaks of Charles Bordes and the way in which the inseparability of his artistic convictions and Christian faith led him back to the purest sources of religious music. Yet Mauclair points out that the small, elite group that initially attended his concerts included those, like himself, who were drawn to both the symbolist and Anarchist movements. He also notes the presence there of Franck's disciples, of Mallarmé's circles, and of the "habitués" of the "Salon de la libre esthétique" in Brussels.[143] As Mauclair observes, the atmosphere of these concerts, characterized by the primacy of feeling as well the absence of histrionics, was later transferred to the Schola Cantorum.

While not religious himself, Mauclair approved of the Schola's placing chant in a position of honor and its attempt to raise the level of the organist's repertoire: both, he believed, helped build the "moral fibre" of the performer, to make the art of the soloist one of the "inner" as opposed to the "outer" world. It is from this perspective that Mauclair draws attention to d'Indy's provocative inaugural address, ignoring the other aspects of it not relevant to his points; he also praises the Schola's venture in independent music publishing, its own influential attempt to print and disseminate the repertoire that it taught. The result was a library that he saw as a document of French music history, especially that aspect of it that was studiously ignored by the Conservatoire's professors.[144] Mauclair lauds the Schola's journal, *La Tribune de Saint Gervais,* as well, for its serious historical purpose and its distinguished group of contributors; these, he notes, include the Conservatoire's professor of music history, Bourgault-Ducoudray, as well as André Pirro, Pierre Lalo, Adolphe Jullien, Julien Tiersot, Camille Benoist, and Camille Bellaigue.[145] He concludes that the Schola's prestige is such that it can invite the participation of the leading scholars of music in the period in its journal. This undoubtedly did contribute to the institution's growing reputation, a fact that would help determine the cultural counteroffensive of the Republic.

Finally, moving from the moral to the purely professional musical realm, Mauclair eulogizes the unprecedented homogeneity and coherence of the Schola's teaching.[146] This he attributes to its founders—a distinguished and unpretentious group who have proceeded with "rigorous logic" in the face of "official timidity." For Mauclair, the principle underlying the Schola is exactly the opposite of what he sees at the Conservatoire, where all the instruction is founded solely on desiccated "formulae"; here anti-Dreyfusard rhetoric is indeed employed by a former Dreyfusard, now to the Left of the Republic, and hence closer to the other extreme than to the center. Mauclair goes on to argue that at the Schola the pedagogy issues from a highly "personal" reflection, but one that is based on impartial study of the "great masters." "Chefs-d'oeuvres" at the Schola are not those works that have been consecrated only by public success but are works that have been heroically saved from oblivion by an intelligent minority.[147]

When turning to opera, Mauclair takes a position very much like that espoused by d'Indy, for he supports the effort of the pupils of Franck to profit from the Wagnerian "revolution"; like d'Indy, he believes that it is in this manner that the French can thus "extinguish" the degenerate Italianism that unfortunately characterizes so much contemporary virtuoso singing in France.[148] Hence, Mauclair condemns the vocal instruction characteristic of the Conservatoire, which is applicable primarily to the works of Meyerbeer, Gounod, and Donizetti.

Mauclair's conclusion resembles that of many of his contemporaries: the Conservatoire, persisting in its perennial "routine," is now being surpassed by the Schola, for underlying its "formulae" is a "fausse science," or a set of pedagogical doctrines that have to do not with the interests of art but with those of the official world. The deeper implication here appears to be the same as that made by d'Indy, and Richard Wagner before him: artistic reform is contingent on prior reform of the state. The Conservatoire, Mauclair asseverates, is an institution with a memory, but in a negative sense: it has neither learned nor forgotten anything since its genesis in the First Republic.

Other Initial Praise for the Schola

Mauclair's panegyric of the Schola was far from isolated; in fact, it was echoed in other journals by more politically moderate and respected figures in the professional musical world; for the Schola, while undoubtedly serving the ideological interests of the league, was implementing important reforms, as well as filling gaping holes in "'l'enseignement officiel." One who perceived the fact was Jean Marnold, the powerful critic of the *Mercure de France,* the readership of which included a highly cultivated intellectual elite. In 1902 he published an article on "Le Conservatoire et la Schola," which opens by boldly proclaiming that the Schola has become the artistic center of the musical world.[149] He points out the extent of its influence through its impressive concerts in Paris, as well as through the trips to the provinces that its directors and pupils frequently make. In this manner, he continues, they are rapidly disseminating not just musical knowledge but the beneficent "cult" of the great musical masterpieces of the past. Although later he and Mauclair would see this cult as neither beneficent or politically innocent, both here perceive its goal, unlike the Conservatoire's, as simply to promote great art.

Marnold proceeds to praise the public pedagogical role of the Schola, especially its concert programs, which served an adjacent instructional purpose; but here there is no mention of the exegetical discourse that surrounded these concerts, or the attempt to imbue the works performed with a larger historical and thus political meaning. Marnold observes that only at the Schola could one listen to the cantatas of Bach and to Beethoven sonatas and quartets; learn the history of the violin sonata through examples; or hear the works of Lully, Rameau, and Gluck.[150] For Marnold, the Schola was thus the natural complement to the Société Nationale—the former opening the ears of the public to the treasures of the past, and the latter creatively exploring their implications for the future. The two organizations had, in fact, already largely fused, and not just in the person and the interests of their common director, Vincent d'Indy. Physically, too, they were joined, since frequently the concerts of the Société Nationale took place in the concert hall of the Schola Cantorum, in its new location.

Marnold, however, is not content to eulogize the Schola's director: he proceeds to vilify that of the Conservatoire, the hapless and beleaguered Théodore Dubois. According to Marnold, it was Dubois's fear that the Schola and the Société Nationale would fuse that led him to forbid Conservatoire students to perform at any concerts held at the Schola. From this incident Marnold draws the conclusion that considerations of a purely musical order were completely foreign to the Conservatoire's stolid and pertinacious director. To buttress his claim, he cites other examples of Dubois's intolerance and intransigence, especially his purported threats to expel students who collaborated in any way with the Schola. Hence, as far as Marnold was concerned, any antagonisms between the institutions did not come from the Schola: rather, it was Dubois who had belligerently declared war.[151] The Schola was thus embattled and inherently in a defensive position since, in effect, it did not yet possess the symbolic legitimacy of the state institution. To be a graduate of the Paris Conservatoire, Marnold points out,

means professional privileges; moreover, the Conservatoire had financial resources not available to a private institution.

But Marnold expands even further on Dubois's "arbitrary hostility," citing
other incidents in which students who manifest any sympathy for the Schola
were threatened with dismissal. And his attack on Dubois includes his teaching
as well as his pedagogical texts, for Marnold calls into question even Dubois's capacity to teach his students both counterpoint and fugue.[152] Already these techniques, given so much priority at the Schola, for the ideological reasons that we
have seen, were accruing palpable symbolic value. Hence Marnold condemns the
"artistic dictatorship" that he believed Dubois and the Conservatoire were exer-
cising over the musical life of the entire country. This charge also implied a critique, later to be made explicit by the Action Française, of the centralizing and
megalomaniac cultural power of the French state.

Such an indictment was certainly not out of place in the *Mercure de France,*
which espoused the socially conservative but politically antiauthoritarian views
of the Liberal Right.[153] Indeed, in a final salvo, Marnold uses the Republic against
itself by citing a report on the Conservatoire made in the name of a prominent
government official: it is a report that explicitly denounces the unfortunate effects of inveterate routine and concludes, in a damaging contrast, with a panegyric of the Schola Cantorum.[154] So effective had been the multifarious rhetoric
of those diffusing the Schola's doctrine that it could be construed in a manner acceptable even to a state official.

THE BATTLE OVER FRENCH MUSIC HISTORY

Not all concurred with these opinions, and, as we might expect, the Republic's re-
buttal to the Schola's attack on its educational system in music was immediate. It
eventually resulted in the appointment of a new Conservatoire director, Gabriel
Fauré, as well as in a thorough reform of its pedagogy under his leadership. But,
most immediately, the Republic responded to the Schola's propagandistic efforts
in music history and aesthetics with similar ones conducted through its own institutional channels. Through various lecture series, palpably in dialogue with
those sponsored by the far Right, the Republic continued to elaborate a conception of French identity through musical discourse. And it did not just employ established venues for scholarly lectures on music; it also developed new ones to
facilitate the spread of its own meanings or codes. We shall see in chapter 2 how
these efforts further contributed to a politicized atmosphere and a method of
reading or responding to works that few musicians in France could escape.

Perhaps the Republic's strongest network of propaganda, in addition to the
press it controlled, was its educational system, of which there were several different levels. On almost all these levels, attempts that recall Bruneau's—to outline a
Republican history of music and culture—became the task of more professional
music historians. It was in this manner, through the escalating political and cultural rivalry between the Republic and its critics, that the discipline of music
history began to flourish in France. Indeed, this had already been the case with

the International Congress of Music History, held in conjunction with the 1900 Exposition.

No one could escape awareness of the growing prominence and popularity of the lectures on music history given by Pierre Aubry at the Institut Catholique and by d'Indy, both there and at the Schola. Particularly well received was the Schola's series of "historical concerts," intended to complement its teaching by illustrating a specific historical point. Such "themes" related to d'Indy's preoccupations and included "La Symphonie pittoresque," "La Musique de scène en Allemagne," and "La Cantate funèbre."[155] "Pedagogical concerts," or those intended to teach music history from a nationalist perspective, would eventually be appropriated by the Republic during the years of the First World War. But the Schola also assumed the lead by establishing a "chair," or permanent position, in music history that was filled by a number of leading musical scholars. Among them was André Pirro, the noted specialist on Bach, whose L'Esthétique de Bach was published in 1907, the year of his doctorate at the Sorbonne. Also included was Michel Brênet (the pseudonym of Marie Bobilier), a widely recognized authority on French music of the Ancien Régime.[156]

Serious studies in the history of music had begun at the Sorbonne in the 1890s but were soon to be intensified in the new ideological and political context. The first scholar to receive a Docteur ès [sic] Lettres at the state institution for a thesis on a musical subject was Jules Combarieu, in 1893; he was followed by Romain Rolland in 1895, and then by Maurice Emmanuel, in 1896, and Louis Laloy, in 1904.[157] Not surprisingly, it was these figures who now began to offer lectures on the history of music under the auspices of Republican institutions, and thus most open to the public. The two primary figures here were Jules Combarieu, who lectured at the Collège de France, and Romain Rolland, who delivered lectures at the Sorbonne.[158]

Romain Rolland and French Music History

Romain Rolland led the way by elaborating on the themes that Bruneau had already outlined, but in a more exacting, convincing, and consistently scholarly manner. Like Bruneau, he helped establish attitudes, idioms, paradigms, and themes that were to become integral to the musical discourse disseminated through Republican institutions; but, like d'Indy and La Laurencie, he traversed different cultural realms, propagating this discourse in journals and publications associated with several fields. And he, too, was ideologically committed. Although his feelings concerning the Dreyfus Affair were ambivalent, his political sympathies were firmly with the Republic and the political Left. This did not prevent his achieving a professional objectivity, however, one for which he was later to be increasingly attacked, for Rolland attempted to mediate positions at a politically dangerous time. Although he was a Republican, he acknowledged d'Indy's contribution and was an appreciator of German music, including the widely acknowledged German masters of the past and embracing more controversial modern masters, such as Richard Strauss.

Rolland had a special interest in the period of the French Revolution, particularly in the kind of theater to which this event had given birth. As both a writer and a scholar, he perceived such revolutionary theater as a revitalization of true French dramatic tradition.[159] This interest had led to Rolland's involvement with the movement for popular theater centered around the *Revue d'art drama-tique,* which attracted both Dreyfusards and Anarchist sympathizers. He became increasingly convinced that art would be transformed not by "genius" but by the "rise of the people" as a result of the contemporary democratic movement.[160] These convictions were to inform his influential tract concerning the kind of the-ater that was now required, *The People's Theater,* of 1903. It bears a close examina-tion since his ideas were to influence not only his music history and his support for Naturalist opera but also eventually the cultural politics of the Syndicalist movement.

Like Bruneau, Rolland reacted strongly against what he perceived as the per-nicious infiltration of "Wagnerian neomysticism" in contemporary France. Rather than turning to Zola, being a scholar, he rather returned to the past, specifically to the writings of Diderot, Mercier, and Rousseau. In addition, he ab-sorbed the "Jacobin patriotism" of Chénier, as well as Michelet's stress on the po-tential of theater for national reconciliation and education of the masses. And, fi-nally, Grétry's *Essay on Music,* written during the Terror, provided Rolland with aesthetic ideas, as well as with technical ones. These included Grétry's advice that the author "paint with a broom"—or avoid both complex psychology and ob-scure symbolism of any type.[161] But Rolland then combined these suggestions with his own personal interpretation of the implications of ancient Greek theater for a modern democratic drama.

According to Rolland, a true "theater for the people" should be characterized by "broad actions of great characters with general lines vigorously traced and ele-mentary passions throbbing to a single and powerful rhythm." He further sug-gested that spoken text be complemented by music, and specifically song, since in a large theater spoken dialogue and individual gesture were less effective. In addition, he believed that the emphasis should be on the strongest dramatic op-positions, or on mass conflicts, articulated through group dialogues, and even through double and triple choruses. Such theater, for Rolland, was integral to the education of French workers, for it would help simultaneously to exercise both their rational and their imaginative faculties; moreover, it would rouse the masses to collective pride in their dignity, thus replacing popular newspapers, worthless novels, and less exalted theater.[162] Rolland's adaptation of the model of ancient Greek theater was thus one that ignored its conservative and platonic implica-tions, emphasizing not communal harmony but, rather, "manifestation"—or ex-pression and involvement.

Rolland's lectures on music history at the Sorbonne reflect similar populist themes and were to lead to a series of influential books on the great musicians of the past. The most relevant studies within this context were his biographies of *Beethoven* (volume 1, 1903) and *Handel* (1911), which treat the composers' lives and works. In both biographies, the topical themes of heroism and combat are prominent, as they were in Bruneau's works, with his argument that great com-posers pursued "sincerity" and "truth," which often led them to suffer. Rolland applies this perspective to Beethoven, seeing him as the most heroic force in modern art: "Il est le plus grand et le meilleur ami de ceux qui souffrent et qui luttent" (He is the greatest and the best friend of those who suffer and fight). For Rolland, however, the reference is less to the recent Dreyfus Affair than to the large social injustices with which he was currently so concerned. Hence, he discusses Beethoven's "faith," although not in religion (in the manner of d'Indy) but rather in his individual conscience and in his communication with nature. Here again we glean the Republican themes of freedom of the individual spirit, as well as the dictates of nature (or the "natural"), as opposed to the force of tradition (or the mystic). This was precisely the point against which d'Indy would soon launch an attack, presenting the composer rather as fundamentally motivated by religious faith.[163]

But the Republican ideas that we saw in Bruneau—of the individual and his conscience as the source of great art—recur in Rolland's writings, not just on Beethoven but also on Handel. Recalling Bruneau, Rolland begins by stressing that Handel had no inclination whatever for mysticism and that, in general, "la réligion n'était pas son affaire." He then emphasizes Handel's universality, as well as his objectivity, presenting him as a true "European," however with a predominance of Latin culture.[164] Most clearly in accordance with the ideology and aesthetic values held by Bruneau is his reference to the "popular" as a source of artistic inspiration; for Rolland asserts that Handel "drank" from the roots of popular music, and, indeed, from that of the simplest and the most realistic sort. And, like Bruneau, he delights in citing the presence of popular street cries in Handel's music—in this case, those that he purportedly heard on the streets of London. From this, Rolland extrapolates that Handel was, above all, an "observer," thus embodying the Naturalist values that Bruneau had promoted in his *Rapport*.[165]

IDEOLOGICAL DIALOGUE AT THE ECOLE DES
HAUTES ETUDES SOCIALES

Rolland also diffused his ideas and values through another influential lecture series, one that reached a small but intellectually powerful group, thus creating yet another network through which to propagate a political conception of music history. It was sponsored by an institution that catered to a segment of the Parisian intellectual and artistic elite, the influence of whom, because of their positions, was considerable. Significantly, this institution had derived its impetus from the Dreyfus Affair as the conception of an ardent Dreyfusard, Jeanne Weill, who used the pseudonym Dick May.[166] Called the Ecole des Hautes Etudes Sociales, it opened in November 1900, although it was, in fact, a reincarnation of an earlier effort; for in 1895 a Collège Libre des Sciences Sociales had been born, based in the Hôtel des Sociétés Savantes and devoted to the study of economic and social doctrines. May, its general secretary, had conceived the project the previous year, as part of her dream of building a "young Sorbonne" that would address more modern needs; she envisioned an institution that could respond to the moral crisis occasioned by both the Panama affair and the threat of Boulangism. Such an institution, she hoped, would give birth to a new democratic elite, one more fully apprised of the most recent developments in the social sciences.[167]

May had also played an important role in the organization of the first International Congress of the Social Sciences, which, like that on Music History, took place in conjunction with the Universal Exposition of 1900. Both may be construed as efforts to place these incipient disciplines under the auspices, and implicitly under the control, of the Third Republic. In the case of the social sciences, this constituted recognition of their place in the intellectual world, for indeed they embodied an approach particularly consonant with intellectual Dreyfusism. But the Congress also helped propagate the desire to further the contact or rapprochement of intellectuals and workers in order to educate all citizens for democracy. This effort, of course, was undoubtedly in implicit dialogue with the ongoing efforts of the leagues, such as the Patrie Française, to educate workers in their philosophy.

The ideal of a democratic elite that could accomplish the ambitious task of disseminating a social education throughout society lay behind the new institution. The Ecole des Hautes Etudes Sociales thus received a government subvention, being entirely in keeping with the social goal of the "Dreyfusard Republic." It was indeed a sort of semiofficial educational institution since almost half its lecturers were associated with the university system.[168] Because the goal of the institution was to bring university figures together with socialists and proletarians, it was considered inherently Dreyfusard; beyond this, such a peripheral institution was designed to supplement university education—to provide a forum for the presentation of new ideas not yet "authorized" for university instruction. Located in a building just across from the Sorbonne, it was partially supported by student fees, as well as by a regular society of "friends" of the institution. This allowed the school to present about five hundred lectures per year, approximately 10 percent of which were delivered by a team of regular collaborators.

At first, the institution comprised three "schools"—"Morale," "Sociale," and "Journalisme"—but in 1903–1904 it added that of "Art." The director of the new "school" was Henry Marcel, the administrator of the Bibliothèque Nationale, who envisioned it as filling in a gap in traditional French education. Although it stressed the disciplines of both literary and art history, it added the study of contemporary literature, including literary criticism. And because this was a period of proliferation of lectures on music history, particularly because of music's role as a political stake, the school also included music. In the spring of 1902, Rolland delivered a series of lectures at the institution stressing the revolutionary period, in keeping with his intellectual emphasis.[169] He was subsequently put in charge of the study of music at the school and seized this opportunity to bring together the leading scholars of music in France. Rolland used the institution as a forum for exchange between the radically different approaches and opinions associated with competing institutions or schools. The "école" was thus to provide another nexus not only for the diffusion of musical discourses charged with ideological implications but for a dialogue between them as well. It was in this manner, through such institutions, that the musical culture interacted even more integrally and consistently with intellectual and political cultures; such institutional venues for the debate over musical values and historiography were an inseparable part of the musical culture, which they would soon affect.

Rolland's goal was to imbue the study of music history with the same legitimacy as that enjoyed by the other arts by placing it in a broader social context.[170] Implicitly, too, it was to rival the Schola, or to follow the lead that it had established, by illustrating lectures with pedagogical concerts, or examples played at the piano. Rolland had already initiated this practice in his lectures at the Sorbonne, a practice admissible now in light of the marked success that it had at the Schola. But the pedagogical concerts here, or those with a specific intellectual point, unlike those of the Schola, were of new works and introduced by the composers themselves. The audience was presented with a wide range of positions—those of the most renowned modern composers, some of whom agreed to come and discuss their works in this intellectual context; these included composers with hortatory tendencies, or those on the ideological extremes—Bruneau and d'Indy—along with others, such as Paul Dukas, Maurice Ravel, and Claude Debussy. We shall see in chapters 2 and 4 the extent to which contemporary musicians, including those named, became part of the dialogue over authentic French values and, by extension, French national identity. It is also important to realize the gap that such a venue filled when artists were prohibited from presenting their "ideas" in the university system.[171]

Indeed, the school accrued so much prestige that, in effect, it became a seat of alternative intellectual legitimization and recognition by the academic world. This may well be why Vincent d'Indy agreed to speak at the school, despite its initial political associations with a Dreyfusard intellectual stance. D'Indy, like Sorel (who withdrew from the institution in 1906), while hostile to the academic world, nevertheless sought a recognition by it.[172] For d'Indy, moreover, this was part of his "battle" for authorization of his principles by the intellectual elite, given their exclusion in official circles. And, as we shall see, the paths of d'Indy and Sorel were again to cross in their common embrace of National Socialism and their rejection of the political center.

We may glean a sense of the nature of the musical discourse at this institution by examining Rolland's article for a publication that commemorated the tenth year of its existence. In it Rolland speaks of the slow development of studies of music history in France and of the isolated efforts toward it, despite the pioneering role of the Schola. The turning point, he argues, was the International Congress on Music History in 1900, which served fundamentally to raise the consciousness of French historians of music; in the following years, courses on music history began to spread, including the "cours libres" at the Sorbonne and the lectures at the Schola, the Ecole Normale Supérieur, and the Institut Catholique. While remaining silent on the ideological battle behind these lectures, however, Rolland does speak of the institutions's desire to put such diverse efforts in contact with each other.[173]

As we have noted, Rolland was one of the very few in the period who was able to rise above ideological antagonisms on the basis of professional interests; for him, it was to this higher end that the Ecole de Musique was founded at the Ecole des Hautes Etudes Sociales, in May 1902. Its other goal was to present to the public the musical treasures that historians of music had been uncovering in their research over the course of the past twenty years. As Rolland explains, when he was placed at the head of this "school," his goal was to show the intellectual elite training the personnel in public schools the importance of the history of music; specifically, he wished to establish its significance for understanding human spirit and thus to claim for music its place in general history, which to that point had been denied it in France.[174] Implicit again was the fact that, while this denial had taken place in the official domain, the gap was being filled aggressively by the French Nationalist Right.

The Ecole, through Rolland, did manage to recruit as impressive a group of lecturers on the subjects of music history and aesthetics as that at the Schola Cantorum; these included Pierre Aubry and André Pirro (who also lectured at the Schola), as well as a wide range of others on almost all aspects of music history. Between the efforts of those associated with the Schola and the efforts of those at the rival Republican institutions, no epoch of music history was being neglected.

- Theodore Reinach and Louis Laloy delivered lectures on Greek music, and Laloy on Gregorian chant
- A. Gastoué and Pierre Aubry spoke on music in the Middle Ages
- Henry Expert and Michel Brênet lectured on the Renaissance
- Henri Quittard, Lionel de la Laurencie, Henry Prunières, Paul-Marie Masson, André Pirro, and Rolland spoke on the seventeenth century
- Pirro, Rolland, Charles Malherbes, Julien Tiersot, Paul-Marie Masson, and Frédéric Hellouin spoke on the eighteenth century
- Lecturing on the nineteenth century were Tiersot, Malherbes (on Berlioz), d'Indy (on Franck), Paul Landormy, Jean Chantavoine, Henri Lichtenberger, Lionel Dauriac (on Wagner), Rolland, and Calvocoressi (on Russian music)
- Speaking on contemporary music were Louis Laloy (whose lectures, as we shall see, were published in the *Mercure musicale*), and Paul Landormy (on Belgian music)

Even more timely were Calvocoressi's monthly lectures (beginning in 1904) on "Le Mois Musicale," which helped prepare for and influenced the reception of specific works.

Other series of courses and lectures included those on non-Western and Popular (or traditional) music, along with those on "Esthétique et technique musicale," in which d'Indy participated. It was through this manner, once more, that the meanings, or associations, of forms and styles that he developed at the Schola were disseminated even more broadly in Paris. Lectures such as d'Indy's "Analyze de divers formes musicales—comment on fait une sonate" was here heard by an influential elite.[175] Moreover, the meanings or codes he propagated were spread even further in the context of the "Salon" that the institution held periodically and in which lecturers, professors, politicians, artists, and even workers mingled freely.[176] In chapters 2 and 3 we shall see the impact of this distinctive intellectual context on French music critics and the manner in which they approached their task. In addition, many of the lectures delivered in this institutional frame were either published as books or as articles in significant musical or cultural journals. Finally, such a context for sociability and intellectual exchanges was undoubtedly not without influence on the composers who chose to participate in it. Those who accepted the invitations to speak or present their music at the Ecole included some of the most prominent figures in the French musical world of the period. Bruneau, d'Indy, Debussy, Ravel, and Fauré gave lectures, and such prominent artists as Cortot, Viñes, and Landowska participated in performances.[177] In such a context, these composers and artists could not help but see that musical forms and styles were being argued for and were being legitimated in terms of historical and political discourses. They could thus hardly escape an awareness of the meanings adhering to style, and they could either work with these significances or manipulate them in novel ways. But they were also aware that there would be a price to pay for ignoring such significations by attempting to communicate the unorthodox through them.

2

CREATIVE AND PROFESSIONAL
RESPONSES TO THE
POLITICIZATION OF MUSIC

In chapter 1 we examined how French music was implicated in the torrid symbolic battle that was launched by two nationalist leagues over the question of French cultural identity and values. We saw that as a result of the central institutional opposition between the Schola Cantorum and the Conservatoire, musical culture was bisected into hostile camps. D'Indy and the nationalist Schola challenged the Republic's educational hegemony and established a discourse that related its conception of national identity to a canon and to style; the Republic responded with alacrity, defining its own set of meanings and values, as well as a canon in the context of both the programs of the 1900 Exposition and academic music history.

It was against the background of this conflict over historical conceptions, pedagogical models, musical meanings, aesthetics, and the canon that composers in France had henceforth to work. This chapter examines those figures who were most prominently implicated in the battle—those who either attempted to inscribe ideology in their works or to whose works were attributed an ideological content. In the first case, we examine those compositions through which d'Indy avowedly sought to communicate an anti-Dreyfusard message—his opera *La Légende de Saint Christophe* and his *Second Symphony*. In the second case, we see

how the context of performance of Charpentier's *Louise,* as well as its framing discourse, became an integral factor in the misconstrual of its meaning by critics.
Here we may observe how the latter applied the codes of meaning that were now
in wide use but had by no means been a factor when the polyvalent opera itself
was composed; we also see how Charpentier took advantage of this misconstrual
to further his own social program through music—his equally polyvalent "Oeuvre de Mimi Pinson."

Finally, we examine the case of an engaged but independent composer who
dared to cross the lines of battle and thus was inevitably to pay the professional
price. Albéric Magnard refused to accept the dominant stylistic code and composed a work that had Dreyfusard content but employed an "anti-Dreyfusard
style." We see in this context that the French press here played a crucial role,
categorizing composers and often victimizing those who did not fall into orthodox camps. The code of meaning they thus further disseminated was soon applied throughout the musical world, affecting not only institutional decisions but
also repertoire choices and financial support.

It is no surprise that d'Indy was among those who, in their compositions,
consciously manipulated the meanings that he himself helped develop and diffuse at the Schola. For d'Indy, ideology could unequivocally be communicated
through music by means of styles and techniques that carried meanings within
the context, or, in the language of semiotics, the "interpretant." We see this not
only in his professed "anti-Dreyfusard opera," begun in these years, but also in
his symphonic music, particularly in his Symphony No. 2.

Written in the wake of the Affair—in the years 1902–1903, the symphony illustrates d'Indy's distinctive sense of the educational role of the genre. As we have
noted, his ultimate model for the symphony was Beethoven, especially the Symphony No. 5 as both he and Franck interpreted it—in terms of the conflict of
dark and light. "Darkness," for Franck and d'Indy, could signify such qualities as
doubt, evil, sadness, and fear; "light," by contrast, could suggest faith, goodness,
joy, and courage.[1] Franck, of course, in such works as his D Minor Symphony remained completely abstract, while d'Indy here assigned a political meaning to
this theme.

Here "X" is the theme of "modernism," or of destructive antitraditionalism,
while "Y" is the theme of tradition, which enters into a symphonic battle with
"X." Significantly, "X" outlines a tritone, since it consists of two ascending thirds
that are separated by a falling second. (The tritone, which as scholars knew, traditionally symbolizes "the devil in music," would also figure prominently in
d'Indy's depiction of the "Jew" in his so-called "drame anti-Juif.") "Y," to the contrary, is a lyrical motive that prominently features a bold and expressive ascending leap on the interval of a minor seventh.[2] Romantic and expressive, it adheres
to Scholiste values, as defined against the nineteenth-century operatic and virtu-
osic models of the Conservatoire.

These motives appear cyclically throughout the work, generating others as
well, and thus the "combat" between them affects all the movements, with "Y"
(or "tradition") predictably triumphing over "X" ("modernity"). Metaphorically,
then, the symphony represents the triumph of traditional forces, not only in

music, as pursued by the Schola, but also in sociopolitical values. At first, d'Indy did not comment publicly on the meanings of the motives, leaving it rather to his allies in the anti-Dreyfusard press to make them explicit.[3] Here again, specific musical meaning was in large part contingent upon the surrounding texts and discourse that served an exegetical role. Producing such commentary was the task of d'Indy's friend and associate René de Castera in the journal *L'Occident* which, as we have seen, proclaimed itself "anti-Dreyfusard." De Castera explained the significance of the two principle themes in the symphony to the journal's readers in the following explicit terms:

> Le premier . . . dessinant un intervalle de triton (*diabolus in musica*) par une suite de tierces alternativement mineures et majeures, a un caractère sombre et menaçant qui symbolise vaguement dans la pensée de l'auteur l'élément moderne de mauvaise influence.
> Le second . . . , c'est l'élément traditionnel, de bonne influence.[4]

> (The first . . . , outlining the interval of the tritone (the devil in music) by a series of thirds alternatively minor and major, has a somber and menacing character that in the thought of the author vaguely symbolizes the bad influence of the modern element.
> The second . . . , is the traditional element, the good influence.)

While de Castera points out that it is not really necessary to attribute specific meanings to the themes, his commentary on the music did strive to instill them in the minds of his readers.

D'Indy, however, was not content to limit his ideological zeal to an abstract symphonic statement that relied on a commentary to make its meaning explicit. He decided to write an opera which he described as his "drame antijuif," in a letter of September, 1903, to his friend Pierre de Bréville whom he recruited for the Ligue de la Patrie Française.[5] Although d'Indy began the opera, *La Légende de Saint Christophe,* in 1903, he worked on it only sporadically until its completion during the war, in 1915. In this, as in his previous operas, d'Indy followed Wagner's example in being the composer and, in addition, serving as his own librettist. As in his instrumental music, his operas stress the triumph of spiritual values, employing the themes of faith and redemption, and they incorporate quotations from Gregorian chant. The selection of the legend of Saint Christopher, and even the source to which d'Indy turned, relates not only to his political preoccupations but also to Wagner's personal advice to him. To a French composer, the *Legende aurea,* a thirteenth-century collection of the lives of saints, was the closest thing to a collective mythos, or a legendary source. Wagner, in fact, had already employed the very same source himself (together with several others) in the heterogeneous libretto to *Tannhäuser.*[6]

The product of a Dominican monk, known in France as Jacques de Voragine, the *Legende aurea* was originally an attempt to popularize ecclesiastical doctrine, but its distinctive contribution lay in its borrowing from popular culture—particularly from peasant beliefs and tales—for an added level of appeal. It was largely owing to this deft intertwining of the popular and the clerical that the collection, one of many lives of saints, gained immediate and enduring popularity. The text was frequently reedited and retranslated, even from the time of Voragine, with no fewer than seven French versions appearing between the thirteenth and the fifteenth centuries. It remained popular in nineteenth-century France, and perhaps it is significant that the ardent Wagnerian Théodore de Wyzewa was one of those who translated it.[7]

D'Indy had long been enchanted by the collection, particularly by the legend of St. Christopher, which he had heard as a child from his governess and then later studied in preparation for his baccalauréat. As an adult, he continued to collect iconographic sources that depict the legend, some of which are included in the original printed score.[8] D'Indy apparently sought to appropriate the legend for his political cause, to reshape the meaning of his beloved story as part of a "grande entreprise politique." To appreciate the nature of his revisions, we must review the original text and then examine the libretto, together with the scenic indications in the printed score.

The tale in the *Légende dorée* begins in Canaan, where Christophe, of giant build and frightening appearance, believes he has found the greatest king in the world. One day, a jongleur comes to perform for the king; one song concerns the devil and causes the king, a devout Christian, to make the sign of the cross whenever the devil is mentioned. Christophe, deciding that the devil must be more powerful than the king, determines to seek out and serve him; he soon finds the devil and promptly pledges his service.

But the devil encounters a large cross in the road and turns to avoid it. Christophe asks the reason, and, when the devil explains his fear, Christophe decides to seek out and serve Jesus Christ. In his long search, he encounters a hermit who both instructs him in the faith and seeks a way for Christophe to serve the cause of Christianity. The hermit decides that, because of Christopher's build, he can help travelers across a dangerous river. One day Christophe hears the voice of a child calling for help; he puts the child on his shoulder and starts to ford, but as he does so, the child becomes increasingly heavy. When he reaches the other side, the child announces that he is Christ and as proof tells Christophe to plant his staff in the sand, saying that the next day it will be covered with flowers and leaves. Christophe does so; the prophecy is fulfilled. He then proceeds to Samos to help the Christians there.

God gives Christophe the ability to speak the Christians' language, and Christophe exhorts the faithful to have courage. One of the heathen judges is angered and strikes him in the face, but, as a Christian, Christophe will not take revenge; instead, he puts his staff in the earth and prays that God may make it flower. On seeing the miracle performed, eight thousand people immediately convert to Christianity. The king sends two hundred soldiers to take Christophe away, but he manages to convert them as well, and together they go to the king. The king is so terrified that he falls off his throne; Christophe accuses him of being the devil's companion.

The king puts Christophe in prison and sends him two beautiful girls, Nicée and Acquilina, to whom the king promises great rewards if they can lead Christophe into sin. But Christophe converts them and has them and the people destroy their idols. The two girls are punished by the king; Acquilina's bones are

broken by stones; Nicée is thrown into a fire and, after emerging from it un-
scathed, is promptly decapitated. Christophe is beaten, and a helmet of red hot
iron is placed on his head, but he remains unharmed. The king has him tied to a
stake and commands four hundred soldiers to pierce him with arrows; the arrows
remain in the air, but one returns and hits the king in the eye.

Christophe announces that his work is almost done, and he informs the king
that if the following day he moistens mud with his (Christophe's) blood and puts
it on his eye, he will see again. The king has Christophe decapitated, follows his
advice, and is indeed healed; he becomes a believer and orders those who blas-
pheme against God or Christians to be put to death.[9]

D'Indy designed his version of the legend not as an opera, but as a mystery
play, which would demonstrate aspects of what he termed the "Judeo-Dreyfusard
influence"—in particular, "orgeuil, jouissance," and "argent" (pride, pleasure,
and money), which he wished to present in conflict with goodness, faith, hope,
and charity.[10] He projects this opposition onto the story and, by emphasizing the
section in which the giant seeks the greatest power on earth, manipulates elements of the legend, as he mixes genres and theatrical conventions.

Although d'Indy locates the action in France (in the Cevènnes mountains,
which run through the region of his birth), the work begins in his version of
Venusberg. The preconversion giant—called Auferus—resembles Tannhäuser
serving Venus, or, as he calls her, "La Reine de Volupté." This idyllic existence is
interrupted when the doors open and a sinister yellow light floods the room, revealing a small man whom d'Indy describes in the printed score as pudgy and
jolly, with frizzy hair and a hooked nose. Behind him appear valets, their leather
sacks filled with gold. Those assembled comment on this "strange man," "not one
of us." Identified as "Le Roi de l'Or," this new character explains that it is useless
for the "chevaliers d'amour" to defend the queen, because he has purchased their
weapons and their ministers. His valets proceed to throw handfuls of gold to the
crowd, which follows them outside. The Roi de l'Or promptly decides to buy all
the "beaux objets d'art" in the room and proudly claims to be immune to love (recalling Alberich in the *Ring*). Auferus converts to his service.

The next scene reveals the summer palace of the Roi de l'Or. The walls, as
d'Indy describes them, are decorated with expensive paintings, and "quelques
meubles de mauvais goût" are strewn pell-mell among the precious objects. (The
king is clearly "bourgeois.") The king asks that a message be taken to his brother
in "la cité hanséatique" (clear ties to Germany), and he boasts of his palace as the
heritage of a noble family he has ruined. He observes that "ce pays teutonique est
bien vraiment le centre des affaires" (this Teutonic country is truly the center of
things), and in the ensuing dialogue claims proudly, "j'ai fait innocenter des
traîtres" (I have had traitors declared innocent). (The king is clearly a Dreyfusard.) Suddenly a goat's head appears, gradually growing to huge proportions;
the room fills with red light, and mephitic vapors exude from the goat's nostrils.
The gold in the room liquifies to yellow mud: the Prince du Mal has appeared,
and clearly the Roi de l'Or is his ally. In the following scene the Prince du Mal
takes on more normal incarnation. Dressed like a "seigneur" from the past, he
chats amiably with the Roi de l'Or, marveling at the way he deftly oppresses the

people while continually invoking liberty. (The prince is apparently not only a traitor, a Dreyfusard, Jewish, and bourgeois, but a Republican as well.)

Next we experience a Wagnerian blending of drama and spectacle, a dramatic idea expressed through visual imagery or contrast, as the "armée de l'erreur" appears.[11] D'Indy describes a series of clouds on the horizon (probably inspired by Baroque conventions), each of which contains a cortège replete with emblems (suggesting *Die Meistersinger*). First are the "faux penseurs" who sing "A bas les prêtres! . . . Nous seuls savons penser librement . . . à bas toute religion!" (Down with priests! . . . Only we know how to think freely . . . down with all religion.) Next are the "faux savants," all wearing gold spectacles; claiming science to be infallible, they chant contemporary scientific words with obvious anachronism, thus fusing the present with the mythic past.

Next we see a large crowd carrying a red banner inscribed with the word "Guerre"; this group sings "Haine aux puissants! Haine aux rois, haine aux prêtres! . . . Détruisons tout." (Hatred to the powerful! Hatred to Kings, hatred to priests! Let us destroy everything.) They are followed by "les arrivistes orgueilleux" and finally by "les faux artistes" (false, so obviously Dreyfusard). These last carry shapeless blocks of stone, canvasses dotted with spots of bright color, and bizarre oriental instruments that they seem unable to play. They sing "Fauteurs d'un art ténu et rare, nous faisons la mode et nous la suivons. Que tout soit abaissé à notre taille. Haine à l'enthousiasme! Haine à l'art idéal! Plus de règles, plus d'études, faisons petit, faisons original."[12] (Fomenters of an art that is thin and rare, we make fashion and we follow it. All should be lowered to our size. Hatred to enthusiasm! Hatred to ideal art! No more rules, no more studies, let's make things small and original.) Then they chant in unison, "Haine au Christ! Haine à la Charité!" (Hatred to Christ! Hatred to Charity!)

The clouds fade to reveal the powerful image of a gothic tower surmounted by a cross. Slowly, the entire "cathédrale triomphante" appears in full and glowing light. (This is a powerful moment of Wagnerian "Verdichtung," or of scenic contrast that "condenses the drama.")[13] As the shadow of the cross gradually fills the stage, the Prince du Mal declares that the cathedral must be destroyed. When Auferus realizes that the Prince du Mal fears it, he sets out to find Jesus Christ, who is evidently more powerful.

Act II takes place in the mountains. Near an overturned altar, a hermit kneels in prayer before a cross of branches. This part of the story proceeds more or less according to the legend, except that Auferus (now renamed Christophe) refuses passage across the river to those representing his former masters—a lover, a merchant, and an emperor, or "volupté, avarice, and orgeuil."

Act III begins in the great hall of the Roi de l'Or's winter palace; he has become "le Grand Juge" and is counting his money. The Reine de Volupté is sent into the prison to corrupt Christophe. He converts her and renames her Nicéa. The final scene takes place in "une grande place de la ville," decorated with various monuments. In the background is a fire hung with pieces of iron. A "bourgeois" brings his children to see the execution, and d'Indy instructs him to "rire bêtement." But during the torture, the armor disintegrates on Christophe's body, and the arrows shot at him do not reach their target. One returns to pierce the eye

of the Grand Judge, who emits a terrible cry and gasps that he is dying. (Significantly, there is no mercy or redemption for d'Indy's Roi de l'Or.) Christophe is
sentenced to be decapitated, but there is no violence to him on stage; we merely
hear his "chant triomphale" (a vocalise), broken momentarily by the fall of the
axe but then continuing even higher. Nicéa, who has been present at the execution, enters, covered with blood. As light slowly pervades the scene, all sing
praises to the glory of God; the chorus ends with the words "Saint Christophe,
priez pour nous" (St. Christopher, pray for us).

The aspect of the opera that we must examine is the "poetic intent," Wagner's
term for the essence of the drama behind music and text, which is revealed
through their union. Significantly, while Wagner expressed anti-Semitic beliefs in
his prose text *Judaism in Music* and a similar social analysis in *Art and Revolution,*
here they are part of the poetic intent. For these and other ideas inform the text,
as well as the musical style, through the use of the stylistic codes that were diffused at the Schola Cantorum.

D'Indy's goal of renewing lyric drama after an epoch he termed "Italo-cos-
mopolite-judaïque" had originally directed him toward the modified Wagnerian
music drama of *Fervaal;* in the *Cours de composition* he claims that *L'Etranger* was
more independent, less Wagnerian in concept and style, although he was still
deeply respectful of Wagner. In *La Légende de Saint Christophe* d'Indy sought a
more authentically French model, while still employing Wagnerian techniques
that served his specific dramatic purpose. Typically, his goal of renewal led him
back to the origins of opera, to what he claimed were its origins—not the Florentine Camerata, but the medieval mystery play.

How much d'Indy really knew about the genre is uncertain, although the prewar period in France saw several scholarly explorations into the subject.[14] D'Indy
obviously found in the mystery play not just the ritualistic but the didactic qualities he thought best conveyed his specific political message. To highlight the didacticism of the legend, however, and to reinforce his political points, d'Indy also
borrowed elements from the oratorio—a narrator and a chorus. But he labeled his
narrator the "historien," having him and the surrounding "choeur récitant,"
draped in white robes against a somber curtain, appear before the beginning of
each act and before the second scene in Act II.

In keeping with d'Indy's fundamentally moralistic approach to musical form,
even the very structure of the opera is didactic and symbolic. Apart from the pro-
logues, he divided the work strictly into threes—it consists not only of three acts,
but each of them contains three scenes. Although seemingly suggesting the trin-
ity in information circulated before the performance, d'Indy cryptically explained
that the "triptych form" was the only truly national one.[15] Church and state thus
once again became one in d'Indy's mind, which identified the basic traits of
French culture specifically with the Catholic Church.

As always with d'Indy, the tonal structure of the work is equally strict and
symbolic, turning Wagner's associative use of tonalities into a rigid didactic system; d'Indy ardently admired what he explicitly termed (and indeed distorted)
Wagner's "usage méthodique des tonalités significatives." Typical of his uses of
Wagner, he sought a more systematic and intellectual approach, employing keys

in association not only with feeling and situations, but also with characters or specific objects.[16]

But perhaps the most symbolic and didactic element in this "drame mystère" lay in the choice and manipulation of themes, which d'Indy carried to unprecedented extremes. Of the opera's twenty-four themes, seven are taken literally from Gregorian chant, which, as we have seen, was one of d'Indy's preoccupations. D'Indy had occasionally employed chant in his previous operas, but here the seven chants bring with them specific liturgical associations that are linked to the drama: several are taken directly from the Common of Martyrs and from the Common of Martyrs Who Are Not A Bishop.[17] But the composer employs more than just melodies in the interest of exegesis; there are also allusions to the masters admired at the Schola (and as interpreted at the Schola), in particular Bach and Beethoven. These references, like the Renaissance motet style that he associated with "les primitifs," appear when the text refers to sincerity, spiritual probity, and the certitude of faith.[18] They are emblematic of the "true tradition" in both a musical and political sense, just as they were in d'Indy's teaching and writing at the Schola Cantorum.

This rhetorical or strategic use of styles extends to the depiction of evil, probably the most pervasive thematic preoccupation in the opera. Not surprisingly, d'Indy reserved for the Roi de l'Or the most devastating devices in his stylistic arsenal, making him repugnant musically as well as morally. The Roi is associated with the same kind of jerky, uneven rhythms, suggesting physical deformity, as Wagner's Aberich in *The Ring*; however, going far beyond Wagner's technique of equating moral shiftiness with tonal ambiguity, d'Indy associates his villain with the harshest of dissonances and the gravest of harmonic faults (see Ex. 2-1).[19] Along with this, we find references to the "Italo-judaïque" style, especially to the squareness and monotony of rhythm that d'Indy associated with Meyerbeer. Although used most consistently for the Roi de l'Or, and (slightly less so) for the Prince du Mal, some of these traits appear in connection with other social groups that d'Indy wished to vilify: the bourgeoisie in the final act, the people whenever misled, and the Emperor's evil soldiers. Open stylistic parody is reserved for the comical "armée de l'erreur," with the "faux artistes" depicted visually and musically through a caricature of impressionism (see Ex. 2-2). All these techniques stand out against the background of a Wagnerian idiom, d'Indy's post-Wagnerian harmonies and fluid rhythms forming the stylistic "ground" of the work.[20]

We might now pause to consider the message that d'Indy intended and its relation to the philosophy of the league to which he was so close throughout these years. It is one of antimaterialism and anti-Republicanism, directed against a world he depicts as motivated by profit and controlled by a corrupt authority structure. Against this greed and corruption are contraposed the values of duty, sacrifice, and heroism, the purity of race and nation, and the primacy of the collective and of social hierarchy. Many of these values indeed relate to those of the Ligue de la Patrie Française, while others transcend the ideological and conceptual limits of the league. For the league's fundamental goal was that the traditional social hierarchy, led by those of both intelligence and property, oversee the education of the masses to guarantee order. While d'Indy's interests and many of

EXAMPLE 2-1   Act I scene 2, Vincent d'Indy, *La Légende de Saint Christophe*. Paris: Rouart, Lerolle et cie., 1918. By permission of the New York Public Library for the Performing Arts.

his beliefs related closely to those of the league, they often went beyond them, particularly as his position evolved after 1905. As we shall see in chapter 3, his conception of the social order and of the place of art within it would lead him to embrace nationalist movements with more "advanced" political tendencies.

D'Indy's relations with the league continued out of loyalty and for pragmatic reasons, even after it became politically inactive, about 1907.[21] However, the nature of his relation with the organization was to change, an evolution we can see through his letters to it, begun at the time of the Affair. The early ones proudly re-

EX. 2-1 *(Cont.)*

port the prominent musicians he was able to recruit for the league and make reference to the lectures it sponsored (by figures such as Jules Lemaître), as well as to their mutual hatred for Dreyfusards like Zola. By 1902 d'Indy was writing letters of appreciation to the league, complaining about the codirection of Charles Bordes and apparently planning a reorganization of the school. The following year, when he assumed the complete direction of the school himself, he was still reporting to the league on its activities, as well as its budget; significantly, he makes reference to the financial problems of the Schola and specifically to "cet imbroglio dont nous suffrons tous."[22] This undoubtedly referred to the serious and embarrassing financial scandal in which the league found itself directly implicated by 1903. The previous year, rumors had begun to circulate concerning the diversion of funds on the part of the treasurer, Gabriel Syveton, who finally committed suicide. Jules Lemaître himself abandoned the league in the fall of 1904, and by 1905 its final liquidation had begun.[23]

Not surprisingly, d'Indy's letter to the league in early 1904 reflects his discouragement over his inability to solicit new "subscriptions," despite his many letters; they also report his horror over the financial state in which he found the school, which clearly could not subsist on the basis of the fees that were paid by the students. Although d'Indy did not sever his ties with the league despite the financial scandal, now his letters simply report on his artistic activities, as well as those of the Schola.[24] The league had played an important role in both defining and launching his project, but now he moved on ideologically to seek out other bases of intellectual support.

As we have seen, d'Indy's artistic interests and goals were inseparable from his political convictions, which initially most closely approximated those of the league; we have also seen how he not only helped to attribute political meaning to aspects of style through his teaching at the Schola but also applied these mean-

EXAMPLE 2-2   Act I scene 3, Vincent d'Indy, *La Légende de Saint Christophe*. Paris: Rouart, Lerolle et cie., 1918. By permission of the New York Public Library for the Performing Arts.

ings in his creative work. For d'Indy, there was thus no dissonance between the styles he employed and the political significances attributed to them by contemporaries, largely because of his personal efforts; but this was by no means to be true of all the composers who were drawn to d'Indy's teaching and to the Schola without, however, espousing its political beliefs. In this context it is illuminating to turn to the case of Albéric Magnard, which illustrates the plight of composers who crossed the lines of battle within this culture. For although he, like d'Indy, was associated institutionally with the Schola, he nevertheless sought to reject the associations it assigned to genres and styles. Magnard, like d'Indy, did wish to communicate a political message through his art, but the message, contrary to the Schola's implicit ideology, was Drefusard.

MAGNARD'S "DREYFUSARD" COMPOSITIONS

D'Indy, a wealthy aristocrat, could confidently declare his political position through art, especially since it was his sympathizers and disciples who explicated his ideological intentions. But it was another composer also protected by wealth and a powerful family who, although a Scholiste, wrote a work with a consciously Dreyfusard message. This was not Alfred Bruneau, whose operas had been retrogressively labeled "Dreyfusard," in the context of the Affair, because of his association with Emile Zola; it was, ironically, a colleagues and friend of d'Indy, and eventually a member of the faculty of the Schola Cantorum, who attempted to write a "Dreyfusard work." Even more ironically, he did so by applying a code similar to that of d'Indy, one born of the conception of symphonic music that was espoused at the Schola. This bold individual who refused to accept the ideology

EX. 2-2 (*Cont.*)

associated with the style he espoused was the son of the director of the Dreyfusard paper *Le Figaro*. Albéric Magnard was indeed a singular figure within the
French music world, and he was to become, in spite of himself, no less than a national legend.

Magnard began his musical studies at the Paris Conservatoire, but, perhaps
because of his belief in the moral function of art, he grew disillusioned and decided to leave; an admirer of Franck, while in Dubois's class he was immediately
drawn to the circle around the former, especially to Guy Ropartz, and eventually

began to study composition with d'Indy. The two shared many ideas concerning musical form and aesthetics, and Magnard happily remained d'Indy's pupil for a period of four years. Fundamentally a Romantic, like d'Indy, he approached music as a representation of the inner life, but, being an idealist, he sought perfect order, as sustained by "beauty" and "justice." Music, for Magnard, was an art of thought, but thought as expressed through tones, a belief that, as we have seen, was generally shared at the Schola Cantorum. And, like the Scholistes, he admired "great works," considering, like d'Indy, the best art to be that which is fundamentally based, at least in spirit, on the classics. Hence his initial attraction to the symphony in the early 1890s, marked in particular by his Second Symphony, of 1892–1895, dedicated to Guy Ropartz.

When Magnard's father died, in 1894, Magnard became a critic for Le Figaro, the paper with which his father had been associated. Here he was among those helping to further the revival of Rameau, writing an article, "Pour Rameau," which convinced Durand to undertake his monumental edition of the composer. When the Affair broke out, Magnard could not stand aside from the tumult and, despite the fact that he was teaching counterpoint at the Schola, he declared himself a Dreyfusard.[25] He became deeply absorbed in the fundamental issues surrounding the Affair, resigning his commission as an officer because his beliefs concerning them were so strong. Despite his strenuous disagreement with d'Indy over the Affair, however, no official rupture ensued, although the nature of their personal relationship was to change.

Like d'Indy, during the height of the Affair, Magnard's interest shifted to opera, and to opera with a political message, although one opposite to that of d'Indy. Between 1897 and 1901 Magnard worked on his first opera, Guercoeur, which would be followed in 1902 by a symphonic work also inspired by the Affair, his Hymne à la justice. The score of the opera (dedicated to the memory of his father) was not published until 1904, and only the first act was performed in his lifetime, at the Concerts du Châtelet, on December 18, 1910. The score was published not by one of the major commercial firms but by one that called itself "L'Emancipatrice" and that identified itself as an "Imprimerie Communiste."

The opening of the work takes place in a kind of platonic paradise, with the principal divinity, "Verité," surrounded by "Bonté," "Beauté," and "Souffrance." Like the philosophic-political operas of d'Indy and Charpentier, it is highly allegorical, freely mingling elements of reality and fantasy. Like Charpentier's Louise, it is concerned with illusion, but in Magnard's opera the misguided are the people, who wrongly pursue their noble leader, Guercoeur, as a traitor. Here the reference to the Dreyfus Affair is subtle and indirect, but in the context of its later performance and commentary, it could hardly be missed.[26]

In 1902 Magnard returned to symphonic composition with his Hymne è la justice, which he had published at his own expense and dedicated to his friend, Emile Gallé, one of the first to sign the petition for Dreyfus and the future treasurer of the Ligue des Droits de l'Homme. The work was premiered in 1903 in Nancy and later performed in Paris, in December 1904, at the Concerts Cortot and, on January 13, 1907, at the Concerts Lamoureux. The basic symphonic technique that Magnard employs in his Hymne à la justice is fundamentally the same as that which we saw in d'Indy's Second Symphony: he utilizes two strongly opposed thematic ideas that, together with the critical commentary around the work, carried specific symbolic connotations. Again, the exact construal depended ultimately on a printed exegesis, as well as on what was perceived at the time to be the relevant political context. Typical of such commentaries is one that immediately followed the work's premiere, appearing in *Le Libéral de l'Est* on January 5, 1903:

> The *Hymne à la justice* is a powerful work of indisputable originality. It has two very different themes: the first, very violent and brutal, symbolizes the revolt of the oppressed; the second, very simple and soft, suggests a prayer and invocation to justice. These two themes alternate and occasionally combine. The impression made by this superb work is one of grandeur and rare musical power. The last part of this poem is extremely beautiful: the strings rise gradually to evoke the supplications of the weak, their appeal for Justice.[27]

If here a social rather than a political meaning was to be extracted, it was nevertheless one that was still within the parameters of Dreyfusard discourse. Magnard would not have objected to the more general construal of his work, and indeed he continued to attempt to express his political beliefs through the medium of music. We shall see how these developed, in chapter 4, as well as the genres and themes through which he sought, with unabating fervor, to translate them into musical terms. This would include another opera, one with the subject of an heroic Jew, although it was not, in the end, to be construed by the press as a "Dreyfusard opera." This was because the critical response in the period preceding the First World War focused not on the content of the work but on its Scholiste, or traditionalist, style. Magnard was not the only victim of this battle, suffering distortion of his message on the basis of his style at the hands of a politicized press. Another victim was a composer who, despite his neutrality in the Dreyfus Affair, was both praised and attacked for writing "the" Dreyfusard opera, on the evidence of genre and style.

CHARPENTIER'S *LOUISE*: ITS POLITICAL USES AND CRITICAL MISREADINGS

As we have seen, in this musical culture it was not simply the interaction of musical text and performative context that determined responses but that of music and the discourse around it. With no work, perhaps, is the semantic role of both the performative context and the surrounding ideological discourse more evident than in the case of Charpentier's *Louise*.[28] A full understanding of the reception of this opera at the time of its premiere is inseparable from an awareness of the ideological context we have traced. The discourse of both the Left and the Right were applied in evaluating the work—both substantially distorting the composer's original motivation and determining the opera's fate. As we saw with Bruneau's *Rapport, Louise* became for contemporaries on the Left and the Right perhaps the quintessential "Dreyfusard opera." But in order to understand its distortion by both sides in 1900, we must begin by attempting to grasp the actual nature of this complex work; in other words, we must try to understand the composer's original conception, the language and genre through which he communicated it, and the way in which both were now read.

Like many other works presented at the Opéra Comique at the turn of the century, Gustave Charpentier's *Louise* was far from a conventional "opéra-comique." Devoid of spoken dialogue, it relied rather on Wagnerian dramaturgy; even its melodic style, as a whole, was distant from the theater's lyric traditions. Charpentier himself proudly emphasized the opera's originality by abjuring traditional generic terms and boldly labeling it a "roman musical"; undoubtedly inspired by the influence of Emile Zola's novels on the opera's libretto, the appellation was without precedent, even in earlier French Naturalist opera.

And yet, in jarring contrast to the composer's avowal of the work's innovations, post–World War II scholarship has dismissed it as a sentimental melodrama in the tradition of "opéra-comique."[29] This was not the case in the decades following the premiere in 1900, when it was presented in conjunction with the Universal Exposition in Paris. Far from being dismissed as a maudlin or vapid "comédie larmoyante," the work incited a debate based at once on aesthetic and political grounds; such politicized responses concerned its subject along with its musical style, which contemporaries equated with the new aesthetic of the triumphant "Dreyfusard Republic." We must then explain this shift in perceptions of its relation to innovation or convention from the standpoint of its complex genre, which is both Wagnerian and novel-like in nature; only in this manner may we understand its "Wirkungsgeschichte," or the manner in which the work was subsequently used and read over time.

Louise, on one level, is a work about language, in both a textual and a musical sense, and thus one inherently subject to different social modes of reading. For the languages employed here had one meaning in the context of the work's composition and another as a result of the politicized discourse at the time of its premiere. Charpentier's original goal was to use musical, verbal, and theatrical language to construct a multilayered projection of his own psychosocial condition and value-tensions.[30] It was in order to do this that he took the unprecedented step of turning to the genre of the novel as a paradigm, or guide, for his operatic project. In understanding its novel-like aspects, the insights of Mikhail Bakhtin are relevant, for, according to Bakhtin, the novel is characterized by the depiction of "images of language," and these images suggest the different social horizons—and thus the styles or modes of consciousness—characteristic of the novel's various characters. From this perspective, each novel is a "system" of such images of language and a dialogue between the social perspectives to which they are ultimately bound. The novel is thus the opposite of myth, which implies a transparency of language: it is characterized rather by linguistic plurality or by this continual dialogue. As others have gone on to observe, the genre is thus inherently incompatible with either a totalitarian universe or a single "tyrannical narrative."[31]

Despite its Wagnerian dramaturgy, *Louise* resembles a novel far more than myth, for at its core is just such a system of "images of language." But, as we shall see, this work "about" discourse, in the case of its discrepant readings, has been interpreted "as" a discourse—its deep irony is thus not perceived. Our focus shall ultimately be on the interaction of text (or work) and the context of reception, or of the "performative context" with the work's polyvalent nature.[32]

To understand why Charpentier wrote an opera about language or conflicting styles of speech, it is essential to explore his background and his resultant complex social identity; indeed, the deeper message of *Louise* is truly autobiographical in the most profound and thoroughgoing sense. As the eldest son, Charpentier, as expected in the period, became an apprentice in the factory where his father worked, in Tourcoing (near Lille), at the tender age of ten. At the same time, however, his father, an amateur musician, was instructing him in "solfège," and at the age of eleven the boy took up the violin. The elder Charpentier was already an active participant in the amateur musical life of Tourcoing, which, like nearby Lille, possessed many such musical organizations, including "harmonies" and "Orphéons."[33]

The child's musical progress was rapid, and by 1877 (at the age of seventeen) he had organized his own instrumental ensemble in Tourcoing. So impressed was his employer that he helped to fund Charpentier's studies in harmony at the Lille Conservatory and then aided him in obtaining a municipal subvention. With this assistance, Charpentier was able, in 1879, to pass the entrance exams of the prestigious Paris "Conservatoire National."[34] But the musician's social identity was to undergo an immediate disorientation upon his arrival in Paris, where he was now cut off from his family nexus; he was forced, because of financial limitations, to find lodging in Montmartre, then a socially intermediate realm where bohemians, workers, and students mingled freely. Charpentier was struck by this mixture and, in his letters home, described in detail the curious mingling of social groups that he witnessed here; he even went so far as to recount, as realistically as possible, the nature of the conversations that he overheard among different groups.[35]

Charpentier himself was becoming confused about his identity, being subjected to both educational and cultural contexts that were completely new. He began to dress as a bohemian and, exhibiting his personal independence in other ways as well, frequently experienced clashes with his Conservatoire professors. Finally, after studying with several less demanding teachers, he found a sympathetic and compatible personality in Massenet; now, while rebelling in behavior and dress, Charpentier sought, in his composition, to conform to the prevailing style and after two years won the Prix de Rome. But his success was evidently due in part to his astuteness and initiative, for his letters to his parents also reveal the program of study that he adopted: while dutifully pursuing his exercises in harmony, he spent his spare time in the Conservatoire library, where, as he describes it, he went to learn the "formulae" of the masters.[36] He specifically mentions his study of Wagner, and also his careful reading of Goethe's *Faust,* and, feeling the necessity of instructing himself in poetic techniques, he speaks of his desire, when financially able, to buy a treatise on versification.[37] Like so many other Conservatoire students of humble origins, Charpentier felt inadequate when approaching dramatic music, armed with only a primary education.

Upon his arrival in Rome, Charpentier continued to find it difficult to adjust, and again he rebelled in his outward demeanor while continuing to conform in his music. Perhaps the most colorful incident occurred when he tried to escape from his "prison" in Rome, returning to Paris and to the Universal Exposition in 1889. There he encountered Massenet, who was horrified and to whom Charpentier facetiously explained that he was in Paris to prepare his candidacy as a Boulangist deputy from Tourcoing. Massenet, of course, instructed him to be on the next train back to Rome, and Charpentier dutifully complied—but only to plot his next rebellion: upon his return, he plastered the walls of the Villa Medici with posters that read, "Gustave Charpentier, Prix de Rome and Boulangiste, solicits the votes of the people of Tourcoing."

This gesture was probably inspired by Montmartre cabaret humor, as seen, for example, in a poster of Rodolphe Salis (the founder of the Chat Noir) that irreverently proclaimed "Boulanger c'est moi." In view of Charpentier's purported "Boulangism," it is also important to note the assistance he received from General Boulanger, through one of his teachers, Pessard; Boulanger helped arrange for the musician to serve his mandatory military service at the Casserne du Château d'Eau, in Paris, thereby allowing him to continue his Conservatoire studies. We should also note that Boulanger was most popular among French workers, for he helped them crystallize their discontent with politicians, developing a kind of nationalism that appealed to the socially deprived.[38]

During this period Charpentier was known to don another provocative social disguise—the garb of a Catholic priest, which he wore while wandering about the streets of Rome. But this inclination toward social subversion assumed a considerably more dangerous form, both before and after his stay in Rome, when he frequented the Café du Delta, a known gathering place for Anarchists. That his contact with them was direct is attested to by the fact that one of them gave him a chanson, the music of which was an adaptation of the revolutionary "Ca ira" and the "Carmagnole," the text of which referred explicitly to the recent Anarchist bombings. Charpentier was later to incorporate fragments of it not only in *Louise* but also in the later sequel to the work, entitled *Julien;* since Charpentier was already at work on *Louise* when he received this particular chanson, several scholars have identified what seem to be references to Anarchism in the libretto.[39]

We might explain Charpentier's attraction to Anarchist circles on several levels; here recent analyses of Anarchist cultural theories are particularly illuminating. Richard Sonn stresses that Anarchism was an antiparliamentary movement like Boulangism, but one that went so far as to reject any politics or organized means of social control. Hence, he argues, we cannot understand the movement solely in political terms, since it was a cultural rebellion against both bourgeois morality and its institutions of power. Particularly relevant for an understanding of the subject of *Louise* are Sonn's observations that Anarchism opposed "the bourgeois institution of marriage as a system of paternal authority" and rejected "the orthodoxies of art and learning" as institutionalized in the academies, the educational system, or any such hierarchical structure.[40] By the early 1890s, Anarchist discourse suffused the French literary world and particularly symbolist circles, for here there was a recognition of common social goals: it was the Anarchists who helped make the symbolist poets "more aware of the necessity of challenging the prevailing rules of prosody."[41]

As a successful Conservatoire student, who had learned the appropriate "formulae," yet at the same time viewed them suspiciously or objectively, Charpentier began work on *Louise*. Moreover, he did so as a young man who was confused in his social identity, eager to succeed in the system, and yet plagued by a sense of having betrayed his origins—for he continued to be close to his family and to be involved in the musical societies that were so important to it, those associated with French workers. Two of the results we can see in *Louise* are a sense of self-loathing or self-irony, and a simultaneous acceptance of and revolt against the "languages" that he had learned. Like the literary "decadents" such as Hysmans, he was to produce a work that manifests an "ironic distance"—that "performs an implicit act of autocriticism and self-destruction through self-parody."[42]

In search of a libretto, Charpentier had initially contacted Massenet's editor. Although a libretto was promised, it was never delivered, so Charpentier began to work on his own. He was encouraged not only by the example of Wagner (which had inspired two trips to Bayreuth) but by Massenet himself, who urged him to create from his own individual experience. Having purportedly had an affair with a young working girl named Louise, Charpentier designed a libretto about her affair with a "poet" and the rebellion against her family to which it led. In writing his libretto, Charpentier turned not to the now-fashionable Symbolist movement but to Naturalism, which had impressed him through the theater of Ibsen and the novels of Zola. And Naturalism was appropriate to his educational level as well, since it was considered a literature of the "unlettered," and thus barred Zola from the Académie.[43]

As we have already noted, there was a precedent for French Naturalist opera in the works of Zola and Bruneau, but one that had led to an aesthetic impasse. It is important to analyze this particular dilemma here, that of shifting aesthetic distance, for it was this that Charpentier would overcome. Bruneau had developed a set of dramaturgical procedures adapted specifically to the setting of Naturalist texts, while retaining others from French operatic tradition. Like the Russian Realists, he attempted to translate the rhythms of the speech and the inflections of the text as literally or naturalistically as possible into his music.[44] But as we have seen, Zola's operatic texts were hardly naturalistic in style, and thus the result was less reminiscent of Mussorgsky than of Lully's settings of the verses of Quinault. Like Lully's, Bruneau's line does not always mirror the inflections of the text exactly; he also often heightens key words for rhetorical emphasis, usually by means of leaps, and at times he attempts to imbue the vocal line with more musicality or, recalling Wagner, to project an emotional component onto the text through such lyric means.

Like Lully, Bruneau understood that such heightened rhetorical declamation, despite a full orchestral accompaniment, required periodic points of relief; so, as in Lully's operas, lyric interludes in "quadratic" or balanced antecedent-consequent phrases frequently appear, ranging from small sections of several measures to simple small-scale lyric arias. As Bruneau's critics immediately noted, and at the time of the Affair would stress, his lyricism was influenced by that of his teacher Massenet, and inappropriate in the context. Also for dramatic relief—and again like Lully and Quinault—Zola and Bruneau employed scenes of "spectacle," but bound to the action with some dramatic plausibility. In Zola's libretti, such moments of spectacle serve an important function as vehicles for visually articulating the symbolic idea that underlies the plot. Thus, what is an extremely slow and subtle process in the novels here appears boldly telescoped and within the context of French operatic convention. Perhaps the clearest example is the ballet of Act III of *Messidor*, the story of which is a conflation of the novels *La Terre and Germinal*. Called the "Ballet de la légende de l'or," it relates to a legend to which reference is made in the text and hence, although highly unrealistic, serves the plot as a "condensation" of its contents. Zola saw no contradiction in employing "féerique" elements in a realistic drama because they represented the very "real" realm of the imaginary and the "marvelous."[45]

Not all of Bruneau's procedures, however, were rooted in French operatic tradition. From Wagner he learned that opera could break free of traditional forms through the use of leitmotifs. Clearly Bruneau did not construe Wagner as had the French Symbolists of the 1880s, who saw him as a "poet," the explorer of new and subtle realms of sensations. In France, by the 1890s, there was a Wagner for the Left and one for the Right; while the former dated back to the 1860s, the latter was the creation of d'Indy and Barrès. As we saw in chapter 1, their view of Wagner as the heroic liberator of collective instinct was felicitously consonant with the political ideals of the Patrie Française. The Wagner of the Left had evolved over several decades, from one associated with democratic collective "release" (under the Second Empire) to one linked to complete legibility, or "transparent truth." Hence, for Bruneau, Wagner opened the way to a more concrete and explicit statement and, through the use of leitmotifs, the possibility of making all "visible," as the Naturalists had sought.[46] Leitmotifs are thus omnipresent, employed more consistently than in any French composer before, although used more obviously and didactically than in Wagner and not in a "motivic web." As we have noted, this was one of the points on which Zola's and Bruneau's operas were denounced, from the time of the Dreyfus Affair, by anti-Dreyfusard writers and critics. Other points concerned the mixture of naturalistic and conventional elements, which caused constant and bewildering shifts in terms of levels of reality in the works.

In *Louise,* Charpentier was able to resolve such illogical contrasts in style, and thus in dramatic verisimilitude that had plagued the Zola-Bruneau operas. He did this in part through his choice of subject—how individuals use and relate to the socially defined and determining languages or discourses that surrounded them. More specifically, the opera concerns the distance between sincerity and the conventions of expression of "high art," as well as the self-delusion that can result from the appropriation of such a "foreign" language. This is the plight of Charpentier's hero in the drama, Julien, with whom the composer identified as someone who has begun to believe in the truth of his own florid rhetoric. Perhaps in his student days, Charpentier, having discovered the "formulae" of the masters, just like his character Julien, had lost sight of both sincerity and truth.

Several scholars have noted the different levels of language employed in the text of *Louise:* poetic language (rhymed verses, alliterations, and assonances), literary language (lyric prose), and "familiar" (colloquial) locutions. According to

Manfred Kelkel, they are used to demonstrate the different social levels of the characters: the poet Julien, for example, expresses himself most often in literary situations, in verse. Even when he employs more informal diction, it is always "correct" in usage, corresponding with the cultural level that Julien represents.[47] The same is true of the allegorical characters in Act III, such as the Pape des Fous, who facetiously expresses himself in the "language of the Muses," or in verse. Except in certain sections of Act III, the other characters from Montmartre speak in popular or colloquial language—including the use of realistic street cries. The exception is clearly Louise, who, although from a lower sociocultural group, frequently expresses herself in the rhetorical manner of Julien.

This apparent inconsistency has been attributed to Charpentier's naiveté and to the rumor that, despite his disclaimers, he sought the advice of his literary friends.[48] Rather, we should see this as a calculated technique, one that takes us to the core of the meaning of this "musical novel." For *Louise* is not only about different social groups and their distinctive languages and thus about the conflicting modes of consciousness that these locutions express; it is also about the corruption and illusion that ineluctably result from the appropriation of a language that is inherently foreign and false. And here the tragic element of the opera discretely emerges: Julien not only deludes himself with his "poetry"—he deludes and corrupts Louise.

In both text and music, Julien employs an idealistic, academic language, with results that are consciously turgid, pretentious, and often also patently comic. The vapid, vulgar quality characteristic of his poetic lines is appropriately mirrored in his Leitmotifs, treated in a manner that is correspondingly crass (Ex. 2-3). As we can see in the example at the opening of the opera, Julien's motive largely comprises intervallic leaps of the fourth and the third, the latter outlining a major triad. Both rhythmically and intervallically, it is as unsubtle and direct as Julien himself and, as we soon see in the opera, as limited and repetitious. Charpentier's critics later were to charge that Julien's motive never develops; we might add that, just like Julien's character, it can only modulate. Its nature is harsh and intrusive, qualities heightened by the garish orchestration: it is thus as incapable of responding to its surroundings as Julien himself. As we see in Example 2-3, his musical line wanders indulgently and obtrusively; being triadic, syllabic, and rhythmically square, it has an empty, rhetorical ring.

Several contemporaries observed that the central conception of *Louise,* especially the ensembles, bears a strong resemblance to *Die Meistersinger,* which Charpentier saw five times in Bayreuth. But although both concern artistic convention and the issue of "true" artistic expression, the distinctive feature of *Louise* is its trenchant and omnipresent irony. This irony is highly personal and is articulated most clearly in the atelier scene (sc. 2, second tableau of Act II) during Julien's "Serenade." Here the poet becomes a curious synthesis of Walter and Beckmesser, for the idealistic hero is controlled by conventions and completely consumed by illusion. And it is also here that Julien briefly deludes the young girls in the atelier who, in a manner that is poignantly ridiculous, appropriate his poetry and his lyricism (see Ex. 2-4). Such lyricism not only is dramatically apt, but also, in a manner recalling *Tannhäuser,* helps provide the lyric interludes that are necessary for relief.

EXAMPLE 2-3   Act I scene 1, Gustave Charpentier, *Louise*. Paris: Heugel et cie., 1900. By permission of the Lilly Library, Indiana University.

EX. 2-3   (*Cont.*)

While the assimilation of Julien's mode of expression and illusions occurs transiently and comically with the working girls, in the case of Louise it is a slow and irreversible process. Like the girls in the atelier, but on a more extensive temporal scale, she gradually abandons her more realistic declamation—and vision— for Julien's poetic rhetoric. Indeed, in scene 1 of Act IV, her father comments with horror, after hearing her impassioned declarations, "Ce n'est pas toi qui parle par ta bouche méchante . . . C'est une étrangère" (It isn't you who is speaking so wretchedly from your mouth, it's a stranger). Louise's assimilation of Julien's language and his self-delusion, already incipient in the opening scene, culminates in her aria "Depuis le jour": occurring at the beginning of Act III, it is the turning

EXAMPLE 2-4   Act II scene 2, Gustave Charpentier, *Louise*. Paris: Heugel et cie., 1900. By permission of the Lilly Library, Indiana University.

EX. 2-4   *(Cont.)*

EXAMPLE 2-5   Act III scene 1, Gustave Charpentier, *Louise*. Paris: Heugel et cie., 1900. By permission of the Lilly Library, Indiana University.

EX. 2-5   (*Cont.*)

point of the drama, and, contrary to common conceptions, its stylistic weakness is clearly conscious and deliberate. Characterized by awkward accents and leaps, both the intervallic structure and rhythms implicitly recall the omnipresent, insidious influence of Julien (Ex. 2-5).

Louise's corruption continues in the love scene that follows her aria, one in which she is completely consumed not only physically by her lover but by his language (see Ex. 2-6). This consumption is mirrored in the rhythmic development: a waltz rhythm subtly and gradually comes to dominate the scene as the lyricism itself continually expands. And here a further borrowing of language occurs, in particular of Wagnerian language, although less in the music than in the text, which further emphasizes the stilted conventions of "high art." There are continual references to "lumière"; here, however, it is not to daylight but, significantly, to the garish artificial illumination of the city. And the characters similarly invoke a "love-death," but here we can see that it is merely profane as they utter such explicit phrases as "mourir sous mes baisers."

It is significant that this inversion of Wagnerian meaning occurs just before a more extensive and symbolic reversal—the fête (previously composed and inserted into the opera) called "Le Couronnement de la Muse" (The Coronation of the Muse), which here serves as the operatic spectacle. As in the operas of Zola and Bruneau, it relives and yet relates to the drama, but in a "carnivalistic" inversion of the kind of popular "fête" that the Republic had been encouraging. In

EXAMPLE 2-6   Act III scene 1, Gustave Charpentier, *Louise*. Paris: Heugel et cie., 1900. By permission of the Lilly Library, Indiana University.

EX. 2-6 *(Cont.)*

these festivities, held on occasions like Bastille Day, spontaneous popular participation was common, as was pseudoclassical allegory and the symbolic use of a female central figure. Here it was Marianne who stood for the Republic and the working people of France; in the context of Charpentier's spectacle, she is the illusory "muse of the people." Charpentier thus links his inversions of meaning in "high art" with those of Republican ritual, which he apparently perceived as similarly false.[49]

A score of le *Couronnement de la Muse* had already been published in 1898, a year after the first presentation of the work in Montmartre and the same year as two more performances in Lille and in Paris.[50] It was sold for the benefit of a project entitled "l'Oeuvre des Muses," one of many attempts to bring theater to the public, which would include both Charpentier's and Republican efforts. The "fête" consists of four scenes, preceded by a march: (1) Le Ballet du Plaisir, (2) L'Apparition de la Beauté, (3) Le Couronnement de la Muse, and (4) La Souffrance Humaine. The printed score explicitly defines the symbolism of the characters: the "petits miséreux," for example, symbolize "l'Avenir." It also explains the action, in the manner of the following passage:

> Durant les danses populaires sont survenus des groupes d'artistes. Ils apportent leurs hommages à la Muse, fille du peuple, et glorifient en elle l'inspiratrice de leurs oeuvres, elle enfin qui les guide vers la Beauté.
>
> (During the popular dances, groups of artists appear. They bring their homage to the muse, daughter of the people, and glorify in her the inspiration for their works, she which guides them toward beauty.)

Charpentier, who crossed several cultures, was very well aware of how to write a work that, on one level, could appeal to both the "people" and to the Republic, but he was also aware of how to make a far more trenchant statement through the systematic use of reversals of normal social roles or expectations. Here Bakhtin can once again illuminate Charpentier's technique, having coined the term "carnivalization" to describe this reversal of conventional relations. For carnival was traditionally associated with "social leveling," or "an equality of unequals"; the festival thus serves to release "the people from the imposed order of daily life."[51] Such reversal is indeed what occurs at specific points in Charpentier's "fête," as we can see in the text at the specific point where the beggars enter: "Voici venir les divins gueux, aux longs cheveux, les jeunes dieux!" (Here come the divine beggars with long hair, the young gods!) One meaning of this incongruity may be that "la foule" that sings these lines is as insensitive and deluded as Julien himself, as unable as he to see social reality. Charpentier appears to underscore this interpretation in his elaboration at the bottom of the score:

> Pour exprimer l'amère ironie des gaîtés humaines, impuissantes, hélas, à nous faire oublier l'éternelle misère, l'auteur a développé en le raillant, le thème du 'Rêve de l'universel bonheur' des Impressions fausses.
>
> (To express the bitter irony of human gaiety, unable, alas, to make us forget the eternal misery, the author has developed, while making fun of, the theme of 'The Dream of Universal Happiness' from Impressions fausses.)

The latter was a work that Charpentier had written in 1894–1895, inspired by Verlaine, and which he here, consistent with his preoccupations, mocks with irony.

In Louise, this ironic manipulation of language extends also to operatic conventions, to which Charpentier continues to make reference in both the music and the text. In the latter, he makes an incisive point about how distant such operatic conventions were from the people and, indirectly, about the current Republican program (in which he himself participated), which sought to bring opera to the "people." For Charpentier was actively involved in plans to establish an experimental "opéra populaire," one that would attempt to make opera accessible to the "humble" who were excluded from the Palais Garnier. But here again he mocks himself, and at one point he has the "gamins" comment on the operas they have seen and in which they obviously found no sense.

Throughout the work Charpentier pointedly invokes operatic conventions when he wishes to demonstrate the insincerity or self-delusion of specific characters. For example, when Louise's mother (an unsympathetic figure) appears to lure Louise home on the pretense of her father's illness, she does so in the guise of the traditional messenger of death, and with an orchestration that recalls Wagner's Erda. The one character who is spared in the opera, and whom many contemporaries found the most sympathetic, is Louise's father, the honest worker, who is always sincere and direct. Although he sometimes resorts to an idiom, as in the case of the lullaby to which he sings to Louise, it is guileless and part of his culture, making him, for Charpentier, the positive model.

Musically, Wagnerian traits are evident, including the web of leitmotifs in the later orchestral introductions and in the large symphonic sweep that characterizes Act III; yet these are not the aspects of Wagner that are most central to the dramatic point of *Louise,* for it is not the Wagner of the *Ring* that Charpentier is emulating here—it is, rather, the composer of *Die Meistersinger* and *Tannhäuser.* This is true in the nature of the leitmotifs he employs; it is also evident is Wagner's way, within the context of the drama, of incorporating separate numbers in the continual orchestral flow. Even more important, Charpentier has drawn from both operas (but particularly from *Tannhäuser*) the technique of conflating the subject of the work (in the case of *Die Meistersinger* and *Tannhäuser* singing contests, in the case of *Louise* the use of the conventions of artistic expression) with the conventional means of opera.[52] In all these works, the composer thus overcomes illogical operatic conventions through the choice of the very subject matter he employs in them; moreover, Charpentier uses artistic and operatic conventions in the opera as the languages or attributes of those characters who are controlled by or manipulate conventional languages. This interaction of manners of expression, of discourse, is the core of his musical novel, one about the way an artist can become deluded and harm others through these false conventions; it is in precisely in this manner that Charpentier arrives at a more complete operatic Naturalism, a more consistent aesthetic distance, than is found in the operas of Zola and Bruneau. And further in accordance with the Naturalist vision, he does not make a moral judgment; he offers only a commentary (recalling Anarchist theories) concerning the corrupting power of academic conventions. In his next opera, *Julien,* of 1913, as we shall see in chapter 4, Charpentier follows the consequences of this delusion in the dissolution of Julien and the concomitant fall of Louise.

The Politicized Reception of *Louise*

Few composers would have been displeased to have the premiere of their opera occur within the context of a Universal Exposition, which brought a mammoth potential audience.[53] Charpentier was undoubtedly well aware of the suitability of his work for the occasion, or for the ideological goals that we have discerned lay behind the Exposition itself. It certainly praised the "common people," and the characters' fascination with the city of Paris, although in the composer's mind a tragedy, seemed good propaganda for the Republic and the city. Even more felicitously, as we have seen, Charpentier's use of Parisian street cries accorded perfectly with the conception of French music that Bruneau now hoped to ensconce.

We have already seen Bruneau's attempt to slant interpretation of the work in the context of his official report on the concerts presented at the Universal Exhibition, but he expanded on its meaning even further in his book *Musiques d'hier et de demain,* which, as we have noted, he published the year before the *Rapport* appeared as a book. In the former he lavishes extensive praise on "Le Couronnement de la Muse," seeing it as the "ennoblement" of the official fête through the beauty of "virile" music and feminine grace. For Bruneau, the work unites the poetry of art, of work, and of rejoicing crowds, making it no less than a "réveil heureux de l'esprit national" (the happy awakening of the national spirit). This national spirit, of course, was one that was diametrically opposed to that which was currently being stridently propounded by the clamorous anti-Dreyfusard Right. According to Bruneau, it is indeed such art that the future requires—one that brings happiness to those who suffer, ideas to those who produce, and glory and beauty to those of imagination and contemplation.

These ideas were to be developed further by a more respected and exacting scholar who would eventually become a major figure of the Republican musical establishment, Maurice Emmanuel. His attempted propagandistic use of the work, like that of Bruneau, distorted its meaning just as badly and also helped prepare the nationalist reaction against it. Emmanuel's article "La Vie réelle en musique" appeared in the *Revue de Paris,* a politically conservative although not narrow-minded journal, in 1900.[54] His task, for which he would later be rewarded by the Republic, was formidable: to convince an inherently skeptical readership of the legitimacy and value of Charpentier's work. His focus is thus on the composer's attempt to avoid mysteries (in the medieval sense), legends (of Germanic association), lies, and conventions, in order to define a "democratic" music. Like Bruneau, he attempts to trace Charpentier's values back in French history, but his focus here is on the decisive point of reference for Dreyfusards— the French Revolution. Indeed, in the context of Charpentier's "fête," he draws attention to the recent publication by the librarian of the Conservatoire, Constant Pierre, *Musique des fêtes et cérémonies de la Révolution Française.*[55]

Like the works of the Revolution, the message of *Louise,* according to Emmanuel, is a moralizing one, concerning the destructive potential of mere sensual pleasure. Yet he takes pains to legitimize the work further for his readers by stressing its traditional and conventional elements—its classic harmonies and the purity of its language, which place it within "les plus hautes traditions." Emmanuel ends with an indictment of the conservative taste of the Académie des Beaux-Arts, which, as we have seen, had been, on the whole, anti-Dreyfusard; this reactionary group stolidly refused to recognize the opera, thus "infligeant un démenti officiel au succès éclatant de l'ouvrage" (thus inflicting an official denial of the stunning success of the work).[56]

Bruneau and Emmanuel were by no means the only critics associated with the political Left who attempted to reduce the complex polyphony of Charpentier's "novel" to Republican "myth." We find consistent support in journals and from figures associated with the political Left, support based on principle or on interpretations like those of Bruneau and Emmanuel. A review in *Germinal,* for example, found the music to be stronger than the libretto (too highly influenced

by Zola's novel *Paris*); yet it lauded the opera.[57] For the Left, the main criterion
against which Charpentier's *Louise* was to be judged was whether it adhered to its
doctrinal conception of an authentic "art social": such an art was one that was
born from and placed at the service of collective life—meaning one that dealt
with the life of the city, the setting of the factory, the home, or the street. This was
indeed the period of a proliferation of works on "social art," which included
Lazare's *L'Ecrivain et l'art social* and George Sorel's *La Valeur social de l'art*.[58]
The original staging of the opera made it seem to conform to these ideals even
more, given the socially realistic costumes and the scenery it employed (see figures 2.1 and 2.2). The most prominent attempt to interpret the opera as conform-
ing to such conceptions was that of Camille Mauclair in his article "L'Artiste moderne et son attitude sociologique." Charpentier himself was already familiar with
Mauclair's writing, having set several of his texts, including "Complainte" and
"Les Trois sorcières," in the early 1890s.[59]

Here Mauclair, the former Dreyfusard and now a prominent Socialist writer,
presents the composer as a "fils du peuple" who reconciles Socialist beliefs with
the temperament of a great musician. Charpentier was not yet a Socialist, and, as
we have seen, despite the nature of his social projects he was not a Dreyfusard,
but rather, like Debussy, one who had signed the "Appel à l'Union." Mauclair, like
Bruneau, however, perceived the composer as contributing to the progressive
refinement of "l'âme populaire" by providing it with examples of taste and thus
leading it toward the "delicate and intellectual." Here again, we see the Dreyfusard stress on the "intellectual," in addition to the Republican stress in the title
on a scientific, "sociological" vision. Yet, for Mauclair, the primary merit of *Louise*
was that it had finally and triumphantly brought the battles and desires of the
"humble" onto the prestigious operatic stage.[60]

FIGURE 2.1   The original production of *Louise*. By permission of the Lilly Library, Indiana University.

FIGURE 2.2   The original production of *Louise*. By permission of the Lilly Library, Indiana University.

Such rhetoric was eventually to cause a reaction among those who were not sympathetic either to the aesthetic espoused or to the social and political vision purportedly subtending these values. As we shall see later in this chapter, attacks on the opera would crest by 1905, at the height of the battle concerning the so-called Nationalistic reaction in art; even more immediately, fellow composers such as the irascible Claude Debussy interpreted and criticized the work in the light of the surrounding Leftist polemic. In a letter from Debussy to Pierre Louÿs of February 5, 1900, it is clear that probably because of such commentary, Debussy had missed the work's deep irony:

> He has taken the cries of Paris which are so delightfully human and picturesque and like a rotten "Prix de Rome," he has turned them into sickly cantilena and harmonies that, to be polite, we call parasitic. The sly dog! It's a thousand times more conventional than *Les Huguenots,* of which the technique, although it may not appear so, is the same. . . . And the man imagines he can express the soul of the poor! . . . It's so sickly it is pitiful. Of course, M. Mendès discovers his Wagner in it and M. Bruneau his Zola. And they call this a French work.[61]

Louÿs, an anti-Dreyfusard, would have appreciated the last remark, since nationalists at the time of the Dreyfus Affair had emphasized Zola's Italian ancestry.

But beyond the Dreyfusard discourse that positioned *Louise* at the pinnacle of the French tradition, Debussy's negative opinions may also have been influenced by the interviews with Charpentier in the press. In these he stressed the so-cial projects to which, as we shall soon see, he would turn immediately after the opera's premiere, in part because of the way in which the work was read. His im-mediate professional response was to take advantage of this misreading and to promote his social goal through projects of a similarly polyvalent nature. The first was the "Oeuvre de Mimi Pinson," a plan that he established in conjunction with Parisian theater directors to distribute free tickets to young girls of the working class and their families. The project ostensibly grew from Charpentier's widely publicized distribution of free tickets to young Parisian seamstresses for the pre-miere of *Louise*. This prompted the Dreyfusard *Le Figaro* to praise the composer's "large" and "generous" theories, as opposed to those of the "artiste-aristocrate" and the society snob. It goes on to present the work as triumphantly heralding no less than "la conquête du drame lyrique par les idées philosophiques et sociales." Moreover, the authors perceive *Louise* as the ultimate realization of Wagner's ideal that the artist find inspiration in "la vie spontanée," as manifest in the people.[62]

Debussy, skeptical of such specious arguments, was also undoubtedly jealous of the work's success, for some eighty performances the first year brought the the-ater a handsome profit.[63] Several years later, however, he was beginning to per-ceive the composer's deep originality, observing in *Gil Blas* that "Charpentier's music is entirely his own as far as fundamentals are concerned."[64] But this more penetrating analysis was a rare one in Charpentier's France, in which both adver-saries as well as supporters projected an ideology onto the work.

THE "CONSERVATOIRE POPULAIRE DE MIMI PINSON"

Charpentier's reaction was, again, in the short term, pragmatic: like d'Indy, he subsequently devoted his time to a socially prosletyzing school of music. But, like his opera, his school could be construed on two very different levels or be seen to serve two different social purposes, according to the perspective that one as-sumed. Having crossed different cultural levels, Charpentier was well aware of the diversity of ways in which cultural products and projects could be appropri-ated, and he could thus play with and profit from this insight.

Sensitive to the political world and to the cultural projects now being fostered not just by the Republic but by its adversaries on the Right, Charpentier devised his own: situated ambiguously between Socialist and Republican visions of the "people's" social and cultural needs, like his opera, it was a long-lived success. And like d'Indy's Schola Cantorum, it was a concrete means to diffuse an ideological vi-sion, and it simultaneously met a need or pragmatically filled in a gap. After the popular success of *Louise* Charpentier perceived a lacuna in the Republican educa-tional system and, indeed, in his own life and career; the triumph of the work, so important and timely for the Republic, was to bring Charpentier, like Bruneau, a series of premature official rewards. Made a Chevalier de la Légion d'Honneur in 1900, he later became a Commandeur, and in 1902 he was elected to the Institut. As we shall see in chapter 4, he became a victim of his own success—a success based upon an ideological misreading—and was henceforth to produce very little.

His second opera, *Julien,* an artistic statement of disillusion, was only a "succès d'estime" and thus subsequently little performed in France, but his multivalent "fête," "The Coronation of the Muse," was, like *Louise,* to live on, being read on only one of its levels and performed in cities throughout France.[65]

As we have noted, the decline in Charpentier's creativity immediately after the success of *Louise* was made up for by his incipient project, called the "Oeuvre de Mimi Pinson," and by a turn to musical journalism, which Charpentier saw as a way to further his vision by other means. After the success of *Louise,* Charpentier was asked to serve as a critic, undoubtedly through the efforts of his already established colleague Alfred Bruneau. Not surprisingly, one of the works he praised was Zola's and Bruneau's *L'Ouragan,* which elicited a personal letter of thanks from Zola, on April 30, 1901. Like Bruneau again, Charpentier would profit from association with Emile Zola, despite the fact that he had not politically declared himself a Dreyfusard. Here Zola, ostensibly with reference to their common social interests, refers, in effect, simultaneously to their shared artistic and political values:

> C'est très bon et très doux, cette embrassade de deux frères d'armes qui combattent le même combat: celui de la vérité et de la vie dans l'art. La victoire est certaine puisque nos coeurs battent ensemble.[66]
>
> (It is very good and sweet, this embrace of two brothers in arms who fight the same battle: that of truth and of life in art. Victory is certain since our hearts beat together.)

Apparently these common values were soon applied to an artistic project in which Zola and Charpentier participated but that proved to be abortive, for this letter from Zola was written approximately five months after d'Indy made reference, as we have seen, in a letter to Guy Ropartz, to an institutional project of Charpentier and Zola. Again, this was, as he phrased it, "le nouveau Conservatoire Dreyfusard sous le titre de 'Collège d'esthétique sincère' que Bruneau, Charpentier, Zola, et Bachelier installent à Montmartre"[67] (The new Dreyfusard Conservatory under the title "The College of Sincere Aesthetics" that Bruneau, Charpentier, Zola, and Bachelier are establishing in Montmartre). Only ephemeral, it was one of many such plans for popular musical education in which Charpentier was currently involved. For in the aftermath of the Dreyfus Affair, popular education was a Republican priority, and various schemes to educate the "people" pullulated throughout France. As we shall see, music was integrally involved in this larger project, perhaps in part because of the efforts of d'Indy at the Schola Cantorum. Moreover, the Ligue de la Patrie Française was currently developing or supporting a vast apparatus of institutions to inculcate its values and ideas on several different educational levels. In response to this tactic, as well as to the Affair, which had brought traditional cultural patterns into question, the Republic was stressing that culture and learning could and should be diffused to the masses.[68] Now more than ever, it thus emphasized the spread of education, as a means to produce good citizens, those who were ultimately capable of discerning "truth." But support for such ideas also came from other sectors, particularly from Socialist intellectuals and leaders such as Jean Jaurès.[69]

This was the period of the flowering of the "Universités Populaires," a massive project of popular education, which included an introduction to the arts. From this conceptual framework issued a whole series of musical projects, a configuration of ideas and plans into which Charpentier's would perfectly fit. The idea for the Universités Populaires was initially launched by a creative and ambitious worker in the French printing industry. His project, which was designed to bring intellectuals and militant workers together, began in October 1899 in the faubourg Saint-Antoine. As a former worker now considered an "intellectual," Charpentier himself participated in the Université Populaire du Faubourg Saint-Antoine, serving as the vice president during the presidency of Anatole France.[70] Accompanying this effort, particularly in the faubourg Saint-Antoine, was the development of small theaters specifically designed to elevate and educate the workers. Born of Socialist faith in the pedagogical potential of theater, they had already begun to proliferate in the decade of the 1890s; indeed, one of Romain Rolland's goals in his book Le Théâtre du peuple was to draw attention to such efforts that had not been endowed with official support.[71]

As we have noted, the government had considered the question of developing a "popular" opera within the larger context of widening access of the lower classes to music.[72] But a central problem here was determining the appropriate kind of repertoire—one that would simultaneously elevate, instruct, and entertain or "distract" the people. Another concern was the logistical issue of how to make opera accessible to the workers, aside from the distribution of free tickets on July 14. Despite this problem, the pressure to expand access to music, to theater, and to opera was particularly great during the period when the Popular Universities flowered. As the "rapporteur" of the budget for the Beaux-Arts put it in 1901, "le public là est avide d'idées, il cherche au théâtre la représentation ou l'explication de ses souffrances, de sa vie" (The audience there is avid for ideas, it seeks in theater the representation or explication of its sufferings, of its life). Hence the vigorous response of the Opéra's director (between 1899 and 1906), Pedro Gailhard, who proposed the establishment of a "théâtre populaire."[73] Gailhard was apparently sincere in his wish to provide the people with access to opera, as we can see in his letter to the Ministre de l'Instruction Publique et des Beaux-Arts et des Cultes on July 14, 1905. In it he complains that the audience that attended free performances on the national holiday was indeed not that for which such performances were originally intended; apparently, those who were financially well-off had adopted the practice of paying the less privileged to stand in line for them in order to obtain the free tickets. Gaillard overtly expressed his outrage over the situation, going so far as to say that he found the practice to be nothing short of "scandalous."[74]

Charpentier, probably for such reasons, had attempted to found a "people's opera," to be subventioned by the city of Paris, although apparently without success. He wrote to the Municipal Council of Paris, pointing out that the Opéra and the Opéra Comique were essentially closed to the workers because of the limitations of their income. But what he now desired was a theater that would create the kind of "spectacle" that would help imbue French workers with both a vision and hope: specifically, he envisioned des fêtes artistiques populaires, où un plus grand nombre de spectateurs viberaient à l'audition d'oeuvres grandioses où seraient célébrés le travail, la vie sociale, les aspirations du peuple vers un avenir de justice et de bonté.

(popular artistic festivals, where a greater number of spectators would vibrate upon hearing grandiose works in which work, social life, the aspirations of the people towards a future of justice and goodness would be celebrated.)

It was for just such ideas that Charpentier would eventually be attacked on political grounds during the First World War by the vociferous Action Française.[75]

Already wary of such a musical theater and its message at the turn of the century, the government did support other efforts to help diffuse music to the lower classes; it is within this context that we must attempt to understand the design of Charpentier's project, as well as the larger social goal that he wished to achieve. We must recall as well that the Schola offered free lectures and tuition for workers, although from all accounts the turnout among this group was not great. The goal of Republican projects, as at the Schola, was articulated in moral terms—an emphasis that we have noted on the far Left as well as on the Right. This was true of that project conceived in 1901 by a "chansonier" and entitled the "Oeuvre de la Chanson Française," which was aimed at working-class women. Its purpose was to provide free courses for working-class women and girls in which the students would systematically be taught a new "mélodie française" each week. Conceived as a "moral project," it was intended to keep its innocent pupils away from dangerous "mauvais spectacles," as well as from "fréquentations malsaines." The project, apparently successful, lasted for more than twenty years; in 1926 its leaders felt justified in requesting an official subvention.[76]

This was not the only project with which Charpentier would be in dialogue, in terms of its goal, as well as of the kind of art it diffused. Also founded in 1901, at a moment of populist fervor and amid the cultural propaganda of the Right, was a Société de Vulgarisation Artistique. Entitled "L'Art Pour Tous," it was founded by Louis Lumet, a pioneer in popular theater, and Edouard Massieux. It, too, would eventually be supported by the Third Republic and incorporated into its network of cultural institutions after the First World War. According to its original statutes, the society's goal was the following: "Faire connaître les richesses de nos collections publiques et privées, la beauté de nos musées et monuments, les découvertes de nos savants, la valeur de nos sites" (to make known the worth of our public and private collections, the beauty of our museums and monuments, the discoveries of our scholars, the value of our sites).[77] Once again, the language and emphasis of this statement recalls Bruneau's *Rapport* and its attempt to define the monuments of French art in specifically Republican terms.

Its method was essentially the same as that of the contemporary Rightest leagues such as the Patrie Française and the Action Française, as well as the Institut Catholique: it would offer public lectures on French art and, when possible, on the physical sites that it considered to illustrate that art most vividly, whether in France or abroad. And, like institutions on the political Right, it also provided evenings of art, literature, and music, as well as a lending library for further reading. As we have seen, it had been the Right, in the period following the Dreyfus

Affair, that had established the utility of a discourse on art in further propagating its ideological message.

Although Charpentier's ambitious cultural project, the "Oeuvre de Mimi Pinson," evinced an awareness of all these precedents, it developed from his unique social vision. He knew well that high culture could be "appropriated" or used by the people in order to meet their own specific needs, so different from those of the bourgeoisie. For art served a very different kind of function in their lives and was integrated into their experience in a highly distinctive way. His project was named after a heroine of Alfred de Musset, a character who by this point had become emblematic of a young working-class woman, Mimi Pinson. As we have noted, the initial project evolved from his widely publicized distribution of free tickets to Parisian seamstresses and their families for the premiere of *Louise*. By 1901 it had developed into a coherent social project on a much wider scale and involved several different Parisian theaters. Already, Charpentier was exhibiting both the enterprise and the business acumen that would characterize his handling of the vast cultural project he was to conceive. Here he succeeded in enlisting the participation of Parisian theater directors, as well as directors of important business enterprises.[78]

Such an effort was not without precedent, for already in 1897 arguments against the exclusivity of the Opéra were being made within the Chamber of Deputies. One project that in fact was proposed was to allocate 100,000 francs to make free tickets available to the workers, using the model of the Socialist municipality of Lille.[79] Charpentier, who had attended the Conservatory in Lille and remained in close touch with the area, undoubtedly was well aware of the potential of this significant precedent. Like d'Indy, he made no clear distinction between his own professional musical projects and those that were ostensibly the products of the contemporary political world. He learned from the Socialist Left, just as d'Indy did from the nationalist Right, and both went on to develop unique cultural syntheses of these two worlds.

From his original venture Charpentier began to develop an interlocking system of projects grouped collectively under the rubric "L'Oeuvre de Mimi Pinson." While some endured for almost three decades, others were never fully realized; yet it is important to examine his total conception to understand his social vision. For Charpentier's musical aesthetic and pedagogical goals were as completely inscribed in his social and subsequently political vision as were those of his nemesis, d'Indy. The "Oeuvre de Mimi Pinson," according to Charpentier's total conception consisted of the following musical and social-service components:

1. Mimi Pinson au théâtre: billets de théâtre gratuits
2. Le Conservatoire Populaire de Mimi Pinson
3. La Chanson de Mimi Pinson: rénovation des chants populaires
4. Les Concerts de Mimi Pinson
5. L'Image de Mimi Pinson: don de gravures et estampes artistiques
6. Le livre de Mimi Pinson: don de lectures instructives et distrayantes
7. Le Journal de Mimi Pinson
8. Les voyages de Mimi Pinson: voyages de vacances, excursions à prix réduits

9. Offres et demandes d'emplois: les renseignements sont reçus et donnés aux cours du soir
10. Consultations médicales et judiciaires gratuites
11. La Maison de repos de Mimi Pinson
12. Le Théâtre de Mimi Pinson[80]

Charpentier exhibited the same astuteness in explaining his goal in the statutes of the project as he had in his culturally multivalent opera, for it too could be variously construed. His rhetoric appealed to current Republican cultural themes and to those of the Socialists, as well as of other groupings on the political Left. As he put it:

> Le but est d'associer en un même et fraternel effort, pour leur relèvement moral et intellectuel, les ouvrières et employées de magasins et ateliers parisiens. . . . En même temps que par des leçons artistiques bien appropriées, l'Oeuvre de Mimi Pinson affine le goût de ses adhérents et leur montre le Beau, les détournant ainsi de tant de vulgarités et de platitudes elle leur offre, par le jeu régulier de ses différentes sections, encouragements, distractions, aide matérielle.[81]

> (The goal is to bring together female workers and employees of Parisian stores and workshops in the same fraternal effort for their moral and intellectual elevation. . . . At the same time "L'Oeuvre de Mimi Pinson" refines the taste of its members and shows them the beautiful by well-appropriated artistic lessons, thus turning them away from the many vulgarities and platitudes, and offers them, by the regular interplay of its different sections, encouragements, distractions, and material aid.)

The emphasis on the importance of counteracting "vulgarities" and "platitudes" may well refer not only to modern urban culture but to the propagandistic efforts by the political Right. Here Charpentier offers female workers a cultural exposure and association that had already long existed for their male class counterparts in the "Orphéons" societies. But Charpentier goes even further, making his "L'Oeuvre de Mimi Pinson" a comprehensive system of social aid and welfare for French female workers. The concept that unites the project, and that recalls Anarchist theory, as well as the moral of *Louise,* is the necessity of working-class independence.

But again, as with the Schola, there was also a pragmatic aspect to his enterprise, for it filled a need simultaneously for those it attracted and for the composer himself. It helped produce those performers needed in Charpentier's "open-air spectacles," such as "The Coronation of the Muse," in which workers themselves were to participate. Like Romain Rolland and Jules Michelet before him, Charpentier believed that a spectacle for the people should, in fact, arise from the people themselves. The Conservatoire drew young women from the Parisian garment industry who learned to sing, to accompany voices on the harp or piano, or to participate as dancers. It held classes twice a week, from 8 to 10 P.M., in classrooms made available to the conservatory by the city and state. Charpentier established different sections of the school in workers' districts throughout Paris, with such a degree of success that many had to be turned away. The project was not without its critics, however, including the dyspeptic Claude Debussy, who commented acerbically on it in an article in *Gil Blas* in 1903:

> For some time now there has been a widespread concern to develop in the hearts of the people a taste for the arts in general and music in particular. . . . I should mention the Conservatoire de Mimi Pinson, where the young genius M. Gustave Charpentier preaches the ideas dear to his heart. In this way he instills the taste for freedom, in life as well as in art in young girls whose likings would otherwise be limited by . . . Paul Delmet . . . and Pierre Decaudelle. Now they know such names as Gluck and A. Bruneau. . . . Instead of being impertinent bourgeoises they are fashioned into nice young ladies.[82]

As we shall see in chapter 3, Debussy also brought a unique perspective to the issue of "culture for the people" and took a considerable interest in it. For he, too, crossed social levels, which resulted in a mixed identity and which helped produce a complex art that could be construed in several ways. We shall shortly examine the way in which Debussy's own art, like Charpentier's, was used for politically propagandistic purposes and the unique nature of his response. But his theory of how to bring art to the people was fundamentally different from Charpentier's, a difference that made it impossible for him to appreciate Charpentier's scheme. Debussy did not advocate an independent workers' culture but advocated instead the search for a common cultural thread that united the different classes. What Debussy may have perceived was the pragmatic and egotistic element in Charpentier's plan, his desire to train young women to participate in his "popular spectacles." But another, more noble motivation might have been Charpentier's sense of falseness and guilt—of having abandoned his proper culture, a preoccupation we saw in *Louise*. The development of this social project was thus another way of resolving this tension and of helping to foster a culture that would obviate a similar danger for others. Ironically, the success of *Louise* provided the composer with an entrée into the official world, which he used to devise a project that both articulated and undermined its ideals. Only gradually would Charpentier find a coherent political expression of the beliefs or inclinations he had discovered through his art and through "Mimi Pinson."

POLITICIZATION IN REPERTOIRE CHOICES, SUBVENTIONS, AND JOURNALISM

Composers were not alone in their awareness of the codes that penetrated the French musical world or of the meanings that now adhered to works, to composers, and to styles. It is also within this context that we may perhaps most fully understand official institutional decisions in this period concerning the repertoire to be performed. In official institutions of music, the political could not be separated from "professional" decisions, so firmly was this code of meaning

entrenched by 1905. And, given the Republic's defensive position, it is not surprising that we may perceive a connection between works performed at the
Opéra and the Republican musical discourse and canon.

A concern with presenting the great French operas of the past had already
arisen in the decade of the 1890s because of the increasing dominance of Wagner
at the Opéra. But even earlier, in the 1870s, the Société des Auteurs, Editeurs, et
Compositeurs de Musique expressed concern that not only French works of the
present but the French "classics"—Lully, Campra, and Rameau—were being
abandoned.[83] After the Affair, with the new political nationalism of the anti-
Dreyfusard Right, this concern was to gain in importance, but accompanied by
concomitant issues: What works were indeed truly French? What was the French
"classic tradition" as it applied to music? And what were the proper aesthetic criteria by which it should be defined?

At first, French Wagnerian composers were in an advantageous position since
they provided the answer to the question of how to respond to public taste while
promoting works by French composers. These included Chabrier (in 1899),
d'Indy (in 1903), Georges Huë (in 1901), Victorin Joncières (in 1901), Erlanger,
and Bruneau.[84] To these we may add those works with Wagnerian elements that
were premiered at the Opéra Comique, particularly Charpentier's Louise, in 1900,
and Debussy's Pélleas, in 1902. Those selected for performance could all somehow
be construed as according with elements of the Republican theatrical aesthetic, as
articulated most fully by Bruneau. This even included Vincent d'Indy's L'Etranger,
in 1903, a work in which his Wagnerism is clearly attenuated and certain Verist
stylistic elements appear. While the work, for d'Indy, was an attempt to marry Symbolism with a more modern settings, for the Opéra it was opportunity to co-opt the
well-known but militant and troublesome composer. Hence the great care taken
with the production and the solicitous concern for the composer, which prompted
him to write a letter of thanks to the Opéra's administration.[85]

But other works performed in this period could be construed within the
framework of the themes or points of emphasis characteristic of Dreyfusard discourse. The year 1900 saw the production not only of Louise at the Opéra
Comique but also of Camille Erlanger's Le Juif Polonais; in 1904 Erlanger's opera
Le Fils de l'Etoile, to a libretto by the (Jewish) Dreyfusard Catulle Mendès, was
produced at the Opéra. But another way to respond to the nationalist Right, as
well as to the Schola, was to revive works both had scorned as associated with the
"style italo-judaïque." Meyerbeer's Le Prophète had brought financial profit at the
height of the Affair, in 1898, even surpassing that of Wagner's works. But there
was undoubtedly a symbolic element in the Opéra's decision to perform his Les
Huguenots for the free performance of July 14, 1901. As the reader will recall,
most Protestants in France were Dreyfusards and identified their own religious
persecution with that which had plagued the Jews.[86] There may well have been
symbolism, too, in the fact that on September 20, 1899, the Opéra celebrated the
nomination of the Jewish composer and critic Ernest Reyer to the status of Grand
Officier de la Légion d'Honneur. Not only was his earlier opera Salammbô performed at this point, but in January 1900, to celebrate the twenty-fifth anniversary of the inauguration of the Palais Garnier, so was his opera Sigurd.[87]

Similarly revived in this period were the works of other composers in Bruneau's canon, including those of the revolutionary period, which held such symbolism for the Republic: Méhul's *Joseph,* for example, was performed in 1899, the same year that Bruneau and Zola's *Le Rêve* was presented in a free performance. But composers revived now also included those who had been appropriated by both the Left and the Right, within the framework of different discourses and thus construed in different ways: this included Gluck, whom d'Indy perceived as leading to Wagner, and whom his adversaries, on the other hand, construed as inspiring the revolutionary rescue opera.

Hence in 1904, the Opéra revived Gluck's *Armide,* which the "rapporteur" of the budget of the Beaux-Arts justified in the following explicit terms: in mounting *Armide,* he argued, the Opéra "a fait revivre sur les programmes le nom d'un maître célèbre qui en avait disparu depuis près d'un siècle"[88] (had revived on its programs the name of a famous master who had disappeared from them for over a century). Such rhetoric here would have been inconceivable without the challenge of the Schola Cantorum, to which the Republic was now responding in so many subtle ways. For so successful had been the Schola in its subtle marriage of ideology and professional innovation that the Republic had now to recognized or co-opt most of its innovations and reforms. The Schola had, in effect, succeeded in reversing the hierarchy of genres, and by 1904 the symphony was assuming more symbolic importance than opera. This was to occur not only at the Conservatoire, as we shall see in chapter 3, but also in official competitions and through subventioned performance societies.

The Fondation Cressent, founded by a lawyer in 1869, had established an annual competition in France for a large dramatic work: the prize was a sum of money that allowed the winner to select the theater of his choice in Paris, in which his work would be produced. But in 1904 the state introduced a fundamental change—one that completely ignored the founder's original intent. Given the growing prestige of symphonic music, due largely to the efforts of the Schola Cantorum, it changed the competition into one for a symphonic composition.[89] The works ostensibly were to be judged not by the criteria instituted at the Schola but by those associated with the Republic and its musical institutions; the jury consisted largely of professors from the Conservatoire, members of the Académie, and, eventually, previous winners of the prize. Significantly, the jury for the first competition made a gesture toward conciliation by including d'Indy, along with Fauré, Gédalge, Hué, Bruneau, Widor, and Saint-Saëns. As we might expect, however, the first winner of the prize, Eugène Cools, was a student of Fauré, Widor, and Gédalge, thus setting a pattern for the future.[90]

This was also the year that another important change was made, one that further demonstrates the impact of the cultural discourse of both Right and Left. There had long been debate over the subsidized "grands concerts," both because of their social elitism (due to high ticket prices) and their limited repertoire. In the Chamber of Deputies, those on the Left were going so far as to argue that the subsidies should be canceled and given to organizations with a broader public. It was within this context that the question of the performance of modern French works once more became important, appealing to both "progressive" and nationalist interests. The Colonne and Lamoureux Concerts were, from this point, required to program three hours of new works by living French composers that had not been performed before, as were other concert societies, including the Société Nationale and the Concerts Pasdeloup, along with the smaller Concerts Poulet.[91]

What Works Are Truly "French"?

It was, of course, a matter of performing both new and older French works, and also as we have seen, of defining which were aesthetically "truly French." Responses to this highly charged issue were to influence the reception of both Charpentier's *Louise* and Debussy's enigmatic *Pelléas et Mélisande*. While these two complex works were indeed multivalent in their social implications, Debussy's, with its more innovative musical language, was to prove more of a critical challenge: perplexingly inconsistent in style from the standpoint of the discourses of both the Left and the Right, Debussy's work would pose problems of "classification" that would be resolved only as the composer's style evolved. In chapter 4 we shall trace this evolution, as well as the gradual appropriation of Debussy's music, by the nationalist Right, most notably by the Ligue de l'Action Française.

Determining if a work composed by a French artist was culturally authentically "French" became a major preoccupation in the press by 1904. Certainly, the discourse of the nationalist Right had been essential in highlighting this issue, but the Republic again was soon to riposte with its own distinctive concerns and criteria. As factions continued to fight for hegemony, or for their definition of what was "French" and hence what should be promoted, the "enquête," or survey of musicians, began to flourish. Born of the Affair, the survey was a means for prominent figures to assume the stance of "intellectuals" or judges and authorities on a wide range of contemporary matters.[92] As France's relations with Germany deteriorated, the concern with German cultural influence and the threat it posed to French identity and French "genius" began to intensify. Accordingly, between 1902 and 1903, in a series of installments in the *Mercure de France,* Jacques Morland launched an extensive "Enquête sur l'influence Allemande." As we might expect, spokesmen for the nationalist Right seized the occasion to define a series of fundamental oppositions between French and German cultural traits.[93]

In 1903 the Enquête turned to the volatile subject of music; it surveyed major figures in the musical world, including representatives of opposing perspectives. The powerful rhetoric of the Right by now had made it impossible not to agree with the importance of attenuating German influence in music and returning to the French tradition, but several figures (including Bruneau and d'Indy) qualified this assertion with the caveat that Germanic influence could be acceptable if it was assimilated with a distinctively French spirit.[94] As we have seen, however, there was little agreement over what this spirit comprised, and thus the opposing attitudes within the political culture continued to resonate.

This fact becomes inescapably clear in another "enquête" the following year on the essential nature of the French tradition. This one appeared in the conservative Republican *Revue bleue.* Conducted by Paul Landormy, it returned again to the essential question raised in Bruneau's 1900 *Rapport,* as well as in the vigorous criticism of it: it asked specifically what should be considered the beginning of this tradition, and not only whom it included but also who should be "expelled." Specifically, it raised the question of whether a "Romantic" composer such as Berlioz could be considered as legitimately belonging within the French tradition. There was already much disagreement over whether Romanticism was inherently "French," an issue that would become only more heated when the Action Française attacked the movement.[95]

The survey, entitled "L'Etat actuel de la musique française," is important for understanding several different aspects of the contentious musical culture. Not only do the attitudes and associations articulated further explain institutional decisions, but also, as we shall see in chapter 4, they illuminate creative choices. In this survey we may again observe the political associations that by now adhered not just to styles and to genres but, in many cases, to specific composers; hence, when inclining to emulate a past master, composers were often responding both to a line of musical development and to the contemporary associations it carried. Seeking to relate to a canon through specific stylistic choices in this context was considered a political gesture, an entry into the politicized aesthetic debate.[96]

Landormy begins the "enquête" by stating his own opinions, and it is here that his inclination toward "d'Indysme," or Scholisme, becomes immediately clear. He argues that proponents of "grand art," or of a music that is serious, severe, powerful, and profound, "do exist" in France, implying that this is not the official mainstream. Specifically, he credits the Schola with having originally launched the "cri de guerre" against the slavery of routine and that of conventional established forms;[97] but, Landormy continues, in order to maintain the "health" and ensure the future of French art, it is essential to continue to regain contact with sincere impressions and profound emotion. This, of course, was Scholiste rhetoric that Landormy was here diffusing, in an implicit critique of the official aesthetic and institutional system.

As one might expect, d'Indy's response centered on the concept of a "great" French art, but here he particularly underlines the importance of recognizing "national" qualities.[98] As he states once again, the French tradition comprises a series of great musicians who have fought for artistic sincerity as opposed to mere fashion or convention. Implicit here, of course, given the standard Scholiste discourse, is that this tradition excludes all Jewish composers, as well as composers associated with the Conservatoire; hence, the cornerstones of his canon, as we have already seen, are specific pre-revolutionary French composers—in particular, Marc-Antoine Charpentier, Couperin, and Rameau. And here d'Indy further propagates his theories of how this tradition was rudely broken by the "Italian" invasion in the nineteenth century but revived by the Société Nationale.

On the basis of his criteria for distinguishing what is "French," d'Indy, although not hostile to Romanticism in art, finds Berlioz to be extraneous, his talent essentially not musical but literary; moreover, according to d'Indy, Berlioz was neither precise nor concise, and, since he was little interested in form, his music does not manifest the "essential French traits." D'Indy further observes, moreover, how easily the Germans have adopted Berlioz, which is, he argues, further testimony to his essentially "un-French" nature. Frenchness is thus defined not by birth but by cultural qualities that can be derailed by contact with the non-French, thus delegitimizing an artist's entire oeuvre. Significantly, long before his colleagues, d'Indy perceives French traits in Debussy, whom he places in this tradition because of the similarity of his techniques with those of other "French" composers. This, however, was a point that would be continually contested in France and was only gradually resolved in the period before and during the First World War. D'Indy's frame of reference is *Pelléas,* in which he stresses the vocal style, one that, as we shall see in chapter 3, for many signified a return to French declamation of the past.[99]

As we might expect, Alfred Bruneau similarly used Landormy's "enquête" as a forum in which to propagate further the ideas he developed in his *Rapport.* On the question of Berlioz, Bruneau asserts precisely the opposite of d'Indy: that it is he who "saved" French music from the Italians, and his influence is still being felt. By "French" he again intends that secular tradition that began with Adam de la Halle and continued, most prominently, with Rameau, Méhul, and, later, Boieldieu; for, once more, French music is essentially simple, a music that issues from the "heart," with a direct if not always profound expression that is nevertheless "generous" and "frank." And denying d'Indy's assertion that symphonic music is by no means "un-French," he argues (like Debussy) that the French go against their own nature in attempting to be symphonic composers.

Yet, Bruneau continues, the German influence did have positive effects, since Wagner's music helped make dramatic music in France even more solid; however, he qualifies this by asserting that Wagner has now ceased to "act on" the French, who are in the process of liberating themselves and becoming more "national" in their art. In this context, contrary to d'Indy, he finds Debussy to be problematic since, while he embodies some traits that are purely French, he is completely lacking in others: although his musical language is simple, he is outside the "great tradition" because he cultivates a musical style that is too "specialized," or unique and thus "exceptional." As we shall see in chapter 3, uniqueness and originality were to be recognized as "French" only gradually, with the development of the aesthetic position associated with the "Liberal Right," but for Bruneau here, Debussy remains a "tempérament d'exception" and thus either incapable or unworthy of founding a tenable "school" in France.[100] He finds d'Indy to the contrary, however, too surrounded by ardent disciples, observing that art is not a matter of erudition—knowledge of the history of form cannot suffice.

Bruneau, while denying that he himself belongs to a "coterie," goes on to point out the social and aesthetic values that he shares with Gustave Charpentier: "sympathie pour la vie, pour le peuple, pour tout ce qui est moderne aussi et qui par là nous touche de plus près" (sympathy for life, for the people, and for all that is modern and hence which touches us the most closely). These aesthetic, social, and political values, so distant from the hierarchy and traditionalism of the Right, according to Bruneau have inspired a similar music in himself and Charpentier: they both seek an expression of nature, of the real, and of the immediate or spontaneous, and to illuminate a philosophical position, a love of humanity. Finally, in response to the question of the true role of the artist, Bruneau once again refers to the still controversial example of the writer Emile Zola: "C'est à lui, c'est à ses oeuvres, c'est à son amitié, c'est à ma collaboration avec ce grand homme que je dois d'être tout ce que je suis"[101] (It is to him, to his works, to his friendship, to my collaboration with this great man that I owe all that I am). These were bold words indeed at a time when Zola, even after his death, continued to be a principal target of animadversions by the nationalist Right.

If Bruneau's position was clearly inseparable from his politico-aesthetic stance, the same continued to be true of his ideological "confrère" on the Left, Romain Rolland. In this survey, the latter asserts his profound belief that a "true" French music cannot exist until the "people" have become musical, which is contingent on social conditions. Here, again, his views on the music of the present and the past in France provide him with a forum to develop his ideas about fundamental social reform; as he points out, there was once a great French music— in the sixteenth century—but it can be reborn only if certain essential social conditions are changed: there must be a broader education in music, which is itself contingent on a fundamental amelioration of the social conditions of the majority. Anticipating the rhetoric of the Popular Front and the Communist Party three decades later, he argues that a true national school can arise only if the appropriate changes in society are made. Rolland here echoes the Socialist belief that the conditions of a country are those of its art and that art is universal and not the monopoly of any one nation.[102]

The other notable figure interviewed in the survey was Debussy himself, who, by 1904, was espousing an increasingly consistent nationalist perspective. But, as we shall see in chapter 4 when we trace his tortuous intellectual evolution, while his nationalist rhetoric grew increasingly orthodox, his musical traditionalism remained unique; the school that developed around him would further develop his singular conception concerning the true qualities of French music that contemporary composers should strive to recapture. This "third" way, which we shall examine in chapter 3 and which argued that music should not uplift or instruct but simply "give pleasure," would become the position of the Liberal Right. In the period around 1905, however, the two major stances continued to be those represented by the nationalist Right and their adversaries in both the Republic and on the Socialist Left. This opposition was exacerbated by political events: in 1905 the tensions between the poles peaked with the definitive separation of church and state in France.[103]

The "Nationalist Reaction" and Music

The political tensions articulated by this event were refracted once more through the medium of critical debates over the question of the authentic French tradition. Again, through these debates, we may clearly perceive the associations now carried not only by particular composers but also by specific genres and musical styles. This is especially true of the prominent controversy between two major critics, both of whom, characteristically, crossed over several professional worlds: these were Louis Laloy, representing a broadly nationalist perspective, and the writer Camille Mauclair, representing the coalition of those who opposed it.

Laloy led the charge with a series of lectures at the Ecole des Hautes Etudes

Sociales, which, as we have seen, attempted to represent the major aesthetic and social positions. Delivered in March and April of 1905, the lectures were subsequently spread to a specifically musical audience through their publication in the *Mercure musical* as "Le Drame musicale moderne."[104] Through the eventual publication of such lectures, the Ecole was able both to further its intellectual aspirations and to have an impact on the musical culture. We have already noted Laloy's dissertation on music at the Sorbonne, as well as his initial approbation for d'Indy and the innovations of the Schola Cantorum; other aspects of his background, however, are important for an understanding of his style and approach in these articles along with his wide network of intellectual influence.

Laloy, who was to become the close friend and intellectual guide of Claude Debussy, had originally been a student of Bergson at the Lycée Henri IV; he then went on to become a pupil of the politically conservative medieval scholar Joseph Bédier at the prestigious Ecole Normale Supérieur.[105] An Agrégé de lettres in 1897, he subsequently studied Greek music and poetry and eventually published articles in the scholarly *Revue de philologie*. This was the context of his meeting both Jules Combarieu and Romain Rolland, who encouraged him, like them, to write a thesis on music for a Doctorat-ès-Lettres. To further his knowledge of music, and since he was unqualified to enter the Conservatoire, Laloy enrolled instead in the Schola Cantorum in 1899. Here he studied counterpoint with Pierre de Bréville and eventually went on to study composition with Vincent d'Indy himself. In 1904 Laloy both defended his thesis on Greek music at the Sorbonne and met the critic and writer on music Jean Marnold at Debussy's home; as we shall see in chapter 3, Laloy's connection with the composer had become increasingly close since the premiere of *Pelléas* and the appearance of his perceptive and highly complimentary article on it. With Jean Marnold, Laloy then went on to found the new musical journal the *Mercure musical,* which promoted "advanced" aesthetic, if socially conservative, views.[106]

In his lectures at the Ecole and in the subsequent articles based on them, Laloy ostensibly attempted to relate to the institution's goals and themes: one was to place the development of the art within the broader context of larger historical and intellectual developments, and from this perspective then to assess them critically. Although the stated subject of the articles is contemporary French opera, an important theme informing them is that ideological movements are determining its current directions; Laloy's specific goal is to condemn one direction that he sees as artistically and, more important, politically noxious—"French Verism," or Naturalist opera.

Laloy begins by distinguishing a new generation of French operatic composers, one that includes, most prominently, Gustave Charpentier, Alfred Bruneau, Vincent d'Indy, and Claude Debussy. Like his contemporaries, he attempts to define an increasing distance from Wagner in all, but particularly a more critical appropriation of the composer's ideas and innovations: as opposed to the generation of the 1880s, these composers embrace the social essence of Wagner's reform, while adapting his philosophical ideas to their more immediate political concerns. More specifically, according to Laloy, for this generation, which reached prominence around 1895, it is a question of how to achieve this simultaneously in text and in musical style; for, given the premises of Wagnerian reform, the ideological stance expressed in the language of the dramatic text determines the nature of the melodic line. In other words, for these composers, Wagnerian reform essentially implies that music must mirror the words of the text in the manner of a "faithful photograph." Hence, in the wake of Wagner, ideological expression in opera inheres not only in the nature and premises of the text but also in the musical style that translates it. We may here recall the similar ideas that had been expressed in the context of the highly politicized reviews of Alfred Bruneau's *Rapport*.

What Laloy sees emerging as a result of the Wagnerian reform is a conflict between competing literary-musical styles and their concomitant ideological associations: he thus proceeds to examine the antagonists, making no pretense of being objective, despite the scholarly or intellectual context of the original lectures. Certain trends he decries as baneful in both their political and aesthetic dimensions, and for him, as for "Willy," the most dangerous is French Verist, or "Naturalist," opera. It is in this discussion that we may most clearly perceive the way in which a coherent political perspective was by this time identified with specific stylistic traits.

Operatic Naturalism as a genre for Laloy is a vehicle of ideology that, like its literary counterpart, edits reality and imposes a theory of representation: despite its pretense of being objective, Naturalism is biased in what it depicts, for it is based not only on a false social vision but also on misleading conventions of representation. Nothing, Laloy trenchantly argues, is "less spontaneous, more strained and pedantic that this art which pretends to be inspired directly from nature."[107] Laloy perceives both a selective social positivism and aesthetic inconsistencies resulting from the propagandistic use to which Naturalist opera is being put. First, as the vehicle for specific ideas, the texts that the Naturalists employ are ponderously didactic, being illogically studded with crude and blatant symbols. These he condemns as especially inappropriate in nonmythological texts and, thus, as theoretically incongruous as the musical leitmotifs that are intended to convey them. Such an argument, we may recall, had been introduced to attack the operas of Zola and Bruneau soon after the publication of "J'Accuse."

Laloy also perceives political didacticism in the style of the language; he considers Zola's operatic texts to be pedantic, turgid, and overblown in diction. The music naturally reflects this trait, particularly that of Alfred Bruneau, still the arch incarnation of the Dreyfusard Republic in the musical world. For Laloy, Bruneau's vocal style translates the weaknesses of the text, being similarly turgid and declamatory, and his musical dramaturgy is academicized Wagnerism. The leitmotifs, which, again, Laloy finds to be incongruous with a Naturalist text, are as "impersonal" as the ideas they represent and as uninspired as their Conservatoire treatment. Significantly, "impersonal" and "uninspired" frequently appear as derogatory terms in the political rhetoric used by the nationalist Right to characterize the Republic's programs. Here Laloy thus condemns the Conservatoire and its pedagogy and, along with it, the Republic's valuation of an objective or scientific social vision. He then goes on to equate operatic Naturalism with the political self-image of the current Republican regime—that of "la démocratie triomphante."

Predictably, Laloy proceeds to ascribe certain attitudes and values to elements of style, as generated by their associations with Naturalism and the discourse of the Conservatoire: the Naturalist style in opera, for him, is what Roland Barthes termed an "écriture," or "le langage littéraire transformé par sa destination sociale"[108] (literary language transformed by its social end): even when purporting to be objective, words become both descriptions and judgments, and language itself becomes "le signe suffisant de l'engagement." As we have seen, in Naturalist opera this applies not just to the literary text but, through the controlling power of language, to the musical values that convey it: from the subject and style of the text evolve certain kinds of musical themes, a manner of treating them, a style of declamation, and, concomitantly, stylistic inconsistencies.

Despite his prolonged castigation of Emile Zola and Alfred Bruneau, for Laloy the prime exemplar of this "écriture" is Charpentier. It is thus on the opera *Louise* that Laloy most fully unleashes his critical wrath, for the symbolism it carried by now existed powerfully, and on several levels. Certainly all the ideologically charged, enthusiastic reviews of the work at the time of its premiere played a role in forming these symbolic associations. But, just as one ideological screen obscured the work's message for the political Left, another rendered it equally opaque for Laloy, who could not see the irony. For him, *Louise* is emblematic of all that is dangerous in Naturalist opera—the fallaciousness of its political presuppositions, the distortions of its language, and the weaknesses of its aesthetic.

According to the critic, Charpentier has undergone a pernicious politicization, which is acting on a subconscious level, distorting his vision and poisoning his creativity. Although he admits that Charpentier is a better composer than Alfred Bruneau, he too is a prisoner of the Conservatoire, practicing an "art du second main": his musical inspiration is nourished by the rules, formulae, and recipes "de l'école," and as a librettist he similarly perceives the world through an ideological veil. Certainly, Charpentier's involvement in the "Oeuvre de Mimi Pinson" and the publicity about it in the press played a role in encouraging this perception.

For Laloy, Charpentier is incapable of truly perceiving the misery he attempts to depict, since "cheap political journals have ruined his judgment and perverted his sensibility." Thus distorted by indoctrination, the composer is in perpetual illusion of himself and the world: he believes in the sincerity of feelings that are, in fact, only cold rhetoric. In sum, Charpentier the "Naturalist" is biased and is incapable of criticism or irony: the product of an insidious indoctrination, *Louise* is hence a "musique bâtarde."[109] The irony, of course, is that Laloy was so blind to the composer's own deep irony, just as had been the critics who originally warmly praised Charpentier's opera.

While it seems odd that these points were made at an originally "Dreyfusard" institution, we must recall that both the far Left and the Right had been receptive to the Schola's ideas: this may have accounted for the invitation to d'Indy to present his works and for the subsequent "d'Indyste" influence that is evident in its published lectures. Not all the original supporters of the Schola—including Laloy—were to remain true to the institution as it grew more militant, however. This group also included Camille Mauclair, who assumed the task of responding to Laloy and defending Charpentier in an anonymous letter to the journal. Laloy, discerning the author, acerbically rejoined by denouncing "un état d'esprit . . . fréquent dans les sectes socialistes et anti-cléricales" (a state of mind frequent in socialist and anticlerical sects). Mauclair's views were widely known at this point, since he was currently engaged in defending his conception of "l'art social" against those who were launching a reaction against it.[110]

Mauclair, however, was Laloy's target for yet another reason: on January 15, 1905, he had published a politically provocative essay. Entitled "La Réaction Nationaliste en art et l'importance de l'homme de lettres," it appeared in the important and widely read journal the *Revue mondiale*.[111] In this highly perceptive article, Mauclair identified a cultural reaction that cut across several fields, the result of the current mutual influence of politicians and artists in France. Here we may observe not only a complete articulation of Mauclair's aesthetic but also the way in which he related the reaction in music to those occurring in politics, literature, and painting. He assumes the same task as his nemesis Laloy, as he attempts to explain how artistic styles had by now developed specific political associations in France and he thus addresses the issue of how a political message is encoded in style, making an even more explicit reference to the role of the Dreyfus Affair.

Mauclair immediately centers on the questions of national identity and tradition, emphasizing the current obsessive search for "origins" in both politics and art. Clearly, the nationalism he is addressing is not the simple French chauvinism that we saw in Bruneau but the antiliberal, antiparliamentary movement that asserted the political primacy of indigenous values.[112] He then goes on to explore the psychological appeal of the conflicting positions and, like Laloy also does, their role in the success of particular operas in France. And once more like Laloy, Mauclair distinguishes the generation of the 1890s, but here he differentiates it from that which was integrally affected by the war of 1870. This was not a generation characterized by the fear, hesitation, and depression experienced by their elders in the wake of the devastating defeat at the hands of the Germans; rather, it was one that, in search of renewal, helped transform French musical taste by consciously turning away from Wagner and his overwhelming artistic influence.

Mauclair pointedly observes that this was the generation affected by the Dreyfus Affair, and hence one that proceeded to divide itself into hostile aesthetic camps. He perceives this division as also relating to preexisting aesthetic divisions in the musical world, between proponents of what he terms "elitist" and "social" art.[113] Predictably, it is in the former group, those who became "anti-Dreyfusards," that he discerns the current marked reactionary movement in artistic taste: it was they who abruptly repudiated their former fascination with non-French art and turned almost obsessively to the criterion of the "purely French." Hence the former Wagnerians of the early 1890s became clamorously anti-Wagnerian—staunch defenders of French taste conceived in terms of "measure" or of the "classic."[114]

Mauclair, of course, includes Barrès as an integral part of this group, as well as Maurice Denis, in whom he traces the same ideological evolution; both had moved from individualism to a reactionary aesthetic posture, Denis now praising Ingres and denouncing French Romantics like Delacroix and Berlioz. As Mauclair incisively notes, Denis and other nationalist "converts" henceforth excised the

Romantic movement as a whole from the canon of the "truly French"; this entire group of artists, he argues, terrified by their earlier audacities—by their former "violent originality"—was now in search of discipline, dogma, and a norm.[115] But what concerns Mauclair is that the influence of this group has spread, and now almost everywhere one finds this obsession with "origins," this "l'inquiétude d'être Français."

It is against the model of classicism, as confected and then propagated by the nationalist Right, that Mauclair, recalling Alfred Bruneau's discourse, proposes his own "French classicism." It is one not based on the academic models of the Greeks and Romans but one that springs from indigenous sources and is thus characterized by "frank realism":[116] Mauclair had already elaborated this point of view in 1903, in an article in the *Revue bleue* entitled "Le Classicism et l'académisme," in which he claimed that, far from representing an authentic, indigenous French style, academicism was only the continuation of a bastardized "Italo-German" style. "True" classicism, to the contrary, was entirely free of foreign art—an authentic French style that sprang from life and addressed current social needs. Here he finds another means to promote those values he shares with Bruneau, by claiming them to be indigenous and, simultaneously, inherently classic. Significantly, however, Mauclair makes it clear that he does not reject the "occidental ideal," a concept originally stressed by the Right but becoming increasingly legitimate; yet this ideal, he continues, is one in which Roman academicism does not belong, and one that certainly does not exclude France's gothic and "realist" past.[117]

Mauclair then points out that French "reactionaries" are motivated by fear of "déracinement," the product of the "detestable" influx of political nationalism into art. Politicians and artists, he argues, share an absorption with "origins" and "race" and, indeed, have a pernicious influence on each other.[118] As we saw when examining the tactics of the Ligue de la Patrie Française, as well as the Republican cultural response, Mauclair was here indeed correct: political and artistic worlds no longer had clear lines of demarcation but were united by common influential figures as well as suffused with a similar discourse. Mauclair argues that the point of view associated with the nationalist Right is increasingly widespread within the general culture: "On parle chaque jour davantage tout récemment d'une certaine tradition mystérieuse qu'on aurait perdue et qu'il faudrait à tout prix retrouver pour sauver l'art français d'une imminente décadence"[119] (Recently, one speaks more and more every day of a certain mysterious tradition that would have been lost and that should be found again at all costs in order to save French art from immediate decadence).

Mauclair explicitly includes musicians in this reactionary spirit, an observation that now impels him to repudiate the Schola that he had once highly praised: now he perceives that the school has strayed from its original and noble goal as a result of its unfortunate "ingestion" of a narrow Catholic spirit. The renaissance of religious music—the one that issued from the spirit of Franck—has all too easily become a rallying point for reactionary clericalism.[120] As we shall see in chapter 3 when examining the Schola in this period, Mauclair's perception was not only correct, but shared by many sectors of the musical world.

Mauclair goes even further: he associates the Schola with a political stance and with a specific social group. He elaborates the canon of the "snobbish" public that supports the Schola Cantorum, as well as that promoted by the pupils of César Franck: it includes not just the religious works that the school originally championed but now Rameau, Gluck, and Mozart have become part of it as well. According to Mauclair, the beatification of these composers is ideological: it does not issue from an admiration of their music but from a pertinacious "esprit rétro-grad." Moreover, he perceives this political reaction as being responsible for the vogue of anti-Wagnerism that is increasingly so pervasive in France. This bias, Mauclair finds, has worked to the detriment of the realist and social drama, especially the Wagnerian-inspired operas of Bruneau and Charpentier.[121] It also explains the success of *Pelléas*—the result not of its inherent value but of the increasingly prominent argument that it is fundamentally anti-Wagnerian. As we shall see in chapter 3, by now there were attempts to construe Debussy within the aesthetic of the Right, an appropriation to which he did not object. For he was indeed, as Mauclair argued, a part of the group that was obsessed with the question of the return to origins and to the purity of "true" French art.

Mauclair astutely perceived that between 1900 and 1905 French music was absorbed into the cultural politics of both the nationalists and their opponents. This was due in large part to the initiative of two nationalist leagues that were born of the Dreyfus Affair, especially the Ligue de la Patrie Française. Both leagues had sought to penetrate fields of culture by employing subtle new means—developing or co-opting critics and sponsoring lectures, publications, and institutions; through such venues they helped make musical legitimacy a political issue and engendered a new, coherent, and compelling discourse about the art. This discourse brought new issues and concepts into musical aesthetics and criticism and even, as we have seen, into the adjacent domains of music history and pedagogy. In bringing new criteria and questions to music, the cultural politics of the nationalist Right thus transformed the way in which French music of the present and past was both evaluated and discussed. It made the question of "how to be French" of central importance in musical aesthetics and, by extension, made the definition of a canon of great French works a political stake. Within this discourse, political values were translated into aesthetic terms and thus aesthetic oppositions implicitly assumed political meaning.

As we have seen, the effect of this phenomenon on French musical culture was direct and eventually extended to almost all aspects of the musical world. The new tactics of the political culture politicized the musical culture, in part through the medium of figures from both worlds like Rolland, d'Indy, La Laurencie, and Mauclair. The result was a distinctive musical culture, one that was divided and wrought with tensions that were simultaneously musical (or professional) and ideological (or political). Although common themes ran through this culture, it was far from homogeneous, being characterized by deep dissensions and bifurcations that would only become greater.

Institutional decisions concerning music were fundamentally affected by this context, especially by the political meanings that now adhered to musical styles; but so, too, were composers, who were forced either to face or to "negotiate" with these discourses and the musical meanings that they helped spread. Yet composers learned to use the new politicized institutions and organs available to them, although sometimes with unwonted consequences for their reputations or connotations; however, some willingly addressed the larger social and political issues that were becoming of central importance to the new politicized musical discourse. For again, political and musical cultures were no longer clearly distinct but were bound by a common web of figures, institutions, concepts, questions, and issues.

II

THE BATTLE ESCALATES
AND IS WON
1905–1914

3

Proliferating Factions, Issues, and Skirmishes

Between 1905 and World War I France experienced the increasing politicization of almost all fields of culture, together with a proliferation of ideological groupings and political factions. The year 1905 marked the ending of the resolutely anticlerical Combes ministry, the legal separation of Church and state, and a new collaboration of Radicals and Moderates in the government. With the evolution of the political situation, existing groups shifted their cultural emphasis, while others entered the dialogue, introducing new social goals and their own aesthetic conceptions. Movements of both the Right and the Left quickly learned how to use French culture to expand the political debate and to communicate their distinctive political visions; they also introduced new means of infiltrating various cultural realms, which resulted in an even more thorough "occupation" of the arts in France. As cultural ideologies, discourses, and tactics proliferated among competing French political factions, so did musical ideologies, along with associated musical programs. Now the boundaries between political initiatives using music and those belonging to the "professional world" grew vague, and frequently French musicians crossed the lines.

Increasingly active was the Action Française, which helped intensify attacks on the Conservatoire through its vociferous and escalating denunciation of Republican educational institutions. We shall see in this chapter that the reforms undertaken by Gabriel Fauré, appointed the new director in 1905, may be more fully illuminated within this context; these changes, forced on the inert institution through the exigencies of cultural politics, balanced innovations from the Schola with symbolically Republican practices.

This chapter also examines the new Socialist initiatives in popular involvement in the arts (including music), which followed upon the unification of the French Socialist Party in 1905. It then turns to the formation of a group that united dissidents of the far Right and Left, defining its own musical aesthetic under the banner of French National Socialism. Far from subsiding, the politicization that we saw in Part I grew even more strident, and the borders between French musical and political cultures were further effaced. Significantly, this was the period when journalists were preoccupied with the war of the compositional "chapelles," which made frequent intertextual reference to issues in other politicized cultural fields; even when partisan, critics perceived and analyzed the ideological and professional interests behind its "Debussyste" and "d'Indyste" camps, born ultimately of the institutional war.

THE ACTION FRANÇAISE AND MUSIC

In the period after 1905, the cultural "war" against the Republic was no longer led by the deliquescent Ligue de la Patrie Française. Now the more ideologically coherent and truculent Ligue de l'Action Française assumed command of the battle and marshaled its forces on all cultural fronts. (Although the Action Française had been founded as a movement and a journal in 1899, it technically became a league only in 1905.) Perhaps more than any political grouping in the period preceding the First World War, this league controlled the discourse of cultural politics in France: it determined the major issues, and it continued, through a variety of means, to assign specific political meanings or connotations to style in the arts. Just like the Patrie Française, it focused the political debate on culture as it continued to emphasize the theme of "authentic" French traditions and values. But it was specifically to stress the importance of preserving the classical tradition in France in its pristine form, free of foreign cultural or racial elements.

As has already been well established, the role of the militantly Royalist Action Française in the ideological renewal of the Right in France was seminal and profound. Despite its relatively small membership, the impact of the league was unequivocally large because of the appeal of its message to the "wealthy, well-born, right-thinking classes." But it appealed to other groups as well, for the movement could be seen in substantially different ways: if it was the guardian of tradition for the established, for the young it was revolutionary, promising a rupture with Republican ideology. A principal theme of its founder and leader, Charles Maurras, was that the Republican-led France of the present was, in fact, not representative of the "true France." Here he made a crucial distinction between the postrevolutionary "pays légal" and the virtual or quintessential, indigenous "pays réel";[1] the latter, for Maurras, comprised at once a national and a regional culture, thus endowing everyone with two "patries," each commanding loyalty in different ways: while one's roots were in one's own regional "petite pays," one nevertheless shared the common destiny and potential of the nation—of "greater France." But this conception would eventually lead to an inner tension within the league between advocates of the authoritarian centralization of the ancien régime and the protectors of regional culture and rights.[2]

Like the pioneering Ligue de la Patrie Française, the Action Française similarly avoided the conventional or legitimate channels of political action in France; for the latter, however, this did not exclude violence or a direct physical intervention whenever this seemed an effective means to make an emphatic political point. In 1908 it formed the Camelots du Roi, a violent action group of young men who sold the movement's newspaper and were deployed on specific occasions. The year this bellicose youth group was founded, the league engaged in clamorous protest against the symbolically aggressive Republican act of transferring Zola's ashes to the Panthéon. In the course of this tumultuous event, Alfred Dreyfus, still a target, was physically attacked and shot in the arm by a politically radical journalist. Although this was not an act that was specifically planned by the Action Française, Maurras publicly and belligerently expressed his approbation of it. Significantly, this was the period when the league was actively seeking supporters not only in the upper but also in the middle and the working classes.[3]

The league's other means of avoiding the conventional channels of political action in France was its focus on the symbolic domain of culture. For Maurras, the political and cultural ideologies of the league were not simply of equal importance—they were inherently inseparable, for they had sprung originally from the very same source. Maurras attributed his original political perceptions to his initial search for the basic principles of order that he believed inhered in all great art. As he put it, "We had seen the ruins in the realm of thought and taste before noticing the social, military, economic, and diplomatic damage that generally results from democracy."[4] For Maurras, beauty was dependent on order, and order on a hierarchy of values; hierarchy, in turn, depended on an authority to "define and endorse it." Since order, hierarchy, and authority in politics ought to arise from tradition, that which similarly followed this tradition in literature would be most successful. In other words, Maurras supported "absolutist" judgments in art, with the aesthetic model being, above all, seventeenth-century France. He thus equated classicism and traditionalism in general with his attempt to restore the French monarchical state that had originally produced such superior art.[5] This also meant a stress on "purity," a concerted attempt to extirpate all those cultural elements perceived as "foreign" or not inherently "French."

The cultural network of the league was powerful, like that of the Patrie Française, and embraced influential institutions, as well as important publications. The latter included the overtly ideological *L'Action française* along with more subtle and scholarly publications with an impressive intellectual veneer. One example was the prestigious *Revue critique des idées et des livres,* edited primarily by those either affiliated with or sympathetic to the Action Française. Founded in 1908, it became, in effect, the equivalent for the Right of what the *Nouvelle revue française* would be for the Left. Like other journals of its kind, it sought to join in solidarity those holding common opinions, and in doing so it

became a new sort of laboratory of ideas. Another venue through which to develop and diffuse Rightest doctrine subtly was the Institut d'Action Française,
modeled on precedents like the Institut Catholique and the Ecole des Hautes
Etudes Sociales. Founded in 1906, the Institut d'Action Française was directed by
Louis Dimier, a teacher of rhetoric and classical language at the Institut
Catholique. Its goal was to organize lectures to be given by the principal theoreticians of the movement; many of these lectures were subsequently published.[6]

The year after the Institut opened, the ambitious young literary critic Pierre
Lasserre delivered a series of lectures that attacked the Romantic movement.[7] As
we have seen, the question of whether Romanticism was inherently French was
already well established and had begun to penetrate the musical world. Lasserre,
not originally a supporter of the political Right, had passed the agrégation in philosophy and then went on to specialize in the field of literature. But his thesis, *Le
Romantisme français: Essai sur la révolution dans les sentiments et dans les idées au
XIXe siècle*, had been poorly received at the recently "Republicanized" Sorbonne.
A subsequent convert to the Action Française, Lasserre, in 1907, published a
book, *Le Romantisme français*, based on his thesis and lectures.[8]

Lasserre's argument is important since it would not only become typical of
the Action Française but also would have wide resonance in France, affecting
several fields, including music. He presents the position of classical philosophers
who argued against the encouragement of all that agitates the vague, wild, and
confused aspects of human consciousness. He points out that, rather, they advocated order and hierarchy in the physical faculties—an order that subordinated
feeling to intelligence, imagination to reason, and the spontaneous to the reflec-
tive. Romanticism, Lasserre asserts, indulges in precisely the opposite values and
thus, as an artistic movement, is inherently inimical to society. He then goes on
characteristically to claim that the Germans have ravaged French culture and
taste, and even the national political order, by their exportation of "the Romantic
model"; for Romanticism affirms the utopian vision of a social order in which all,
instead of being by nature unequal, are identical in their capabilities. He concludes that Romanticism inherently favors decomposition, not just in the realm
of thought and feeling but, by extension, in the political world.[9]

As a spokesman for the Action Française, Lasserre by no means ignored the
art of music; rather, like his nemesis, Mauclair, he crossed easily from literature to
the other arts. Indeed, the Action Française was to take a substantial interest in
music and to use it more overtly in its ideological campaign than had the Ligue
de la Patrie Française. For the Action Française also perceived that music could
be a major stake in the symbolic battle and that, being nonobjective, it could be
used to combat the Republic's stress on logic. Both leagues perceived that music
might be a prime anti-Dreyfusard symbol, since, like tradition itself, its meaning
was necessarily ineffable and intuited. And so in the period, when the political
Right was generating powerful new symbols, both leagues took advantage of the
fact that music, for the Republic, was a vulnerable field.[10] For the Action
Française, music would continue to serve as a valuable weapon in the larger contestation over political myths, or central collective values. And so it developed a
musical aesthetic that was inseparable from its political discourse, employing the

same system of concepts, meanings, values, and historical references. And this discourse was eventually to have a substantial influence in French musical culture in the period immediately preceding, during, and after the First World War.

The Action Française, with its stress on the "classical" and on French as opposed to German "modes of thought," would promote a different range of styles than the Ligue de la Patrie Française. We may see this clearly in Pierre Lasserre's attack on Wagner as articulated most fully, perhaps, in his polemical book, based on his thesis, *Des Romantiques à nous.*[11] The critic castigates Wagner as an arch Romantic, unlike those writers associated with the Patrie Française, such as Maurice Barrès. Lasserre attacks the composer's disingenuousness and what he calls his "impurity," by which he means what he perceives as Wagner's constant quest for an "artificial complexity."[12] Lasserre elaborated this idea further in *L'Esprit de la musique française,* a book that was published during the war but that was still consistent with his prewar beliefs. Here, in this widely quoted volume, he denounces Wagner as "opulent" and "sumptuous," suggesting that the possibility that Wagner's Jewish stepfather was his real father accounts for the "éclat oriental" of his style.[13] In *Des Romantiques à nous* Lasserre contrasts Wagner's style with the "purity" of that of Fauré. But his other positive model is the Russian composer, Modest Moussorgsky. The latter, he argues, is strongly and positively marked by his national character and, as all the Russian "Five," is both "naïf" and "raffiné"; for this was a group whose members opened their hearts to the "songs" of the Russian soil—here implying not an irrational act but rather the instinct passed on by their "race." He then concludes that the same kind of music cannot possibly spring from every soil since each people, each race, formed by tradition and blood, has its own kind of "song." As he puts it metaphorically (and as Maurras himself was similarly to do) such a "song" essentially is "le chant de leur âme, de leur pensée, de leur rêve."[14]

It was undoubtedly because of d'Indy's Wagnerism that, while the Action Française, in general, approved of the Schola and its traditionalism, it was hesitant about d'Indy himself. Articles in the *Revue critique des idées et des livres* frequently reported on the Schola's activities and discussed its teaching, as codified in d'Indy's *Cours de composition musicale.* Moreover, August Sérieyx, who taught at the Schola and prepared the manuscript from the notes he took as a student, was a founding member of the journal. *L'Action française* did praise d'Indy for his efforts on behalf of the French musical past, hailing him as the energetic defender of the "true" national tradition in music.[15]

Other members of the Action Française expressed themselves stridently on the subject of music and especially on the topical question of who was an authentically "French" composer. They were thus once more to bring to prominence the question that had already been raised initially by the Société Nationale de Musique Française: "How does one write 'truly' French music?" The question of what was "French" in music was henceforth to become a prime concern and again was to be generated from its political nexus to the entire musical culture. This would affect not only the significances carried by styles, forms, and techniques, as already defined at the Schola, but the question of whom the French canon should embrace.

The prominent nationalist writer Léon Daudet was among the first to perceive the way in which Debussy's music could be construed within the movement's doctrine. In his *Salons et journaux,* Daudet deftly sketches the composer's distinctive appearance and manner and pronounces *Pelléas* a "chef-d'oeuvre," a judgment based on nationalist criteria. Anticipating articles on the composer in *Action française* during the war, he pronounces Debussy a "classic" in the tradition of prerevolutionary France.[16] In chapter 4 we shall see the extent to which this was true and to which Debussy was not only beguiled by such discourse concerning his music but began to adopt it himself. For as the prestige of the movement mounted with the prewar nationalistic tide, it was to the advantage of an "independent" or nonofficial composer to have such support.

The Action Française not only encouraged its members to comment on music but also, like d'Indy and the Patrie Française, actively approached sympathetic musicians. This was demonstrably the case with Louis Bourgault-Ducoudray, a composer and a professor of music history at the Paris Conservatoire. Originally an anti-Dreyfusard before it was clear which faction would win in the period following the Affair he attempted to rehabilitate himself with the Republic. In 1903 he published an article in the *Revue musicale* on the then timely subject "L'Enseignement de chant dans les lycées."[17] Here he sounds like Bruneau, stressing the importance of expressing "real," living, palpitating feelings in music and, indeed, in every genre. And, like Bruneau, he emphasizes models that are drawn from the revolutionary period, which, in the orthodox Republican manner, becomes a central point of reference.

It was in this period, he argues, that the state first attempted to exalt "real" human feelings and therefore to follow the models of Greek antiquity and the Protestant Reformation.[18] He goes on, however, (like d'Indy) to regret that the repertoire of the workers's choral societies, or "Orphéons," is so inferior to that of the other social classes: performing music of the "third order," such societies are made to stand apart, in essence disqualified from being a member of the recognized musical world. He argues that if all the classes are truly to share common feelings, their access to the one art that is capable of expressing them should be essentially the same; for the goal of all great art, he concludes, is in essence fundamentally political, being, in short, to "faire l'unité dans le coeur d'une nation" (arrive at unity in the heart of a nation).[19] As we shall see later in this chapter, such ideas were soon to be realized in France as they were taken up and politically adapted by the nascent Syndicalist movement. Although this group would seek to appropriate the patrimony and "capital" of great art, it would do so in a distinctive manner that precluded a facile or orthodox assimilation.

Bourgault-Ducoudray's reference to Republican themes was apparently only a tactic intended to redeem his good standing in the Republican institution that employed him, for sometime probably between 1905 and his death in 1910, he expressed political ideas of a far different ideological nature. In an undated letter to an unidentified correspondent, apparently associated with the Action Française, he speaks of a visit from someone whom the correspondent had sent to see him.[20] (Bourgault-Ducoudray was apparently writing this letter upon the specific request of the visitor, who had served as an intermediary in the exchange.) The purpose of the visit was to solicit Bourgault-Ducoudray's opinion concerning the planning of a "séance musicale et littéraire" for the benefit of the Action Française. Bourgault-Ducoudray responded by pointing out the difficulty of such an undertaking in a season already so crammed with so many competing concerts in Paris. But he eventually proceeded to give his larger philosophical opinion of the venture and of the general idea of using concerts as a means of diffusing nationalist propaganda:

> Selon moi, l'Action Française, comme la Patrie Française, devrait chercher dans l'art et particulièrement dans l'art musical moins un moyen de recette qu'un moyen de propagande par le sentiment. Puisque l'idée de patrie est battue . . . il importe de formuler avec toute la puissance qu'il comporte les augures du sentiment national. Je lisais dans le *Gaulois* cette définition du Nationalisme: le sentiment profond, les traditions, les rêves, les energies de toute une race. Savez-vous l'unique moyen de formuler cela? C'est la musique *chorale*. . . . Organisez un culte musical de la patrie et de la tradition française et donnez une audition de musique patriotique au Trocadero. . . . Vous affirmerez avec une puissance de rayonnement incomparable l'idée que nous servons.

> (In my opinion, the Action Française, like the Patrie Française, should seek in art, and particularly in musical art, less a means of revenue than a means of propaganda through feeling. Since the idea of the homeland is beaten . . . it is important to formulate with all the power it carries, the auguries of national feeling. I read in the *Gaulois* this definition of nationalism: the deep feeling, the traditions, the dreams, the energies of a whole race. Do you know the only means to formulate this? It is choral music. . . . Organize a musical worship of the homeland and of the French tradition and give a concert of patriotic music at the Trocadero. . . . You will affirm with an incomparable power of influence the idea that we serve.)

The Action Française was indeed to follow Bourgault-Ducoudray's advice concerning the use of music as a means of propaganda for the cult of French tradition and nationalist sentiment; however, it would not be in the specific manner that he advocated, for choral societies were to remain more characteristic vehicles for the political Left. The Action Française preferred, in the arts, to concentrate on "high" culture and, in posing as its protectors, to profit from the symbolic legitimacy it brought: eventually it would sponsor concerts—in the period following the First World War, when patriotic concerts had become common—through the Schola d'Action Française.[21]

Other influential figures in music were close to the league in this period, including the powerful critic of the conservative *Revue des deux mondes* Camille Bellaigue: not only was he sympathetic to it, but also later, when the movement was officially censured by the Pope, Bellaigue, a representative of the latter, acted as an intermediary between the two. Like the league, he was anti-German, and particularly anti-Wagnerian, which led them both to animosity toward anyone who exhibited Wagner's influence, including César Franck.[22]

The themes of the Action Française were to penetrate the musical world, but not simply through the medium of musicians and music critics who were sympathetic with or close to the movement; as we shall shortly see, the Action

Française propounded its beliefs through the writings of cultural critics whose themes were related to or drawn from the movement. The issues such critics targeted would become omnipresent in musical discourse, which more or less overtly made intertextual reference to them. We shall later examine two cases— that of the "new" or reformed Sorbonne and that of the current cultural tendencies of French youth.

FRENCH SOCIALIST INITIATIVES IN MUSIC

The political Left, as well, would continue to influence the musical world, particularly as the Third Republic itself grew more moderate or centrist in nature.[23] The role of the Left would increase after 1905 as a result of the unification of the Socialist Party in France, which previously had been splintered into competing Guesdist and Jaurèsist factions. From this point on until the war, the party's percentage of the popular vote would continue to grow, until it finally emerged as the second largest political group in the chamber. Like the Right, the Left would develop or recruit individuals who moved with ease between the political-musical world and the more narrowly professional world of music. It, too, would sponsor concerts as well as musical organizations that eventually would themselves form a part of the more comprehensive musical culture in France.

As the Republic became more moderate and abandoned its earlier Dreyfusard cultural rhetoric, it was the Socialists who now maintained it, along with its associated musical ideals; for they continued to emphasize the role of education as a means toward "liberation," of achieving a free, untrammeled social consciousness and intelligence. They sought not only the establishment of balance among the different human faculties—leading to a free and conscious choice—but the cultivation of true human fraternity.[24] It is also important to note that after 1905 French Socialism was both ideologically anticapitalist and pronouncedly antinationalist. Indeed, this was to throw the party's aesthetic into strong relief against the rising tide of nationalist feeling and associated themes in the center as on the Right.

In literature, French Socialists still charged the writer with the task of education, or the depiction of social realities using the specific means of the art; their leader, Jaurès, however, was eventually to articulate a related theme—that French workers possessed an inherent right to partake of the national cultural heritage.[25] But we shall see that, as far as the "musical heritage" was concerned, the Socialist movement went about defining and appropriating it in a unique manner. This would be particularly true in the chauvinistic prewar period, when French Socialists implacably equated great works with both universal and humanistic values.[26]

Camille Mauclair remained active in both the literary and the musical worlds, elaborating his earlier social themes in literary, political, and musical journals.[27] But he was not alone among the Socialists in mediating the worlds of politics and music, for figures based primarily in the musical world would serve a similar function. Such was the case with J.-G. Prod'homme, the music historian and specialist on Gluck and the long-time librarian of the Paris Opéra. Still an ardent Wagnerian at a time of mounting anti-Wagnerism among those in musical circles, Prodhomme contributed articles on music to the *Revue Socialiste*.[28]

The most lucid statement, however, of the Socialists' developing aesthetic position with regard to the art of music may be found in Jean Richard's journal, *L'Effort*. A bimonthly revue of literature and the arts, it was also concerned with music, and it is here that we find echoes of the rhetoric of Romain Rolland and Alfred Bruneau. Like other political journals, it was aware of the major questions in the musical world and, like they, helped contribute further to their definition and assumed a stance on them. On June 15, 1910, for example, it cited two surveys on prominent questions—the first, in the *Paris journal,* on the "prétendu renaissance classique" and the second, in the *Revue du temps présent,* on the subject that was presently bifurcating the musical world in France—that of "Debussysme." Both surveys concerned preoccupations associated largely with the political center and Right, and *L'Effort* thus perceived them as evidence of the current decadence because of their distance from more central concerns.

Like other political perspectives that we shall examine, the journal also perceived contemporary criticism of the arts as itself a sign of social and political "disorder"; it denounced current criticism, presenting it as essentially an arrogation of power by a "critical establishment" that was using the wrong criteria for evaluation. In a supplement of June 1, 1910, it specifically derided critics through a political analogy, describing them as "artistic parliamentarians," a class of the "elected," but without "electors." Significantly, this was a period of antiparliamentary feeling on the part not only of the extreme Right but also of the far Left, which was disillusioned with the evolution of the Republic. The three years under the leadership of the Radical premier Georges Clemenceau, from 1906 to 1909, had evoked increasing labor agitation, eventually peaking, in 1909, in the mythic general strike, which Clémenceau suppressed without mercy by calling in French military troops. Hence the notable hostility in the contemporary Socialist press not only toward the government but also toward the parliamentary model, although French Socialists, in general, supported the Republic.

In the June 1, 1910, supplement, the author accuses critics of perceiving themselves as invested with the mission of interpreting the thought of the "masters" of the past for the incompetent or uncomprehending masses.[29] As we have seen, this indeed was occurring, not only in the Republican political press but also in contemporary lectures and books on music associated with the far Right. Those within the musical world, as we shall shortly see, were similarly to denounce this propagandistic effort, while, at the same time, participating in it.

L'Effort had its own perspective on the central question of what kind of theater would meet the needs of the masses and on current proposals concerning it. In 1910, Jean Richard published a series of articles entitled "Le Théâtre du peuple: critique d'une utopie," in which he addressed these timely issues. In them, he sounds very much like Claude Debussy several years earlier, as we shall see in chapter 4 when we examine his position in this politicized debate; for Richard asserts that the bourgeoisie is still far from being able to furnish the people with the kind of theater they truly need; he then questions whether the bourgeoisie can, in fact, ever share the same intellectual representations, feelings, and emotions as the other social group.

Richard's subsequent point relates very closely to that which we perceived as one of the central messages of Gustave Charpentier's "roman musical," *Louise:* the people's approach to language, both in terms of modes of construal and as modalities of usage, is fundamentally different from that of the upper classes. A word enters the vocabulary of the "people" because of its subtle etymological associations, and they construe it distinctively, immediately translating it into terms of "movement" or action. Any theater for the people must necessarily take account of this basic fact and must possess, in addition, what Richard here terms an "odeur de foule." Finally, it must relate to contemporary enthusiasms or feelings in the manner of Romain Rolland's monumental work *Le 14 juillet*.[30] Rolland remained an important figure in mediating the perspectives and concerns of the political Left and the musical world before World War I.

As *L'Effort* maintained its own paradigm of effective "people's theater," like Mauclair, it also held a conception of what authentic French classicism comprised. Ironically, its conception closely resembles that of Wagner; both are implicitly based on a similar conception of ancient Greek theater: "Les époques qu'on appelle classiques sont celles où l'unanimité idéale dans la nation contraint les artistes à produire des oeuvres animées de cette foi, et toutes pénétrées de ces mythes puissants" (The epochs that one calls classic are those in which the ideal unanimity in a nation constrains artists to produce works that are animated with this faith and penetrated by these powerful myths).[31] Certainly, the French far Left, after the compelling rhetoric of Georges Sorel, was as aware of the power of the myth in unifying the nation as the far Right. But it was the basis of this unity in the nation, or the content of its centrifugal myth, that remained a fundamental point of contestation between the Left and the Right. Classicism was no longer the question, nor was it exclusively the property of the French nationalist Right: at issue, rather, was the values it embodied and the content of its myth.

The question of a "motivating" myth thus became a central concern of the journal, and particularly Sorel's myth of "l'âme moderne" as articulated in his *Réflexions sur la violence*. On June 15, 1910, *L'Effort* addressed the Sorelian myth, agreeing with Sorel that the current motivating myth of the people was neither that of the Republic nor that of equality and liberty but, rather, that of "la guerre sociale," a myth that would eventually triumph and, in turn, inspire great art as well.[32] As we shall shortly see, another aspect of the Sorelian myth was indeed to attract the attention and collaboration of a composer—Vincent d'Indy. D'Indy was not attracted by Sorel's belief in the inevitability of social "war" but by his faith in the fundamental, irrational, unifying power possessed by the nation.

L'Effort had little question concerning the qualities that constitute great art, and its ideas recall those that Mauclair originally perceived in the Schola Cantorum: "Pour être forte et grande, l'oeuvre doit enfin être écrite conscieusement, avec probité" (To be strong and great, a work should be written conscientiously, with probity). It goes on to specify that by "probity" it means sincerity of artistic feeling, as well as, on the level of execution, sincerity or integrity of craft.[33] Once again, it is no coincidence that some of the ideas we find in the journal seem to recall those of d'Indy and the Schola at the turn of the century; for, as we have noted, it was at that point that the two political extremes on the Right and the Left had joined forces against the mediocrity of the Republican center. This would continue when d'Indy and other figures on the French nationalist Right attempted, if briefly, to join their forces with those on the Socialist Left.

Given the fact that many of the journal's social ideas relate to those of the "Dreyfusard Republic," it is not surprising that this was also true of artistic taste. Both its prophetic populist ideas on theater and its musical interpretation and taste resembled those of Romain Rolland. For example, an article of November 10, 1910, entitled "Un Poète" is a tribute to Beethoven that immediately recalls the approach of Romain Rolland: it praises many of the very same qualities that Rolland had perceived, and its rhetoric recalls that of both the writer and Alfred Bruneau: "S'il ose l'y voir, il y trouvera tout: le style, la composition, la grandeur sans emphase, la gaîté sans fadeur, le pathétique sans effet, la variété la plus prodigieuse et la source de l'émotion" (If he dares to see it, he will find it all: style, composition, grandeur without bombast, gaiety without tastelessness, the pathetic without effect, the most prodigious variety and the source of emotion).[34]

Grandeur, gaiety, strong emotions, variety—as we have seen, these were precisely the values that Bruneau had initially promoted as essentially "French." In addition, the journal points out the absence in Beethoven of anything that inhibits the directness of the statement, or of "La vie, la force, et la nature," once again recalling Bruneau. And even more explicitly, another article, of March 1912, echoes Bruneau's *Rapport* of 1900 and the "credo" of his Dreyfusard aesthetic. Its subject is the utility of art and thus the necessity of its closeness to life, art being, in essence, not a metaphysical, but a "human" manifestation.[35] Like Bruneau, it asserts that not only popular but also high art could be close to life, while still elevating and educating, each according to its own distinct conception. The Left in France continued to stress the necessity of effacing the boundaries between art and life, perceiving the two as essentially lying within a continuum.

In the period before the war, the Socialist daily *L'Humanité* propounded its own specific views of what kind of culture to promote for the people. It was interested in literature, of course—it serialized the works of Murger and de Maupassant—but it also exhibited a sustained and substantial interest in both theater and music. On January 16, 1913, it reported on a new kind of venture undertaken by the theater of the soon-to-be director of the Opéra—Jacques Rouché's Théâtre des Arts. The journal praised its "concerts illustrés," with musicians in period costumes acting out concerts from the historical past, while at the same time performing the music. Recalling those of the Schola, each of the concerts served a pedagogic end by not only depicting the history of music, but suggesting links between present and past. One concert on which the journal reported attempted to exemplify a specific conception of the "true" French canon by juxtaposing excerpts from works of Lully and Fauré.[36] *L'Humanité* approved of this venture, for it attempted not just to assimilate the people to the culture of the bourgeoisie but to educate them in the national patrimony, imbuing them with awareness and, thus, power.

The journal, however, was not exclusively interested in increasing access to high art: it also promoted programs of more popular art, recalling those born immediately after the Affair. This included the "Chansons du Peuple," which performed poetry and music from different regions of France, thus appropriating French folklore for the workers, as opposed to its association with peasants by the political Right.[37] Held at the Maison Commune du 18ème goguette familiale, it was to profit what was revealingly called the "Muse révolutionnaire du 18ème." Recalling Charpentier's "Muse du Peuple," the journal announced that the "Camarades de la Muse" was to present what the journal referred to as a "grand concert de solidarité en faveur d'un camarade."

The Left, like the political Right (and specifically sympathizers like Bourgault-Ducoudray), was thus planning concerts instinct with simultaneously pragmatic and political ends; again recalling the projects of Charpentier, the journal also announced a "concert vocal" to be given by the Chambre Syndicale des Coiffeurs de Paris, performed by "véritables artistes de tous genres."[38] For the far Left, the idea of the concert was still informed by nineteenth-century traditions that we may trace to the influence of workers' clubs and the Utopian Socialist movement: it still carried not just the association of fraternity and mutual aid but, in addition, the Fourrierist metaphor of social harmony and cooperation. During the First World War this model, along with that of the "patriotic" Right, would enter the mainstream of French musical culture, affecting it in vital ways.[39] But already, through mediating figures such as Gustave Charpentier, the political-musical and professional musical cultures were beginning to fuse.

The "Fêtes du People"

Another venture initiated now, and one with a distinctly political goal, would also eventually be absorbed into the Third Republic's musical culture. This was the Fêtes du Peuple, which, like the long-lived L'Art Pour Tous, sought to propagate the love of great works of art while simultaneously "aiding humanity." Associated with the syndicalist movement and organized originally by the working class, its ultimate goal, like that of Socialism, was "l'affranchissement des hommes." Its metaphorical "heart," a chorale, was to provide a center not only for leisure and friendship, but also, through the agency of music, for both culture and education.[40]

Like the Schola, the Fêtes du Peuple is an apt illustration of the fluid movement throughout this period between properly musical and political cultures: we may trace the ideas behind it not only to intermediary figures such as Romain Rolland but also to a young composer and protegé of Gustave Charpentier. The organization was born shortly before the outbreak of the First World War—in the spring of 1914—from an idea of the composer Albert Doyen. Although formally a student of Charles-Marie Widor at the Conservatoire, Doyen nevertheless considered his real masters to be Bruneau and Charpentier. Their examples and their rhetoric were central to his project, which was eventually to have a substantial resonance in both the political and musical cultures.

Doyen had assisted Charpentier in the "Oeuvre de Mimi Pinson," and in 1907 he met Romain Rolland in the circle of the *Revue d'art dramatique*.[41] But he came to public attention when his "fête" *Le Triomphe de la Liberté* won the prestigious Concours de la Ville de Paris in 1913. Recalling Charpentier's earlier "fête populaire," it is dedicated to the "people of Paris" and is based on the "fête" and the text that concludes Rolland's play *Le 14 juillet.* For Doyen it became "la fête du peuple d'hier et d'aujourd'hui, la fête du peuple éternel" (the celebration of the people of yesterday and today, the celebration of the eternal people), who are represented in the work by the continual presence of the "foule anonyme." In order to suggest the crowd, he even included a line in the score for "les clameurs, les murmures, les grondements, les soufflets et les cris" (clamors, murmurs, rumblings, whistles, and cries).[42]

It was fortunate for Doyen that Charpentier, now a member of the Institut, served between 1910 and 1912 on the jury of the competition that was sponsored by the city. Other members were drawn not only from the political world but from the Académie, as well as from the official musical world: among them were the Préfet de la Seine (the president), a Conseiller Municipal (vice president), Alfred Bruneau, and Albert Carré, director of the Opéra Comique. Fortunately again, Charpentier was the "rapporteur" for the group when Doyen won the prize, and in his report we may witness the rhetoric with which he supported the work. Charpentier begins by noting that pieces of many genres were submitted, including a "poème symphonique avec soli et choeurs, légendes, actions populaires, comédies lyriques, drames, et mélodrames."[43] Clearly, by now, the influence of such figures as Rolland and d'Indy, and the opposing hortatory genres that they established, were firmly established in the next generation.

Despite the range of the entries, however, according to Charpentier, it was one work above all that seemed best to realize the idea behind the "concours": this was Doyen's *Le Triomphe de la Liberté,* a work conceived for execution "en plein air" and integrally incorporating both professional and nonprofessional performers. After lauding its powerful musicality, its vast proportions, and its general "enthusiasm," Charpentier goes on (recalling Bruneau) to draw attention to its realistic elements: "En vérité, son oeuvre est . . . bizarre, impulsive, indisciplinée, tourmentée, bariolée comme la foule d'émeute et de fête qu'elle veut représenter, enfantine et brutale comme l'âme d'un peuple qui fait de l'histoire" (In truth, his work is . . . bizarre, impulsive, undisciplined, tormented, motley like the crowd of a riot or a celebration that it wishes to represent, childish and brutal like the soul of a people who make history).[44] Charpentier, a master of multiple meanings, as we have seen, here, in describing the work, was pointing out not only its populist but also its Romantic traits: at a time when Romanticism and all that it represented politically and socially was under attack by the Right, he seized the occasion to support it through his encomium of the "fête."

As Charpentier perceived, Doyen was following in his footsteps, having developed certain political implications of his original conception, and was the perfect person to found such a venture. Legitimized by the professional musical world, he was inspired not only by Charpentier's goals but also, as we have noted, by those of another mediating figure, Romain Rolland. Doyen's ideas concerning popular theater were prepared by those of Rolland, specifically his model as articulated in his earlier *Théâtre du peuple.* At the same time, they were characterized by an original appropriation of other ideas that had previously been associated with d'Indy and the Schola Cantorum. While the "fêtes" he proposed would be "new," they could be based on traditional legends, as well as on medieval mysteries (recalling d'Indy's *La Légende de Saint Christophe*). As Doyen put it, they would resemble "les mystères qui rassemblaient le peuple de la ville sur les parvis des Cathédrales, puisaient dans les Evangiles, *La Légende dorée,* la vie des Saints" (the mysteries that gathered the people of the city in the square in front of the Cathedral, drawing from the Gospels, the *Légende dorée,* the lives of the saints).

Doyen's ideas were drawn from a fund that was similar to those employed by d'Indy himself—one that included both Wagner and the medieval past. But here they are employed in the service of a distinctly different social vision: Doyen, again like his mentor, was adept at both assimilation and "appropriation." Although d'Indy's goal was submission to an ineffable authority, Doyen's was rather a collective "liberation": the new "fêtes" were to be vehicles of ideas that were neither religious nor national but, rather, in the tradition of the political Left, essentially universal and "human." Doyen, like d'Indy and Wagner, sought to create a social ritual centered on music, although their ritual models were substantially different in nature. While d'Indy's paradigm derived from a conservative conception of ancient Greek drama, Doyen's fused a more radical interpretation of such drama with the example of the revolutionary "fête."

Doyen's "fêtes" were to be characterized by the abandonment of individual interests or intrigues, being synoptic or "synthetic," resembling a fresco as opposed to a painting. As in Rolland's model, his "fêtes" were to be of vast proportions—monumental works, destined for the "crowd" and requiring its participation. The result was compositions such as Doyen's *Le Chant du Midi,* which employs characters that have no names and that are identified only as, for example, "trois jeunes veuves" or "la mère douloureuse." Concomitantly, the visual focus is on simple, decorative lines, but, as in *Louise,* the costumes employed are distinctly of the present day, and, again as in portions of *Louise,* the action is to be articulated in a Wagnerian manner, or in other words, by the orchestra, "tout intérieur et symphonique." But the principal actor is always "the people," which for Doyen, as for Romain Rolland, was unquestionably the very fundament of any true "popular art."[45] Significantly, such ideas, drawn from stalwarts of the musical world like Doyen and Rolland, here enter the cultural politics of the French Left. Eventually, however, they would migrate back to the domain of professional musicians, as would occur most notably two decades later, during the Popular Front.[46]

The first of the "Fêtes du Peuple" took place on April 4, 1914; organized by the Bataille Syndicaliste, it drew three thousand spectators to the Salle Wagram. There they heard in juxtaposition readings from famous poems and performances of musical works of the past and present (some with new words), which were to be illuminated by such propinquity or substitution. As the Action Française had already observed, a "soirée musicale et littéraire" could be a powerful means of propaganda, combining the agency of ideas and feelings. Here the audience was presented with readings from poems of Whitman and Verhaeren, along with the "Hymne à l'universelle humanité," an adaptation of the finale of Beethoven's

Ninth Symphony to a poem of Maurice Boucher; it also heard Méhul's *Hymne à la Raison,* from the revolutionary period, the final scene of *Die Meistersinger,* Gustave Charpentier's *Ronde des Compagnons* (to a poem of Verlaine), Alfred Bruneau's *Les Mauvaises fenêtres* (to a poem of Catulle Mendès), and Albert Doyen's *Chant Triomphal* (to a poem of Victor Hugo). Other programs included readings from Maupassant and Vallès, a Beethoven trio, a fragment of Doyen's *Le Triomphe de la Liberté,* and the *Hymne à la paix,* based on the largo from Handel's *Xercès.*[47]

Symphonic and operatic works were thus to be construed in a distinctive way, becoming unique enunciations when performed in this specific manner and context. Specifically, by supplying new texts to works that already belonged to the national patrimony, Doyen was developing a way to appropriate them in the workers' interests. Although the Right had led the way in the political appropriation of high culture and particularly music, now the Left followed suit, responding politically in kind: on the Left as on the Right, commentary or texts surrounding the works performed helped shape the meaning or cultural connotations they carried for a targeted audience. Both Right and Left used the works of great composers like Beethoven and Wagner, but each in conjunction with a different discourse, for its own ideological goal. Neither side perceived the canon of great works as transcendent or politically neutral—as abstract and isolated from the concerns of political or social life.

This becomes clear in the period just before World War I, when the "Fêtes du Peuple" performed "great" works in order to unite social groups in opposition to the threat of combat. Thus even works such as *Die Meistersinger* become associated not with nationalism, despite explicit references in the text, but rather with the universal solidarity of workers. French syndicalists argued that participation in the war would destroy the "patrimony of humanity" that was represented by these masterworks in favor of the interests of finance and industry. The "fêtes" brought together groups who were boldly opposed to the war, as well as, as in the earlier Dreyfusard ideal, intellectuals and the "people." It was only after the war, however, when the "Fêtes du Peuple" were revived and in the context of the postwar ideology of the Left, that these "fêtes" achieved their most complete efflorescence. They became a part of the larger French musical culture, and, in the 1930s, they provided a model for the cultural programs of the Popular Front.[48]

THE NATIONAL-SOCIALIST MUSICAL AESTHETIC

In the prewar period, the boundaries between the political and the musical worlds in France were further effaced by other notable musicians and political groups. As we have noted earlier, this included a political grouping that was characterized by the joining of factions from the Left and the Right against the center, as at the turn of the century. By 1907, Georges Sorel, a former Marxist and a former Dreyfusard, now increasingly disillusioned with both Socialism and the Republic, was in search of a new direction: his hopes of a social renovation based on his heroic vision of a "pure" new proletarian mass, with its "natural leaders," were beginning to crumble. Now he perceived the growing power and appeal of the nationalist movement, which stood in such pronounced relief against what appeared to be superannuated French Socialism. Sorel moved toward nationalism and was promptly "discovered" by the Action Française. In 1909 it published one of his articles and heralded him as the "brilliant and profound theoretician of anti-democratic socialism."[49]

However, it was not the center but rather the "outer wing" of the Action Française that briefly joined politically with Sorelian syndicalism; for, while both detested "liberal democratic intellectualism and bourgeois culture," those from the Action Française were dissatisfied with specific limitations of the movement.[50] This was the group that took issue with the implacable rationalism of the league, maintaining that belief could not be fostered by intellectual constructions or purely rational analysis. Rather, after the imposing paradigm of the Catholic Church, belief was to be based on an irrational sense of purpose—here of national mission and destiny.[51] We shall shortly see how the rejection of rationalism (and, by extension, of classicism) and this espousal of the irrational would lead to an endorsement of Romantic values.

These common beliefs resulted in a number of projected collaborative publications, beginning with the aborted La Cité française, which brought French syndicalists and nationalists together. In the spring of 1911 it was followed by another, more successful effort, L'Indépendance, with Sorel as the editor-in-chief and an editorial board that included Vincent d'Indy. Its collaborators included not just Maurice Barrès and Maurice Denis (already in d'Indy's circle) but the writers Paul Bourget and Francis Jammes. Clearly, the collaborators knew, having observed the models of both Socialism and the rightist leagues, how important a musical aesthetic could be to articulating an ideological cause. But although the journal, calling itself "National-Socialist," was patriotic, nationalist, and anti-Semitic, it did not espouse a coherent political stance.[52] Still, it is not difficult to discern what now attracted Vincent d'Indy to this particular political grouping, as opposed to the Ligue de l'Action Française.

D'Indy, like Sorel, harbored a strong nostalgia for a distant past when individuals were united by forces that transcended all rationally constituted "theories."[53] Undoubtedly, Sorel's advocacy of the use of "warmly colored images," of the heroic, and of "the ethics of infinite and mysterious obligation" appealed to d'Indy.[54] Unlike Barrès, d'Indy was not reluctant to reject the Republic or, as we gleaned from La Légende de Saint Christophe, to embrace the Sorelian belief in the necessity of violence; d'Indy, like the members of this group, condemned the sentimentality and corruption of liberalism, believing in the ultimate importance of faith in achieving political change. This common doctrine was further amplified in an ideologically related journal, the Cahiers du cercle Proudhon, which counted Georges Valois among its contributors. Here Valois expanded on Sorel's aesthetic theories, and we may observe a strong resemblance to those articulated by Vincent d'Indy; the ideal of both was a primitive purity, an antiintellectual art that is rooted in collective, prerational emotions, as opposed to the individualism and "intellectualism" of modern art. Aesthetics, from this perspective, was an integral branch of ethics, for the most important aspect of a work was the "moral" result to which it led. This philosophy implied (recalling Wagner) a belief in the use of the arts, including music, to instill collective values and, in doing so, to release the latent national "energy."[55] In addition, as Sorel's disciples stressed, he (like d'Indy) condemned Renaissance art, which, he argued, had initially released dangerous individualistic forces: "modern" art, as opposed to the "primitive," selfishly rejects the social and requires a technical knowledge that makes appreciation into a science of both reasoning and intellect. For Sorel, to the contrary, as for Proudhon before, the principal value of all art is social, and one of its primary goals is to ennoble manual labor.[56]

Sorel's aesthetic ideals were apparently one of the factors that drew d'Indy to L'Indépendance, together with the publicity for the Schola it provided. Alienated by the anti-Romantic rhetoric of the Action Française but still in search of legitimation from outside the state, he found the journal suitable to his purpose. D'Indy thus used L'Indépendance as he had L'Occident, to publicize the Schola's ideas, activities, and publications to a sympathetic intellectual elite. In the issue of March 15, 1911, for example, he reprinted an excerpt from the lecture given by Blanche Selva on virtuosity, already published in Les Tablettes de la Schola. In it the prominent Scholiste further develops d'Indy's ideas concerning honorable and praiseworthy, as opposed to ignoble and meretricious, virtuosity.[57] The former variety seizes the performer's deepest feelings and thought; the latter is concerned primarily with the "effect" and the remuneration it will bring. The readers of the journal learned that, just as a piece of music does not become a "sonorous monument" unless it is generated from a rigorous logic and plan, a performance does not become a "true interpretation" unless it arises from a similar foundation.[58] This concept of structural probity was related to the Schola's ideal of "la grande musique"—music not divorced from life but linked metaphorically to its ethical dimensions. Such a conception was to remain within the aesthetic of those circles that were either associated with "national socialism" or ideologically sympathetic to it.[59]

The same issue of L'Indépendance reported on a concert of motets, chansons, and madrigals at the Schola and reprinted an article by Michel Brênet, originally published in Les Tablettes de la Schola. In addition, it contained an excerpt from d'Indy's book—or, more properly, his hagiography of his idol, Franck, which was published in 1906. The excerpt reprinted stresses that Franck was not in search of success but wished only to express his thoughts and feelings, to the best of his ability, through his art; it also emphasizes the extent to which the composer, like those who were unquestionably great, was a true believer, ultimately perceiving the source of all art to be faith. This, as d'Indy argues, places Franck in the noble line of development of figures running from Palestrina to both Bach and Beethoven.[60] Although d'Indy had originally implied that religious, as opposed to social, faith was at the root of true art, the ambiguity of his reference to it here was apt for the journal's purpose: for faith in its ideological context implied an instinctual and irrational belief, an implication to which d'Indy was not averse, as we perceived in his anti-Dreyfusard opera.

CULTURAL POLITICS IN FRENCH MUSICAL JOURNALISM

We have already noted the ideological infiltration of artistic criticism and the battle between opposing perspectives within this politicized culture. By 1910 such
politicization was pervasive in music criticism, with the Action Française as well
as the Socialist Left playing leading roles. Many observers were led to comment
on this phenomenon and to identify music criticism as another venue for political propaganda. In music we see this most clearly in a book by Frédéric Hellouin,
his *Essai critique de la critique musicale*, originally written as lectures at the Ecole
des Hautes Etudes Sociales. Hellouin, a respected and regular lecturer at the institution, spoke there on a number of musical topics between 1902 and 1909; his
subjects included various issues in eighteenth-century music, as well as "le Can-
tique musical" and "Les Nationalités musicales."[61] But the lectures on music
criticism, as Hellouin points out, were the result of a course on the subject that
the School of Journalism offered, along with one on dramatic criticism. Ironically,
the approach that Hellouin decorticates—one that places aesthetic questions in a
political frame—had been furthered at the Ecole by "mediating" figures like
Laloy. Here Hellouin himself discreetly applies this very approach by (as Laloy)
castigating politicized criticism from an ideological perspective. Later in this
chapter we shall look at the role of the critics involved in the escalating battle
over politicized compositional factions.

Hellouin divides the major critics of music into a number of categories and
then proceeds to offer a studied opinion on each. The critics mentioned comprise
the "critiques littéraires—nonmusicales," such as Combarieu, and "musiciens in-
tuitifs," such as Fourcauld, Gauthier-Villars ("Willy"), Lalo, and d'Udine. It also
includes musicians such as Alfred Bruneau, about whom Hellouin, like d'Indy before him, has largely negative things to say. According to the author, the literary
aspect dominates Bruneau's judgment and, of course, in particular and unfortunately, that of Emile Zola; again, like d'Indy, who ostensibly had an effect on the
Ecole des Hautes Etudes Sociales, he criticizes Bruneau as an historian, especially
his 1900 *Rapport*. He then proceeds, in effect, to disqualify the musician Bruneau
as a critic on the basis of the absence he perceives of any critical faculties and of a
true musical sensibility. He sounds very much like his colleague at the institution, Louis Laloy, when he describes Bruneau's style of writing as "heavy" or "en
mal d'éloquence."[62]

Not surprisingly, given the institutional context of the lectures, Hellouin proceeds, by contrast, to lavish praise on his colleague at the school, Laloy. Pointing
out his academic credentials, he also revealingly mentions Laloy's having had the
good fortune to study composition with d'Indy at the Schola Cantorum. But the
author finds other occasions to praise d'Indy and the Schola and to denounce "la
critique sociale," which he associates with the Left, especially with the Socialists.
He argues that this perspective approaches art in terms of its narrowly practical
end and hence judges music only in reference to its ultimate utility to the
"masses": treating music, above all, as an educational and social tool, it thus de-
prives the artist of any other more lofty artistic or aesthetic goal.[63] As we have
seen, however, this charge was not entirely true, for the Socialists were not the

only group to approach and judge music in terms of its social utility. As we may recall, Hellouin's colleague at the institution, Louis Laloy, had made a similar point in his lectures on opera and subsequent articles in 1905.

Laloy continued to diffuse the ideas that he had developed at the Ecole in the musical and political press, as well as in his scholarly writings. He became a prominent contributor to *La Grande Revue* and grew increasingly close to its editor, the powerful and ambitious Jacques Rouché. The latter was similarly an intermediary figure: soon to become the Opéra's director, he had originally begun to pursue a political and bureaucratic career. A former "Polytechnicien" and a diplomé de Sciences Politiques, he subsequently became an attaché at the Ministère du Commerce. But a "beau mariage" had made Rouché the owner of a perfume firm, which allowed him to purchase a journal, the *Grande Revue,* in 1907. Increasingly interested in the theater, in 1910 he published a book entitled *L'Art théâtral moderne,* which subsequently led to a theatrical venture: he took over the Théâtre des Arts between 1910 and 1913, an enterprise that would eventually result in his appointment as the Opéra's new director.

Laloy became closely associated with Rouché at the Théâtre des Arts and, subsequently, at the Opéra, as the Republic grew more "centrist." At the former theater, Laloy was put in charge of the musical performances; in 1919 he assumed the role of Secrétaire général of the Opéra.[64] In addition, Laloy continued to contribute to a number of journals that were associated with either the political center or the moderate Right: these included the journal of theater and art entitled *Comoedia,* begun in 1907 and thereafter steadily to grow in importance and influence.[65] They also included another journal of the more moderate nationalist Right, the venerable *Gazette des Beaux-Arts,* to which he contributed between 1905 and 1908. Ideologically, it was eminently compatible with the ideas Laloy had expounded in the lectures on music that he delivered at the Ecole des Hautes Etudes Sociales, for it advanced a conception of the "true" French spirit as one that reconciled the Christian and the Greek, thus maintaining the ideals of measure, sobriety, and national solidarity.[66] As we shall shortly see when we examine Laloy's writings on Claude Debussy, he easily transferred his ideas, so compatible with this press, to purely musical journals, but it is in the context of the more general and politically conservative journals that these ideas, and thus the aesthetic-political position that Laloy occupied, becomes the most fully coherent.

Considered a minor figure today, in his period Laloy was both influential and highly respected by musicians and major intellectual figures. The aesthetic spokesman for Claude Debussy in the period after 1903, he was highly thought of by Rolland, his colleague at the Sorbonne and the Ecole; it was the open-minded Rolland, who, already a contributor to the *Grande Revue,* had initially put Laloy in touch with its owner, Jacques Rouché.[67] Laloy's critical approach to music, one that addressed aesthetic questions in music within both a cultural and a political framework, was in great demand. Developed initially in the elitist context of institutions like the Ecole des Hautes Etudes Sociales, it was to grow particularly prominent as the nationalist tide mounted in France.

As the reader may recall, Laloy, having been associated with the *Revue musicale,* went on to become a founding editor of the new *Mercure musical;* together with Jules Ecorcheville, he gradually transformed the journal into the organ of the French section of the Société Internationale de Musique. Called at first the *Mercure musical et bulletin français de la Société Internationale de Musique,* in 1912 it fused with Combarieu's *Revue musicale* and was renamed the *Revue musicale S.I.M.* (Société Internationale de Musique).[68] It was to become the most important musical journal of the prewar period, one that would continue to provide a forum for the kind of discourse developed at the Ecole. But Laloy was also associated with the parent journal of the *Mercure musical,* the *Mercure de France,* which had gradually developed a distinctive political stance. Founded in 1890, it originally had promoted the Symbolist aesthetic but had eventually waxed more conservative, espousing a variety of traditional French humanism. Although articles on politics played a relatively minor role in the journal, a political orientation became increasingly evident in its cultural posture: while it grew more socially conservative and nationalistic, it maintained the importance of individual freedom and assumed an economically liberal stance, as did the liberal Right. This position, while espousing traditional French values, recognized—unlike that of more extreme nationalists—that these values could be realized in individual, artistically innovative ways. The *Mercure* thus became the journal that most fully supported the music of Claude Debussy, and contributors included sympathetic critics such as Jean Marnold and Emile Vuillermoz.[69]

Laloy was by no means the only critic who mediated between musical and political presses and thus diffused values originally developed within the nexus of French cultural politics; other figures whom we have already examined continued to play important roles and to influence not only institutional decisions but musicians themselves. Camille Mauclair continued to write for journals in the political press and for musical journals such as the *Courrier musical.* Thus, not surprisingly, musical journals entered the fray and responded vigorously to state policies on music in the period when these policies were being castigated in the nationalist press.

The *Revue musicale* regularly published the yearly subvention amounts awarded by the state to musical institutions and to specific concert series. The journal was clearly not unaware of the major political issues concerning the social priorities that should determine the allocation of cultural funds. For example, an article entitled "La Musique et l'Etat," published in 1910, argues (recalling Mauclair) for the importance of maintaining the inexpensive tickets at the subventioned Colonne and Lamoureux concerts; in addition, it points out the value of Charpentier's "Conservatoire Populaire de Mimi Pinson" and thus the social importance of its continuing to receive a subvention. Moreover, it suggests that the funds for this project can easily enough be found by using those previously accorded the Ecole Niedermeyer, which the state had voted to suppress.[70]

But the article also evinces an interest in popular education in music, observing that between seven and eight thousand adults attend the singing classes held in municipal schools; yet they meet as a collective group only once a year, which is clearly inadequate in terms of either a musical or a social program. It therefore encourages the efforts of l'Association pour le développement du [chant] choral, under the direction of d'Estournelles de Constant in the Administration des

Beaux-Arts. Particularly revealing here is that the author goes on to praise the specific kind of repertoire that is being promoted by this particular society: it includes the work not only of the great French musicians of the past, as advocated by d'Indy, but of those who were inspired by the musicians of the First French Republic.[71] Here we may see one effect of the cultural politics of the Republic, in response to that of the Right, as manifest within the musical world.

This close interaction of perspectives, concepts, and issues in the political and musical press was not unique and was in fact characteristic of other kinds of publications as well. The books that were published in the prewar decade are similarly informed by intertextual references to the politicized cultural discourses characteristic of this period. By 1905 writers who had been associated with the Schola Cantorum were publishing important studies on the subject of music in France. Of special significance here is Lionel de la Laurencie's still frequently cited book, *Le Goût musical en France,* originally published in 1905.[72] La Laurencie was an advocate of d'Indy in the Catholic, the artistic, and the French musical press, and he was to become the first president of the Société Française de Musicologie. In all of these contexts he would continue to serve as an advocate of the ideals of the Schola, as well as, more subtly and by extension, of the nationalist and traditionalist Right. Particularly evident here is the proximity of La Laurencie's ideas and concepts to those that were currently being diffused by the Ligue de l'Action Française.

Perhaps the most striking feature of La Laurencie's book on French musical taste is his prolonged attack on both Romanticism and the Italian stylistic influence. Here his rhetoric clearly resembles that of Vincent d'Indy, as well as that of the Action Française advocates of classicism, such as Pierre Lasserre. La Laurencie denounces the "absolute subjectivity" of Romantic individualism, its egoism, its desire for "sensation," and its quest for immediate gratification; the latter, he then argues, harmonizes perfectly with the sensualism of Italian music, which explains the great enthusiasm for it in the nineteenth century. Hence Rossini becomes a target, in terms that recall Lasserre's equation of Italian and Jewish influences, for La Laurencie denigrates his "oriental" ornamentation. As a positive French model (if incongruously so, given his anti-Romantic stance), La Laurencie defends Berlioz, although in an ingenious if specious manner: he points out Berlioz's propensity for attempting to evoke extramusical associations through music, which, undoubtedly with the clavecinistes in mind, he presents as a distinctive French trait.[73]

When discussing the present, La Laurencie admits that taste is deeply divided and seems to be splitting off continuously in a multitude of different directions. We shall shortly see the extent to which this observation was true, as well as the deeper intellectual and cultural tensions that ultimately lay behind it. La Laurencie's own position, as well as its basis, becomes immediately clear, since, like Laloy, he does not hide his own ideological and aesthetic inclinations: recalling the "regionalist" theme that we noted within the Action Française, he observes with approbation that French folklore is inspiring some composers to the discomfiture of others.[74] But also evident, and not surprisingly, given his loyalty to d'Indy and the Schola, is La Laurencie's antipathy towards the Conservatoire, which emerges in his discussion of Debussy. He argues that Debussy had evaded the tyranny of its desiccated scholasticism not only in the suppleness of his melody and rhythm, but in the freedom we may perceive in his form. Hence La Laurencie concludes: "Un souffle de liberté et de simplicité paraît donc agiter nos tendances musicales, en même temps qu'avec l'aide franckiste, le classicisme français reprend ses droits, s'affirme constructeur et économe d'effort, partisan résolu des architectures solides et logiques"[75] (A breath of liberty and simplicity would thus seem to agitate our current musical tendencies at the same time as, with the help of "franckisme," French classicism is again reclaiming its rights, affirming itself as constructive and economical in effort, a firm partisan of solid and logical architecture).

La Laurencie thus attempts to claim Debussy for the nonofficial "independents" and to equate French classicism with the qualities that were so highly valued at the Schola Cantorum. This position was in implicit opposition to that of Camille Mauclair, as was La Laurencie's perspective concerning attempts at a "social art." He notes a tendency in French musical taste to reflect "le mouvement social en le soumettant à une manière de symbolisme démocratique" (the social movement, subjugating itself to some kind of democratic symbolism). But La Laurencie then implies that social concerns are by no means the exclusive property of the Left, which attempts to equate them categorically with its democratic goals. While acknowledging the works of Charpentier and Bruneau, he lavishes praise on d'Indy's L'Etranger as truly singing the hymn of the humble, of "les petits." As in his other writings, La Laurencie includes an encomium of the Schola, pointing out the leadership it has assumed, particularly in the area of music history.[76]

INTERLOCKED BATTLES OVER THE "NEW SORBONNE" AND THE PARIS CONSERVATOIRE

The battle between the Conservatoire and the Schola that we may perceive in La Laurencie's remarks was by no means abating in this period but was growing even more intense. One of the reasons for this increasing intensity was, again, the current war being waged in cultural politics and especially the renewed assault on Republican educational institutions. The nationalist Right perceived the French educational system—from primary schools through university education—as a conduit for Republican ideology and thus made it a target. Once again, the questions raised and the positions assumed in this particular skirmish were to be refracted through the concerns of the musical world by mediating figures.

The issue in French education was the Republican reform of the venerable Sorbonne, an attempt simultaneously to update and to democratize the kind of education it offered. This reform had been met immediately with hostility on the part of the traditionalist Right, which assumed the posture of the implacable protector of the humanistic disciplines. One of the sallies in this war was led by the tireless Pierre Lasserre, in a series of lectures at the Institut d'Action Française in 1908 and 1909; in 1912 these lectures were published as a book, under the title of La Doctrine officielle de l'université: Critique du haut enseignement de l'Etat, *défense et théories des humanités classiques.* Only the previous year, under the pseudonym "Agathon," Henri Massis and Gabriel de Trade had published a related attack: entitled *L'Esprit de la Nouvelle Sorbonne: La Crise de la culture classique, la crise du français,* it consisted of a collection of articles that had appeared in the journal *L'Opinion* in 1910.[77]

A primary target of the Right was current literary history as it was now being taught by Gustave Lanson, whose intellectual bias was both Republican and democratic. This perspective determined his selection of "great" French writers, just as it had determined Bruneau's pantheon of truly great French composers. For Lanson such a canon was intended to implement the creation of a new national bond, an integrated community that celebrated the same aesthetic and political values.[78] We have already noted attempts shortly after the turn of the century to arrive at a similar goal through the implementation of Republican musical programs. Now "Agathon" was to charge that Lanson, together with historians such as Seignebos and Lavisse, was not teaching his students to honor the "true" French cultural and political heroes; moreover, he was "sullying" his students by teaching them "scientific" or scholarly techniques, such as documentary and literary criticism—a charge in which most of the Académie and Institut concurred. The authors condemned not only the current emphasis on "research teams"—a democratic approach to knowledge—but also the democratization of knowledge itself: the end result of such reforms, they charged, would eventually be a cultural leveling and thus a lowering, they would "faire de notre culture une culture de pauvres" (make of our culture a culture of the poor).[79]

Perhaps most seriously, the authors accuse the Sorbonne of dispensing "la science Germanique," especially German philology, thus triggering reaction among the "truly French"; they incisively note that this reaction is coming from both political extremes—from Socialists (many of whom were former "Normaliens") and from the neomonarchist defenders of classical culture. Moreover, the authors boldly claim support for their positions from the journals *Le Temps* and *Le Journal des débats,* as well as from many of the students presently at the Sorbonne.

The book does attempt to explain the Sorbonne's rationale for adapting its teaching in the direction of the practical and utilitarian to meet the needs of the modern age: "éducation de l'esprit par les sciences, véritables humanités modernes; développement démocratique de notre société incompatible avec la culture littéraire et philosophique"[80] (education of the mind by the sciences, the veritable modern humanities; the democratic development of our society, incompatible with literary and philosophic culture). But they then pose the central question, one that would be prominent in prewar cultural politics: Is such a teaching in conformity with the qualities of our race? They here explain that in every nation there is a "reserve" or a "capital" of intellectual forms that it is incumbent on the system of higher education to maintain. "Our French genius," they continue, "which comprises order, clarity, and taste, was one that was acquired and tested over centuries and hence must necessarily be maintained." In conclusion, they aver, "nous défendons la culture de l'intelligence contre la culture de la mémoire, l'effort spirituel contre le labour matériel"[81] (we defend the culture of intelligence against the culture of memorization, the spiritual effort against material labor). For "Agathon," minute research in source studies, chronology, and bibliographic techniques has gradually obscured the substance of "true" French education, imperilling no less than the future of the race itself; the transfer of a scientific approach to French literary studies has led French students both to fear and to disqualify all that is original and individual.[82]

Even before "Agathon"'s diatribe, d'Indy had begun his systematic assault on all state educational institutions through which a knowledge of music was dispensed. This attack was only to escalate under the impact of the question of the "Nouvelle Sorbonne," the discourse of which he appropriately adapted to the case of his own profession. In 1904 the Schola's journal, *Les Tablettes de la Schola,* published a warning to all young musicians, one that it would henceforth implacably repeat: "N'entrez pas à la Sorbonne pour écouter les inutiles verbiages universitaires, mais pour contempler dans l'hémicycle le pur chef-d'oeuvre de Puvis de Chavannes, qui ne fut jamais membre d'aucune académie" (Don't go to the Sorbonne to listen to the useless university verbiage, but to contemplate in the hemicycle the pure masterpiece of Puvis de Chavannes, who was never a member of any academy). The warning included the courses and lectures at not only the Faculté des Lettres but also the Faculté des Sciences, the Ecole des Chartes, and the Ecole des Hautes Etudes Sociales (before it invited d'Indy). Significantly, this warning was reprinted for all to see and for some to condemn in the *Revue musicale,* a journal that was generally sympathetic to the Republic in 1905.[83]

In addition, this was the period when the Ligue de la Patrie Française, although in decline, was targeting the issue of the defense of religious education. Its last large public gathering, in fact, took place in 1907 and included a lecture by Maurice Barrès on the topical subject of "Les Mauvais instituteurs." This meeting was the prelude to the league's campaign to launch numerous associations for the defense of Catholic educational institutions, now under Republican attack. D'Indy, still in touch with the league, was quoted as saying, in a book on state administration published in 1910, "Je considère l'enseignement des arts par l'Etat comme une simple monstruosité"[84] (I consider the teaching of the arts by the state a simple monstrosity).

The Republic was well aware of the politicized campaign against the Conservatoire, and particularly of the prestige of the Schola, which indeed had instituted important reforms; it finally responded in 1905, but typically in a manner that was indirect or implicitly in dialogue with its ideological opponents. This was the year that Théodore Dubois, the much maligned director of the Conservatoire, resigned from the position he had occupied since 1896 and was replaced by Gabriel Fauré. Dubois's resignation has been frequently attributed to the so-called scandal Ravel, when Ravel (Fauré's pupil), already a recognized composer, was not chosen as a finalist in the Prix de Rome on the grounds of "harmonic errors." This event threw the pedagogical intransigence of the institution into strong relief but was itself probably not the immediate cause of Dubois's resignation. For the Prix de Rome was awarded in May and Dubois, now increasingly ostracized, had already announced his impending retirement from his position the previous March.[85]

The question of Dubois's replacement was a delicate one indeed, for it was inseparable from the central issue of the future evolution of music in France. On the surface Fauré seemed an unlikely choice: he was not a graduate of the Conservatoire, not a Prix de Rome winner, and not a member of the Institut de France.[86] But within the context that we have seen, there were other factors to recommend him as someone who could help resolve the still escalating battle between the Conservatoire and the Schola Cantorum. Moreover, the political conjuncture is significant, for 1905 was the year not only of the separation of church and state but also of important ministerial changes. In January 1905, the ardently anticlerical Prime Minister, Combes, was replaced by the former Minister of Finance, Maurice Rouvier. With this change came the creation of the Sous-secrétariat d'Etat des Beaux-Arts, which replaced the former administrative category of Directeur des Beaux-Arts. The painter Dujardin-Beaumetz now became Sous-secrétaire d'Etat des Beaux-Arts, and it was he who named Bonnet and Fauré as the directors of the Ecole des Beaux-Arts and the Conservatoire, respectively.[87]

THE CONSERVATOIRE'S RESPONSE THROUGH FAURÉ

The rationale behind Fauré's selection becomes clearer if we examine the address of Dujardin-Beaumetz to the Conservatoire students and faculty in August 1905. Implicit in his statement are references to the Schola's innovations—innovations that, as we shall see, Fauré was well prepared to adapt for the Conservatoire. Indeed, such official appropriation of innovations that challenged the state institution was an effective means of disarming opponents and critics of the beleaguered Conservatoire. Hence, as Dujardin-Beaumetz told the assembly, "If the Conservatoire is to preserve the old traditions which are the foundation on which innovators' explorations are now based, let us not forget that the artist needs support from the past and not regrets."[88] He then went on to stress the importance of a "stricter, more solid, and more diversified" education and to request specific reforms within the program of the Conservatoire's instruction. As we can see, it took the pressures of cultural politics to implement at last the reforms that d'Indy and others had proposed in 1894.

By now the Schola and its supporters controlled the dialogue between institutions, since they had defined the terms of the challenge and thus forced the Conservatoire to respond in kind; the key question for the latter would be which of its institutional traditions to preserve, or how to make concessions while still symbolically affirming the principles underlying its identity. No one, perhaps, was better equipped than Fauré to undertake this task, on the basis of his background and training—and because of his temperament and personality as well.

Fauré came from a family that, while not wealthy, was nevertheless cultivated; his mother was of the "petite noblesse," and his father became the director of the local Ecole Normale. One brother became a prefect, another an officer in the Marine, and the third, following his father's earlier occupation, an Inspecteur de l'Académie.[89] Years later, in a letter to his friend and mentor Paul Léon, Fauré described the impact of his background on his comportment as the Conservatoire's director:

> Je dois vous avouer . . . qu'élève sous le Second Empire, fils, frère, et beau-frère d'universitaires, j'ai grandi dans le respect de la hiérarchie à un point que vous ne sauriez imaginer. Converser avec un ministre me cause encore aujourd'hui un profond émoi."

> (I must confess . . . that student during the Second Empire, son, brother, brother-in-law of academics, I grew up with the respect for hierarchy to a point that you wouldn't imagine. To converse with a minister causes me still today profound agitation.)

Always a moderator, Fauré would prove to be the consummate conciliator in the musical world, able to befriend both sides and to win their confidence and cooperation.

His training, in addition, was ideal for the task that he now faced. Fauré had attended Niedermeyer's Ecole de Musique Classique et Réligieuse. Founded in 1853, with a state subvention, by the Swiss composer and teacher Louis Niedermeyer, the school was intended to train church musicians—organists, and choirmasters.[90] Niedermeyer's focus, like d'Indy's later, was on the masterpieces of the past, especially those dating from the period between the fifteenth and the eighteenth centuries. Hence, the core of the curriculum centered on Palestrina, Lassus, Bach, and Handel, as well as the illustrious school of "clavicinistes" in France.

Just as at the Schola later, the students at the Ecole Niedermeyer received intensive instruction in plainchant and in modal harmonization; it too was a school concerned with education of its students in a broader sense, although not from the standpoint of ideological indoctrination, as was the case at the Schola Cantorum. Recruiting its pupils young and keeping them as boarders, the school used the clergy of Saint-Louis d'Antin as faculty to teach them academic subjects, including Latin, history, geography, and literature.[91] Fauré had entered the school in 1854, at the age of nine, and remained there eleven years, during which time he formed a strong bond with Camille Saint-Saëns. The latter, a teacher at the school, had become a powerful figure in French music by 1905 and was doubtless important in Fauré's appointment as the Conservatoire's director.

In addition, Fauré had social contacts that probably aided him as well, since he frequented important salons in which government officials and high society mingled. Since 1871 he had been a regular at Saint-Saëns's salon, and later he frequented those of Mme. de Saint-Morceaux and the Princesse Edmond de Polignac; moreover, he was present in the Clemenceau's salon, together with other former Dreyfusards and Republican politicians.[92] Besides these connections, Fauré had the distinction of having been chief organist at the Madeleine since 1896 and of succeeding Massenet as a composition teacher at the Conservatoire. And he had already held positions in the educational bureaucracy, having been an Inspecteur des Beaux-Arts as well as an inspector of the provincial conservatories.[93]

Fauré himself was apparently delighted with the new appointment, writing to Martin Loeffler of his joy over the unanimous approbation of his election; musical conservatives applauded it, and, he proudly added, so did those musicians who held the most "advanced" positions. As an article on his appointment in the *Revue d'histoire et de critique musicale* confirmed shortly after the event, "Il n'a pas d'ennemies."[94] Fauré's first statements indicate how clearly he understood his implicit charge of absorbing the Schola's innovations without sacrificing any of the Conservatoire's basic principles or symbols:

> I want to be the auxiliary to an art that is at once classical and modern, which sacrifices neither current taste to established tradition nor tradition to the vagaries of current style. But that which I advocate above all else is liberalism: I don't want to exclude any serious ideas. I am not biased toward any one school and censure no genre that is the product of a well-conceived doctrine."[95]

But, as we shall shortly see, Fauré would soon have a substantial amount to say about the spread of musical "dogma" that he considered to be a danger.

Paul Léon, at the time in the cabinet of Dujardin-Beaumetz, later recalled how Fauré was able to subtly impose his will despite opposition. Léon remarked on how he succeeded in bringing in new talent, as well as in giving the institution the new breath of life that it so badly needed. In his letters to Léon, Fauré indeed sounds very much like Vincent d'Indy when speaking of his desire to make both singers and composers into more "complete artists"; as Léon pointed out, once again recalling the Schola's standing challenge, this new education was no longer aimed at merely forming "premiers prix." Fauré, he reported, was determined not only to enlarge the repertoire of works performed but also to teach the students to execute them with a higher degree of historical accuracy.[96]

Until this point, as we have noted, Conservatoire students took harmony before being admitted to the composition classes in which they learned counterpoint and fugue. This was the basis for the charge that students at the Conservatoire approached the analysis of music primarily in terms of chord progressions and little more. In response, Dujardin-Beaumetz, in his address to the institution, proposed those very reforms that had been recommended and rejected in 1892 and 1896: after a year of harmony, both harmony and counterpoint would be taught simultaneously, and, to implement this decision, two new classes in counterpoint were to be created. To encourage an historical approach to the analysis of form (again, as at the Schola), Dujardin-Beaumetz requested that Bourgault-Ducoudray create a new class for students of harmony and composition that would analyze forms within their historical succession, or in terms of "schools";[97] moreover, once more as at the Schola, this would be accompanied by the creation of an ensemble class that would provide live illustrations of the historical repertoire.

Finally addressing the other issue so often raised by the Conservatoire's critics, he asked the teachers of voice to "no longer consider the theater as the only purpose of study"; instead, he proposed the inclusion of classical arias, German, Italian, and French cantatas, and the lieder of Schubert and Schumann—

once more as at the Schola. The canon taught at the Conservatoire was thus to include such composers as Monteverdi, Peri, Caccini, Bach, Beethoven, Weber,
Schumann, Lully, Rameau, and Gluck.[98] The implications of this inclusion were
profound, not only because of the role of the Conservatoire in perpetuating a
canon but because of its role within the configuration of state institutions: it was
Conservatoire students who would teach later generations in France, would hold
the major positions in French musical institutions, and would serve on official
committees and juries.

The other important change now made in the Conservatoire's program of
study, one that was similarly inconceivable without the Schola's challenge, was
the inclusion of the symphony. But, while the symphony would now be taught, it
would be presented in a different way, in the context of a discourse that differed
substantially from that of the Schola: it could be included as a genre only if its
symbolic connotations were substantially changed or if the social and political associations that it carried were thoroughly redefined. As Brian Hart has shown, for
Scholistes the symphony was inherently both a solemn and a spiritual genre, the
purpose of which was to convey metaphorical ideas or concepts through the
medium of tones. Hence, they approached sonata form as well as the sonata cycle
in the manner of Franck—as a struggle between dark and light, with the final triumph of light, or good. Indeed, Scholistes as well as Franckists before considered
the symphony the equivalent in the sphere of absolute music of the philosophical
Wagnerian music drama.[99]

As we have seen, the source of these beliefs was Franck's and d'Indy's construal of Beethoven, who they believed had made the symphony a medium of
self-revelation. The symphony was henceforth an expressive vehicle—a means
not only to convey the composer's thoughts and feelings but also, in so doing,
eventually to both educate and edify its listeners. We find testimony to current
perceptions of the symphony in such terms in Romain Rolland's fictional picture
of the Schola Cantorum in his novel *Jean Christophe,* where he implies that the
Schola produced what he refers to as "doctoral symphonies," or symphonies so
completely imbued with ideas that they resembled Sorbonne theses. Indeed, for
the Schola it was the symphony that, in a period of tension or trouble, could convey uplifting messages of faith and inspiration to the masses.[100]

Under Fauré the Conservatoire no longer derided the symphony or excluded
it completely from its curriculum as it had before; yet it did attribute very different purposes and qualities to the form, defining as well as teaching it in a fundamentally different way. Before Fauré, the Conservatoire treated the symphony as
it treated the fugue—as an exercise to establish professional skill, but not as a living genre; once it was recognized as a "legitimate" genre, however, the Conservatoire did acknowledge its "meaning," although it conceived this in a manner distant from that of the Schola Cantorum. The symphony was not a philosophical
medium conveying ideas or moral lessons, but either a vehicle of sensual sounds
or a metaphorical "celebration of nature"; if a symphony was "French," it was by
virtue of its emphasis on balance, clarity, and logic or of the specific musical quotations that it employed.[101]

As we shall see, the battle between these conceptions was exacerbated by the major critics, who tended to espouse one or the other institutions's symphonic models. Pierre Lalo, Gaston Carraud, and Paul Landormy were quite clearly supporters of the philosophical "expressive," Scholiste paradigm of the symphony; Julien Tiersot and Jean Marnold, by contrast, promoted the Conservatoire's emphasis on the way it could display French qualities of balance, order, clarity, and logic.[102]

Despite the Conservatoire's reforms, the onslaught did not abate, and during the period of "Agathon's" attack the state institution was once more a target. Now the major charge was that the Conservatoire's reforms were neither sincere nor profound, but only illusory, touching the mere surface of the institution's approach. In 1910 Jules Combarieu, who firmly believed that the institution should not discard its roots in the French Revolution, nevertheless impugned it directly: he charged that its pedagogy was still outdated, immobilized in practices that were contrary not only to reason but, by now, to public opinion as well.[103] As he pointed out, so widely spread was the perception of its weakness that the journal *Comoedia* launched a survey entitled "Y a-t-il lieu de réformer le Conservatoire?" As he notes, among the responses was the accusation that the counterpoint it taught was not really counterpoint but, in essence, still simply the progression of chords.[104]

As several of the respondents to the survey charged, the students at the Conservatoire (unlike those of the Schola) never analyzed the real contrapuntal masterpieces of the past; as Combarieu observed in a subsequent article, although music is not a science like geometry, the Conservatoire persisted in treating it as such, teaching the same immutable rules. He concluded that, despite all the criticism and the resultant so-called reform, the emphasis at the institution remained the competitions at the end of the year.[105] Combarieu, of course, as a lecturer at the elite Collège de France, could speak from a protected position that was unique to his institution: unlike the university, which was so directly affected by the Republic's politics, the Collège, while state-funded, provided a realm of ideological liberty for its professors. It also provided a broad public forum and thus played a unique intellectual role, since the lectures delivered there were not just free but open to the general public. Combarieu was indeed the first to lecture on music at the august institution since the Revolutionary period, and, as we shall soon see, his role was to be significant.[106] Here, as an advocate of the Republic, his concern was to make it more competitive, less vulnerable to Nationalist attacks, hence his ingenuously critical tone.

NEW COUNTERATTACKS ON THE SCHOLA

Most others, even those in less protected positions than Combarieu, were far less temperate in their remarks, feeling obliged ideologically to support one or the other of the institutions. By this point, many were openly hostile not only to the Schola Cantorum but also to the cultural, social, and political ideology that they now perceived it as supporting. This was particularly the case with Emile Vuillermoz, a former student at the Conservatoire, a defender of its reform, and a

proponent of Debussy and Ravel. Originally from Lyon, Vuillermoz had been
Fauré's pupil at the Conservatoire, as well as a close collaborator with (a ghost
writer for) the music critic "Willy."[107]

By no means a defender of the Left, Vuillermoz could accommodate his position easily to the aesthetics of the "centrist" coalition and particularly that of the
"liberal Right." Hence, he was very much at home in the circle of the *Mercure de
France,* where he published an incendiary article, "La Schola et le Conservatoire,"
in 1909. This was not his first attack on the Schola: already in March and June of
1906 he had published a scathing satire of it in the *Mercure musical.* The latter is
facetiously written from the standpoint of music historian in the twenty-first century, in which France is now a socialist state, with the Beaux-Arts subsumed by
the "Chambre Syndicale." Its fictional point of departure is the task assigned to
historians of assembling a dictionary, both biographical and critical, of major
French musicians over the past two centuries. Predictably, France is still arguing
over who represents "the true French tradition," and specifically whether Romantic composers such as Berlioz ought to occupy a place in its canon. Vuillermoz
presents d'Indy "historically" as a "riche amateur" who founded the "Ecole des
Chanteurs," a school that propagated "dogma," especially the importance of rigorous form. Its pupils accordingly consisted of "les timides, les amateurs, les fils
de famille et les gens refusés aux examens d'entrée au Conservatoire"[108] (the
timid, amateurs, sons of notable families, and those refused at the examinations
for entry into the Conservatoire).

Vuillermoz points out that d'Indy had the valuable aid of the press, in particular of a powerful critic from the nobility ("Gaulthier de Villars"), one from
the bourgeoisie (Pierre Lalo), and the third from the "basse populaire" ("Willy's"
fictitious "l'Ouvreuse"). Mocking the Schola's ideal of professional "désintéresse-
ment" and "noblesse," he derides its students by referring to them as "réfractaires
à toute sensation musicale." He goes on to speak of how they gradually extended
their influence throughout the French musical world, infiltrating commissions,
committees, and juries through a powerful organization. And he emphatically re-
minds his readers of the significance of the fact that this school flourished at the
very moment of the "loi sur les congrégations religieuses et sur la séparation de
l'Eglise et de l'Etat" (the laws on the religious congregations and the separation of
church and state). Making the connection even more explicit, he refers to "les
manifestations politiques des prétendus élèves de musique en certaines circon-
stances historiques"[109] (the political demonstrations of so-called music students
in certain historical circumstances). In this piece Vuillermoz boldly dared to expose what he and others now perceived as a fundamentally political project that
was clothed symbolically in the garb of an art.

Vuillermoz was to go even further in his subsequent article of 1909, the point
of departure of which is his response to Marnold's "Le Conservatoire et la
Schola," of 1902. While Marnold's article had cast the Paris Conservatoire in an
unfavorable light, Vuillermoz now reverses the terms, charging the Schola with
being pedantic and rigid. And not only that: he now accuses it of incarnating a reactionary spirit in its artistic approach, as well as in its more fundamental political intentions.[110] Vuillermoz openly charges d'Indy with attempting to challenge

"l'enseignement officiel" by conceiving his institution implicitly as a criticism of the Conservatoire. But, he immediately points out, d'Indy's critique is, in fact, probably unfair, for the Conservatoire is not the rigid, immobile institution that the Scholistes claim; it is, to the contrary, a "multitude of small and autonomous living cells" that are capable of creating a "prodigiously abundant musical nourishment." This biological metaphor, of course, was intended to associate the Conservatoire not only with the "scientific" but also with "life," as implicitly opposed to a desiccated tradition. Vuillermoz further suggests a Darwinist argument in his defense of the competitive system, which, as he argues, serves to "weed out" the mediocre and to promote only true talent.[111]

One of the author's primary points is the Schola's excessive devotion to the past, which, he contends, alienates musicians from the influence of their own time: an overzealous reverence for tradition distorts its students' sensibilities and judgment and ultimately ends up by instilling them with anachronistic artistic aspirations. They are taught to denigrate all that is modern and to hold in reverence all that is associated with the past, especially the sacred period of the Middle Ages. Its students thus learn to speak with horror of the artists of the Renaissance period—those who had the audacity to break with the Christian tradition and to return to pagan antiquity. From here, Vuillermoz condemns the way in which Scholistes persecute, throughout music history, "tous les compositeurs présumés circoncis," distinguishing the Semitic from all others.[112]

Finally, the mania for history, he charges, has another unfortunate consequence: it has imbued the Schola's students with a kind of "fétichisme de la forme." Since they are trained to study the development of "musical molds" throughout the ages, they accord a preponderate place to what is, in fact, a mere accessory to creation. The "masters" of the Schola, he continues, are concerned not with the beauty of a theme but only with the academic correctness of the form or the "plan" employed in the work: in sum, they denigrate "l'acte brutal de la création, ce spasme cérébral, cette exaltation émincée qu'accompagne souvent une sorte d'orgeuil quasi sexuel"[113] (the brutal act of creation, this cerebral spasm, this thin exaltation that is often accompanied by a quasi sexual arrogance).

But form for Vuillermoz is not the only aspect of musical language that the political and philosophical doctrine of the Schola has imbued with a social meaning. Harmony, too, is condemned there on the same basis as originality or creativity—for its pure sensuality, considered again to be a socially dangerous trait. Yet Vuillermoz does admit that the Conservatoire makes the mistake of presenting conventions as natural laws, and hence its "science" of harmony is an "orgeuil un peu puéril"; this does not, however, justify its total exclusion from the Schola, or d'Indy's dismissal of harmony as "the simultaneous emission of several different melodies." Arguing as a Conservatoire graduate, Vuillermoz claims that to deny the phenomenon of chords is to annihilate the "soul" of music, the living force that assures its development over time: counterpoint, to the contrary, he argues, is a technique that does not "progress"—a "procédé artificiel d'élocution," perfected by Bach, it is no means of expression for the present. Harmony, by contrast, is capable of being enriched each day as, one by one, music lifts the "veils" that enshroud the true "natural" phenomenon. And so Vuillermoz apodictically

concludes that to deny the objective phenomenon of harmony is, in fact, tantamount to denying the very phenomenon of nature itself.[114] As we shall shortly
see, this "scientific" argument was to be carried much further by Vuillermoz's
friends and colleagues who founded the renegade Société Musicale Indépendante.

The core of Vuillermoz's attack on the Schola is reserved for the end of the article, where he turns to the linkage between d'Indy's political convictions and his
theories of art. Vuillermoz observes that the teaching at the Schola is burdened
with "une foule de considérations morales, politiques, religieuses, et sociales du
plus fâcheux effet" (a host of moral, political, religious, and social considerations,
with the most deplorable effect). He charges that the Schola is collectively and officially not only nationalist but also anti-Semitic, as well as ideologically anti-
Dreyfusard. And hence, with puerile ostentation it has committed the unpardon-
able error of subordinating aesthetic questions to preoccupations that ought to
remain outside of Music.[115] The Schola, of course, as we have seen, was by no
means alone in this "error," for we may also perceive a cultural politics informing
Vuillermoz's critique.

Although it appeared in the intellectual and literary *Mercure de France*,
Vuillermoz's article elicited immediate responses in a range of purely musical
journals. *Le Monde musical* soon published three articles, all of which, in some
way, responded to or commented on the specific points that Vuillermoz had
made. One, by Louis Combes, that appeared on October 15, 1909, corroborated
many of the critic's claims and similarly undertook the Conservatoire's defense.
Combes contrasted the artistic freedom and creativity offered by the Conservatoire with the cerebral and pedantic uniformity demanded by the Schola Cantorum, and he repeated Vuillermoz's biological metaphor when referring to the
"natural selection of talent" as opposed to the military metaphor that he and
others employed for the Schola. The Scholistes, he argued, "acceptèrent tous le
même idéal, celui de leur généralissime et s'appliquèrent à le réaliser
méthodiquement" (all accepted the same ideal, that of their general, and attempted to realize it methodically).[116] The implication of the military metaphor,
in the context of the discourse of cultural politics, is that the Schola advocated
such military authority, in the manner of the nationalist Right.

In the interval that separated the publication of Vuillermoz's two articles,
Louis Laloy had joined the chorus of the Schola's detractors, using *La Grande
revue* to articulate his new perspective. In an article of 1907, entitled "Les Partis
musicaux," he labels d'Indy a "Gothic"—someone who is driven by reason and
classification.[117] He excoriates d'Indy's propensity for moral allegory along with
the spirit of the Schola in general, which he compares to that of a religious sect.
At the Schola everything is made sacred and mystical, and only works in conformity with its ritual canon are considered to merit praise. Finally, Laloy refers to
the artificial works that emerge from the "laboratories" of the rue Saint Jacques,
asking facetiously, "L'Art a-t-il vraiment d'autre but que de faire souffrir?"[118]
(Does art truly have another end than to make us suffer?).

Other critics seized the occasion to comment on d'Indy's biases when the second volume of his *Cours de composition musicale* appeared in 1910. The *Revue
musicale* stressed his willful manipulations of numerous historical facts, espe-

cially his attempt to force music history into his own intellectual molds. This included his preoccupation with the cyclic sonata, which he traces back to Beethoven and then follows through to its culmination in César Franck. Also impugned is his tendency to slight many important forms and styles in the interest of his fetishistic models and his stress on religious vocal polyphony.[119]

As tensions between the institutions mounted in tandem with the ambient battles over the official educational system, Fauré responded true to form: always the conciliator, he now attempted to achieve a minimal degree of reconciliation with the Schola, at least on a symbolic level. In 1912 he invited d'Indy, still at the head of the Schola, to teach a class at the Conservatoire on the seemingly neutral subject of orchestration.[120] Typical of the prudent and oblique tactics of Fauré, it had the effect of co-opting d'Indy without affecting any fundamental issues. But, by 1913, under the impact of Fauré's reforms, the Conservatoire had, in many respects, co-opted the pedagogy of the Schola Cantorum. By this point students were required to pass a preliminary examination in fugue in order to gain admittance to a class in composition, and courses in the history of music were no longer simply optional (and thus unattended) but, as at the Schola Cantorum, required of all students. Finally, the repertoire taught to the performers, especially to the singers, no longer drew exclusively or even primarily on that of the theater. Yet distrust of the Schola remained, as we may discern in an article of 1913 by the teacher, composer, and former Dreyfusard Charles Koechlin. Here he not only refers to aspects of the Schola's teaching as dangerous but, like others, emphasizes its dogmaticism, based on both ideological and religious beliefs.[121]

Scholars Join the Battle

The battle with the Schola Cantorum continued in other venues as well, including lectures on music delivered at both the Sorbonne and the Collège de France. For the Schola's conception of music history could not go unchallenged any more than could its idiosyncratic approach to musical education and to performance. Now, however, the more "centrist" Republic, which was waxing conservative, sought an appropriate spokesman for its concomitant artistic ideals. It found one in Louis Laloy, whose profile in the French academic world was increasingly prominent, who thus undertook this specific intellectual charge: not only did he take over Rolland's position at the Ecole des Hautes Etudes Sociales, but in 1906 he became "chargé de cours de l'art" at the Sorbonne, lecturing on music history. As we might expect, here he concentrated on the now central issue of the "French tradition," with an emphasis on opera between the periods of Lully and Rameau.[122] Laloy, however, employed the latter composer in an ingenious way— to defend both the Conservatoire and Debussy's style as a model for French youth. Laloy undertook the defense of harmony (and, implicitly, of Debussy's musical style) in his book *Rameau*, undoubtedly based on his earlier lectures. Here he thus attempts to valorize Debussy by linking him to a concept of the French tradition that recalls the rhetoric of "Agathon."

After arguing that harmony is the invariable and absolute "truth" of music, Laloy characterizes Rameau's oeuvre as "la musique de raison"; moreover, he asserts, since Rameau's work has remained in the repertoire (which, as we have noted, was not entirely the case), he has achieved the status of "classic."[123] As we shall shortly see, by placing Debussy in the canon that leads back to Rameau, Laloy was able to construe the former as definitely in the French classic tradition; as we shall see in chapter 4, not only did the composer openly embrace this argument but also, indeed, he later attempted to manifest it creatively in specific works.

Laloy's efforts on behalf of the Conservatoire (and hence the more conservative Republic) did not go unnoticed, and neither did they go unrewarded by official recompense. In 1910 the faculté des lettres of the Sorbonne took a vote on who would replace Rolland in his courses on music history while he was away on leave. The candidates were Laloy and André Pirro, who, as we have noted, had held the chair of music history at the Schola Cantorum. In preparing for the vote, Rolland presented the credentials of both but, remaining professionally objective, refused to state his own personal preference. He did, however, observe Laloy's remarkable literary talent, the fact that he was an excellent hellenist and gifted in languages, knowing German, Russian, and Chinese. He further noted Laloy's position as critic for *La Grande revue*, as well as his very "modernist" tendencies as the critical representative of "Debussysme."[124] Laloy's influence in the larger intellectual world was undoubtedly considered an asset, as was his association with "progressive" tendencies.

When speaking of Pirro, Rolland observed that his thesis and subsequent writings represented the most substantial scholarship done on Bach since that of Spitta. He continued, however, that although Pirro had renewed the study of Bach, he was modest, isolated, and less known in France than in Germany, where his value was acutely appreciated. Given the complicated network of power within the French university system, as well as the mounting tensions with Germany, this was not to be in Pirro's favor. Rolland concluded, however, that both of the candidates had certainly proved themselves not only very good teachers, but, in general, excellent lecturers.

The noted sociologist and leading figure of "la nouvelle Sorbonne," Emile Durkheim, as we might expect, supported Louis Laloy; he pointed out that Laloy had already taught as an assistant, which would make a refusal of him now seem to be a disapprobation. But three others supported Pirro, and Durkheim, apparently worried, then suggested a compromise position—that the two alternate lectures. When the vote was finally taken, however, it was, predictably, in Laloy's favor, given the current attacks on the Schola and Pirro's former association with it.

The Conservatoire also found a defense in Combarieu's lectures at the Collège de France, despite his objective and guarded criticism of it. His lectures were further diffused through their publication in the *Revue musicale,* making them an important and influential forum that reached a considerable audience. Combarieu, the former organizer of the Congrès d'Histoire Musicale, of 1900, gave one series of lectures on "L'Organisation des études d'histoire musicale en France dans le second moitié du XIXe siècle."[125] In his talks, undoubtedly in answer to the Schola, he pointed out that all the fertile innovations in such studies were the result of "a keen sense of the French genius and of the unity in France's political history." Combarieu presented the Conservatoire as the incarnation of this awareness, pointing out its conception in opposition to the monarchist Opéra, and hence its suppression during the Restoration, as a source of Republican propaganda.[126]

In his subsequent lectures, Combarieu offered suggestions for the present day, particularly concerning the way in which musical instruction could serve the Republic. Probably with the Schola, as well as suggestions like those of Bourgault-Ducoudray and the Action Française, in mind, he recommended the use of music in national primary education; through instruction in singing on a national scale one might act directly on "l'esprit publique," as in the revolutionary period, and thus help to form the right kind of "sentiment national."

Combarieu's conception of this emerges in another one of his lectures on music history, and also subsequently published in the Revue musicale. It too is staunchly anti-Scholiste, sounding in places like Bruneau's Rapport, for it similarly traces the origins of music back to the "chanson populaire."[127] Moreover, his treatment of Beethoven resembles that of Bruneau and Romain Rolland, for he presents the composer as the incarnation of the universalistic, humanitarian, Republican ideal. As we shall see in chapter 4, d'Indy, infuriated by such interpretations, was soon to publish a book on the master that stressed the role of his religious faith.

POLITICIZATION IN THE WAR OF THE "CHAPELLES"

The battle launched by the Right on official Republican educational institutions was by no means the only one whose reverberations were felt and refracted by the musical world; other battles of cultural politics waged initially by the nationalist Right had profound implications for the musical culture, whose tone they help to set. Once more, these battles interacted in a complex manner with the professional concerns and divisions in the field that already existed; this was certainly the case with the famous "Guerre des Chapelles," the war between compositional "camps," to which a substantial literature in France was immediately devoted. Again, as in the battle between educational institutions that we have seen, this battle for professional hegemony was subtended by far deeper value-tensions. Here, too, the discourses of politics, literature, and music interpenetrated, once more through the medium of intermediary figures who cut across them all. Indeed, the word employed now to describe the hostile factions, with their conflicting configurations of beliefs and values, originated in the literary world.

The term "chapelle," which now entered general usage to describe the antagonistic factions vying for leadership in the professional world of music, first appeared in literature. In 1920 Pierre Lasserre, in Les Chapelles littéraires, addressed the phenomenon, which, he argued, had existed for the past twenty years. What he describes here are parties of zealots, grouped around certain major figures and acting with a tyranny and intolerance reminiscent of religious sects: their tactics consist of emphasizing certain politicized values associated with an author and often, in doing so, obscuring the writer's actual source of merit.[128]

In the field of music, the "chapelles" were similarly grouped around major figures, and the question of aesthetic legitimacy was linked to more comprehensive political values. With the approach of war, all factions were arguing in
the name of "true" French tradition, while maintaining different political and
cultural conceptions of it. The values of each camp were related to the political realm in a manner more subtle or indirect than that in the field of literature, which deals with "ideas." Still, no one could escape awareness of the
"spirit of violent combativity" that pervaded the musical world and was immor-
talized by Romain Rolland in his novel *Jean Christophe*.[129] Each "chapelle" was
associated not only with the advocacy of certain values but also with their associated styles and forms, as well as with specific historical canons or models.
As we shall see in chapter 4, hardly a composer could avoid being critically
being "classed," and often wrongly so, on the basis of style, by a polarized press.
This would have a significant impact on the decisions that composers in this period would make and on the creative tactics employed by some to confound such
classifications.

The "Debussystes"

As we might expect, one "chapelle" was grouped around d'Indy and the Schola
and the other around Claude Debussy, now the idol of young Conservatoire students. In this context, the battle between educational institutions reappeared, but
now with a new set of galvanizing issues, questions, and aesthetic conceptions.
The question of Claude Debussy, of his "legitimacy" as a French composer, was
clearly the central issue, eliciting responses on all sides. Mauclair remained a central figure in the battle over Debussy, bringing the issue to a head in a controversial article published in 1905. Entitled "Le Debussyste" and published in the
Courrier musical, its focus is on the fanatical adulation of the composer on the
part of young Conservatoire students. He was by no means alone in this perception, for Léon Vallas as well observed that it was the rebellious Conservatoire students who idolized him, despite the reserve of their professors. Although the
Conservatoire did not officially recognize Debussy's harmonic language, it did at
least consider him an advocate of their "vertical" conception of music. It was thus
the institution's opposition to the "horizontal" or contrapuntal conception associated with the Schola Cantorum that led to its recognition of Debussy.

What now concerned Mauclair was the frenetic manner in which young
Conservatoire students defended and vaunted their idol, often to the detriment of
other fine composers. It was becoming increasingly characteristic of this group,
after the example of Debussy himself, to deride Berlioz and Wagner along with
Beethoven.[130] While Mauclair distanced himself from such fanaticism, he did
point out his appreciation of Debussy, having been among the first to hear him
perform *Pelléas* at the piano in 1893. However, it was not in the opera that the
writer perceived the best of Debussy's work but rather in the composer's more recent work, which he considered more "healthy." Already in *Pelléas,* however,
Mauclair perceived certain elements of the composer's new style—a simplicity
and clarity that would elevate him to the status of a model or guide. In chapter 4

we shall examine the impetus for this evolution and the way in which it related to values diametrically opposed to those of Mauclair.

What now alarmed the writer was the way in which his nemesis, the redoubtable Louis Laloy, was explicating this new stylistic phase. Once more, it was a question of the values that he was reading into the style—values that Mauclair still equated with the menacing "nationalist reaction." Again, as we shall see in chapter 4, Laloy's interpretation was to prove in keeping with the image that the composer apparently wished to project of himself. Mauclair's key point of contention was whether Laloy's academic credentials endowed him with the "competence" to pronounce upon the deeper intentions informing Debussy's art. As a man of letters, he did not admit that Laloy had more of a right than he to speak of the larger cultural meaning of Debussy's musical style; he thus proceeds to belittle Laloy by referring to him as a "professor" and by observing that, in France, where diplomas are valued, art is considered a consequence of "instruction."[131] He thus exacted his revenge on Laloy, who, in the earlier debate over "Verism," had made a scathing reference to Mauclair's "universal incompetence." Mauclair concludes ironically by noting that apparently Debussy himself is not "competent" to understand the intentions being imputed by Laloy to his art.

The debate over the interpretation and evaluation of Debussy became so heated that, in the same year, Emile Vuillermoz published an article about this so-called affaire in the Mercure musical. Again implying the deep divisions of values underlying opposing sides, as well as their ultimate sources, he refers here to music's "Dreyfus Affair"; moreover, Vuillermoz perceives these deep conflicts over values as homologous, and he proceeds facetiously to carry the analogy to the point of confounding the two "affairs":

> Il se peut que les traités d'histoire ancienne enseignent un jour qu'un chef de musique militaire, nommé Achille Dreyfussy, fut accusé de haute trahison par un expert en harmonie qui avait étudié de près son écriture.
>
> (One day treatises on ancient history might teach that a chief of military music, named Achille Dreyfussy, was accused of high treason by an expert in harmony who studied his writing closely.)

Vuillermoz reveals his allegiance to Louis Laloy, his colleague in the journal, through his own dismissal of the position represented in the debate by Mauclair. He equates the latter's diatribe with that of another writer of the Left of whom he disapproves and whom he considers dangerous, the author of Pelléastres, the fashionable novelist, Jean Lorrain.

The author of a damning social characterization of Debussy's followers as aesthetes, Lorrain indeed had begun as one, modeling himself after Oscar Wilde,[132] but, once "reformed," he venomously targeted those who were unrepentant, focusing his attention briefly on the ardent young followers of Claude Debussy. In his articles and subsequent book, published in 1909, Lorrain devastatingly portrays the group of fanatics that coalesced around Pelléas et Mélisande. He observes that it was the same group that attended Lugné Poé's premieres, that praised the nostalgic melodies of Grieg and the "learned orchestration" of d'Indy's *Fervaal;* as Lorrain goes on to argue, what drew them to Debussy was, in effect, nothing more than the self-indulgent titillation of the senses they derived. For him, such quasi-sexual pleasure was simply the latest delight of a group he disdainfully characterizes and dismisses as both "snobs" and insincere "poseurs."

Lorrain then proceeds to contrast this group with those who had worshiped Wagner, for the latter were, he argues, sincere and drawn from all social classes. The "religion" of Claude Debussy, in contrast, for Lorrain, is much more elegant: its members are of "le monde" and accordingly occupy the most expensive seats.[133] Although Lorrain was not a man of the Right but of the Left, he shared the traditionalist's moral probity and disdain for the merely sensual. The picture that he painted of Debussy's followers is one they would have to combat, in part through the development of their own coherent social rhetoric; once articulated, it would enter in dialogue with the other positions around it, each seeking to provide a political and philosophical justification for an aesthetic preference.

Here the way was prepared, once more, by the omnipresent Louis Laloy, who became the spokesman and defender for the group that was labeled "Debussystes." He would soon be joined by both Emile Vuillermoz and Jean Marnold, after the latter's apostasy and renunciation of his former Scholiste sympathies.[134] As the reader will recall, Laloy published an article on the subject of "musical parties" in Jacques Rouché's *La Grande revue* in December 1907; here Laloy, like Vuillermoz, but in a less facetious tone, remarks on the way in which French political culture has ineluctably impinged on French musical life. For him, this is manifest in the spirit of "parties" and their increasingly fierce opposition, which, in the musical world, is refracted into the opposition of d'Indysme and Debussysme. (Since the opponents of Debussy on the Left did not propose an alternative model—other than the German Wagner—Laloy omits them as a compositional "party.")

I have noted Laloy's attack on the Schola, especially on its atavism and pedantry; in the article, this becomes the foil against which he presents Claude Debussy. As opposed to d'Indy's passion for reason, "classification," and moral allegory, Debussy composes music that is, for Laloy, the opposite in almost every sense: "Elle se présente seule, sans garanties, sans argument, forte de sa grâce unique et d'une intime cohésion qui dispense des appuis des théories" (It presents itself alone, without guarantees, without argument, strong in its unique grace, and of an intimate cohesion that does without the support of theories). According to Laloy, Debussy's only logic is that of sounds and harmonies; his achievement is to have "discovered" the true character of chords and to have connected them according to their inherent "laws."[135]

Like Vuillermoz, Laloy, in essence, preserved and further elaborated the scientific rhetoric of the Conservatoire, in opposition to that of the Schola; such rhetoric, however, bore increasingly less relation to that of their idol who, as we shall see in chapter 4, attempted increasingly to disassociate himself from "Debussysme." But the circle around Debussy used it to differentiate itself from the Schola, which it represented as dogmatic and moralistic, less interested in music than in political goals. Hence, they argued, the Schola, being a school of amateurs, devoid of talent, who could only follow rigid rules, condemned genius, novelty, and the original. Debussy and the Conservatoire, in contrast, represented precisely the opposite: genius, independence, purely musical goals, and liberalism of approach. Despite their disclaimers of political allegiance, it is by no means a coincidence that the movement's major spokesmen published in those journals that were associated with the "liberal Right."

Like the adherents of other positions, the Debussystes held their own conception of the French tradition and began to discuss it more articulately as the Nationalists tide mounted before the war. They agreed with Debussy, who in this period was arguing that the French tradition was one of clarity, concision, elegance, simplicity, and a desire to please the senses. It thus characteristically valued pleasure, the "picturesque" or descriptive, a pagan sensuality, independence, grace, charm, and wit, or humor.[136] These, consequently, were the qualities they perceived in the works within their own French canon, one that they did, in fact, share with their idol, Debussy. It centered on the secular masters from the sixteenth through the eighteenth centuries, especially Jannequin, le Jeune, Couperin, and, of course, Rameau. It did not admit any composer of either foreign influence or blood, which excluded not only Gluck but also César Franck, dismissed as "Belge."

Debussy and his followers emphasized Couperin and the "clavecinistes," who, in general, were excluded by the camps around both Bruneau and d'Indy; while the Schola denigrated most of the popular nineteenth-century composers, the Debussystes pointedly honored Gounod, Bizet, Lalo, and Massenet.[137] As we might expect, they emphatically excluded those figures and genres that were too closely or exclusively associated with the pedagogy of the Schola Cantorum: this prominently included the symphony, which the Debussysts continued to revile, even after it won some degree of legitimization at the Conservatoire. Their primary argument against it was that the genre was not a legitimate one for French composers because it was neither historically nor endemically "French."

For Debussy and his supporters, such as Laloy and Vuillermoz, the symphony embodied none of the traits that they believed defined the authentic French tradition in music. Not only did it value form over content, but the kind of content that it embodied was overly intellectual and moralistic, abjuring the sensuous play of sounds.[138] Instead of emphasizing freedom and "the natural," it encouraged personal emotional confessions and required adherence to rigid rules, which curtailed the composer's individual choice. Here, clearly, the Scholiste propaganda concerning the nature of the symphony had been so powerful that the Debussystes conceived its model as synonymous with the genre itself, but, given the growing importance of tradition, it was necessary to acknowledge the fact that there had been a tradition, if minor, of symphonic composition in France. Hence, according to Charles Koechlin, who decades later repeated these views, while the French did not slight tradition, they abandoned what they considered too dogmatic or narrow; he, like his Debussyste colleagues, argued that the authentic French tradition is essentially one of freedom, of continual renewal and invention.[139]

Again, this point of view precluded an acceptance of the symphony—and especially the Scholiste conception of it—as an appropriate vehicle for French composers. Vuillermoz explicitly argued that the symphony was by now not only obsolete but also an essentially Germanic genre more suited to ideas than to art. In addition, in the hands of ardent Scholistes it was a medium of nefarious propaganda, or, more specifically, of Nationalist, authoritarian, and Catholic ideology. As Vuillermoz later expressed it:

> The connoisseur of symphonies loves order and discipline above all. . . . It pleases him to see art renounce its attitude of eternal rebellion. The symphonic formula is an acquiescence to social order. The partisans of authority have always been instinctively grateful to artists who have consented to this profession of faith and hostile to those who have refused to carry out this rite.[140]

Although this description was written after the war, it reflects the opinions held by Vuillermoz and his Debussyste colleagues throughout the prewar period. It was these fundamental disagreements over values, genres, and styles that fostered a growing perception of the persistence of antagonistic "poles" within French music. This appearance was further reinforced by those who continued to pit the "horizontal" conception of music, as disseminated at the Schola, against the "verticalism" of the Conservatoire.[141] In 1909, in the widely read *Le Monde musical*, Alfred Casella published an article on the subject of "Musiques horizontales et musiques verticales."[142] Here he perceptively analyzes the basis of the conflict between "harmonistes" and "contrapuntistes" as deriving from the profound incompatibility of the Debussyste and the d'Indyste aesthetics. As we have seen, these conflicting sets of values had a deeper foundation, one extending ultimately to the level of conflicting political and cultural models. It was for this very reason that, despite the attempts of Casella and others to effect a reconciliation of hostile positions, this did not, in fact occur; for, again, it was not a matter of purely artistic logic or taste, so inextricably were aesthetic and political stances in France by now intertwined.

The "Case" of Debussy

Further testimony to this fact emerged the following year, in 1910, when two books on the rancorous divisions with the French musical world appeared. One was by two journalists, C. Francis Caillard and José de Bérys, the latter of whom was associated with the moderate Republican *Le Radical*. Entitled *Le Cas Debussy* and aimed at a broad potential audience, its principal subject was the legitimacy of Debussy's style from the perspective of what is "French."

Here we see even more clearly the intertextual references to larger ideological issues that the question of the legitimacy of Debussy's musical style evoked. The authors begin by drawing attention to the current acrimonious battle, aptly and incisively comparing it with the famous eighteenth-century musical "Querelles":

> "On se rend compte que jamais peut-être dans l'histoire musicale de la France ne s'était élevée polémique plus curieuse . . . plus passionnée . . . depuis la légendaire querelle des Gluckistes et Piccinistes."

(One realizes that never perhaps in French musical history had a more curious . . .
more passionate . . . polemic arisen since the legendary quarrel between the Gluck-
istes and Piccinistes.)

Indeed, in both cases political and artistic ideologies had become inseparable,
and hence conflicting political ideals were fought out obliquely around the art.

Le Cas Debussy begins by juxtaposing an unpublished interview with Debussy and an article by Raphäel Cor, "M. Claude Debussy et le snobisme contemporain." The latter, which appeared in the Revue du temps present in October
1909, was, like Lorrain's Pelléastres, an act of cultural politics, similarly attempting to delegitimize Debussy as "French" by associating him with contemporary
"snobisme" or "le monde." In the interview juxtaposed with the article, Debussy
claims that there are no more "chefs-d'école," which leads the authors to insinuate that the composer has hypocritically assumed precisely such a stance; moreover, they claim that the "school" he heads is indeed the most intransigent group
of composers that has ever been known in the history of French music.[143] As we
have seen, this was the impression often given by Debussy's defenders in the
press, although Debussy himself remained aloof and abjured such a "school." The
article by Raphäel Cor sets the tone for the rest of the book, being in essence a
scathing critique of the Debussyste social clique; like Lorrain, its author clearly
holds Wagnerian sympathies, is inclined to the political Left, and admires Gustave Charpentier's Louise. Resembling other spokesmen for this aesthetic-political
position (such as Mauclair), he condemns Debussy for avoiding what he terms a
truly "musical result"; for all real art, Cor continued, is both a rich and passionate
experience, one that Debussy repudiates in search of only minute and rare
sonorities.[144] This criticism recalls d'Indy's cruel satire of the Debussystes in the
tableau of the "Faux Artistes" in La Légende de Saint-Christophe. Here again, the
Left and the Right, in search of a moral and "substantial" art, are joined in their
critique of a more independent or "liberal" approach.

According to the book's authors, it was on the basis of the article's "success"
that they then undertook a survey, which was published in the Revue du temps
présent. This, they explain, was inspired by one conducted on the occasion of the
twenty-fifth anniversary of the death of Wagner and that appeared in 1908 in
L'Eclair.[145] The authors of the poll had asked the most notable living composers
in France for their opinions on the other key question of the moment—the influence of Wagner on French music; now, Caillard and de Bérys argue, it is time to
consider Claude Debussy and to question contemporaries on the advisability of
his becoming a "chef-d'école." Once more, the deeper implications concern the
future of French music and the legitimacy of Debussy's art as a potential major influence upon it.

The authors posed the following specific questions to those they approached:

Quelle est l'importance réelle et quel doit être le rôle de M. Claude Debussy dans
l'évolution musicale contemporaine? Est-il une individualité originale, seulement ac-
cidentelle? Représente-t-il une nouveauté féconde, une formule et une direction susceptibles de faire école, et doit-il faire école?

(What is the real importance and what should be the role of Mr. Claude Debussy in
the evolution of contemporary music? Is he an original individuality, only accidental?
Does he represent a fecund novelty, a formula or a direction that is capable of founding a school, and should he found a school?)

The question of leadership was tied not only to that of "schools" in general but to
the now central question of a representative "national school"; as we have seen,
the future direction of the nation's culture, including its art was an increasingly
pivotal question in the cultural politics of contemporary France.

Tied to this issue as well was that of French youth and its cultural proclivities, a question that entered into complex counterpoint with that of Debussy's
musical influence. The culture of the next generation was increasingly a profound concern, and the battle over it would grow only more intense in the years
preceding the war. One of the forms that this battle assumed was that of "genera-
tional portraiture," descriptions and explanations of the cultural tendencies of
French youth. In 1912 the two Rightist sympathizers Henri Massis and Alfred de
Tarde published a survey of French youth in the Parisian daily *L'Opinion*. It was
subsequently published in the form of a book the following year, which bore the
bold and arresting title *Les Jeunes gens d'aujourd'hui* (The young people of today).
The survey was not innocent: as Massis and de Tarde later admitted, it was an act
of cultural politics—it had a specific ideological goal. They wished to influence
French youth by offering an "image" of themselves that imbued them with motivation, as well as with a "sense of power and pride."[146] This image, as we might
expect, given their book on the "new Sorbonne," was closely associated with the
nationalist ideology of the far Right. Here they contended that French youth, on
the basis of those they polled, admired such contemporary figures as Maurras,
Bergson, and Péguy, as well as Sorel.[147]

Similarly, Caillard and de Bérys attempted to show, on the basis of their interviews, that Debussy's position in the canon was fragile and his influence on youth
not substantial. The individuals surveyed included critics and those with a professional background in music along with literary personalities, especially those
concerned with the direction of French art. Maurice Barrès, however, demurred,
commenting that Debussy was too great an artist for someone so ignorant of the
field to pose as one of his "judges." Given Barrès's Wagnerism, a negative response was probably expected, although as we shall see in chapter 4, by this
point Debussy was philosophically close to Barrès. Camille Bellaigue responded
as could be expected: "J'estime cette importance minimale et je souhaite que le
rôle soit aussi"[148] (I appraise this importance as minimal, and I hope that its role
is also). Again, Bellaigue, a man of the Right, was expressing an aesthetic view
that accorded with that of the political Left, as against the dangerous "liberal" or
center Right.

Mauclair, too, was predictable, commenting, "le Debussysme est un snobisme haïssable . . . la gēnialité [de Debussy] ne suffit pas à constituer un génie
complet, puissant, et humain" (Debussysme is a detestable snobism . . . [De-
bussy's] cleverness does not suffice to constitute a complete, powerful, and
human genius). Debussy's music was still being judged through a discourse that

had been developed originally by figures like Bruneau in the wake of the Dreyfus Affair. Romain Rolland also supported the authors, commenting, through the fictitious personage of Jean Christophe, "Je n'aime pas beaucoup toute votre musique française d'aujourd'hui et je ne suis pas fou de votre Debussy"[149] (I don't like all of your French contemporary music a lot, and I'm not mad about your Debussy). Although Rolland was open-minded, given his strong appreciation of German music and his socioaesthetic ideals, this position is hardly surprising. "Willy's" response was similarly predictable because of his support of the Schola Cantorum; indeed, he begins by quoting d'Indy on the "haute valeur" of Debussy. But he then proceeds to praise d'Indy as the composer who has remained "complètement fidèle à notre tradition musicale française" and whom no one can accuse of incompetence or snobbism.[150] The nature of the French tradition was still the principal issue, and lying behind the different conceptions of it remained conflicting cultural and political conceptions of France.

The "Société Musical Indépendante"

The polarity in French music, the "guerre des chapelles," was not merely a perception of critics; indeed, so deep was the rift that it led to a secession from the Société Nationale de Musique. A number of younger composers, particularly those who admired Debussy, had long complained about the repeated rejection of their works for the society's programs; given d'Indy's leadership and the dominance of his fellow Scholistes, there seemed to be no choice but to found a rival "Debussyste" performance society. This was the Société Musicale Indépendante, which professed to have no dogma, and thus to be open to all musical works of authentic merit. But, in fact, this was not really true, for a larger socioaesthetic and political position did indeed emerge within the writings of its members and associates. They, too, attempted to "appropriate" composers in support of their common aesthetic cause, even those whose aesthetic and political views were, in fact, substantially different.

The society's founding members included Charles Koechlin, Louis Laloy, Jean Marnold, Emile Vuillermoz, Maurice Ravel, and Jean Huré. As we shall shortly see, it was the latter who would reveal the larger sociopolitical presuppositions that implicitly underlay their aesthetic within this dialogic context. Fauré agreed to become president of the society, despite the fact that he still felt a loyalty to the Société Nationale, which had done so much for his career. But it was to promote young talent, particularly his former Conservatoire pupils, that Fauré nevertheless reluctantly acquiesced and took on the new post. Debussy, however, remained aloof and avoided serving on its juries, not liking the tone of the society, which he perceived as too "mondain." Ironically, he agreed with critics like Lorrain, Caillard, and de Bérys that the social milieu of the so-called Debussystes was high society, or "le monde." Indeed, the Société Musicale Indépendante, actively cultivated "le tout Paris" by distributing tickets and thus ensuring a firm basis of social support. And, like Fauré, Debussy himself (as opposed to his ardent admirers) was not hostile to either the Société Nationale or to its leader, Vincent d'Indy.[151]

PERCEPTIONS OF THE CONFLICTING MUSICAL "DOGMAS"

For the founders of the new society, hostility to the opposing faction extended from the aesthetic level to the social and political presuppositions beneath it. This we may perceive in Jean Huré's analysis of the battle between the "chapelles" and their contentious philosophies, his *Dogmes musicaux* of 1909. The book was one of several analyses by musicians in both opposing factions of the fractious state of the French musical world and its ultimate ideological basis. In all of these we may observe the way in which purely technical or professional issues were laden with deeper layers of cultural and political associations and conflicts. Here, denying that the Debussyste position was itself a "dogma," Huré attempts to identify such creeds, the ways they are spread, and their ideological foundations. In a sense, Huré's analysis resembles that of Massis and de Trade in their own minute dissection of the ideological roots of the "Nouvelle Sorbonne"; for it is in the same critical spirit that Huré "exposes" not only the political basis of support for the teachings of the Paris Conservatoire but for the Schola Cantorum as well. As we shall see, his exposé was also informed by a specific professional goal— to lay the intellectual foundations for a new school of music he was currently planning.[152]

As we might expect, Huré both criticizes and supports the Paris Conservatoire, speaking on behalf of its most aesthetically "advanced" former students. This, in part, explains the preface to the book, by Gabriel Fauré, whose interest here was ostensibly in defending the institution of which he was in charge. Reinforcing the argument of the Conservatoire's defenders concerning its "liberalism," he impugns "le règle étroite et accepté sans contrôle" as inimical to creative genius. Undoubtedly with the Schola in mind, he then identifies such "eternal routine" not with the Conservatoire but with fear and hate of progress and the new.[153]

Fauré also emphasizes the seriousness of the current problem of "dogma," observing the important place that music occupies in contemporary intellectual preoccupations. Here, perhaps, he is referring to the omnipresent discussions of music in almost all the major contemporary French political and cultural publications. He thereby affirms the usefulness of the book at a time when so many people, without either preparation or predisposition, have become interested in the art. The implication, which Huré develops, is that, depending on how it is taught or from what ideological angle, the knowledge of music can, in fact, be dangerous. Fauré goes on to point out the value of a book that argues that the purported "laws" of music are really based on exceptions and badly generalized by ignorant theoreticians. Clearly, the Schola Cantorum with its curious and elliptical music history, as codified in d'Indy's idiosyncratic *Cours de composition musicale,* is intended here. But, once more, Fauré qualifies his comments by observing that one should not confuse such "laws" with the fundamental principles of order that guide the creator of a work of art.[154]

Huré begins his book by explaining precisely what he means by "dogma": any affirmation imposed as an absolute truth, but without exact verification. He then facetiously characterizes the Conservatoire's dogma as the simplistic conviction that a musician is basically someone who has learned solfège, harmony, and counterpoint. From this perspective, he observes, the physical senses count for nothing; indeed, "geometric calculation" or literary inspiration are considered far more important. But to this he adds the new dogma of Conservatoire students—which transcends even Debussyste beliefs—that harmonic writing is "le langage naturel des musiciens avides de sonorités savoureuses"[155] (the natural language of musicians avid for savory sonorities). Huré then distinguishes his own "scientific" position against this view by discussing his plans for a study on the topic of "les lois naturelles de la musique": in it he intends to trace what he calls "the natural progression of hearing" as it develops in each individual, according to the degrees of auditory comprehension. Like the other Debussysts, Huré attempts to provide his aesthetic with a covert ideological foundation, citing "science" as his authority.

It is on the basis of a more rigorous "science" that he attacks the orthodoxies of Conservatoire instruction, sounding very much like Claude Debussy when a skeptical and recalcitrant student. Debussy, like Huré, questioned the practice of teaching only major and minor scales, to the complete exclusion of both the church and the oriental modes.[156] In addition, both challenged the convention of ordinarily limiting chords to four or five notes along with the conventions of contrapuntal writing that they were taught. Huré asks why certain rhythms are "authorized" in contrapuntal textures, observing that the "contrepoint d'école" is not that of Palestrina and Bach but rather that of Franck. Based on the major and minor modes, it studiously ignored those of the church and admits neither absolute diatonicism nor the chromaticism of Wagner.[157] Once again Huré recalls the young Debussy when he discusses the peril to the composer's spontaneity and imagination of the conventional Conservatoire instruction; both are aware that the young composer, after having learned all the exigent "rules" of modulation, form, and style, is finally granted his freedom, only to find that he has lost it.

Huré then attempts to situate this "official" approach within the social and political world that, he argues, is responsible for maintaining it. For him it is "l'esthétique officielle, bourgeoise, l'esthétique du public éclairé, aux goûts modérés, du public centre droite et centre gauche (the official bourgeois aesthetic, the aesthetic of the enlightened public, of moderate taste, of the Right center and Left center public)."[158] This indeed was the position of the Republic by the time of Huré's book, for it was inching ever closer toward the position occupied by the more moderate Right.

Huré has no sympathy for Naturalism, and, although he professes to admire *Louise,* like Debussy he argues that music, by nature, is antithetical to social reality.[159] His aversion to the orthodox Left is patent in the course of his discussion of the "dangerous" musical instruction that is currently being dispensed from above to "le peuple." Seeing such free courses in music as tantamount to mere indoctrination, he claims that the naïve audience that attends them is essentially "told" what to think. Huré proceeds to deride such partisan attempts to "initiate" the people to art, which, he argues, only serves to alienate them from their own essential nature. For Huré, such politicized socialization in music distorts what he perceives as the social and cultural "essence" of the people, which must be maintained. Now "les gens du peuple" no longer compose "sublime chansons" and no longer work ably with their hands as they did in the Middle Ages; rather, they possess the dubious distinction of knowing, for example, that Wagner, Michelangelo, Phidias, Racine, and Homer were true men of genius. Huré concludes that dogmas are not only the refuge of the timid and pedantic, but, in France, they are equally the refuge of those without power.[160]

Huré then proceeds to a discussion of the controversial Schola Cantorum and the aesthetic, social, and political philosophy on which he believes it is based. Although he appreciates the merits of its many pedagogical innovations, he still considers the school to be dangerous on the basis of its philosophical foundations. Huré objects especially to the school's "artificial" view of music history as a series of transformations over time that are born of human will. This, he challenges, precludes acknowledgment of all "instinct" on the part of the artist and, moreover, teaches the student to follow abstract "laws" instead of the ear.[161]

Huré deplores d'Indy's projection of philosophy onto music, as well as his naïveté in concocting a formula for the fabrication of musical "masterworks." Like others before him, he ridicules the blindness and pretension of those at the Schola who pretended to be the "depositories" of the teaching and aesthetic of the dead masters. Just as Debussy does, Huré argues to the contrary that the "greats" should be seen as exceptions, and most certainly not as providing simplified models for students to follow. Finally, he condemns those associated with such teaching as inimical to nature, since they have replaced it with qualities that are artificially derived from intellect, deduction, and reasoning. Yet, as we have noted, Debussystes, including Huré, were not categorically hostile to tradition, although they maintained a distinctive conception of it. Huré lauds the Schola's efforts to develop an historical approach but points out that d'Indy was not alone in stressing the importance of music history.[162]

Huré, then, does not disapprove of the fact that students at the Schola begin by learning to write monodic melodies free of the major and minor modes or that they proceed to learn counterpoint from an historical perspective, first in the form of simple organum and then later advancing to motets and chorales. Only after this background, he observes, does the student finally learn and gain perspective on tonal counterpoint by proceeding to write both canons and fugues.[163]

For Huré, however, the conclusions that the Schola draws from this teaching are wrong, once again being narrowly based on its particular philosophical and social dogma. Such dogma, however, is spread by the press, which Huré, like Hellouin, perceives as contributing integrally to the escalating phenomenon of "chapelles." Here he particularly draws attention to those dual figures who cross cultural domains and attempt to apply their psychological, philosophical, or literary doctrines to the criticism of music. Indeed, he sounds like his colleague Laloy when he acerbically observes that to be a critic of music it can suffice simply to be a brilliant "hommes de lettres." Such criticism, he continues, is self-referential, referring constantly either to a "dogma" of music history or simply to other critical writings; for it is from such texts that the critic appropriates a vocabulary, a critical code, or the "catechism" of the specific "religion" that he will then proceed to profess.[164]

But Huré does not neglect to expose his own aesthetic philosophy, one that, as noted, was itself erected on an ideological foundation. He argues that the transformations of musical style in the past were the result not of human intent but of the development of "hearing," or the human ear. From this he deduces that education in music should serve primarily to perfect the ear through the study of sonorous sensations, moving from the simplest to the most complex: the student may study the masters, but it is from this study that he will learn that the polyphonic style is incompatible with contemporary, more complex harmonies.[165]

Students will also learn that "charm," or the force of a piece of music, does not derive exclusively from the form or mold in which it is written: rather, he argues (recalling Debussy), the idea and the form interact, form being, in essence, "l'ensemble des moyens employés pour obtenir, l'emotion esthétique" (all the means employed to obtain the aesthetic emotion). Terms like "sonate," Huré argues, again as Debussy does (in distinction to the Schola), should be employed in their original historical sense—as a medium-sized composition of "musique pûre." And finally, again like Debussy and as once again distinct from the Schola, he opines that there should be no distinction between "le style élévé, le style familier" and "le style bas." In other words, he opposes the Schola's conception of "la grande musique," with all the moral, social, and ideological implications it carried.[166]

Underlying all Huré's arguments is a conception of the "natural order," one that in several respects, but especially aesthetically, recalls Jean-Jacques Rousseau. With Rousseauistic nostalgia, Huré speaks of the "coins de Bretagne," not yet deformed by modern civilization, where there are still "mélodistes de génie." He argues that these are "true" musicians, people whose innate musicality has been allowed to develop unencumbered and according to "natural laws." As a typical Debussyste, he continues that the "true" musician is one who possesses not just a perfect ear but a "noble sensuality" as well.[167] Yet his conception of the natural, as we can see, was not itself value-free, uniformed by a larger social and cultural perspective—like the other chapelles. For Huré and the majority of the Debussystes, it most closely approximated that of the liberal Right, being socially conservative while maintaining the importance of personal freedom or "liberty."

Huré was by no means the only one to attempt to understand the French musical world in terms of its conflicting musical, social, political, and cultural ideologies. Others were equally concerned with how the different parts of this culture interacted and how even its most seemingly technical conceptions ultimately arose from an ideological base. One was the composer Déodat de Séverac, who, on January 15, 1908, published an article in the *Courrier musical* entitled "La Centralisation et les petites chapelles." In it he attempts to analyze not only the characteristics of the predominant "chapelles" but also the reasons for their existence within the French musical world.

The provenance of the article is revealing: it was based on the "thesis" that Séverac was obliged to write when he terminated his studies at the Schola in 1907. In competition with official institutions, the Schola required a thesis, which it considered an equivalent, although less extensive, of a doctoral thesis at the Sorbonne. Such studies were not without impact, as we may perceive by the fact that Séverac was able to publish an adaptation of his in a major musical journal. D'Indy's requirement, moreover, was a manner of developing an "alternative" musicology, one that addressed the issues of interest to the Schola, and from its distinct perspective. The impact of this on the Société Française de Musicologie would be direct, since many of its early members would come from the circle around the Schola Cantorum.[168]

The article is undoubtedly an adaptation of the thesis; although many of its conceptions derive from the Schola, it is highly critical of the institution itself. Séverac himself never fit the mold of the institution completely, being an ardent admirer of Claude Debussy, whose music strongly influenced his style. Hence he refers to "Scholistes" as reactionaries and, like Emile Vuillermoz, points out their compulsive adulation of "musical architecture," considered as an end in itself. And he mocks the singular preoccupation at the Schola with cyclic themes, which (recalling the words of Rolland) they treat as a "sujet de thèse mécanique rationnelle."[169]

Although otherwise critical of the Schola, Séverac does not neglect to mention its strengths: its artistic probity, its contempt for vulgarity, its horror of all histrionics. But he does point out that despite the fact that it represents the "chapelle de droite," it nevertheless has not given rise to any serious regional current.[170] Séverac then describes d'Indy facetiously as a "monk of the Middle Ages" who propounds the great classical traditions as well as the necessity of a "discipline sévère": his "dogma" is that art must progress ineluctably along the path that the "great" or classical masters of the past have already firmly established. But Séverac notes d'Indy's peculiar conception of this classical tradition—his reduction of it to certain contrapuntal procedures and unchanging tonal "laws"; it is a conception that places an inordinate priority on formal definition, or, once more, what d'Indy refers to as "architectural beauty in music."[171]

In his analysis of d'Indy's place in the French musical world, Séverac, like several others, considers him under the rubric of "independent," as opposed to "official"; the former are those who work outside the context of state-sponsored institutions and thus must seek both financing and symbolic legitimacy through other channels. This rubric includes "chapelles" of the Right and the Left, with d'Indy clearly being the leader of what Séverac and others commonly termed "la chapelle de droite." In contrast, Séverac considers Claude Debussy to be—despite his Conservatoire background and young Conservatoire admirers—the "officiating priest" of the independent "chapelle de gauche." Debussy, as its leader, preaches the love of music in itself, although his followers reduce his creed to the simple primacy of harmony.[172] As chapter 4, shows, they distorted a great more than this, and indeed Debussy disavowed the role of leader and belief in this "chapelle."

Séverac astutely identifies the reasons for these divisions in the musical culture that force those outside state institutions to seek sponsors in the "elegant" world; it is the latter, he argues, who further encourage such factionalization by displaying a pronounced propensity for one "chapelle" or dogma over the other. As we have seen, this "elegant world" indeed included those with manifest political sympathies and those with a proclivity for cultural politics. This was certainly true of amateurs who supported the Schola Cantorum—socialites who had previously been members of organizations like the Ligue de la Patrie Française. Séverac correctly perceived that independents are forced to identify with a particular clique—to don a "uniform" or a label that indicates their position. And this position or association with a "chapelle" is construed immediately as indicative not only of a composer's aesthetic, but of his ideological stance. Séverac also perceives that if a composer refuses to assume a position, he entertains the peril of having a label assigned him by his enemies or his friends: through a mere gesture, a word, or even the use of a particular form, the composer finds that he is immediately categorized or classed in a camp, and without recourse. Chapter 4 describes the extent to which Séverac's perceptions were true and the tactics to which this situation led among composers who were "mis-classed."

The Role of "Salons"

Significantly, as Séverac implies, the salons were not a realm apart, above the antagonisms between "chapelles" and the cultural politics that underlay them; the "elegant world" of the Parisian salons could not avoid awareness of the debates in the press, the meanings it propagated, or the "labels" it assigned French composers. Moreover, many salons had been infiltrated by proponents of different political positions who, like d'Indy, found them a useful medium to pursue their cultural politics. Hence there was a simultaneously social, political, and cultural logic to the musical taste of important patrons who held salons in Paris.

Aside from Scholiste salons and those frequented by major Dreyfusard figures, perhaps the clearest example of this phenomenon is that of the Princess de Polignac. Originally an American (née Wineretta Singer) and thus although an aristocrat outside the "mold," she was further marginalized by being a homosexual married to another homosexual. Although she was not overtly political, it was nonetheless clear at the time of the Affair that she was not an anti-Dreyfusard and that she believed in the innocence of Dreyfus. Indeed, not all French nobles were hostile to the Republic or held atavistic artistic tastes: some, like the princess, inclined far more towards the artistic progressivism of the liberal Right.[173]

Hence the princess (unlike her husband) was no d'Indyste; her salon seemed to favor the opposing "chapelle" and included those with ties to the official world, such as Fauré. Other salons similarly favored composers in the "chapelle" associated with the "Debussystes," as opposed to the Naturalists or "bien pensant" supporters of d'Indy. The "Debussyste salons" included that of Ida and Cipa Godebski, which welcomed such figures as Ravel, Fauré, Roussel, and Satie. Misia Sert, as well, encouraged the nonofficial Debussystes, in addition to major figures such as Fauré, Debussy, and Ravel. Chausson's salon, on the other hand, was palpably d'Indyste, receiving personalities such as Franck, Chabrier, d'Indy, Dukas, and Duparc.[174] Several of its members, as already noted, had been successfully recruited by d'Indy for the Ligue de la Patrie Française at the time of the Dreyfus Affair.

Séverac was undoubtedly correct in arguing that the salons and the "chapelles" were closely intertwined and equally unavoidable for "independent" composers who were forced to navigate within them. His analysis of the "official composers" and their situation is equally penetrating, if more overtly influenced by the cultural perspective of the nationalist Right. The "officials," he explains, are those associated with Republican musical institutions; "protected" by the state, they are obliged to provide appropriate music for official occasions. His description of such occasions is scathing. For Séverac they consist of such events as the inauguration of a statue of a "grand citoyen" to the greater glory of "la démocratie triomphante." His political sympathies become even more overt in his dyspeptic analysis of the education of young, potential French official composers at the Paris Conservatoire. He describes the plight of students from the French regional conservatories who learn their harmony, win a prize, and are sent to study in Paris, where their personalities are promptly extinguished.[175]

For Séverac, the result of such state protection is to distance young musicians from identity with their own region, and thus with the source of their identity. He holds the regional conservatories partly responsible as well, since they have no true regional characteristics but only prepare their students to go to the capital. It is in this context that Séverac's political sympathies become explicit, for he cites Barrès's charge that such uniform instruction forces student pensioners of the state "à se déraciner"; moreover, Séverac explicitly identifies the historical roots of such disdain for regional traditions in France as the destructive and malevolent French Revolution. His cultural and political values here appear to approximate those of that branch of the Action Française that emphasized the regional, as opposed to the centralizing force of a monarchy; indeed, Séverac's larger discourse and analysis, as we have seen, are conceptually bound to those of the monarchist league and, more generally, the nationalist Right.

As noted, the intertextual references in Séverac's discourse were not unique but were increasingly characteristic of contemporary French writings on music. In part, this was the result of the more aggressive cultural tactics employed throughout the political world, which were helping transform the musical culture. The fact that that world was losing autonomy, as so many analysts now perceived, was to have a direct impact on the experience and decisions of French composers.

4

Responses of French Composers to the Traditionalist Victory in Politics and Music

As discussed in chapter 3, in the decade before World War I political ideology and musical values were no longer discrete: the two realms had fused. In chapter 4 I examine the implications of this fusion as the war loomed ominously ahead, and French nationalists and conservatives banded together, achieving hegemony in both politics and culture. Musical life was profoundly to feel the impact of this dual dominance, particularly in the areas of the repertoire and canon, as well as in criticism and music history; moreover, the major French composers were henceforth expected to respond in their art to increasingly traditionalist expectations, the general desire to seek "roots" in the past.

However, they responded differently: Charpentier's political disillusionment led to further engagement in leftist cultural programs, while d'Indy's triumph only reinforced his bellicosity. The situation of those who refused simple dogma was now even more professionally difficult and some proceeded, for various reasons, to thwart expectations by manipulating stylistic codes. Debussy, for example, found it creatively impossible to subordinate his own musical interests and inclinations to his increasingly nationalist, right-wing ideology. Although his political sympathies did not determine the character of his music, they nevertheless affected it from now on in subtle ways. For, while his style was not orthodox, adhering narrowly to conservative codes and expectations, his nationalism was an impetus to his deep creativity, providing him with an "identity."

Satie's clever games with current musical meanings, on the other hand, led him to the creation of a polysemic style that could be appropriated ideologically in multiple ways. Although he was implicitly opposed to nationalism (he joined the Socialist Party), a nationalist but modernist journal of the "liberal Right" appropriated him for its cause. Finally, I examine other composers who fit into neither "chapelle" and who continued, with recalcitrance, to assert their right to differ, against the political tide. For, despite critical retribution, opposition to the imminent traditionalist victory perdured, provoking conciliatory mediators to prepare for a wartime musical "union sacrée." But, as they would discover, virulent passions persisted and would explode in the final vociferous and violent skirmish of the war—over *Le Sacre du printemps*.

DEBUSSY'S NATIONALISM

If Gustave Charpentier was a victim of the politicized battle over Naturalism, Debussy was victimized by the more subtly politicized "guerre des chapelles." The deep-seated ideological differences that underlay different aesthetic positions led to a blindness toward and even to a distortion of his art. For, as we have seen, the question of Debussy's influence and its implications for contemporary French youth had been a polarizing question in the vitriolic "camp war." Yet Debussy's music was still evolving, and, as he himself was painfully aware, by the height of the "guerre des chapelles," it was distant from the Debussystes' dogma. While the reasons for this aesthetic and stylistic evolution are by no means simple, they are not without logic or coherence when we examine all the relevant contexts.

Camille Mauclair was correct in his psychological and political analysis of the "nationalist reaction" and in his perception of the place of Debussy's conceptions and tendencies within it. His comparison of Debussy with Barrès and his movement from the "culte du moi" to the larger "moi collectif" illuminates the composer's critical writings; it also helps explain the evolution of Debussy's ideas and the tensions they engendered in his creativity, which we may discern within the music itself. While doctrinaire in his prose and in his purely verbal utterance, Debussy, the most subtle of artists, found it impossible to be doctrinaire in his art. His aesthetic proclivities, together with his search for a social identity, led him toward a political dogmatism, the limits of which he would transcend in his music. This resulted in his highly problematic relationship to the nationalist musical dogma, which equated certain stylistic orthodoxies with a set of political and social values.

Like Charpentier, Debussy's social identity was highly complex, a fact that influenced his early explorations, as well as his later artistic search for "roots." Both artists came from outside the culture that fostered the artistic language they learned, and both remained objective toward it, seeking something more "authentic"; while achieving eventual success in the state-sponsored academic system, they both retained an emotional, ironic distance from it and the musical language it taught. Finally, both sought to escape marginality through larger political and cultural doctrines as a way to anchor their identities and consequently their

creativity and art. Debussy, like Charpentier, was well aware of the social meanings carried by artistic styles or languages, and he too could not resist subverting
such dogma: he maintained a creative objectivity toward the political position to
which he gradually inclined by continuing to play with orthodoxies—now the
meanings assigned to style.

We cannot fully understand Debussy and the later development of his music
apart from his place in the politicized musical culture that surrounded him after
Pelléas; hence, we must attempt to situate him within it and from this perspective
to examine the evolution of his ideas, his professional status, and, finally, his musical style. As noted, he took a stand on almost all the major issues, but we must
compare his response in prose with the one we find in his music. Since the tensions between his political beliefs and his creative needs impelled his style, we
must begin by examining his ideological evolution and its psychological roots. In
the case of Debussy it is essential to recognize his social liminality—his inability
to identify fully with any one cultural level or social group: his deep originality,
his inability to imbibe a constituted language, culture, or dogma—even that of
the nationalism he professed—emanates fundamentally from this source.

Like Charpentier, Debussy's social origins were, according to contemporaries, "modest," although he did not come from "le peuple," or from a properly
working-class background.[1] His father had successive occupations; he was at different times a soldier in the infantry, a simple adventurer, and, finally, later, a
small merchant of faïence. Politically, Debussy's father was apparently sympathetic to Anarchism, having participated in the Commune and having subsequently been sent to prison for four years. It could well have been this fact that
led Debussy, even after his transformation into an ardent nationalist to declare,
when war broke out, that he had no "esprit militaire."[2]

The composer's brother was an agricultural worker, as well as a cesspool
cleaner, and his sister, Adèle, was an employee in a lingerie company. The only
member of his family to rise in social status was his aunt, who became the mistress of the rich Achille Arosa and opened a "maison de couture."[3] Debussy's first
exposure to music came when he served as a choirboy in his family's church,
where, according to his sister, he formed his first conceptions of music. This has
led to speculation that his later horror of the cadential formulae that he encountered at the Conservatoire derived from this early exposure to chant. Later, indeed, he became a fervent admirer of the "Chanteurs de Saint-Gervais," and in
1893 he made a trip to Solemnes in order to hear plainchant performed. His other
important exposure to music and art as a child was the theater, where, despite
their limited means, his family frequently took him.[4] This experience may lie at
the origins of his emphatic views on "people's theater" and his insight into how
the lower classes experience drama and spectacle.

But when Debussy entered the Conservatoire, his general manner was far
from refined, and his fellow students noted his "gaucherie," or his extraordinary
social awkwardness: it was clear that he, like Gustave Charpentier, did not come
from a social or cultural milieu comparable to that of the majority of the other
students.[5] But they also noted that, in spite of his origins, he had developed an
aristocratic taste, a marked preference for the delicate and fine and particularly

for "objets d'art." Although he was by no means a docile student, rather continually questioning all he was taught, a number of professors admired his talent, particularly Marmontel, Bazille, and Guiraud.[6] Thus, like Charpentier, despite a social marginality and rebellious streak, he succeeded in the system, winning the Second Prix de Rome in 1883 and the Premier Prix in 1884.

Debussy arrived at the Villa Medici in 1885 and immediately began to write M. Vasnier, an architect who had become his mentor. Clearly feeling the need for social and intellectual refinement, he had frequented the comfortable, bourgeois Vasnier family while a student in Paris. But in his letters Debussy constantly speaks of his isolation from his comrades, who, he claimed, accused him unfairly of always wanting to stand apart; moreover, he complained that they wrongly accused him of espousing ideas drawn from the brasseries of the boulevard Saint-Michel which, in this period, implied Anarchism. (Since, as we have noted, part of the Anarchist creed was to question all constituted cultural authority, as indeed did Debussy, this may have underlain the charge.) While thus isolated in Rome, Debussy explored the music performed in the churches, becoming enamored of what he termed the "pure and simple" style of Palestrina and Lassus;[7] in particular, he marveled at the fact that, in their hands, counterpoint was not "forbidding" but rather served to underlay the feelings expressed in the words.

Another manifestation of Debussy's desire to explore modes of expression that lay outside those that the Conservatoire recognized was his interest in the music of Chabrier. It was in this period that he, as so many subsequent composers in France were to do, studied and performed the music of this non-Conservatoire or "amateur" composer. While a Prix de Rome, Debussy was systematically rejecting his training, constantly revising those works that seemed to be marked too strongly by his formal instruction. This included his *Fantaisie pour piano et orchestre,* which Debussy now repudiated because of what he saw of its "predictable" developments and contrapuntal "scaffolding."[8]

His desire to reopen his imagination led him, in addition, to two other interests: the music of Wagner and the Javanese gamelan, which he heard at the Universal Exposition of 1889. Debussy went to Bayreuth in 1888 and 1889 and began an opera, *Rodrique et Chimène,* to the libretto of a Wagnerian, Catulle Mendès, in 1890. But already by 1889 he was beginning to grow disillusioned with Wagner, perceiving him as the last of the "classics"—not a stylistic beginning, but rather an end.[9] What fascinated Debussy now were alternative means of the development of musical ideas, those that had nothing to do with his conventional and constricting Conservatoire training. As Maurice Emmanuel (a fellow student) recounts, he argued, for example, that a development should not have to be "cette amplification matérielle, cette rhétorique de professionnel façonné par d'excellentes leçons" (this material amplification, this rhetoric of a professional, shaped by excellent lessons) but could be conceived in a more "universal" and psychological sense.[10]

Upon his return to Paris, Debussy was, more than ever, aware of the insufficiency of his "general culture," and he set about to expand it by exploring others. But now he rejected the "moeurs bourgeois" of his former friends the Vasniers in favor of (like Charpentier) the "bohemian" literary circles in Montmartre.

Although having an "entrée" into the official and bourgeois words through the Prix de Rome, Debussy peremptorily turned away, rejecting all for which it stood. His desire now was to acquire a "culture," but conclusively not that of "society," in which he clearly felt he did not and could not belong. His intermediary now, in this new social transformation was Edmond Bailly, an editor and the owner of the bookstore and gathering place called "L'Art Indépendant." The culture that Debussy encountered here was far different from that to which he had been exposed through his perfunctory primary education and through his contact with the Vasniers. To "improve himself," Debussy was, according to contemporaries, an avid reader, always ready to form an opinion on almost every subject.[11]

During this stage of his search for an artistic, social, and cultural identity, Debussy's closest friendships began to undergo yet another transformation. It was now, in the early 1890s, that he formed a friendship with Erik Satie, then in his own "bohemian" phase and working as a pianist in Montmartre cabarets.[12] Debussy was also close to Pierre Louÿs, who, as a writer, was highly influential in directing his reading and forming his literary taste in this period. Louÿs had strong political opinions, as well as virulent anti-Semitic feelings, which crystallized during the Dreyfus Affair in an anti-Dreyfusard stance. In addition, Debussy was friends with Robert Godet, who not only was an ardent Wagnerian but also intractably espoused Houston Stuart Chamberlin's racist views.[13]

Yet Debussy remained open-minded, for, in the later 1890s, during the period of the composition of *Pelléas,* his friends included Mauclair and other figures on the Left.[14] During the period of the Affair, while Debussy was at work on *Pelléas,* he remained politically ambivalent, in a period of transition, although his friends chose opposing sides. René Peter, who, like Camille Mauclair and Debussy's first wife, was a Dreyfusard, persuaded Debussy to hear Anatole France and Jean Jaurès speak in support of Dreyfus;[15] but Debussy remained noncommittal, and the most decisive stance that he was able to take was, as already noted, to sign the petition circulated by the Comité de l'Appel à l'Union. It appeared in the conservative Republican *Le Temps,* which moved from an anti-Dreyfusard position to a reevaluation—not an unusual phenomenon during the Affair, which sometimes cut across poitical categories. Debussy read its editorials assiduously during the years of the Affair, and would continue to read and then subscribe to this conservative or centrist paper. His unwillingness to assume a firm stance in the Affair is undoubtedly related to his crisis of professional and social identity—his still liminal position between social worlds, as reflected in the wide diversity of his freinds.

Until the production of *Pelléas,* Debussy was far from financially secure and, according to René Peter, was "as much a Montmartre bohemian as a man of the world." Despite his increasing reputation, he still remained ill at ease in society, generally reserved and avoiding conversation, except with his closest friends.[16] But he was, as an "independent" had to be, a frequenter of important salons, including those of Misia Sert and of the "Franckist" Ernest Chausson.[17] Yet Debussy affirmed his social origins by marrying Lilly Texier, a "fille du peuple," and by continuing to live an essentially simple, unsophisticated life.[18]

This was a period of deep self-searching and uncertainty for Debussy, as reflected not only in his contacts, friends, and political sympathies but also in his art. He continued his attempt to "escape" or disengage himself from his previous influences, in the realm of music, as well as in larger artistic movements. As so many texts have recounted, musically he exploited sources outside the Western tradition, particularly the new rhythmic, melodic, and structural ideas he encountered in his exposure to the Javanese gamelan, in 1889. In addition, he turned back in time to elude the orthodoxies of "Conservatoire language," finding a compatible model in eighteenth-century France in his *Suite Bergamasque,* of 1890. Already, his aesthetic sensibility was leading him toward a paradigm for which he would later find intellectual justification, in his search for cultural "roots." But the decisive influence on Debussy in this seminal stylistic period was the aesthetic direction provided by his exposure first to the pre-Raphaelites and then to the Symbolists; both movements had conclusively rejected the conventions of academic rhetoric, one turning toward the distant past and the other exploring an entirely new mode of discourse.

Debussy inclined, in particular, to the muted poetic values of the Symbolists, to their "nonintellectual" emphasis, their desire for suggestion as opposed to statement. This would bear fruit in the work often said to herald his first maturity, the *Prélude à l'après-midi d'un faune,* of 1894, based on Mallarmé. Here we see a coherent language both defined against contemporary conventional musical discourse and guided by a new set of consistent aesthetic goals. Now he is no longer interested in the traditional development of ideas or in any mere stereotyped form but attempts to redefine the relationship of musical elements in the definition of form. Hence his turn to a continually evolving melody or motivic idea that guides all other dimensions and itself helps determine the formal shape. Debussy here exploits the sonorous as opposed to the "tension-building" effects of chords and avoids emphatic climaxes in order to follow the evolution of the melody and the musical "moment."[19]

Debussy was in the process of a thorough "revolution," reinventing not only his musical language but also his personal and social beliefs. His search for self-definition in this period emerges most clearly in his one dramatic effort—the only play that Debussy ever wrote. It is in *Frères en art,* the play that he coauthored with René Peter between 1897 and 1903, that we may observe his evolving social and political perspective. In this highly autobiographical work, the ironic distance that the author still manages to assume regarding his presumed self-presentation recalls Gustave Charpentier's *Louise;* like *Louise,* it contains ambiguous references to Anarchism, or rather an ambivalent attitude toward specific aspects of Anarchist theory.

Like Charpentier, Debussy could not help but encounter Anarchist ideas in the literary and social circles in which he moved in Montmartre in the 1890s; as we have seen, his father had been known to espouse Anarchist beliefs, although later in life Debussy claimed to have loved, but never shared any ideas with, his father. Debussy most certainly came into contact with Anarchist ideas in the circle of the *Revue blanche,* where he spent six months as a critic in 1901. The issue of Anarchism thus becomes the reason for the author's ironic attitude toward his own self-depiction (recalling *Louise*), here as the Anarchist hero. Debussy, like

Charpentier, expresses his disorientation and self-irony through an ambiguous artist-hero with whom he ostensibly identifies. Significantly, the period of the play's composition spans that period of time when Debussy began to seek the certitude of "tradition" in both his political views and his art.

The theme of the play is a "brotherhood," the proposed communal sharing of collective income by artists from different fields, to promote unity as opposed to competition. It has already been posited that the painter Maltravers is Debussy himself and that his mistress in the play, Marie, is Lilly Texier; also proposed is the theory that, ashamed of his humble origins, Debussy could express himself freely on culture only through a character like Maltravers.[20] In addition, we should note the particular significance of the hero's name, which literally means "crosses badly," implying perhaps a reference to both culture and class. Maltravers's ideas indeed resemble those of Anarchism, especially his desire to destroy all libraries, which contain only "changing aspects of the same human truth"; in addition, a concern of the group is to develop a taste for their "revolutionary" art, not among the bourgeoisie but among the as yet "uncomprehending masses."[21]

We shall see how well acquainted and concerned Debussy was with the issue that was currently raging in cultural politics concerning the people and art. He indeed was to sound like Maltravers in his commentary on the subject so personally sensitive to him, the relationship that existed between culture and class. Here, according to the character:

> I also believe that from this melting-pot of suffering and hatred, and only from this strength represented by the people, will the most beautiful works arise. The only problem is that the common people do not like art . . . they feel rather like intruders or poor relatives! You see traces of this in almost all Anarchist schemes which apply to them: the propagation of art is not included.[22]

In the play, the goals of liberty, equality, and fraternity that are idealistically professed by this group prove to be difficult to realize in the actual world.[23] The emphasis on this problem may well have related to Debussy's own perception of the inherent contradictions in Anarchist theory from the standpoint of creative artists. For Anarchism was characterized by a rejection of partisan struggles, as well as of any means of organized control by a constituted structure of social authority; hence, many artists abetted the movement solely because they perceived it as a theoretical justification for complete artistic autonomy. Such autonomy from the "market" requires the kind of solidarity or independent organization that is attempted by the "Frères en Art"; yet this inevitably eventuates in its own authority structure—again, one that is imposed, as opposed to rising from simple consensus within.[24] In this skeptical attitude were the seeds of Debussy's later propensity for a conservative social model based on instinctual or prerational bonds. This is where he would finally locate the sources of an "authentic" culture that transcended the boundaries of social class and undercut all academic convention. Eventually he was to find in this model, now being propagated by the nationalist Right, both creative inspiration and the answer to his problem of social and cultural identity.[25]

Debussy's Transition in *Pelléas*

The tensions we have noted in Debussy between his search for an identity or cultural "order" and his need to explore his own sensibility appear in several early works. This is particularly true of his opera *Pelléas et Mélisande,* in which Wagnerian influence is both present and countered by specific elements of traditional French style. Many analyses of the opera exist, and so my purpose here is simply to relate the tensions within the work to their construal within the context of French cultural politics. As we shall see, one position in particular would soon approximate Debussy's own arguments (as it developed after 1902) concerning the implications of the French tradition for modern art.

Debussy discovered Maurice Maeterlinck's play in 1892, and by 1893 he had decided to write an opera based upon it. His first version of *Pelléas et Mélisande* was completed by 1895, and another in 1897, the year it was accepted at the Opéra Comique. But Debussy thereafter persisted in continually "improving" the manuscript, even during the final period of the dress rehearsals in 1902.[26] Given what we have observed about the tension in Debussy's personality, the reason for his attraction to the thematic material of the play here becomes particularly clear: one of the work's major themes is the proper nature of the connection between the individual's own inherent inclinations and search for truth and the demands or needs of society. Another, as opposed to the passion at the heart of *Tristan und Isolde,* is the isolation of the individual trying to comprehend the unknown, or "fate," and his lack of an intimate "connection."[27]

In his search for artistic "truth," or for the most appropriate musical means through which to translate Maeterlinck's play, he arrived at a singular stylistic solution: in order to allow the characters to express themselves naturally as "real people," to capture their true humanity, he developed a vocal declamation that recalls the distant French past. One of Maeterlinck's aims was, through the use of a more natural diction, to suggest the mysterious realm beneath the apparent realities of existence. Since Debussy's goal was to set the French language as authentically or naturally as possible, he turned to that composer whom he considered the last master of French musical parody, Rameau.[28] As opposed to the heightened, declamatory style of both Lully and Gluck—whose native language was not French—Debussy emulated the subtlety and grace of Rameau; moreover, as in the French tradition, he gives primacy to the text, which is here set almost exactly, with the exception of a few omissions. The musical development is never allowed to obscure the meaning or flow of the text, once more placing Debussy firmly within the French operatic tradition.[29]

Yet, elements of Wagnerian musical dramaturgy are indeed present in the work, if transformed or adapted to Debussy's specific dramatic intent. Like Wagner, in search of both psychological and musical continuity as well as the integration of dramatic levels, he employs a kind of "leitmotif." But his are substantially different in nature from those that Wagner characteristically employs; they are primarily rhythmic, intervallically more subtle, and more psychological in their associations, which they gradually absorb; moreover, the only consistently symphonic development of these motives occurs in the interludes between the

scenes, composed during the rehearsals to allow for scene changes and to transform the ambience. In general, his motives, unlike those of either Wagnerian or
Naturalist opera, serve not to clarify meaning but to enhance its fundamental ambiguity; as in the French tradition, the orchestra remains subordinate to the text,
but still in a Wagnerian manner, reinforcing the multiple dimensions of its meaning. As Laloy astutely observed, it often serves to reveal what the characters in the
play experience but do not consciously understand; it simultaneously creates a
mood, largely by the reiteration of motives (especially rhythmic, recalling Mussorgsky), as well as through the harmonies and timbres.[30]

The Critical "Processing" of *Pelléas*

In *Pelléas et Mélisande,* French critics were confronted by a stylistically complex
and novel work that they proceeded to "process" or interpret according to the
principal critical discourses: hence, the logic of their responses relates to these intellectual frameworks, as well as to the contemporary issues of cultural politics
that we have already examined.[31] As we have noted, however, like so much of
Debussy's subsequent works, *Pelléas* confounded the dogma of the existing factions, leading to a curious and inconsistent reaction. Hence, again, in 1902 Debussy's "place" was far from clear and his classification as an authentically
"French" composer not yet secure. Unlike *Louise,* the work could not be easily
appropriated for a "side," so inimical was its language to a simple reduction to
the standards of any one discourse. The case of *Pelléas* reveals how inconsistently
and willfully critics espousing the current ideological perspectives could "construct" or even distort the work.

The performative context of the opera also may well have played a significant
role in predisposing certain critics to a specific politicized reading of it. For *Pelléas* was presented (with the financial aid of a Jewish aristocrat) along with a series of works that were part of Bruneau's purportedly "true" French canon. It was
perhaps in an attempt to "rehabilitate" himself in the "Dreyfusard Republic" that
the former anti-Dreyfusard director of the theater, Carré, presented Bruneau's
l'Ouragan and *Le Rêve* and Charpentier's *Louise.*[32] Yet within the Dreyfusard *Le
Figaro,* views concerning Debussy's work were divided, so complex, novel, and
seemingly contradictory was its style. Eugène d'Harcourt found the "vagueness"
of the opera to be alarming and ended by asking for a "conception plus saine de
l'art musical"; however, another critic for the paper, H. Bauer, emphasized the
presence of an element we have seen in the Dreyfusard aesthetic—the originality
of the work.[33]

Others, such as Arthur Pugin, writing in *Le Ménestrel,* saw Debussy's innovations as "dangerous" and even labeled him an "Anarchist in music." This is not
surprising considering Anarchist cultural theories, which, as we have seen,
stressed the importance of deconstructing the dominant language.[34] Yet there
were critics who, like Raymond Bouyer, also employed the aesthetic perspective
that was associated with the Dreyfusard Left in order to criticize Debussy, as
would Mauclair and Lorrain. In an article entitled "Le Debussysme et l'évolution
musicale," published in the *Revue musicale,* he, as many others, compares De-

bussy with Richard Wagner. Here Bouyer argues that, far from having defeated or exorcised Wagner, he has merely transposed the "German giant" "dans un ton plus fin." He concludes that Debussy is to Wagner essentially what Maeterlinck is to Shakespeare: "une petite ombre qui parle bas aux pieds du grand maître" (a small shadow that speaks softly at the feet of the great master).[35] Bouyer's perspective and argument is far more explicit in a review that he published the preceding month in the Republican journal *La Nouvelle revue:* here he openly pits the Scholistes and fellow neo-Wagnerians against the "naturistes," implying both Debussy and his young acolytes.[36] Bouyer, however, does credit Debussy with being far more concerned with reality and truth than with lyric beauty in his declamation, and he makes a point of noting that the critics associated with the Schola thus perceive the work's connection with the early operas of Claudio Monteverdi. D'Indy, in *L'Occident,* did compare Debussy's treatment of the text with that of early Florentine opera and praised its solid thematic construction: but he censured its harmonic departures, decrying an aesthetic of "sensation" and concluding that it was an "inferior art"—beautiful, but nevertheless "dangerous."

Indeed, Debussy's attempt to recapture traditional French declamation won the praise of both Right and Left, if for very different reasons: one side saw the anti-Dreyfusard turn to the past or to the "great tradition," while the other perceived the Dreyfusard values of realistic depiction and "truth." As Bouyer notes, both sides were concerned with the now central question of whether "classical" elements—considered truly French—were present in the opera. Once more, Left and Right agreed on the inherent value of the classic, some critics from both sides perceiving it as present in the work, but according to substantially different conceptions. Perceptively, Bouyer observes that, if there is classicism, it inheres not in the form but rather in the rejection of now hackneyed formulae or clichés. As Maurice Emmanuel points out, other critics on both sides agreed: André Hallays cited his avoidance of prolixity and Paul Dukas a classicism that no "system" can teach. Hallays, writing in the conservative *Revue de Paris,* expressed his approbation for Debussy's use of such refined understatement in the following terms:

> Si M. Debussy n'est point un musicien classique au sens qu'on entend ce mot dans les conservatoires, il n'en a pas moins le goût vraiment classique d'un art concis, sans emphase, ni verbiage.[37]

> (If M. Debussy is not a classical musician in the sense that one understands the word in the conservatories, he has no less the truly classical taste for a concise art, without emphasis or verbiage.)

Yet some journals of the Right, employing similar criteria for the "truly French," emphasized the opera's seeming lack of classical qualities. *La Libre parole* criticized the work for its "perpetual cacophony"; for Bellaigue, in the *Revue des deux mondes,* it was devoid of melody, motives, and rhythm. Louis de Fourcaud, a professor at the École Nationale des Beaux-Arts and a critic for *Le Gaulois,* found only a craving for novelty, an indulgence in cerebral subtleties, and hence a doctrine of "complete negation." Here again, far Left and Right agreed in their quest for a more "substantial" and thus what they considered to be a more healthy or moral" art. Bouyer, in the end, reveals that he does not wish Debussy to head a "school," so distant are his theatrical values from those the critic considers "truly French":

> Un impressionnisme assez morne et peu théâtral va-t-il aider, par un détour, à la re-vanche de notre art, à la resurrection de la papillonnante musique française, récem-ment alourdi par tant de plagiats?[38]

> (Will a rather gloomy and un-theatrical impressionism help, by a detour, the revenge of our art, the resurrection of French music which has flitted about, recently weighted down with so many plagiarisms?)

Other critics of the Left perceived different features in *Pelléas* and were able to construe it within the framework of Bruneau's canon of French works. Julien Benda, for example, writing in the *Revue bleue,* supported the opera enthusiasti-cally on the basis of its human, true, and logical qualities.[39] Still others, writing in journals associated with the political Left, praised the opera on the basis of its reality in the treatment of the French language. This was the case of Camille Sainte-Croix in the Dreyfusard *La Petite République,* who emphasized the fluidity and richness of the rhythms that followed the inflections of the language so faith-fully.[40] Here the stress is less on its "classic" features than its realism, the same quality the journal had praised in the operas of Zola and Bruneau.

Debussy and "Tradition"

Despite these dissensions, however, after the premiere of *Pelléas* a group of sup-porters construed Debussy's music as "traditionalist," to which the composer did not object. One of these was Jacques Durand, the important Parisian editor of music, who, himself a self-avowed traditionalist, had no doubt as to where De-bussy belonged: it was on the basis of the success of *Pelléas* and his perception of the work as belonging firmly within the French tradition that he offered to pub-lish all of Debussy's music. For, as he avers in his memoirs, the central question posed was whether or how it might renew ties to the lost "French tradition," and for him it had.[41]

Although Debussy would increasingly encourage this interpretation, he com-plicated the critical construals of the work by making statements about it that ap-pealed to both factions. Writing in the Dreyfusard *Le Figaro,* he stressed his desire to be realistic in the declamation but still implicitly distanced himself from Char-pentier and Bruneau: "The characters in this drama endeavor to sing like real per-sons, and not in an arbitrary language built on antiquated traditions . . . the feelings of a character cannot be continually expressed in melody."[42] Yet, in a sur-vey that was published in the journal *Musica* in 1902, on the question of the di-rection of French music, his emphasis was on classical traits: "Perhaps in the end we will see the light and achieve conciseness of expression and form—the funda-mental qualities of French genius."[43] From now on the renewal of contact with "French genius," conceived as "classic," was Debussy's continual preoccupation, one that would crest during World War I. The theme of the "truly French," initially introduced into the discourse by the cultural politics of the Right, was now to provide him with a major source of creative direction. For it allowed Debussy to transcend his sense of social and cultural marginality, of participating in, and yet not belonging to any one strata or world; indeed, as he rose in status and class through his success and a second marriage while becoming even more ill at ease in his surroundings, this theme became a virtual obsession. And, concomitantly, no less than an artistic transformation was to follow the social, political, psychological, and aesthetic metamorphosis that he now experienced.

Debussy was becoming aware of the political or ideological implications of the emerging aesthetic basis or "roots" of his own artistic creativity. The surrounding discourse of cultural politics associated with the French nationalist Right would provide him with both the conceptual and emotional grounding that he sought. This may well have been abetted by his contact with figures like Pierre Louÿs and by his increasing proximity to the circle of the Schola and the Société Nationale. In 1903 he became one of the music critics for the journal *Gil Blas,* together with the writer Colette, with whom he was henceforth in frequent contact. They were mingling in the same salons, which included the most prominent figures associated with the Schola Cantorum—Pierre de Bréville, Vincent d'Indy, Louis de Serres, and Charles Bordes.[44] Colette, along with her husband, "Willy," praised the efforts of the Schola Cantorum; Debussy did as well, but in a more selective or guarded manner. Although disliking the dogmatism and religious atmosphere of the school, he admired its restoration of Rameau, but complained that it had no idea of how to perform him correctly.[45] However, in 1903, he wrote enthusiastically about d'Indy's *L'Etranger* and its curious but powerful combination of Symbolist elements with a Naturalist setting: "The work is an admirable lesson to those who believe in that crude, imported style which reduces music to dust under a pile of realism."[46] For Debussy, again, Naturalism, even in its French adaptation, was not inherently French but fundamentally an Italian import.

It is also significant to note that, despite the "Debussystes," Debussy remained close to the Société Nationale, which continued often to perform his works; indeed, important premieres of his music took place under its auspices between 1889 and 1917, or until the end of his active career.[47] The polarity his supporters wished to create was indeed not present in Debussy, who, like Fauré, chose not to alienate the important d'Indyste camp. And, as Charles Koechlin later made a specific point of noting, Debussy, by personality, was drawn to the Schola's contemplative atmosphere: being "peu mondain," and thus not at home in the circle of the Société Musicale Indépendante, he preferred the "meditative," serious aura of the Schola, free of "snobism" and devoted to "art."[48]

The theme of foreign importations now became dominant in Debussy's writings, manifesting itself increasingly in relentless attacks on Gluck and praise of Rameau. According to Debussy (and Laloy), the former, whose nationality was not French, had not mastered the language, did not write "French music," and had no place within the French canon:

> You turn French into an accented language when it is really a language of nuances. (Yes, I know you are German.) Rameau was lyrical, and that suits the French spirit

from all points of view. We should have continued this tradition of lyricism before, not waited for a century to pass before we discovered it. . . . Finally, you have been the subject of all the many varied and false interpretations people give to the word "classical."[49]

Debussy was astutely aware of the principal themes of cultural politics and of the stakes currently involved in defining the true French "classic tradition"; for him, as indeed for his politicized culture, this was to remain perhaps the most prominent issue in French music, one that would culminate during the war.

But the other theme of cultural politics to which he was especially sensitive now, for social reasons we have already noted, was the question of "people's theater." In 1903 Debussy, more than ever, was caught between cultures and, in a more personal or immediate sense, caught between two women and two "lives": although married to a "femme du peuple," Lilly Texier, he was romantically involved with the wealthy and cultivated Emma Bardac. In 1903 the subject of "people's theater" was especially timely, given the recent publication of Romain Rolland's book *Le Théâtre du peuple*. As we have noted, this was the year when Debussy had nothing but caustic criticism for Charpentier's educational venture, the Conservatoire Populaire de Mimi Pinson.[50] But he also made reference to his own involvement with current attempts to "take art to the people" and was far from sanguine about the results. Speaking perhaps from his early experience Debussy observed: "In general, the people who make such efforts act with the kind of condescending good will that ordinary people feel to be both forced and artificial. . . . It's dishonest! There is an instinctive feeling of envy hovering over this vision of luxury brought for a single moment into their dull lives."[51]

On the question of "people's theater," Debussy had clearly defined ideas, which drew on the more conservative models we have noted of a "democratic" open-air theater. According to Debussy, the ideal kind of theater for the "people" would be modeled not on the revolutionary fête but on the drama of the ancient Greeks, according to his specific conception: "In Euripides, Sophocles, and Aeschylus, do we not find all the great human emotions drawn in such simple lines, and with such naturally tragic effects that they could be understood by the most virgin and cultivated minds?" His ideal is enlightenment and common understanding as opposed to "manifestation" or participation, a blurring of the boundaries between art and actual life. Debussy concludes by proposing that we "rediscover tragedy and enhance its primitive musical accompaniment with all the resources of the modern orchestra and chorus and innumerable bodies."[52]

Debussy was even more specific concerning the theatrical environment he envisaged and about the role or responsibility of the state in helping to realize this vision: such a theater was to be "a cheerful room where everyone would feel at home. . . . And seats should be entirely free—If need be, a loan must be raised: never would such a loan have been made for nobler reasons, nor so much in the national interest."[53] Again, for Debussy, unlike Charpentier, the final goal was not a "people's culture" but a reconciliation of cultures in the interest of national harmony: his identity was now increasingly to be vested in the nation as a means to unite and reconcile the maze of social levels, cultures, and experiences through which he had passed.

Debussy's solution, as we have seen, was by no means unique in the period, as Mauclair had observed in his article on the nationalist reaction in art. His inclusion of Debussy and Barrès within the same grouping was insightful, for this particular analogy does explain a great deal about the composer. Just as Mauclair implied, Debussy had gradually moved from the egotistical "culte du moi" to a conception of the encompassing "moi collectif"; like Barrès's characters in his series of Le Culte du moi novels, he attempted to escape from his "unattached personality," untethered from a social or cultural identity. For both, earlier attempts at escape had included intuition, mysticism, sensuality, and "pure art," but all of them, having proved futile, were eventually to lead to another solution: both Debussy and Barrès were to find an answer in the rediscovery of a national identity and the concomitant conception of the heritage of a "race."

Like Barrès, Debussy turned from doubt to the certainties provided by history, from the cult of the individual to that of the nation and the collectivity. Both believed that the "self" must recognize the cultural identify that precedes and defines it, positively embracing this identity in order to be fully "realized."[54] But an inconsistency emerged in the composer, for, while professing the primacy of national values and the "truly French," he continued to praise the intuitive freedom of the individual artist. He thus departed from the Scholistes' belief in the constraints implied by tradition, construing it rather in terms of the creative instincts that were inherent in a national "race." For Debussy, as we shall see, the implication would be that, after removing "impure" or foreign elements, being true to oneself was being true to one's race. But ironically, for Debussy, highly influenced by non-Western music, "purity" did not require the extirpation of the non-Occidental; while arguing for a "truly French music" he not only avoided heading a school but independently pursued his individual freedom and highly personal aesthetic inclinations.[55] An undying proponent of the "natural," of the model or dictates of nature, Debussy came, philosophically, to confound this with the instinct that is determined by race or blood.

By 1903 Debussy's life was undergoing a substantial transformation again, from both a personal and social and a professional perspective. This was the year that he received the distinction of election to the Legion of Honor as a result of the efforts of Jules Combarieu, at the time the Chef de Cabinet at the Ministère de l'Education.[56] This was to bring him more prominence and a stature in the profession that was continually to grow; by the time of the war, his influence was rivaled only by that of d'Indy. In 1904 further changes transpired: Debussy's life was fundamentally transformed when he abandoned his wife, Lilly (leaving her resourceless), to live with Emma Bardac. One immediate effect of this action was to cut him off from most of his friends, who generally disapproved of his heartless treatment of the now nearly destitute Lilly. This included Pierre Louÿs, who not only sympathized with Lilly's plight, but also, as a rabid anti-Semite, disapproved of the Jewish Emma Bardac. The one exception was Louis Laloy, whom he had known since the premiere of Pelléas and who now became increasingly close to and influential on the composer. Already, this friendship was influencing the musical journals that Debussy read, for by 1905 he was an appreciator of the *Mercure musical,* of which Laloy was an editor. And it was to Laloy that he expressed his frustration with Landormy's survey of 1904, complaining that this "soi-disant musicien" apparently did not hear what he said.[57]

Laloy was to prove of invaluable help as Debussy's style began to change, serving as a mediator between the composer and the dismayed "Debussystes"; by 1905 it was clear that traditional procedures were reappearing in Debussy's work and that now he was no longer making any attempts whatsoever to expurgate them. This was a particular embarrassment to his younger supporters like Huré, who had emulated the composer's attacks on traditional forms and his advocacy of those modeled on the musical content. The first crisis transpired with the premiere of *La Mer* in 1905, when critics promptly drew attention to Debussy's return to more traditional compositional procedures. Although Debussy pointedly subtitled the work "Three Symphonic Sketches," many of the commentators on the work perceived concessions to symphonic form. By avoiding the rubric of "symphony," despite his use of symphonic processes, Debussy was consciously avoiding the undesired associations of the genre. This meant not only those of the Schola—tradition, the metaphysical, and the Germanic—but also those of the rival Conservatoire: architecture, balance, and logic. Yet elements of both models are present—a cyclic theme unifies the entire work; the first movement loosely adheres to a sonata-like scheme in its key relations; the second movement suggests an ABA structure (defined by key); and the third is a kind of rondo in its use of a recurring refrain.[58]

But while the work does employ traditional procedures, it is by no means anachronistic: for Debussy, the past was always an inspiration for contemporary artistic creativity. Here, as in his subsequent compositions, he drew from a fund of traditional techniques, while preserving those compositional elements that were most unique to himself. He also sought to preserve what he construed as traditional French values—the quest for elegance, pleasure, and "color"—yet he inimitably made them his own; for just as powerful as the emotional and intellectual pull of tradition for Debussy was a creative drive that impelled him to appropriate it in his own way. Past models, for Debussy, served to stimulate imagination; in *La Mer,* for example, they are used only where they are metaphorically appropriate to the subject.[59] From the beginning of the work we find elements already integral to Debussy's style, particularly those that he had previously derived from his study of gamelan music. This is suggested in the constant textural shifts and the complex stratification, as well as the pentatonic pitch material. And, despite the presence of some traditional procedures such as conventional imitation, the themes themselves are antimelodic and subject to constant reinterpretation and variation.[60]

Debussy, having had the audacity to cross the lines of antithetical dogma, now required a "defense," a task that was promptly assumed by Laloy. In 1908 Laloy published an ingenious article in *La Grande revue* that justified Debussy's increasing traditionalism by invoking his authentic "French roots." Indeed, since the premiere of *Pelléas,* Laloy had stressed what he perceived as profoundly French and deeply traditionalist aspects of Debussy's style. Writing of *Pelléas,* he observed, "Il a retrouvé en lui par un de ces efforts d'intuition qui font les chefs-d'oeuvre, un peu de la vieille âme de notre race"[61] (He has rediscovered in himself by one of the efforts of intuition that make masterpieces a little of the old soul of our race). Laloy presents *La Mer* as a conflation of symphony and symphonic poem, but with emphasis on the latter, which allowed for "inspiration," as opposed to "rules." He then argues that this enables Debussy to employ symphonic processes that are useful to his purposes, yet without strict adherence to "tradition."[62] Clearly Laloy, like Debussy, understood the current connotations of the symphony in France, as propagated by both "chapelles," and wished to dissociate Debussy from them.

Laloy, as Debussy's apologist, here argues for a logical evolution in Debussy's style, claiming the new direction surprises only those ignorant of the "secret solidity" of his work. He then goes even further in his linkage of Debussy to "true" tradition by proposing that there has not been a comparable master in France since François Couperin. Debussy's "youth" is over, he continues, and this has resulted inevitably in not only greater maturity and equilibrium but a reconciliation with real "life":[63] his style is now tight, determined, affirmative, and full; it has, in sum, followed a necessary evolution to the point of becoming "classic." Here Laloy draws a direct comparison with tendencies both in literature and in visual art—with their proclivity toward a greater "construction" as well as probity of design. Debussy, he claims, is thus within the line of evolution of all French art, of what is "truly" French—moving toward an essentially classic model.[64] Significantly, Laloy's argument was not distant from that of the Action Française, which held that the laws of equilibrium are the condition of true or "classic" art. As we may recall, it also argued that a work must contain an interior harmony, an elementary truth which the Romantic revolt had either disdained or simply forgot.

Debussy was pleased with Laloy's interpretation and explication of his work, as becomes clear in a letter to Laloy of April 29, 1909. Here he states directly and succinctly, "Vous êtes le seul qui sachiez ce qu'est Claude Debussy, sans grosse caisse ni broderies"[65] (You are the only one who knows who Claude Debussy is, without bass drums or embroideries). Debussy himself had no qualms about admitting that his musical style had changed, and indeed he always welcomed the thought of undergoing stylistic evolution. As he put it revealingly, "There is no greater pleasure than going to the depth of oneself, setting one's whole being in motion to seek for new and hidden treasures. What a joy to find something new within oneself; something that surprises even ourselves."[66] Debussy's goal remained to seek an identity by adhering to instinct, which he came increasingly to identify with pure "French blood." This, as we have noted, would cause consternation among his followers, who preferred that he remain in the earlier style that they admired and had made the focus of a cult. The problem, however, would grow even more intense in the course of the next few years as the war between the contentious "chapelles" escalated and reached its peak.

By 1906 Debussy was chafing against the barriers of the opposing cliques, a frustration on which he elaborated at length in several different letters. On March 10, 1906, he wrote to Louis Laloy, reflecting on the aesthetic result of the pernicious battle of values now in full force: "La musique est présentement divisée en tas

de petites républiques où chacun s'evertue à crier plus fort" (Music is presently divided into so many little republics where each struggles to cry louder). He also remarks to Laloy about the amount being written on music and on the fact that now
artists themselves feel compelled to expand at length on aesthetic issues.[67] He
himself, of course, was by no means exempt from this very trend or aloof from the
issues and battles being propagated by figures like Mauclair and Laloy. Debussy
understood well how the politics of this musical culture worked and passed the
benefit of his knowledge on to his stepson and pupil, Raoul Bardac. In a letter to
Raoul of 1906, he explains the reality of these cliques and their power, attempting
to comfort him after having a piece rejected by the Société Nationale. This hap-
pened, he explains, because Raoul does not belong to one of the "parties"; however, pointing out their "nullity," he presents this as an advantage.[68]

Debussy thus seized every possible occasion to confound the established
"parties," including that of his own admirers, from association with whom he
fled. By 1907 his tastes were becoming increasingly distant from those of this
group in terms of musical style, as well as in literature and drama. Now he considered composing a version of the old Tristan legend—but one that did not "de-
form" the historical nature and legendary character of the story. It was undoubtedly through Laloy, a former pupil of the politically conservative medievalist
Joseph Bédier, that he discovered Bédier's adaptation of the legend of Tristan and
Isolde. Although the project never succeeded, it nevertheless remained in Debussy's thoughts as a serious possibility for an opera over the next several years.
In 1909 he was working on a libretto for the opera himself and was still concerned with the plans for it as late as 1912. Debussy's "rivalry," as a Frenchman,
with Wagner was still alive, as it had been in his *Pelléas* and in humorous reference to the composer in works like his "Golliwog's Cakewalk."[69]

Now, more than ever, Debussy was absorbed by the question of an "authentic
tradition," as shown in his writings and interviews, as well as his musical language and style. His interest in Rameau grew increasingly strong, further encouraged, perhaps, by the promotion of Rameau at the Schola and by the studies of his
friend Laloy. Yet the sources of this emulation were deeper than a mere admiration for Rameau's style: by invoking it, Debussy was identifying himself with the
cultural values for which Rameau stood. Within the rhetoric being propagated by
d'Indy, Laloy, the Monarchist press, and Debussy himself, Rameau represented the
"purest," unadulterated French tradition. This, of course, was to ignore the
strong Italian influence on Rameau's style and his ability to integrate the techniques and innovations of other great European composers. But if Rameau for
them all was a "myth," essential to the tactics of their cultural politics, he was for
Debussy an "instrumental" myth that stimulated his creative imagination. Again,
typically, Debussy sought intellectual confirmation for what was already emerging in his own creative personality and aesthetic. This perhaps accounts for his
virtual identification with Rameau, his tendency to view himself as the great composer's modern reincarnation.

In a letter to Laloy of 1906, Debussy is explicit about his perception of the
cultural meaning of Rameau's musical style. He contrasts Rameau's "goût parfait"
and "élégance stricte" with contemporary taste, which he perceives as sullied and

characterizes disdainfully as "cette mélasse cosmopolite" (this cosmopolitan murk).[70] As we have seen, such terminology was currently being popularized by, among other groups, the Action Française, and denoted the "un-French," the impure, and, often, specifically the Jewish. As with his interests in non-Western music, Debussy here overlooked the contradiction inherent in the fact that this statement came from someone who was married to a Jewish woman. For his creativity required the myth, as a source of identity and direction; like d'Indy's, his anti-Semitism was "de principe" and could overlook Jewish friends.

Debussy's conviction that his "national instinct" was that of Rameau appears not just in his critical writings but in his creative work as well. In 1907, as part of the first volume of his series of *Images* for piano, Debussy included a small piece entitled explicitly, "Hommage à Rameau." The work is neither a parody nor a syntactical imitation of eighteenth-century style but rather an attempt to reinterpret Rameau's musical values in Debussy's own idiom. The stately rhythm, the punctilious attention to sonority and color, the graceful and expressive melodic treatment, the texture—all evoke the eighteenth-century master's style. But Debussy's identification with Rameau was both technical and aesthetic, as he would later make explicit in his articles on Rameau before the war. In them he praises Rameau's discovery of harmonic "moments" to caress the ear, as opposed to the mere propagation of easily understood academic formulae. As Debussy observes, "Rameau's major contribution to music was that he knew how to find a sensibility within the harmony itself; and that he succeeded in capturing effects of color and certain nuances that, before his time, musicians did not clearly understand."[71] Rameau thus provides a justification or Debussy's own musical values, which he was now increasingly attempting to identify as quintessentially "French."

The past for Debussy was a source not of nostalgia but of inspiration: his goal was to grasp the mood and character of its music within his personal style. Hence orthodoxy or respect for the "rules" derived from the "masters" as taught at the Schola, its concern with rediscovering great "laws," was never tenable for Debussy. His hatred of orthodoxy, as we have seen, was bound to his social liminality, his inability to identify with a culture, class, or dogma—his quest for "freedom." And yet, he required a conceptual base, a set of values capacious enough to suggest a direction, to "root" his personality—and this is what French nationalism provided. But Debussy's brand of nationalism, as it emerged in his creative work, was as unique and personal as his interpretation of its primary musical icon, Rameau.

Models and Inspirations

There were, however, other figures in Debussy's nationalist Pantheon, figures through which he expressed his political engagement and explored his artistic "roots." It was amid the atmosphere of nationalist agitation and the concomitant political tensions that, in 1908, Debussy completed his *Trois chansons de Charles d'Orléans*. The work, in fact, was begun in the period when the Schola was providing the artistic lead in the return to the music of the past, in part, for political reasons. Debussy had already set the first two poems in 1898, but he did not return to complete and publish the set until 1908. It had taken ten years for the psychological and political moment again to be right, although after *Pelléas* Debussy had been rediscovering French poets of the distant past. His two "Rondels" of 1904 are set to texts of Charles d'Orléans and his *Promenoir des deux amants* to poems by the seventeenth-century French poet Tristan Lhermite.

The *Trois chansons,* ostensibly inspired by the high Renaissance masters, are set for unaccompanied chorus, but in a provocatively inconsistent style; although its harmonic language is clearly not that of the Renaissance period, its contrapuntal texture—which shocked the Debussystes—most unashamedly is.[72] The first of the pieces is motet-like in style, employing imitation and modal harmonies; the second (of 1908) suggests Jannequin and employs Renaissance word-painting; the third, more chromatic and varied in texture, displays Debussy's knowledge of the historical evolution of music and is closer to the late madrigal style.[73] Here, as in his previous works, Debussy consciously illustrates the way in which the past need not be a rigid model but can be a living source of inspiration for the present.

Debussy had much to say about the wrong kinds of uses of the past, both in his letters and criticism and in his incisive musical commentary. Despite his "traditionalism," Debussy's opposition to dogma or "chapelles" was to become even stronger as the tensions between the "camps" grew ever more intense. This becomes particularly evident in his controversial *Images* for orchestra, which was composed between the years 1905 and 1912.[74] In 1908, while at work on the score, Debussy wrote to his editor, Jacques Durand, describing what he was attempting to do stylistically in the work:

> J'essaie de faire "autre chose"—en quelque sorte, des réalités—ce que les imbéciles appellent "impressionnisme," terme aussi mal employé que possible, surtout par les critiques d'art qui n'hésitent pas à en affubler Turner, le plus beau créateur de mystère qui soit en art.[75]
>
> (I'm trying to do "something else"—in a sense, realities—what imbeciles call "impressionism," a term as badly employed as possible, above all by art critics who do not hesitate to attach Turner to it, the most beautiful creator of mystery in art that there is.)

Debussy no more liked the label "impressionist" now than he had earlier in that phase of his career when he concentrated on setting French Symbolist texts. The "realities" here were of several sorts, relating not only to the subjects but also to the suggestive material incorporated, as well as to the resonant techniques employed. Each of the pieces refer to a country, or more properly to a "nationality"—to England in "Gigues," to Spain in "Ibéria," and to France in "Rondes du Printemps." "Gigues" employs material that relates to a traditional Northumberland song, "The Keel Row," although in an untraditional manner, distorted by unexpected modulation.[76] Most provocative of all is his treatment of the material used in the "Rondes du Printemps," which represents and mocks all that Debussy deplored in contemporary French culture. One element of this was its lack of "purity"; the work begins with an inscription from material that is not French but is drawn from an old Tuscan song.[77] He then does introduce an authentic old French popular song entitled "Nous n'irons plus au bois," just as the Scholistes had long recommended: but Debussy proceeds to put it tortuously through the various "academic" procedures that were emphasized at the Schola, particularly rhythmic transformations.[78] Throughout the work he thus uses, and distorts, material that was either systematically banned by nationalists (like himself) or recommended by the less imaginative.

Debussy's projection of an ironic attitude in his music angered several groups, including the Debussystes and, as we might expect, the Scholistes. Gaston Carraud responded immediately by devoting an article to the question of the evolution of Debussy's musical style in the *Revue S.I.M.* Here he observes that, ever since *Pelléas,* Debussy has disappointed his original supporters, and, indeed, a different group is now gaining enthusiasm for his work.[79] As we might anticipate, one of these—Laloy—leaped to Debussy's defense, writing also in the *Revue S.I.M.*, in August–September, 1910. Once again he acknowledges the fact that Debussy's style has substantially changed but argues that his recent works have all been examples of a new, more "substantial" type of art.[80]

Debussy's irony in returning to the use of blatantly academic techniques may have been a satire of the Schola, but, once again like Charpentier, they were also a cruel self-irony. Indeed, this was the period of Debussy's increasing reconciliation with those very academic and official institutions that he had once so vociferously denounced. They were, after all, unequivocally a part of the nation's tradition and culture, and, as the nation veered to the center and the Right, Debussy became less aloof toward them. In February 1909, through the concerted efforts of Gabriel Fauré, he was appointed to the Conseil Supérieur of the musical section of the Conservatoire.[81] Part of his responsibility was to adjudicate competitions, and it was within this context that he wrote the clarinet piece for the 1910 competition. The irony is that only two years before, in a public interview, Debussy had condemned the state for instituting competitions in almost every field, including music.[82] This, of course, had long been a theme of the cultural politics of the Right in France, which believed in a natural hierarchy, as opposed to "careers open to talent." This competitive system was indeed how Debussy, not in the hierarchy by either privilege or birth, had been educated in music and achieved his first acclaim. Now he was both "outside" and "inside," as he had been in some manner throughout his life, sharing the experiences but not the culture of the group into which he had moved.

By 1911 Debussy was also serving on an important jury—that of the Crescent Prize, awarded for symphonic composition, a genre that he had professed to despise. Other members of the jury included official composers such as Fauré, Bruneau, Vidal, Dukas, Erlanger, and Gédalge. Moreover, it was Debussy himself, together with Paul Vidal, who agreed to play the works at the piano for the other members of the jury to hear. Two years later he again served on the jury and once more agreed to read the works submitted at the keyboard, this time with Gabriel Pierné.[83] Perhaps in Debussy's mind such active participation was a significant way in which he could help determine the future direction of French music, a subject now of great personal concern.

Throughout this period Debussy's efforts at "self-improvement" continued, and, given his recent interests and roles, it is no surprise that his reading matter changed. By 1906 he was reporting to Laloy (who may have been guiding his choices) that he was engrossed in reading the work of Paul Simon. Simon, a philosopher and politician of the late nineteenth century, was the author of a number of books on the condition of the working class. This indeed would be in keeping with the range of interests that Debussy had exhibited when discussing the timely question of the "people's theater," three years before. By 1909 he was reading the English conservative thinker Thomas Carlyle, to whom he made reference in a letter to André Caplet on August 25, 1909. In the letter he speaks, in part facetiously, of reading this early-nineteenth-century social philosopher as part of "le traitement que je dois suivre chaque matin"[84] (part of the treatment that I must follow every morning).

The following year Debussy returned to the poets of France's distant past, this time to François Villon, the French Humanist of the fifteenth century. In his *Trois ballades de François Villon* he once again blithely ignores the doctrinal orthodoxies of the warring "chapelles," regardless of the price he would pay. He employs both modality and counterpoint associated with the Schola Cantorum, but in order to set the kind of text—from the Renaissance—that it would have decried. And, to complicate matters further, he concerned himself with the appearance of the score, directing that the typescript itself be evocative of the fifteenth century.[85] But while critics like Emile Vuillermoz were castigating the overzealous concern with tradition, or the "anachronistic aspirations" of the Schola, Debussy was evoking the past musically in his own way. He thus was carefully positioning himself between the two poles of the French musical world—those who wished to recreate or return to the past, building carefully upon it, and the young iconoclasts of the S.M.I.

But Debussy's strategies in the period of the wars between ideologies and musical "camps" grew even more devious and caused no end of dissention among French critics. This was particularly true of his provocative "pseudoreligious" work, *Le Martyr de Saint Sébastien,* which he composed in 1911. The piece was the product of a collaboration with the politically reactionary Italian poet Gabrielle d'Annunzio, to whom Debussy now became close. Although the commission for it was from the Russian dancer Ida Rubenstein, Debussy's motivation to participate came in part from his attraction to the poet. But Debussy was probably also drawn to the project because of the occasion it provided to invoke the Renaissance contrapuntal style, an object of admiration since his stay in Rome.[86] Sounding like a Scholiste, Debussy declared in an interview in *Excelsior* that true religious music ceased to exist after the sixteenth century. After this, he said, the "fresh, child-like souls of the time" disappeared, along with their "untainted fervor in music free from worldliness."[87]

Was he being facetious here, or at least disingenuous? Indeed his invocation of religion, not out of belief, but as a means of social conservation, recalls the Action Française. Maurras, a rationalist, held a similar position, although there were apparently limits to what the league would tolerate in terms of patently "sacrilegious behavior." *Le Martyr* received a largely negative review in Action

Française's affiliated journal, the *Revue critique des idées et des livres,* in 1911, upon its premiere: it disapproved not only of d'Annunzio (who was an ardent Wagnerian) but particularly of the woman who commissioned and danced the work, Ida Rubenstein, who was Jewish. The journal not only condemned the dancing as sacrilegious but went on to denounce the fact that it was "subventionné par les Juifs."[88]

Yet critics close to Action Française did not criticize Debussy, and indeed from this point on the movement was increasingly to laud the composer's work. Writing in the Catholic *La Croix illustrée,* the Abbé F. Brun, whose works were later performed at the Schola d'Action Française, praised *Le Martyr's* musical style. In particular, he drew attention to the frequent use of Gregorian models and paid hommage to the composer's "lofty conception" of religious music.[89] Debussy's music had finally found its own bastion of ideological support, although occasionally sympathetic Republican critics would continue to interpret similar qualities in different ways. But, significantly, Debussy would not object to French nationalist support for his art; indeed, his own rhetoric came now increasingly to approximate that of the Action Française. Just as for Vincent d'Indy, the aesthetic and the ideological realms became more and more inextricably intertwined for Debussy as he matured. But again, this did not compel Debussy to follow the musical dogma that institutions such as the Schola had developed from a nationalist position.

Despite the praise for Debussy in the right-wing Catholic press, however, *Le Martyr,* as a piece for the stage, ultimately did not meet with the Church's approval. Objecting not simply to the text but to the representation of the saint by a woman and a Jew, the Archbishop of Paris condemned it as "offensive to Christian consciousness."[90] Beyond its condemnation by the Church, the other aspect of the work that drew attention and commentary from the contemporary press was its pronounced return to "tradition." Paul de Stoecklin, in the *Courrier musical,* pointed out: "And now he is writing tonal music with characteristic themes, full of common chords that recalls *Parsifal.*" Those who had considered Debussy's earlier work to be "too insubstantial" were, to the contrary, pleased, particularly Alfred Bruneau (in *Le Matin*) and Gaston Carraud (in *La Liberté*).[91] As with *Pelléas,* the very same qualities were being construed in critical frameworks that were diametrically opposed, each tied to a distinct ideological creed.

Debussy as "Classic"

From this point on, the press was increasingly to emphasize Debussy's "classic" qualities," although the composer had his own distinctive conception of what the "classic" comprised. In 1908, when asked why he was so hostile to the "classics," Debussy replied by raising the still volatile issues of what, precisely, "classic" means: "What do you call classics? . . . most of these are classics in spite of themselves, and that quality has been forced upon them without their knowledge, consent, or even expectation."[92] Clearly, for Debussy, a composer to whom "classic" qualities were being attributed by a number of different groups, this was a highly sensitive issue. By 1912 Emile Vuillermoz (recalling Louis Laloy before) was referring to Debussy in the *Revue S.I.M.* as the "petit fils de Rameau."[93]

Although Debussy would not object to being placed in this canon because of all that it represented culturally, there were other canons that apparently he did not wish to enter. The very same year an attempt was made to make Debussy academically acceptable by construing his harmonic language as being built on a recognized, traditional foundation. In 1912 René Lenormand sent his soon to be published book *Etude sur l'harmonie moderne* to a number of the composers he discussed for their commentary. Debussy, while not negative about the author's treatment of him, was clearly guarded and notably unenthusiastic about the book.[94] He now found himself in the midst of a concerted attempt once more to categorize his music, to impose an inappropriate intellectual order upon it.

But it was continually resisting such order. Works like his two books of *Preludes* for piano (1910 and 1913) recall Rameau and Couperin in stressing traditionally French pictorial qualities. At times (unnationalistically), however, they evoke the Orient and Spain in an advanced, if heterogeneous harmonic idiom, which includes the use of bitonality. This tension with nationalist orthodoxy would continue to activate his works and become prominent in his wartime compositions such as the *Etudes* for piano and the sonatas (which fall outside the range of this study).

The unfortunate attempt to force one-sided coherence on his oeuvre was, in part, the result of the desire to justify it as "French," within the context of the current politicized discourses. As we have seen, this was already highly problematic at the turn of the century, when Debussy seemed to fit into none of the categorical conceptions of the "French." But now, given his change in style and his own rhetoric (as well as that of Laloy), there was no question that he deserved this label—the problem was the conceptual limitations it imposed. As we saw, in each of the "camps" this label involved a process of exclusion, of an excision of those elements of his style that lay outside their conception of "the French."

Debussy himself could see that, despite his own pronounced nationalist sympathies, these discursive systems that attempted to "construct" him as an artist led to a "selection" that continued to distort his style.[95] But they equally distorted his aesthetic, for to argue that his music belonged in the canon implied that he considered it to be concert music in the "grand" tradition. This was a conception that Debussy deplored, as he persisted in attacking "la grande musique," or the "serious" music in traditional form, as propagated at the Schola Cantorum. Given his background and his confused identity, in social and cultural terms, it is not difficult to see why this conception was such an anathema to him: it represented a body of works on a specific cultural "level," imbued with all the other undesirable traits that this, in turn, implied. Hence Debussy, as well as the "Debussytes," following in the master's footsteps, praised the "galant" and graceful, the desire "humbly to please," as distinctively French.[96] As we recall, this challenged the original goals of the Société Nationale de Musique Française, which attempted to disprove the German slander that the French were essentially "frivolous." For Debussy, the desire to please belonged to no one cultural level: it was the property of the national spirit and hence made no such class distinctions.

The label of "classic" also implied that Debussy was a staunch traditionalist, which, as we have seen, was true, but in a highly individual sense. Once more,

his traditionalism transcended "schools," and it never prevented him from identifying with the spirit and values of the past through his own unique technical
means. Debussy's response to Igor Stravinsky's *Le Sacre du printemps* is revealing,
for, in the midst of his turn to the past, it illuminates his reaction to truly radical
innovation. In 1912 he wrote to Stravinsky concerning the latter's recent performance of the work at the piano, for selected company, at the home of Laloy:

> Cela me hante comme un beau cauchemar et j'essaie vraiment d'en retrouver la terri-
> ble impression. C'est pourquoi j'en attends la représentation comme un enfant gour-
> mand auquel on aurait promis des confitures.[97]

> (It haunts me like a beautiful nightmare, and I truly try to recapture the terrible im-
> pression. That is why I await the performance like a gluttonous child to whom sweets
> have been promised.)

Either Debussy was being disingenuous and manipulative—which was not
atypical—or his position did change when he experienced the performance, as
we shall soon see.

But the positive tone of Debussy's letter might also have been influenced by
the significant fact that he was enclosing the proofs for his own ballet commissioned by Diaghilev, entitled *Jeux*. Although Debussy had been unhappy with
Nijinsky's choreography of *L'Aprés-midi d'un faune* the previous year, Laloy, who
admired Diaghilev and Stravinsky, encouraged the connection.[98] *Jeux* provided
Debussy with the opportunity to rival Stravinsky, and once more to refute the "impressionist" label, to confound his followers and to explore a new path. For Debussy, creativity was a constant process of "self-reinvention," and of finding new
ways or techniques to realize those values he believed to be "French." Confronted
by to those who considered the "classic"—the very essence of "Frenchness"—to
be inseparable from specific procedures and forms, he could prove precisely the
opposite.

Debussy's style in the work is a world apart from that of *Le Martyr de Saint
Sébastien,* for here he investigates a new set of radically experimental harmonic
and orchestral techniques. Indeed, his tendency throughout this period was either to maintain a high tension between tradition and innivation in a work or to
jump forward after having grounded himself in the past. In the course of *Jeux,* for
example, he superimposes major and minor seconds which briefly, at least, seem
to generate a kind of polytonal effect.[99] Moreover, the orchestration employs not
only pointallistic effects but also woodwind timbres and even folklike themes
that recall *Le Sacre du printemps.*

Jeux premiered at the Théâtre des Champs-Elysées on May 15, 1913, and,
predictably, given the direction of taste toward the "traditional," it was not a
success. As we have noted, in the acrimonious battle between the warring
"chapelles," as the threat of war approached, the traditionalists were clearly in the
ascendance. For Debussy, himself a part of the nationalist aesthetic and political
tide, *Jeux* was to remain a bold but isolated technical experiment. Although he
did not cease to experiment harmonically during the war, as he had before, it
would generally be within the framework of genres that were anchored in the

past. Indeed, the same year as *Jeux*, Debussy retreated, producing his *Trois poèmes de Stéphane Mallarmé*, in which he returns to broad melodic outlines in the vocal part. Yet, despite the fact that the second song employs a slow minuet rhythm in the accompaniment, he pointedly defined his traditionalism, once more, against that of the Schola's dogma. According to Léon Vallas, the biographer and a personal friend of Debussy, he quipped, "I venture to say that they do not stock this article on the rue Saint-Jacques."[100]

Debussy's musical traditionalism was unique—rooted not in the re-use of forms but rather in what Laloy incisively described as an instinctive conception of what was "French." In other words, descending into himself, in the deepest and most fundamental sense, was for Debussy, as for Barrès, a descent into the basic characteristics of his nationality, or "race." Hence, some of his verbal utterances, clearly within the framework of nationalist discourse, do bear a loose relation to the concepts being realized in his art. In his political ideas we find a recurring emphasis on race, that which issues from what he considered to be unalloyed or "pure French blood." As we have seen, this was the only sense in which Debussy was able to feel that he belonged to a larger cultural unit or collective group identity. Indeed, well before the war, discussions of race and music were pervasive in nationalistic circles, especially among partisans of the Action Française. Already it was treating race not as a simple synonym for national features (as in previous periods) but as a synthesis of culture and blood.

We may perceive this tendency in Debussy's private correspondence concerning Paul Dukas's successful opera, *Ariane et Barbe bleue*. In a letter of May 8, 1907, to Dukas, he praises the work, while in another, this one to Jacques Durand the following year, his response is different. In the latter, Debussy notes Pierre Lalo's attack on the "invertebrate descendants of *Pelléas*." But what disgruntles him here is the nature of Lalo's praise for Dukas. The critic apparently referred to *Ariane et Barbe bleue* as a positive embodiment of "les qualités essentielles de l'esprit de l'art français" (the essential qualities of the spirit of French art). Debussy feels compelled to point out:

> Ce que je trouve de plus pénible dans cette histoire, c'est la bassesse des moyens employés et qu'en somme le 'bon Juif' soit défendu par le "mauvais Jésuite."[101]
>
> (What I find the most distressing in this matter is the baseness of the means employed and that in sum the "good Jew" is defended by the "bad Jesuit.")

By 1912, in a letter to Vittorio Gui, Debussy's attitude is clearer. Here he remarks that the opera is a "chef-d'oeuvre, mais ce n'est pas un chef-d'oeuvre de musique française"[102] (a masterpiece, but not a masterpiece of French music). Perhaps because of his marriage to a Jewish woman, Debussy would not say in public that he did not believe art by a French Jew to be "French" but could confide such feelings in private.

The theme of race became predominant in Debussy's writings immediately preceding the war, which were often published in the *Revue musicale S.I.M.* In 1913, for example, apropos of the influence of César Franck, whom Debussy considered not French but Flemish, he made the following trenchant comment:

> Croire que les qualités particulières au génie d'une race sont transmissibles à une autre race, sans dommage, est une erreur qui a faussé notre musique assez souvent.
>
> (To believe that the qualities particular to the genius of a race are transmissible to another race, without damage, is an error that has falsified our music often enough.)

Once more, this sounds very much like the rhetoric being diffused by the Action Française, particularly his remark that the French should return "au rythme de notre pensée."[103] The league, as we have seen, like so many French nationalist groups, maintained that the French had a distinct style of thought that was a basic attribute of their blood or "race." This had been a major issue in the debate over the "Nouvelle Sorbonne," and here it was recurring, this time in the context of creativity or art.

Debussy's ambiguous conception of race, which fused national cultural traits with "blood," or genetic characteristics, was not unique and would not soon disappear. It would become even more widely spread in the course of the First World War, when nationalist fervor reached its highest pitch, extending to even more groups.[104] Debussy was to end his life no longer on the cultural margins, the peripheries of several different social groups, but in the center of his national culture. He had finally located an identity, one that would provide direction for his later style without hindering his compulsive need to remain free of all constituted cultural dogma.

SATIE'S CREATIVE POLITICS

The case of Erik Satie provides a highly illuminating comparison, for we may identify important parallels with and differences from that of Claude Debussy. Satie suffered from many of the problems that afflicted his friend Debussy—problems endemic to the social, cultural, and musical worlds in which they both lived. Like Debussy, he was to suffer from a "liminal" social identity, as well as from exposure to a plurality of cultures, to none of which he felt he belonged. His cultural alienation similarly led to an inherent antagonism toward any kind of authority structure or dogmatic point of view. Satie also preferred to say "something other," to avoid all dogma, in the interest of maintaining a perspective on the relative, an objective vision. But he too would be victimized by the "guerre des chapelles," the misrepresentation of his art by those factions that wished to use it to prove their own aesthetic point.

Like Debussy, Satie's response would be an ironic "play" with musical meanings and codes to express his own distance from the dogma of the contentious "chapelles."[105] He too would manipulate the connotations of specific styles, particularly at that moment when the battle reached its height and the Traditionalist victory seemed certain. Finally, like Debussy, Satie defined his own version of a political stance, and the stylistic tactics he devised to articulate it would also be unique. Both composers drew creative inspiration from the inherent tension between their independent, "unrooted" personalities and the musical dogma their political orientations implied. For Satie, as for Claude Debussy, the context of this

musical culture in the period preceding the war illuminates the seeming para-
doxes of his life and his art.

From the very beginning, Erik Satie lived between several different worlds,
none of which provided him with a firm emotional or cultural base. He was born
in Normandy (in Honfleur) of an English, Protestant mother and a Catholic, An-
glophile father, who was a maritime broker by profession. Erik's mother died
when he was four, and his grandparents took custody of the child and raised him
themselves while his father went off to settle and work in Paris. Since the child
had been baptized an Anglican, they promptly had him re-baptized a Catholic;
even though his grandmother was pious, his grandfather was an "unbeliever."
Perhaps the strongest influence on the child was an eccentric uncle known as
"Seabird," who, together with the boy's quixotic father, probably served as a
prominent role model.[106]

Like Debussy's, Satie's first exposure to music was through the Catholic
Church, where both were introduced at a very young age to chant, and thus to
the Gregorian modes. As soon as he was old enough, Erik was sent to the local
church for piano lessons with its organist, who had been a pupil of Louis Niedermeyer. But Erik's young life would soon undergo a series of jolting ruptures, beginning with the death of his grandmother in 1878 and the consequent religious
conversion of his grandfather. Now Erik was sent to live with his father, still in
Paris, who, disillusioned with traditional education, decided to undertake the
child's education himself. He accomplished this by taking Erik to lectures and
classes at the Collège de France and later engaging a tutor to instruct him privately in Latin and Greek.

The child's idyllic life was jolted once more when, in 1879, his father married
a piano teacher and former student at the Paris Conservatoire. This has led to
some speculation that, since Satie soon came to hate her, his subsequent defiance
and distrust of the Conservatoire stemmed ultimately from this source.[107] Erik
was sent to the Conservatoire (in 1879) to study piano and solfège, and he finally
graduated to the study of harmony in 1885. In 1886, however, he was forced to
leave Paris for Arras to serve his mandatory military service in the Thirty-third
Infantry Division. Unable to adjust to the experience, he solved the problem by
bringing on an illness through exposing himself, while almost naked, to extreme
cold temperatures. He became so sick as to obtain a prompt release, and by 1887
he was composing and published his first work—a set of waltzes.[108]

This was easily accomplished, for now both his parents were involved with
music, having opened their own school of music, a venture that, however,
quickly failed. They subsequently purchased a stationery store, to which they
added a counter for music, but his father soon abandoned this venture to become
a publisher of music. This allowed him to publish some of the early songs that
Erik had written, along with café-concert tunes and some compositions of Erik's
friends. Already Satie, like Debussy, cared little for the notion of cultural levels, or
for the notion of a serious "grande musique," as opposed to the "petite." But
none of father Satie's enterprises yielded a financial profit and so in time the elder
Satie lost his modest inheritance, just as the younger was soon to do.[109]

By 1887, Erik had discovered "bohemian" culture and began frequenting the

Chat Noir cabaret, becoming its second pianist in 1891. A strong influence on him now was D.-V. Fumet, a pupil of Franck who had lost his scholarship because of his "advanced" musical and political ideas, which included Anarchist sympathies. Also highly influential on Satie in this period was a young writer of Spanish origin who called himself J.-P. Contamine de Latour. It was the latter who introduced Satie to the work of Gustave Flaubert, as well as to the Rosicrucian movement, led by Josephin Péladon.[110] Satie, raised to be independent and autodidactic, now spent much of his time at the Bibliothèque Nationale, reading Violet le Duc on Gothic architecture. For he, like Satie, had a purely secular interest in the Gothic style; the architect, a left-wing Republican (of the early Third Republic), was attracted to its inherent rationality.

For Satie the appeal was precisely the opposite, although again without religious connotations: it was the mystical, atemporal quality of medieval music that so drew him. Works like *Ogives* suggest Gregorian chant, although somewhat facetiously—imitating its fluid rhythm, its texture of solo and response, and its lack of cadential articulation. This "faux naïveté" also appears in his *Gymnopédies,* written in 1888 (under the influence of Flaubert's *Salambo*) and his *Gnossiennes* of 1889.[111] These works were followed by a move to "bohemian" Montmartre in 1890, where Satie met Debussy at the Auberge de Clou and soon also met Péladon. Now he began to set Péladon's texts, beginning with his Wagnerian-influenced drama *Le Fils des étoiles,* for which Satie wrote the incidental music. The following year he wrote more music for the so-called Sâr Péladon, but now specifically for his Rosicrucian movement, *Sonneries de la Rose-Croix.* At the same time, however, as Debussy was also eventually to do, Satie considered setting his own unique version of the old Tristan legend. But for Satie, this was *Le Bâtard de Tristan,* an opera that he began to plan, but apparently never completed, to the text by Albert Trinchant.[112]

Satie, however, did complete a purportedly Christian ballet, *Uspud,* already again seeking out the inherently contradictory, with the whimsical Contamine de Latour. In the first of many provocative gestures and challenges to official institutions, Satie boldly sent the ballet to the current director of the Opéra, Bertrand. However, the composer experienced the humiliation of not even receiving an acknowledgment of the work, and he promptly proceeded to challenge the director of the Opéra to a duel. Moreover, he subsequently published the work with a false announcement on the title page that it had been performed at the Paris opera in 1892. But this behavior, however eccentric, was not completely unique: Satie had models, first in Péladon himself, who had proposed his own works to the Comédie Française.[113] Another source was surely the culture of the Montmartre cabarets and the peculiar brand of cabaret humor that Satie had promptly absorbed. Characteristic of such humor was the practice of lavishing praise on one's own achievement, as well as of assuming the pose of a moralist lamenting the depravity of the world. But most characteristic was a parody of the academic world, and indeed of every kind of official cultural pedantry. Long before Satie, humorists, prominent among whom was Alphonse Allais, were systematically engaging in this particular brand of cabaret humor.[114]

We can see a similar pose reflected in several of Satie's projects, as well as in specific acts or gestures throughout the 1890s. In 1892, for example, he founded his own facetious church, the so-called Eglise Métropolitaine de l'Art de Jésus Conducteur. His stated goal was to combat those "who have neither convictions nor beliefs, not a thought in their souls or a principle in their hearts." This was a particularly trenchant irony for the nihilistic Satie, whose only "culture" at the time was that of cabaret humor, or farcical absurdity. Just as ridiculous is his diatribe against the culprits who were supposedly behind what he pompously denounced as "the aesthetic and moral decadence of our times." Compounding the farce was his "excommunication" of those whom he considered to be his "enemies," including Lugné Poé, Alexandre Natanson, and the music critic "Willy."[115] The latter was undoubtedly included for having publicly reproached Satie for being the musician officially associated with the "Sâr" Péladon. This was only the beginning of a series of hostile confrontations and bitter exchanges between the two men, whose political and cultural stances would grow diametrically opposed.[116]

Like his father, Satie soon managed to deplete his modest inheritance through a series of short-lived fanciful ventures, none of which ever yielded a profit. While still presiding over his "church," he published a series of accompanying pamphlets, as well as a facetious paper titled the *Carticulaire de l'Eglise*. He also participated in a literary circle grouped around the journal *Le Coeur,* edited by Jules Bois and devoted to "esoterisme" in literature, science, and art. But then, in 1895, followed a brief period of seemingly authentic religious conversion (recalling that of his grandfather) during which Satie published his *Messe des pauvres* for organ.[117] Here, as in the ballet *Uspud,* the upper line is derived from ancient Greek modes, and the progression of chords is essentially free of established tonal conventions. And here, too, there is no development in any traditional academic sense; it is replaced instead with simple repetition, and symmetry alone defines the form.[118] Satie was clearly outside the culture that propagated academic conventions and was absorbed by the mysticism that Mauclair had seen as the earliest escape from "le culte de moi." His eventual path, like Debussy's, would lead him toward an engagement with the social and political world, although from a diametrically opposed perspective.

Satie, too, was going through a social transformation in this period: his financial status was declining so precipitously that he was forced to move outside Paris. His new home was the working-class suburb of Arceuil, an environment to which he gradually grew close and that would eventually provide him with another element in his cultural alloy. This move was accompanied by two changes of "costume," changes that were both a part of his social "poses" and, like Debussy, a quest for a public social identity. He switched from a "bohemian" costume to one of grey velours, but by 1900 he had switched once more to his henceforth distinguishing garb: in the midst of this workers' suburb, he assumed the costume that has been variously described as that of a "petit fonctionnaire" and that of a teacher of physics at a provincial lycée.[119] For Satie, social identity, like musical language and prose, was to be a game, although a serious one, beneath the seeming facade of simple farce. All were a means to question or test current ideas of reality and representation; eventually, through such "play," he, like Debussy, would confound established dogma.

Satie's compositions now were varied and ignored the distinctions of cultural "levels": he wrote chansons for the popular Vincent Hyspa, as well as for "la reine de la valse lente," Paulette Darty.[120] But the most significant and revealing work of this period is his *Geneviève de Brabant,* written with "Lord Cheminot"—alias Contamine de Latour—in 1899. This was the first of Satie's works in which he played a new game of "style," one that would become more complex as he discovered the meanings born of cultural politics. Here, the game is to go back and forth between the styles associated with "la grande" and "la petite musique," like Debussy effacing the rationale of the distinction. But, for Satie, this juxtaposition of styles from "high" and "popular" art would eventually involve a game of citations that carried a deeper cultural meaning.

It has been speculated that Satie and de Latour were inspired by the concert version of Schumann's *Genoveva,* performed in the Salle d'Harcourt in 1894. It has also been suggested that another motivation for Satie was Debussy's *Pelléas et Mélisande,* with which Satie may have felt competitive in this period. Indeed, both composers were interested in Maurice Maeterlinck, and both had already expressed a desire to make an opera out of his earlier successful play, *La Princesse Maleine.*[121] There are, in fact, striking points of resemblance between *Geneviève* and Debussy's *Pellèas,* including the setting—a forest in the Middle Ages—and the character of a vulnerable long-haired young woman victimized by male cruelty. In addition, it even employs the same names—phonetically—for the villain, who here is Golo; and both Maeterlinck and "Lord Cheminot" borrowed their principal characters from popular tradition.[122]

But Satie's work roots itself more thoroughly in a newer or more recent version of this tradition. The text itself, both in style as well as in visual presentation, evokes a common kind of fin-de-siècle French popular imagery. But the other predominant influence here is the humor of the cabaret, which appears unequivocally in a number of the specific techniques employed. As in cabaret theater, facts are presented in the opposite order from that in which they occurred, and there are deliberate departures from the historical realities referred to in the work. There are even departures in the legend, especially the end of the story, which depicts not the heroine's pathetic death but, rather, her "rehabilitation."[123]

Most startling of all is the musical style, in which, with studied incongruity, Satie moves between reference to chant-like melodies and those that ineluctably suggest Jacques Offenbach (who composed his own *Geneviève de Brabant*). Why does he juxtapose citations of styles that are thus deprived of their original significance? What is the real intent or purpose of this odd concatenation? Here an analogy is illuminating—an analogy with a genre that was used in the culture to which Satie had been introduced as a child—that of ancient Greece. The ancient Greeks developed a literary genre referred to as "Meneppian discourse," which employs a series of citations from texts that are intended to avoid any unequivocal or "fixed" meaning: as distinct from the postmodern play with styles, originality, and citation, the expressive goal is to suggest the distance of the author from these sources and, consequently, from his own text; this indicates a profound cultural alienation. Later, when Satie's stylistic resources were to expand—at the time of the "guerre des chapelles"—another aspect of the attraction of this genre would emerge. For it was conceived as being a form of literature that was inherently inimical to any kind of authoritarian or ideologically dogmatic society.[124] From Satie's pseudoreligious phase, when he invoked styles with a parodistic intent, he had moved on to an alternative manner of expressing distance, alienation, and the relative.

This was also the period when the tunes and practices commonly associated with the cabaret milieu were another source of inspiration for Satie. One such practice, which he was later to carry to a new extreme (as would Debussy as well), was the use of well-known tunes in new satirical or unusual contexts. This included old chansons such as "Maman les p'tits bateaux," and also revolutionary chansons like "La Carmagnole" and numbers from operetta and opera. All common cultural property (although belonging to different contexts of that culture), they could be creatively mingled into a complex new compound. In this objective manipulation of common references and in his use of mundane materials in disorienting, abstract ways, he anticipates the cubist painters. Compositions such as Satie's *Trois morceaux en forme de poire* of 1903 (a facetious response to the charge that his work had no form) mix melodies drawn from this "popular" repertoire with new or original tunes.[125] In addition, the appearance of Satie's scores now owe much to his roots in the cabaret milieu, especially his practice of providing a running verbal commentary over the staves of the score. Characteristic of Chat Noir scores that were intended to accompany shadow plays are descriptions of the action or characters, together with illustration, running over the music.[126]

By 1905 Satie apparently believed that he had exhausted this vein or that he needed another fund of material and techniques to enrich his style and his "commentary." It has been posited that he grew tired of being dismissed as a "naïf," or an amateur composer; now, wishing for greater professional respect, he decided, at age thirty-nine, to resume his education. But it is particularly important to be aware of how Satie chose to do this: not by the logical method for someone his age—engaging a private instructor—but by making the provocative gesture of enrolling in the Schola Cantorum, at the height of the controversy over it, and, moreover, to study counterpoint.

Numerous colleagues tried to dissuade him, including Debussy and the professor with whom he was to study at the Schola, Albert Roussel.[127] The latter, who saw Satie as a musician of true quality, with a new and rich musical sense, argued that he already possessed a "métier" and thus had nothing to learn. But Satie persisted, and, according to Roussel, this "prodigious musician" became, at the Schola, a tractable, docile, and assiduous student.[128] Satie got along well personally with d'Indy, whom he apparently grew to like, as he himself indicated when reflecting on his experiences at the Schola: "Avec d'Indy j'ai beaucoup travaillé et je conserve le meilleur souvenir des sept années auprès de cet homme, si bon et si simple"[129] (With d'Indy I worked very hard and I retain the best memory of those seven years with this man, so good and so simple). Again, it is not clear whether Satie was here being facetious or accentuating the irony of d'Indy's caring personality toward individuals, as opposed to his ideology.

There is, however, little question as to the facetious nature of the works that

Satie promptly proceeded to compose upon his graduation from the Schola Cantorum. Roussel himself was to admonish Satie not to write "ironiquement," a tendency he immediately perceived in works that Satie composed in this period.[130]
And in 1908 Debussy was to write Francesco de Lacerda, commenting:

> Votre ami E. Satie vient de terminer une fugue où l'ennui se dissimule derrière des
> harmonies malveillantes, dans quoi vous rencontrez la marque de cette discipline si
> particulière à l'établissement cité plus haut.[131]

> (Your friend E. Satie has just finished a fugue where boredom dissimulates itself be-
> hind malicious harmonies, in which you will recognize the mark of that discipline so
> peculiar to the establishment cited above.)

Satie was indeed simultaneously referring to and defying the rules of the Schola,
just as Debussy was to do in his own orchestral *Images*. Both were able through
such means to confound not only the Schola but also, by employing its associated
techniques, those "chapelles" that were hostile to it.

For Satie, the new stylistic references that he could now deploy allowed him
to comment on an even wider spectrum of the cultural and musical world around
him. But these references were to join with the techniques or languages he had
learned in the cabaret, in particular, the running written commentaries and the
use of humorous titles.[132] Such titles can often be read as Satie's own personal
commentary on the dogma that Huré and others had denounced or satirized in
prose: the *Préludes flasques (pour en chien)*, for example, makes fun of Scholiste
training—of its rhetoric of "elevation" and of formal rigor, as well as its favored
techniques. Not only is the implicit message that such formal training is more appropriate to a dog, but the titles and techniques of the pieces betray Satie's perspective on this "chapelle." "Voix d'intérieur" has a double meaning within the
context of the Schola's dogma—it refers not only to the proper behavior of a dog
in the house but to the Schola's doctrine of art as an inner "calling." Further reinforcing the message of such "spiritual" associations is the facetious chorale that
Satie prominently includes in the composition.

The following "Idylle canine" is a revealing contradiction in terms, for this
"scholiste idyl" is, in fact, a rigorous two-part invention. "Avec camaraderie"
probably also makes fun of the doctrine so dear to d'Indy and the Schola of
cooperation as opposed to competition among pupils. But despite its popular-
sounding theme, it is cast in a kind of sonata form, complete with the requisite
"scholastic" modulation to the dominant key. Just as telling is Satie's *Véritables
préludes flasques pour un chien*, which contains a parody of the Baroque style, so
central to the Schola's canon. "Sévère réprimande" includes a citation from an appropriately severe chorale, and "On joue" plays facetiously with a simple contrapuntal texture. Incongruously combining the atmosphere of the Schola and that
of the cabaret, the work is studded with Latin annotations, once more presented
in a mock solemn manner.[133]

In such works Satie is toying with a phenomenon later to absorb psychoana-
lysts like Jacques Lacan—how meanings become "attached" to objects that are, in
fact, multivalent. What interested Satie was the conjuncture in an object of mean-

ings from different aspects of his culture, which could give rise to new meanings, an ability to say something "other." In his life as well, Satie pursued this goal of destabilizing established meanings by combining elements that were seemingly radically opposed to articulate something "else." This is perhaps the context in which to understand Satie's otherwise enigmatic decision in this period to join the French Radical Socialist Party. This decision, too, was both an ideological gesture and a rejection of dogma, for the nature of Satie's contribution to the party was by no means orthodox.

Satie became a member of the Comité Radical et Radical-Socialiste d'Arceuil-Cachan, the largest French party, in 1908.[134] Significantly, this was the year that he completed his studies at the nationalistic Schola, armed with an official diploma in counterpoint and a new fund of stylistic references. The question of why Satie was persuaded to join the party is indeed complex, but one essential fact to remember is his fascination with contradiction and illusion. For Satie, in both his life and his music, this was a manner of maintaining objectivity, of remaining apart, free of established identities, in order to question all authority and orthodoxy. Now, in the context of the "guerre des chapelles," he was able to do just that—by using ambiguity and irony to cast light on the battle and on the deeper conflicts behind it.

Satie had chosen to join the largest and most important political party in France between 1901 and 1914, the first large party on a national scale.[135] Perhaps in a deep psychological sense, being a member endowed him with power—a power he certainly did not possess in any other aspect of his life. But we must also remember that he joined a political party of "social illusion"—something that, as we have seen, already deeply attracted Satie. Its very name was adopted by the left-wing Radical Republicans in an attempt to manifest an awareness of the current "social question," and thereby to garner working-class votes.[136] In other words, it sought to impart the illusion that it was of the Left, despite the fact that its conception of equality was political, and indeed not social. Again, as with the Schola, Satie may well have sought to undermine from within, or to accomplish his own personal goal in the context of an atmosphere inimical to it.

But yet another possible source of appeal of the party for Satie, after his experience at the Schola, was its emphasis on "laïcity." A major component of its doctrine was the strict separation of Church and state, making it all the more ironic that it could recruit a member fresh from the Schola Cantorum.[137] But "laïcity" was ostensibly the aspect that here attracted Satie: although it was not formally incorporated in the party's principles, it informed its cultural program, to which Satie was drawn. While he never missed a meeting of the party, he did not participate in any of them but merely sat in a corner smoking and listening attentively to the speakers' discourses. What stimulated him to activity, however, was the party's program of "patronage laïque," a system of clubs for youth devoted to developing lay education and culture. Within this context, Satie's adopted "costume" assumes all the more social sense, since such "patronages" typically were the projects of provincial "instituteurs": they were an oblique, extracurricular means of opposing the insidious influence of the curé and the Church on the culture and values of French youth.[138]

After his experience at the Schola and his exposure to its subtle diffusion of ideology through musical pedagogy, Satie may now have found such a cultural undertaking to be particularly resonant. Hence Satie, the "mauvais élève" of the Conservatoire Nationale and the quiet, observant pupil of the Schola, undertook his own pedagogical enterprise. Here, he had the additional model—either perversely or nostalgically—of his whimsical, quixotic parents and their own short-lived school of music. If Charpentier had undertaken to introduce the seamstresses of Paris to music, Satie now took it upon himself to do so for the children of Arceuil-Cachan: not only did he teach them solfège on Sunday mornings, at 10 A.M. (a time when good Catholic children were in church), but also he organized inexpensive concerts and fêtes for them. Indeed, it was here that he succeeded in gaining the recognition denied him in the "legitimate" musical world, from which he, like d'Indy before, had resolutely turned away. Both had inclined instead to the cultural projects of the French political world, thereby making their own unique contributions to the complex dialogue of cultural politics. It was through this political-cultural world that, in 1909, Satie received Palmes Académiques for "services civiques," awarded by the Prefect of the Seine.

There was even an official ceremony, duly reported by the local paper, in which Satie's songs "Je te veux" and "Tendrement" were performed, apparently to an enthusiastic response.[139] So multivalent were Satie's works (like those of Gustave Charpentier) that they could be appropriated on different levels and, as we shall soon see, from different ideological perspectives. Satie was apparently pleased with his reception in Arceuil, having, like Charpentier and Debussy, no respect for stratified cultural "levels"; he subsequently expanded his program of cultural politics through music (as had both Charpentier and d'Indy) to include regional "patronages laïques." Like Charpentier and d'Indy once more, Satie's political and professional interests and motivation in such an undertaking were here indeed indistinguishable. He even became, if briefly, a contributor to Arceuil's paper, writing a regular column on his activities entitled "Quinzaine des Sociétés." Eventually, however, as his works were rediscovered by the musical culture as part of the ongoing "guerre des chapelles," he withdrew from his program of cultural politics—at least overtly. But he still continued to contribute what he could to the children of Arceuil, taking them on short outings to expose them directly to the riches of the cultural world.[140] This perhaps was Satie's response to the Republic's similar programs for adults, of which he, like Debussy and Charpentier, was certainly well aware.

Despite his distance from the musical dogma, immediately after his years at the Schola, Satie, like Debussy, was inevitably drawn into the acidulous internecine quarrels of the "camps." He became a victim of a group of supporters who selfishly wished to enshrine an earlier phase of his style for their own purposes, thus ignoring his recent evolution. For Satie, as for Debussy, it was the clique of "Debussystes" associated with the Société Musicale Indépendante who wished to "reclaim" him from the Schola. Satie was deeply irritated by this anti-d'Indyste tactic and later responded by mouthing pseudo-Scholiste dogma, but, of course, facetiously:

En musique je vois quatre phases importantes: Contrepoint—formule primitive—Harmonie—réglementation sonore—Résonance—impressionnisme musical—Néocontrepoint—nouvelle formule. Chacune de ces phases correspond à une évolution de l'esprit humain.[141]

(In music, I see four important phases: Counterpoint—primitive formula—Harmony—sonorous reglementation—Resonance—musical impressionism—Neo-counterpoint—new formula. Each of these phases corresponds to an evolution of the human spirit.)

Satie here subtly accentuated one point shared by Scholiste and Debussyste dogma—their arguments based on "evolution," although conceived in philosophically opposite ways.

But the S.M.I. persisted in its efforts, and on January 16, 1911, it performed Satie's early compositions for its elite and sophisticated audience. The program notes, which attempted to appropriate his style for the Debussyste faction, emphasized the boldness, novelty, and influence of Satie's harmonic language. In addition, on March 25, 1911, for a concert of the Cercle Musical that was devoted to Satie, Debussy conducted his orchestral version of the early *Gymnopédies;* moreover, the "progressive" or Debussyste press abetted this appropriation through an article by Calvocoressi, in the *Guide du concert* and one by Jules Ecorcheville, in the *Revue musicale S.I.M.*[142]

Nevertheless, Satie recalcitrantly continued to compose in his "post-Schola" style, and he now incorporated references to both popular and historical musical idioms. In addition, he included reference to the Debussyste "chapelle" in his *Descriptions automatiques* of 1913, the very title of which was an anti-impressionist gesture, although, it was more anti-Debussyste than anti-Debussy.[143] Significantly, the piece entitled "Sur une lanterne" (On a street lamp) makes reference to a revolutionary chanson that includes the phrase "les aristocrates à la lanterne" (or, hang the aristocrats).[144] Perhaps this juxtaposition of references was also meant to suggest that, in Satie's view, from the perspective of Arceuil, the Debussystes represented the artistic "elite."

In his *Choses vues à droite et à gauche (sans lunettes)* of 1914, Satie once more satirizes the other "chapelle" and its dogma—that of d'Indy and the Schola. The piece includes a "Hypocritical chorale," a "Groping fugue," and a "Muscular fantasy," all obvious parodies of Scholiste ideas, characteristics, and themes.[145] With his *Embryons desséchés,* Satie enters into yet another key issue of contemporary musical and cultural politics—that of the proper definition and role of the musical "classics." Here we see his irreverent conception: an exposition and conventional re-exposition; no development, but a grandiose finale, consisting of the same cadential chords repeated to absurdity. Moreover, in the section where he depicts "le grand gémissement des crustacés en famille" (the great creaking of the crustaceans in a family), we find a literal quotation from a funeral march of Chopin. For Satie the classics, conceived as such, are themselves "dessicated embryos"—now a foreign idiom, and ridiculous in a modern creative context, although solemnly invoked as canonic models at the Schola.[146]

If Satie could not escape attempts at appropriation by "chapelles" and their dogma, neither could he escape those of current politicized cultural journals. A case in point is that of *Montjoie!,* a self-proclaimed "organe de l'Impérialisme artistique française," progressive artistically, but with a strongly nationalist bent. It was one of many such journals of art that served as conduits for French nationalist ideas through an aesthetic discourse, if interpreting "tradition" in various ways.[147] The tone of the journal was aristocratic, and its politics were not only nationalist but also anti-Semitic and antidemocratic. Its ideological sympathies were announced by its title, which it borrowed directly from the traditional "cri de guerre" of the early kings of France. But while it placed great emphasis on the "pure" or the "real" artists of France's past, it, unlike the Action Française, promoted "advanced" artistic tastes.[148] Its director, Riciutto Canudo, did not espouse a classical artistic doctrine or any other kind of narrow ideology or aesthetics. Hence, *Montjoie!,* although to the Right, was not slavishly tied to tradition but encouraged artists to salvage only that part of the past that truly merited preservation. This led to an attack on all official institutions (as we saw in the Action Française), but the journal then went on to exalt such qualities as "life, force, energy, and will." Yet, like the Schola, it emphasized discipline, unselfishness, nobility, and spirituality, as well as the doctrine that all true art must emerge from the melting pot of the "collective."[149]

Ironically, Canudo, a political nationalist, was an Italian who had settled in Paris and engaged in multiple professions including poet, novelist, and commentator on music. Already presciently anticipating wartime aesthetic orthodoxies, Canudo considered France to be perhaps the pinnacle of the "latin" cultures. He bridged several artistic worlds through the salons that were regularly held by the journal, which included such "advanced" artistic figures as Léger, Cendrars, Satie, and Varèse. Because of its musical contingent, as well as the interests of its editor, the journal included articles on music in addition to short extracts from actual scores: it published works of Florent Schmitt, Stravinsky, Albert Roussel, and Satie, whose *Les Pantins dansant* appeared in issues number 11 and 12. Apparently, the journal's authors were impervious to Satie's sophisticated play with signification and his modernist self-consciousness about how the construction of meaning occurs.[150] Florent Schmitt wrote an article entitled "Erik Satie" in which he praised the composer and attacked the Institut de France for completely ignoring him. Probably realizing the utility of such promotion, Satie did not clearly distance himself, despite the radically different politics and aesthetics that he professed. His answer, however, was soon forthcoming, and once more with trenchant irony, in the period of his greatest political and aesthetic subversion—the First World War. This more overt politicization was heralded by Satie's response to the assassination of Jean Jaurès on July 31, 1914: he joined the internationalist French Socialist party.[151] Revealingly, this was his immediate reaction to the simultaneous victory of the Traditionalist and the nationalist factions in the intertwined realms of French politics and art.

CHARPENTIER'S DISILLUSIONMENT AND POLITICS

The other composer who responded publicly to the assassination of the Socialist leader was Gustave Charpentier, who prepared the music that was performed at

Jaurès's funeral.[152] Charpentier had grown disillusioned with the social programs of the Third Republic, with which he astutely identified immediately after the success of *Louise*. Like Satie, the greater his success, the greater his distrust of un-equivocal "truth," which would become pronounced in both composers during the war. Moreover, for both, this distrust was to lead not to renunciation of politi-cal engagement but to an identification with another contemporary French ideo-logical solution. But Charpentier's artistic response, like those of Debussy and Satie, was subtle, even if his political response, at least as overtly stated, was most certainly not.

It was undoubtedly in large part because of the continuing success of his opera *Louise* that Charpentier was elected to the Institut de France in 1912, suc-ceeding his teacher, Massenet; but this supreme recognition occurred during the period when he was completing an opera, *Julien,* that would be far more difficult to misinterpret or appropriate with simplistic optimism. The sequel to *Louise, Julien* concerns the later, disappointing life of the poet and his "muse," with whom he now lives, disillusioned, in a less than idyllic "ménage."[153] Irony again is prominent, for the work, revealingly, is prefaced by an epigram that Charpen-tier drew from Alfred de Musset's Romantic *Confession d'un enfant du siècle:* "Vous cherchez autour de vous comme une espérance . . . et la destinée qui vous raille vous répondra par une bouteille de vin du peuple et une courtisane" (You look around you for something like a hope . . . and destiny that mocks you will reply with a bottle of cheap wine and a courtesan).

The setting is an artist's room in the Villa Medici in Rome, for Julien, now successful, has apparently succeeded in winning the Prix de Rome. He quickly falls asleep, and the entire first act transpires supposedly in Julien's dreams, in the so-called fanciful "Pays du Rêve." Here Louise and Julien together with the "poètes déchus" (dethroned poets), confront the abyss, and futilely invoke inspi-ration of the "divine flame." As in *Louise,* the conventions of literature and high art are again invoked in connection with Julien's blindness and falsehood, the lack of the authentic and sincere. Julien here prays against the background of the celestial sounds of harps, while a psalmodizing or monotone chorus simultane-ously prays to beauty.

The second act depicts a "paysage slovaque," while the third is set in Bre-tagne, amid ruins undoubtedly intended to be suggestive of hopelessness. The fourth act takes place in Paris, once more equated with debauchery, as becomes patently clear in a lascivious dance by a prostitute. Here, in addition, another popular carnival crowd appears, but one in which students and prostitutes to-gether sybaritically praise absinthe and wine. Once more, Carnival is associated with the reversal of social expectations—with the same alliance of people and poets that leftist critics had praised in *Louise*. But now, with poignant irony, they drunkenly sing of "la splendeur du vrai"; the work concludes as Julien collapses, and the vision of the Temple of Beauty disappears. Such art is not a true art for the people but is a delusion-inducing opiate, purveyed by figures like Julien, whose conception of culture can only do harm.[154]

Like Debussy, Charpentier was now in search of a political identity or an ideo-logical orientation that would provide new direction for his art. For both composers, apparent disillusion with Anarchist cultural liberties was leading toward a search for certainty within an established doctrinal frame. But while Debussy escaped the "culte du moi" by embracing the "moi collectif" of the Right, Charpentier rather turned to the collectivism of the Socialist Left. Indeed, this was to be the solution of many former Dreyfusards, who now found the ideological seat of their ideals not in the Republic but in the Socialist Party. As we have noted, this was the period when Charpentier supported the political-cultural efforts of his ambitious protégé, the young composer, Albert Doyen. Apparently, more than ever he believed in an art that would incorporate the people, who would construe it in their own manner, as opposed to an art imposed on them by those of a different class. Self-sufficiency was still his aim, just as it was in his project to create a protective system for female workers, his "Oeuvre de Mimi Pinson."

d'indy's triumph and his enduring obsessions

As we have noted, this was the period when Vincent d'Indy was at work on his own allegorical and political opera, entitled *La Légende de Saint Christophe.* We have also seen his ideological evolution toward new groups and journals such as *l'Indépendance,* which joined together the nationalist visions of the extreme Right and Left. In the period before the war, d'Indy continued to move between two cultural worlds, those of music and politics, and he had a palpable influence on both. But his older preoccupations remained—those that had originally emerged from the Dreyfus Affair, and especially the politicized cultural war that had invaded French musical culture. Despite the immenent "traditionalist" victory, d'Indy could not move beyond the original political obsessions that had first helped to focus his artistic creed.

In 1907 he was still absorbed with the same issues and themes, as we may see in a letter to Guy Ropartz of August 7, 1907. Ropartz was considering artistic collaboration with the Conservatoire in Strasbourg, and d'Indy advised him to go ahead but to be wary of the many Protestants. He considered Protestantism dangerous from both a political and an artistic point of view, citing Schweitzer's treatment of Bach, which he believed made the composer into a sectarian. Such people, d'Indy warns, are adroit as well as dangerous: moreover, he claims, since the Affair they have done much harm to France. D'Indy goes on to observe, sounding already like "Agathon," that they continue to do harm through the university, of which they are now in control. He urges Ropartz in the letter to distrust all Protestants—and indeed to distrust them even more than the menacing Germans themselves.[155] This was consistent with his belief that there was more danger within France from those who were not "truly French" than from the so-called enemy from without.

As we have noted, despite his new involvements in "advanced" political groups, d'Indy continued to correspond with members of the Ligue de la Patrie Française. Although by this point it was effectively defunct, he was still sending letters to it in November 1912, reporting on his activities in Brussels and at the

Schola.[156] D'Indy, now unequivocally powerful in both the politicized and the "legitimate" musical worlds, continued to move between the two with both dexterity and skill: by 1912 he was teaching at the Conservatoire and the Schola, and he was omnipresent on important juries such as the Concours Cressent.

As the leader of one of the "chapelles" or "poles," d'Indy, like Debussy, was also a frequent contributor to the important *Revue musicale S.I.M.* Here he employed political rhetoric that indeed would not be out of place in the various journals of the Action Française or other proximate nationalist groups. We find intertextual reference to their common mobilizing political themes, which were now becoming increasingly legitimized as the threat of war approached. For example, he asks:

> Comment se fait-il qu'en art nous ayons laissé s'égarer ce bon sens qui pendant si longtemps, de Montaigne à Molière et Beaumarchais, de Rameau à Gluck et Méhul a sauvegardé l'originalité de notre création française?
>
> (How is it that in art we have let go astray this common sense that for so long, from Montaigne to Molière and Beaumarchais, from Rameau to Gluck and Méhul has safeguarded the originality of French creation?)

He observes that the reasons are complex but posits that they could be attributable to "métèques," whose promiscuity "a détruit le véritable esprit de notre pays"[157] (has destroyed the true spirit of our country). As we can see, the leaders of both "poles" of independents before the war were arguing for the purity of the French tradition using terms popularized by the Action Française.

The following year d'Indy turned to another substantial symbolic stake in the war of the dogma or "chapelles"—the proper intellectual interpretation of Beethoven. After Romain Rolland's *La Vie de Beethoven* of 1903, other, more recent books had appeared that further provoked the response of d'Indy. In 1905 Raymond Bouyer published *Le Secret de Beethoven,* and in 1906 Jean Chantavoine also published a book on the composer.[158] In 1913 d'Indy answered with his long-awaited *Beethoven* (completed in 1911), which he conceived, in part, as a refutation of Rolland's book. Whereas Rolland presented the composer as heroic, a friend of the suffering, motivated by a humanitarian and civic faith, for d'Indy this faith was religious, as seen in such works as the *Missa Solemnis:*

> Musique liturgique, non . . . mais musique religieuse au premier chef, de plus, musique essentiellement Catholique. Nous sommes bien éloignés de suspecter la bonne foi de ceux des historiens de Beethoven qui ont prétendu attacher à ce monument unique de l'art religieux un sens simplement philosophique, faire de cette Messe une oeuvre en dehors de la foi chrétienne, une manifestation de "libre examen."[159]
>
> (Liturgical music, no . . . but religious music in the highest degree, moreover, essentially Catholic music. We are far from suspecting the good faith of those historians of Beethoven who pretended to attach to this unique monument of religious art a simple philosophic sense, to make of this mass a work outside of Christian faith, a manifestation of free thought.)

Clearly, the oppositions defined at the turn of the century were still in place, and the "chapelles" deeply engaged with them, as their contentiousness peaked in the years preceding World War I. This was not problematic for d'Indy, whose aesthetic continued to coincide with his politics, following the boundaries defined by the "camps," but this was not the case for several prominent Scholistes. It is important to examine these composers together, along with the equally independent Maurice Ravel, for all of them confounded the dogma so obstreperously proclaimed by the litigious "chapelles." Albéric Magnard, Guy Ropartz, and Albert Roussel, together with Ravel, provoked critical passions in the period that defy explanation apart from this context.

Magnard and the "Chapelles"

As we have already seen, Magnard had been deeply involved in the Dreyfus Affair and, although he was a Scholiste, had staunchly supported the Dreyfusards. Not surprisingly, given his uncompromising nature and his subsequent refusal to adhere to the ideological orthodoxies of the existing "chapelles," Magnard's music was little performed. He demonstrably paid the price for his defiance and pertinacious independence, his highly personal mélange of the beliefs and techniques of different cliques. But if one can give credence to Gaston Carraud's impassioned book on Magnard, written after the war and the composer's "heroic" death (defending his home against the Germans), his social ideas were indeed complex. For according to Carraud, Magnard believed himself to be "democratic," but, in fact, this was less the case than the composer actually thought: although claiming to be sanguine toward French workers and peasants, by 1909, in a letter to Ropartz he was complaining of their power or, as he put it, "la tyrannie ouvrière." This was perhaps a reference to the attempted general strike by French workers in 1909, which brought down the premiership of Georges Clémenceau that year. Apparently Magnard's interest in the lower classes was fundamentally paternalistic, that of someone who espoused an idealism that was protected by the privilege of wealth. Yet his idealism persisted and led to further complications for him and the reception of his works in the politicized musical world of the prewar period.

In 1911 his opera *Bérénice,* was performed at the Opéra Comique, which, in fact, had made a specific request to perform the work.[160] *Bérénice* was based on an original play of Racine, but the story was inherently provocative in the context of early-twentieth-century France. It concerns the emperor's lover, Bérénice, who is Jewish, and whom for this very reason the people of Rome do no want as empress on the throne. In the end, however, Bérénice performs the noble and altruistic act of sacrificing her love for the emperor in the Roman people's political interest. Within the cadre of the nationalist Right, and even of the Schola itself, a noble or altruistic Jew was considered an anomaly, an inherent contradiction.

Hence the quandary of the nationalist press, which, while approving of Magnard's musical style, nevertheless faced the problem of the content of the libretto.

The *Revue française politique et littéraire* (the continuation of *Les Annales de la Patrie Française*, the journal of the Ligue de la Patrie Française) solved the problem by limiting its comments to the musical style. After noting that the work's simplicity ostensibly upset some of the listeners, it goes on implicitly to contrast Magnard's music with music written in the "Italo-Judaïque" style:

> On a pu sentir là à quel point les grandes oeuvres italiennes, en altérant le goût du public, ont desservi l'école française et la musique tout entièr.[161]
>
> (One could feel to which extent the great Italian works, in altering public taste, have harmed the French school and all of music.)

Ultimately, for this press, Magnard's "message" inhered in his style and his association with the Schola Cantorum, as opposed to the ideas expressed in the text.

The Case of Maurice Ravel

If Magnard was the positive stylistic model for the *Revue française politique et littéraire*, Ravel was a model of all it condemned in contemporary French musical style. Ravel, too, was caught in the crossfire between the conflicting "chapelles" and labeled a "Debussyste" despite his personal tensions with Debussy himself. On February 11, 1912, the *Revue française politique et littéraire* attacked Ravel's *Ma mère l'oye*, currently being presented at Rouché's Théâtre des Arts. Its critic dismisses the work as no more than an "amusement d'artiste raffiné," under the influence of Fauré and Debussy, as opposed to the "noblesse" of Vincent d'Indy. Ravel had incurred the wrath of the Schola and its sympathizers by boldly confronting them, even when it was clear that this faction was assuming the hegemonic professional position. Although his political engagement would not come until during and after the war, Ravel was already outspoken concerning the dogma that he found so repellent: on numerous occasions, in private letters as well as in published articles, he made it clear how insidious he believed the Schola's aesthetic and social doctrines to be.

Already, in a letter to Jean Marnold in 1906, Ravel referred to the Scholistes dismissively as "morose followers of this neo-Christianity":[162] by 1912 he was voicing his negative opinions concerning Franck and "Franckism," and its later incarnation, Scholisme, in the *Revue S.I.M.* Here he attacks a symphony by Henri Witowsky, a prominent "scholiste," as well as the founder of an important branch of the Schola Cantorum in Lyon. In the article Ravel treats "scholisme" as an equivalent of academicism, much in the same manner as did Debussy and Satie creatively in their prewar compositions. In his description of the Witkowski work, Ravel notes:

> Quelques suites brèves de notes, traités par des procédés d'école: augmentations, renversements, constituant le principe de la mélodie. L'harmonie est presque toujours le résultat de rencontres contrapuntiques. Le rythme, de déformations industrieuses. De sorte que ces trois éléments de la musique, dont la conception devrait être simultanée et avant tout instinctive, sont ici élaborés séparément et unis par un travail purement intellectuel, dirait-on.[163]

(Short series of notes, treated by academic procedures: augmentation, reversal, constituting the principle of the melody. The harmony is almost always the result of contrapuntal encounters. The rhythm, of industrious deformations. With the result that the three elements of music, of which the conception should be simultaneous, and above all, instinctive, are here elaborated separately and united by what one would call a purely intellectual work.)

Here Ravel sounds like a good Debussyste and member of the Société Musicale Indépendante, a group that, as we have seen, was systematically hostile to the Scholiste conception. Although Ravel himself considered writing a symphony at several points, like Debussy, he could never bring himself to do so, undoubtedly because of the connotations that it now carried. As we saw in Vuillermoz, the symphony, for the Debussyste "chapelle," was equated with "reactionary politics, autobiography, and slavish adherence to rules."[164]

Like Debussy, one of Ravel's "countermodels" was the music of Emmanuel Chabrier, which he affectionately parodied in a collection of "pastiches": "A la manière de Chabrier" begins with the very kind of false solemnity that Chabrier himself loved to present and then proceed to ridicule.[165] But his other idol was Claude Debussy, whose music Ravel defended despite the fact that Debussy was reserved about some of his rival's works. When Ravel's *Histoires naturelles* was attacked by the Scholistes in 1907, Debussy, who found it artificial and chimerical, did not come to his ally's aid,[166] but when Debussy's *Images* was censured by Pierre Lalo and Gaston Carraud, Ravel leapt to Debussy's defense in the *Cahiers d'aujourd'hui*. Here, in 1913, he published an article, "A-propos des *Images* de Claude Debussy," in which he addressed the issue of the "guerre des chapelles" and the role of critics.

Ravel recounts the fact that there are presently two major "schools" in France—that of the disciples of Franck and that of the followers of Debussy. He also points out the adherence of critics like Lalo and Carraud to such factions as well, a fact that, as we have seen, both Hellouin and Huré had noted. As Ravel advances, their sympathy for the Schola undoubtedly accounts for their anomalous opinions concerning the historical place of the music of Claude Debussy. Ravel then observes that, although they were both originally partisans of *Pelléas*, describing the work as sublime, they considered it not "French" but an "exception." However, he adds, a group of younger composers by no means sees his work as exceptional or an aberration within French music, one leading ultimately to an aesthetic impasse.[167]

Ravel particularly takes exception to Carraud's observation that, subsequent to *Pelléas*, Debussy's earlier clique of admirers was replaced by a substantially different group. Carraud characterized the former as "les musiciens et les sensibles," specifically intending by the latter designation both painters and men of letters. Ravel incisively notes that this thus makes him a "littéraire" or a painter, as it does Stravinsky, Florent Schmitt, Roger Ducasse, and Albert Roussel.[168] He, unlike some Debussystes, by no means objected to Debussy's evolution, despite the attempt of certain critics to claim it for the nationalist camp; even after Ravel later assumed a political stance, he abhorred the categorical and remained "independent," if not in politics, then in art, like Debussy.

Ropartz's Defiance

Such independence of spirit was also characteristic of another figure, although one who was drawn aesthetically to the opposing scholiste "chapelle." This was Guy Ropartz, who incarnated the same contradictions as his friend, Magnard—aesthetic attraction to a style considered inimical to the philosophy he professed. Ropartz, although a staunch "Franckiste," a devout Catholic, and a friend of d'Indy, was not a Scholiste in the strict sense of the word. And yet he did espouse some of the same ideas as d'Indy, particularly the belief that "one can think in music the same way as one can think in prose and in verse."[169] Apparently, after the Affair, d'Indy saw Ropartz as ripe for conversion, as we gleaned from a number of letters of d'Indy to Ropartz throughout this period. Recall that in 1902 he wrote to Ropartz complaining about the "Naturistes'" condemnation of the symphony, equating this view with "artistic Dreyfusism."[170] A year before, d'Indy had warned Ropartz about musicians in Lyon, cautioning him about the Jewish-Socialist alliance around Dreyfus and urging him to "take precautions."[171]

But d'Indy's warning were futile, for in 1905 Ropartz was at work on his Symphony No. 3 in which he sought to express ideas that could be construed as both "Dreyfusard" and Socialist. It is a symphony with a text by the composer, which opens each of the movements: after the texted section (with soloists and chorus) comes the instrumental "commentary," in a tradition form.[172] An excerpt from the text makes Ropartz's ideological position abundantly clear, for it invokes those terms and concepts that were the stock of the Dreyfusards:

> Aimons-nous les uns les autres! La justice et la vérité, la paix et la bonté se partagent la terre. Aimons-nous les uns les autres! L'Humanité transformée monte vers la cité de joie et d'idéale liberté où les rois ne sont plus, ni les maîtres, où l'unique loi d'amour a remplacé les lois désormais inutiles!
>
> O Nature, maintenant sois en fête! . . . Et toi, Soleil, lève-toi radieux! Unis ta lumière éclatante aux feux de l'idéal soleil de Vérité, de Justice, et d'Amour.[173]
>
> (Let us love each other! Justice and truth, peace and goodness share the earth. Let us love each other! Transformed humanity rises toward the city of joy and ideal liberty where there are no more kings or masters, where the one law of love has replaced the henceforth useless laws!
>
> O Nature, now be in celebration! . . . And you, sun, raise yourself radiantly! Unite your brilliant light with the fire of the ideal sun of truth, of justice, and of love.)

The invocation of nature, justice, truth, and egalitarianism in the year of the separation of Church and state was rife with ideological implications. Hostile critics were quick to perceive the clues and to respond in kind, as shown in the review of the work by Pierre Lalo in *Le Temps* in 1907. Once more, as an appreciator of the Schola, it was not the style to which he objected but the ideas expressed, which were in clear contradiction with the stylistic "code." Lalo compares the text with those of Zola, perceiving in both the same utopianism, the same "false amplitude," and the same "superficial banality."[174] Clearly, the memory of Dreyfusard rhetoric was still vivid and the anti-Dreyfusard discourse still very much alive in critics who held nationalist political sympathies.

But in addition to recalling that the references to Zola derived from the Affair, we must remember that the French Socialist Party had been founded in 1905. Hence, it is not surprising that Lalo would see the reflection of these two influences—those that d'Indy particularly dreaded—Socialism and Dreyfusism. Nor is it surprising that Guy Ropartz, like Debussy and Ravel as well as Magnard, would suffer from critics during the zenith of the "guerre des chapelles"; for, as Séverac acutely perceived, every composer was expected to take a stance. To assume one with a foot in each camp only incited the militant French critics to rage.[175]

Tensions in Roussel

The other composer to feel the strain of attraction to the style associated with the Schola but not to its dogma or political ideology was Albert Roussel. Like Magnard, his background was patrician, and, like him as well, he began a career (as befitting his class) in the military, which he later abandoned for music. But, like Gustave Charpentier, he originally came from Tourcoing, although from the opposite end of the social spectrum—that of the wealthy industrialists. His family was part owner of a firm that was known for manufacturing carpets and tapestries; Tourcoing, as we have noted, had long been associated with the textile trade. Roussel's family was also prominent in the city because of its civic service; his grandfather had served as mayor of Tourcoing.[176]

Roussel was sent to the École Naval but simultaneously studied music privately with a former pupil of the traditionalist École Niedermeyer. He imbued Roussel with a love of the German classics, as well as with a skill in contrapuntal writing and a mastery of traditional forms. In 1898 Roussel was introduced by a friend of Giguet to Vincent d'Indy, which led to his formal enrollment in the flourishing Schola Cantorum. For the next nine years, Roussel attended classes in composition, as well as in orchestration and, of course, in the history of music. It has been postulated that it was not d'Indy's ideology but his personal qualities, and his impressive knowledge of music, that had initially attracted Roussel. Roussel never approved of the sectarian atmosphere and dogma of the Schola, and it was perhaps for this reason that he was never an intimate friend of d'Indy.[177]

Out of respect for Roussel's abilities, d'Indy appointed him professor of counterpoint in 1902, during the period of his own studies, which were completed in 1908. In 1914, however, Roussel resigned from the Schola Cantorum, sensing that further association with it would be detrimental to his independence. Moreover, he felt himself growing away from d'Indy's principles, although this did not eventuate in a personal rupture between the two composers.[178] Always respectful of talent, d'Indy never imposed his judgment on such accomplished figures, even if he personally disliked the artistic result. Eventually, Roussel became the champion of those young French composers in the 1920s and early 1930s whom d'Indy would most vociferously denounce. And, in the course of the political polarization of the 1930s, Roussel would publicly defend those political ideals that the Schola had earlier so stridently attacked.[179]

FINAL ATTEMPTS AT A RECONCILIATION

In the period preceding the war, the theme of French music as a manifestation of the "âme nationale," or of the cultural qualities of the "French race," became increasingly common. By now, this and related ideas, appropriated and adapted from the nationalist Right, were widely considered tenable and, within the changing political climate, legitimate. With the assumption of power by Poincaré in 1912 came an emphasis on the military and on authority, as well as on tradition and order. As Barrès himself was led to comment triumphantly in 1913, "our terminology can be rejected, our doctrines are being realized."[180]

Yet as the inevitability of war became clearer, the polarization of musical aesthetics and factions reached its apogee, a situation many now perceived as baleful; even before the formal declaration of "Union sacrée" during the war, the belief in the importance of French solidarity in all areas was widely spread. We see this in much of the musical discourse, now consumed with the problem of reconciling or justifying the aesthetic polarities within the French musical world.

Characteristic of this attempt is the collection edited by Paul-Marie Masson, entitled *Rapport sur la musique française contemporaine* of 1913. Masson, an "agrégé," was a professor "chargé de conférences" on the history of music at the Institut Français de Florence (an annex of the Université de Grenoble). The volume he edited was the result of papers that were presented at the Congrès de Musique sponsored by the Section d'histoire musicale de l'Institut Français de Florence and held in conjunction with the Exposition Internationale de Rome.

In the volume, Masson attempts to trace the development of French music from the advent of the Third Republic in 1870 to the present. His major concern is to explain certain tendencies once rejected as "un-French" as indeed French, although representing a recessive strain of the "âme nationale." This, however, does not include all stylistic tendencies, as we shall see, only those associated with the so-called indépendants. Masson begins by attempting to justify the d'Indyste faction and the particular formal and stylistic proclivities widely associated with it. We can see this in his treatment of the growth of "la musique pure" in France, which he presents as fostered by an intellectual elite, interested in the relation of music to the unconscious. As he argues, this was also the group that in literature fostered the reaction against Naturalism, helping to propagate the taste for mystery and the irrational being promoted by the Symbolist writers. In this manner, Masson also justifies the French taste of the period for Wagner, but he explains that the French have gradually recognized his true historical place. In the end (like Debussy), they have perceived that he was, in fact, a "musicien classique," in the line of development that began with Beethoven and ran through Carl Maria von Weber.[181]

According to the author, today one may perceive a rejection of both those procedures and modes of feeling that do not accord with the qualities of the French "race." In his attempt to reconcile the two dominant poles or "chapelles" as both authentically French, he perceives each as embodying different aspects of these traits. D'Indy turned to the past in order to arrive at musical forms that could provide inspiration for the present, while still maintaining essential French qualities; Debussy, on the other hand, turned decisively away from Wagner and embraced instead those profoundly French qualities of "la mesure" and "la clarté." Here we may perceive the effect of Laloy's explication of the historical basis of Debussy's style that, as we have seen, was also propagated by the Action Française. To present these antipodes as complementary aspects of the French national character, Masson designates them, respectively, "musique contemplation" and "musique discours." Both are essentially French, for both exhibit those inherent French traits of "la discrétion et la sobriété dans l'expression des sentiments personnels, l'horreur du lyrisme intempérant ou déclamatoire" (a discretion and sobriety in the expression of personal feelings, a horror of intemperate or declamatory lyricism).[182] Already, the way is being prepared for the wartime conceptual orthodoxy of French music as inherently classic or as an embodiment of these traits. Such qualities are in implicit distinction to contemporary German music and to that French strain represented by Charpentier and Bruneau—who are thus not "truly French." This faction, once dominant, was increasingly discredited with the cresting of the French nationalist tide and its doctrinal conception of the proper attributes of the "French race."

For Masson, it is now "la musique impressionniste" that embodies the French desire for "vérité," for inspiration from nature as opposed to the inner passions. Coining yet more labels, he opposes the impressionist "musique des choses" to its complement in the French national character, the Scholiste "la musique de l'homme." Although Masson admits that at present impressionist tendencies are dominant among young composers, he posits that a reaction will soon occur, as it already has in both painting and poetry.[183] He was indeed correct, for even before the advent of war, an attempt to reorient French public taste toward the past was already well under way.

SCHOLISME AND THE MUSICAL MAINSTREAM

The increasingly pervasive nationalist climate in France was having a substantial impact on the shifting hegemony in the musical culture in favor of the supporters of tradition. As nationalistic rhetoric escalated with the imminent approach of war, the stress was on tradition as the root of French values, which were now under ostensible threat; hence, arguments that were originally the province of extreme nationalist groups were becoming more common, especially after Poincaré's ascension to power in 1912. The network of cultural meanings and values generated by the French nationalist leagues thus penetrated the musical world even further in the shadow of crisis and war. Within this context we may perceive an attempt on the part of official culture to promote Scholiste or d'Indyste values, particularly when examining concert programs. César Franck was now much performed at the major concert societies, which had the delicate task of reconciling official exigencies with public taste.[184] And d'Indy, at the height of his influence, was promoted from Chevalier to the prestigious level of Officier de la Légion d'Honneur in 1912. In addition to this honorific reward, his early opera Fervaal, which had premiered not in Paris but in Brussels, was presented at the Paris Opéra.

D'Indy's influence by now extended to most domains of the French musical world—to scholarship, to pedagogy, to compositional models, and to repertoire. It was perhaps because of the Schola's success in legitimizing the symphony as "French"—an appropriate genre for French composers—that symphonic premieres proliferated as nationalism crested. No fewer than eight such premieres took place in the 1911–1912 season, with the Concerts Lamoureux promoting Scholiste works and the Concerts Colonne, the Conservatoire's model.[185] This may also have been closely related to the fact that government officials were becoming increasingly punctilious concerning the so-called three-hour rule. The Lamoureux and Colonne concert societies annually received a subvention of 15,000 francs from the state, but with an important stipulation: within their seasons of concerts, they were required to perform at least three hours of modern French music by living composers that had never been presented before.[186]

By 1910, however, there were official complaints that, if the rule was generally respected to the letter, it was honored far less so in spirit. Often conductors would simply select a number of very short works, of fifteen minutes each, and then cunningly tally them up collectively at the end of the year. This desperate attempt of the concert societies to balance official strictures with public taste was finally thwarted unequivocally by the government in 1910: it now imposed the stipulation that the Cahier des Charges of the societies proscribe the inclusion of works of less than half an hour to count toward the total three hours.[187] The result, as we might expect, and as the government undoubtedly wished, is that, by the 1911–1912 season, symphonies by French composers were appearing on concert programs.

D'Indy's influence can also be seen in the choice of societies that were supported, if only nominally or honorifically, in the period preceding World War I. The meanings that he helped establish concerning repertoires as well as genres, and which he had spread through the intellectual network that he cultivated, were being generally applied. The major points of emphasis in the subventioned or recognized concert societies were now the "classics" (as defined at the Schola) and the revival of the music of the distant past. Also evident, however, was the continuing interest of the Republic in the diffusion of culture and hence in those organizations striving to make music accessible to many more listeners. Societies such as the Concerts de l'Art Pour Tous, for example, continued to receive subventions, as did Charpentier's burgeoning "Oeuvre de Mimi Pinson."[188]

But an emphasis on history was perceptible, a stress on tradition, on rediscovery of the musical classics by foreign as well as by French composers of the historical past. Once more, the rhetoric of the Action Française, as well as that of the Schola, was now palpably affecting both the peripheral and the mainstream musical cultures. For example, in 1910 the Société J. S. Bach was awarded the honorific sum of 200 francs and the Société Haydn, Mozart, Beethoven 600 francs. In addition, the larger societies manifested an interest in the historical repertoire and attempted to diffuse this older repertoire to a greater number of listeners. This was the case, for instance, with the Concerts Symphoniques du Trocadero, which were placed under the musical direction of Alfred Cassella. The concerts were historical in emphasis, devoted to works, both well known and not so well known, that had been written in the period between 1700 and 1900. Ticket prices were low enough for a less affluent public to attend—the very kind of public that frequented the lectures of L'Art Pour Tous.[189] Here the idea of a "musical museum" was designed to serve a political role by fostering those values that the more conservative Republic now sought to diffuse.

The themes of nationalism and traditionalism were being actively implemented elsewhere in the official French musical world well before the outbreak of the First World War. This was clearly the case with the Opéra, which found itself pulled between the dominant nationalist rhetoric and the insatiable public demand for Wagner. By 1910, as at the turn of the century, the concern with the domination of Wagner's works was acute, as becomes clear in the deliberations over the budget to be allocated the Opéra.[190] It may well be that French Wagnerian operas such as d'Indy's *Fervaal* were being selected for performance in order to counter the German Wagnerian threat; nevertheless, Wagner's *La Crépuscule des dieux* was performed in 1908, followed by *L'Or du Rhin* in 1909 and *Parsifal* in 1914.

To resist this "invasion" further, the Opéra's Cahier des Charges became increasingly strict, stipulating the performance of even more of the great masters of France's past. As the reader will recall, this emphasis on great French composers of opera, such as Lully, Rameau, and Gluck, had been stimulated initially by the Schola Cantorum.[191] Already, in response to it and to the fear of Wagnerian dominance, in 1901 the Minister of Education and Fine Arts had changed article 11 of the Cahiers des Charges: now, instead of requiring two premiers by French composers—one of which was to be in three to five acts—it required six premieres in one to three acts. This trend was to strengthen and to culminate during the war, when the Cahier required seventeen new works, fourteen of which were to be by French composers. This was probably also a reflection of the pressure being placed on the chamber by the "groupe de la musique," still actively protecting the interests of French composers.[192] Here, political, economic, and purely professional concerns would merge and together further foster the resuscitation of numerous French musical masterworks.

THE LAST SKIRMISH: *LE SACRE DU PRINTEMPS*

Tensions before the war were to increase still further because of two factors: German political aggression and the untimely centenary of Wagner's birth.[193] This was decidedly not the moment for an aggressively modernist work—one by a non-French composer who was rapidly achieving success in Paris. Given the increasingly dominant aesthetic discourse of tradition, there was only one small politico-aesthetic space in which to legitimize such a style. This we can perceive most clearly in examining the premiere of Stravinsky's ballet *Le Sacre du printemps,* which, in effect, brought the acrimonious "guerre des chapelles" to a head. It became the final battleground in the war over French "traditionalism," a war that the modernists or Debussystes were now on the verge of conclusively losing. By this point, as we have seen, cultural, political, and musical attitudes had achieved so intimate a fusion that no one aspect could be easily separated from the others: French musical culture was by now a tightly strung field of cultural and political tensions that were ineluctably to explode under the detonating impact of *The Rite of Spring.*

The story of the work's tumultuous premiere is, by now, well known: the response of its opponents was violent, the uproar so great as to drown out the music. Physical blows ensued between the ballet's supporters and detractors, assembled in the newly opened and architecturally modernist Théâtre des Champs-Elysées. The reasons for such violent emotions are not difficult to discern if we examine their verbal articulation by both sides in the contemporary press. As we might well expect, the "families of reception" of the work largely adhered to the established rhetorics or perspectives characteristic of the different "chapelles." Georges Auric was to remark in the early 1920s that the battle was fought around the "préjugés d'écoles," each with their own aesthetic polemics and "superstitions."[194] Scholistes and traditionalists, of course, were quick to respond with condemnations in print, which ranged from the restrained to the violent, mirroring the dynamics of the premiere itself.[195] In the *Revue musicale S.I.M.,* d'Indy, making fun of his habitual adversaries, pronounced the work "un chef-d'oeuvre selon les rites de la petite église moderniste" (a masterpiece according to the rites of the small modernist church). This view was seconded by d'Indy's biographer and friend Léon Vallas in his negative review published in the *Revue française de musique.*[196] Modernism, it is important to note, by this point had derogatory connotations: it was associated with Germany and then, throughout the war, with the even more capacious epithet "Boche."

As we have noted, Debussy read *Le Sacre* at the piano with Stravinsky in 1912 and responded to it in a polite, guardedly positive manner; while sitting with Misia Sert, a supporter of the Rissian Ballet's impresario, Serge Diaghilev, at the premiere, he is quoted as exclaiming, "It is terrifying—I don't understand it!"[197] Similarly, Debussy's faithful editor, the self-proclaimed traditionalist Jacques Durand, had essentially the same reaction to Stravinsky's aggressive score. He was later, in retrospect, to blame the "unfortunate" postwar directions taken by younger French composers on the destructive influence of Stravinsky's *Le Sacre.* He observed that each time French music is in full efflorescence, a "disruptive" movement comes from "outside" and promptly proceeds to demolish it.[198]

Nevertheless, there was a vociferous circle that supported Stravinsky's work, one drawn from essentially the same ideological groupings and social circles that backed the Ballets Russes financially. Once more, this was the "liberal Right," or that strain of the Right in France that had descended not from the "Ultras" of the Restoration but from the nineteenth-century "Orléanism." As we have already noted, this group was philosophically economically liberal, but, unlike those of the Left, it remained conservative in its basic social conceptions. Although "patriotic" and nationalist, its judgments in art were not "absolutist" but tended rather to emphasize freedom, as opposed to official restraints.[199] This group included a significant portion of the French aristocracy and embraced such figures as the Comtesse de Greffühle, one of the supporters of the Ballets Russes. Other such figures in this circle included Misia Sert, the Comtesse de Chevigné, and, as we have already seen, the prominent Princess de Polignac.[200]

Musically, Le Sacre's supporters came from the group that had been Debussystes and included Maurice Ravel, who was enthusiastically present at the ballet's premiere. According to reports, when Ravel exclaimed, "Génie, génie" and then turned to quiet a neighbor so that he could hear the music, he was taunted as a "sale Juif."[201] So strongly had the discourse of the extreme nationalist Right, including the Schola, equated "modernism" with Judaism that this was an automatic conservative response. Jean Marnold, a spokesman for the liberal, aesthetically progressive Right, was predictably highly positive about the work in the Mercure de France. Equally supportive was another Debussyste, Emile Vuillermoz, writing in both Le Journal and the Revue musicale S.I.M.[202] Similarly enthusiastic about the score was Florent Schmitt, whose article in La France reveals part of its appeal for this group of composers. Schmitt refers to Stravinsky as no less than the "Messiah" that composers in France have been awaiting ever since the time of Wagner.[203] Far less threatening than the German, Wagner, he was still someone from outside the narrow disputes within the French musical world, who could lead the way out of the impasse. Louis Laloy, who was becoming more progressive in his aesthetic taste than his long-time close friend Claude Debussy, was also positive about the work. Even before the war, Laloy was praising cabarets and music hall for their "actuality" and social realism, which, however, did not threaten the social order.[204]

In the Revue musicale S.I.M. on May 1, 1914, Laloy comments on Stravinsky's statement about Le Sacre, "J'ai accompli une oeuvre de foi." Laloy then continues:

> Cette foi, il nous l'a communiquée. Avec lui nous avons célébré les mystères de la Mère éternelle, nous avons contemplé sans horreur le sacrifice humain et nous nous sommes partagés les chairs égorgés.[205]

> (He has communicated this faith to us. With him we have celebrated the mysteries of the eternal mother, we have contemplated human sacrifice without horror, and we have shared the bloody flesh.)

Laloy's lurid imagery inescapably suggests a psychological preparation for war and adumbrates his particularly virulent strain of wartime chauvinism. Such imagery was soon to become common in the musical discourse during the war, particularly in the writings of both Laloy and his friend Debussy.

It was from a similar perspective that the journal Montjoie! immediately lauded the work, and even published a page (dedicated to its editor) from the ballet's score.[206] Canudo published this excerpt together with an article by Stravinsky, enticingly entitled "Ce que j'ai voulu exprimer dans Le Sacre du printemps." In it Stravinsky emphasizes his interest in the fundamental forces of nature—its cyclicity and universality, as well as its own "essential rhythms." The same issue of the journal published an article on the work by Roland-Manuel that particularly praises its rhythmic power and pronounces the ballet "superbly new."[207] Given the ideological inclinations of Montjoie!, which we have seen, the work, according to such interpretations, was entirely consonant with its basic values: it was rooted in the "collectivity," but not in a narrow, academic sense, and, although foreign, it could be construed as stimulating French national values.

Important figures of the younger generation who were based in both literature and in music greeted *Le Sacre* as a way out of the impasse between the two equally desiccated "chapelles": for Jacques Rivières, writing in the *Nouvelle revue française, Le Sacre* was "le premier chef-d'oeuvre que nous puissions opposer à ceux de l'impressionnisme"[208] (the first masterpiece that we can oppose to those of impressionism). Later, in the early 1920s (in the same journal), Georges Auric expressed a similar view of what the new work appeared to offer young composers: it represented clearer or franker values, as opposed not only to "le bon goût" associated with the Schola Cantorum but to an impressionism that was now "demeaned."[209]

As we can see, impressionism was under attack, not only by the powerful and older traditionalist faction but also by the younger generation of composers. The dialectic of the dominant "chapelles"—that of tradition and harmonic "exploration"—was no longer of interest to French youth, who saw it as inimical to the "truly modern."[210] But they were shortly to find that with the advent of the First World War there was no politico-cultural position for such a conception of the musically modern. It would have to become subversive by outwardly adopting popular or traditional forms, and be framed by a rhetoric that would construe it as in keeping with the "French tradition." By the time of the outbreak of war, a traditionalist musical discourse was firmly in place, having gradually moved from a peripheral to a hegemonic position. In this move, it had followed the political trajectory of the Republic itself—from the Dreyfusard Republic to one that was centrist, or conservative and nationalist. This more nationalistic stance drew integrally on the discourse of two Rightist leagues, which, as we have seen, had helped transform both musical discourse and culture. Through this discourse musical and political values in France had become inseparable, a fact that affected every aspect of French musical life and would continue to do so throughout the war.

CONCLUSION

Music is inscribed in the historical landscape in a vast variety of ways and has assumed myriad social meanings dependent, in part, on its specific location.[1] As we have seen, in France it shifted its position in the cultural terrain as a result of the seismic shifts in political culture following the earthquake of the Dreyfus Affair. As a result of this shift, the French musical world shared a common border with the political, for the Ligue de la Patrie Française, through d'Indy, launched an invasion of the musical culture. Music, which had been associated with centralized power since the days of Louis XIV, now became as implicitly ideological as it had been in the days of the "Querelle des Bouffons."[2]

The distinctive mechanism of this ideological penetration was the genesis of a new musical discourse at d'Indy's Schola Cantorum, centered on the criterion of the "authentically French." Its power lay in the way in which it articulated an otherwise ineffable fusion of aesthetic, moral, and political concepts, as opposed to rationalist Republican rhetoric. Moreover, while nationalist writers impregnated their fiction with ideological concepts, writers on music, beginning at the Schola, assigned political meanings to styles and forms. The Republic was quick to follow suit, ascribing political meanings to musical styles and defining a new canon of French works through its own powerful institutional channels. The result was a structural opposition between nationalist and republican institutions of music, which created a professional confrontation without equal in either literature or the visual arts; but as in these two fields, this nationalist incursion into the art was fundamentally to redefine the critical standards by which French music was henceforth judged.

As in Augustan literature in England, style became freighted with political meaning, affecting music in various ways, as it enlarged the territory of ideological debate.[3] The fact that politics absorbed French music symbolically, making it political, inevitably led to a loss of autonomy in the professional musical world. As the sharp distinctions between the musical world and the political world in France collapsed, so too did musicians' ability to define their own proper aesthetic criteria. However, the dynamics were complex, for the political, ideological incursion served to buttress and polarize professional and aesthetic divisions that were already incipient. But, from then on, major questions in French music were subtended by deep political roots, resulting in dissensions that transcended the realm of purely aesthetic debate: yet larger ideological issues here assumed a unique dimension when refracted through the prism of this particular aesthetic discourse.

The use of music as a symbolic tool in both challenging and legitimizing power had positive and negative musical results, limiting options but stimulating change. The Republic entered into a dialogic relation with its political adversaries. It did not conceive its program from an ideological blueprint; it responded to an aggressive challenge.[4] In this way, political power implemented decisive change in order to answer a threat to its symbolic legitimacy from an independently legitimized opposition. We have seen the development of rival musical institutions in France, for both professional and political reasons that cannot be separated within this context. We have also seen the manner in which such contestation forced changes in the educational system, redefined priorities in the awarding of subventions, and stimulated the growth of French music history. But here there was not even a pretense of the "scholastic," or artistic and scholarly objectivity and professional disinterest that the arts as well as the academy have subsequently claimed. This politicization of music history led to the formulation of rival canons that would eventually fuse for political reasons and to a new conception of the "classic."[5]

The question of the traditional values to be reflected in the musical canon was both academic and political, for in France the two domains were structurally fused. Hence, the redefinition and final institutional installation of a canon in France was linked not to a conviction as to music's autonomy but to political contestation over "national traits." The moral dimension of the canon was thus fundamentally ideological, since moral values were inextricably implicated in contestation over the "authentically French." Canon formation in this period is inexplicable apart from the political realm; the academic, critical, and institutional networks involved were all thoroughly politicized. The same holds true for the reinterpretation of already canonic composers in France, as we saw in the dispute over ideological constructions of Beethoven between the Left and the Right.

Such politico-aesthetic confrontations were equally to impinge on French composers, exerting discernible pressures and affecting artistic motivations and career choices. Most perceived that their professional stakes were not without a political dimension—that the value-tensions they confronted were simultaneously both professional and political. They responded in various ways. Many willingly accepted existing divisions and espoused the ideology that was considered the cognate of their musical style. Some, far from isolating themselves hermetically from the surrounding political dissension, developed artistic-social projects or engaged in prose that addressed the ideological issues. Others reacted independently and attempted to ignore the existing stylistic codes, although, as they were well aware, there was a professional price to pay. Just as in French literature, with writers such as Léon Blum, there were those who were attracted aesthetically to the Right but rejected it politically, although in music the professional consequences were severe.[6]

As we have seen, in the aftermath of the Dreyfus Affair, most musicians, like their colleagues in the other arts, considered themselves to be responsible and engaged "intellectuals." As such, and as a result of the discourse around them, they perceived the relation between the aesthetic dimension and the institutional, political, and social orders. They responded in accordance with the positions they had assumed in both the professional and social worlds—and as a result of the political identities that most of them arduously defined. While some, like d'Indy and Charpentier, espoused an established ideological position, others, like Debussy and Satie, assumed a unique and individual perspective. But none of them attempted to serve "social truth" by pristine isolation or perceived the necessity of complete transcendence of the encroaching political world.[7]

In their work, however, the stronger composers did not mirror their politicized projects or prose but responded to ideologically generated meanings through the matrix of their aesthetic sensibilities. As in visual art, their subtler responses are no longer transparent to us today without a thorough knowledge of the codes and contexts in which they worked, and thus how they were "read."[8] Composers were well aware of the existence of meanings behind both forms and styles, and they well knew that powerful critics and commentators were "initiated," propagating and applying the "code." Some composers, realizing that forms, techniques, and styles could address political values within this structure of meaning, responded to them in ingenious ways. This was the case, as we have seen, with Satie and Charpentier, whose polyvalence and bivocality extended equally to their educational "projects."

Knowing that such meanings existed, if for a small but influential elite, other composers felt compelled to engage them in order to make a socially "authentic" statement; they recognized the possibility of misconstrual (as in the case of the defiant Magnard) but also of communicating a positive message (as in the case of Ropartz). Whether they worked within or consciously against the system of meaning, they knew that their message would interact with its structures—that it provided a communicative context. Hence, again, to read simple homologies or metaphors into specific forms and styles, to impose our own sense of their meaning, is to ignore what these composers sought, even if unsuccessfully, to say. The culture reveals these meanings through the surrounding musical discourse, one that, as we have seen, was pervasive in the musical world. Within this context, as well, we have noted that the so-called anxiety of influence—the sense of relation to overpowering predecessors—necessarily carried with it an ideological dimension.[9] To assume a position via a canon meant to assume an ideological stance, one that could be highly complex, as demonstrated by the case of Claude Debussy.

Artistic and political goals were not easily sundered during this period, as we have observed in the careers of composers, in the commentary around them, and in the bases of their support. But, again, political intentions were by no mean inimical to artistic excellence, for the great composers arrived at a balance between particular interests and aesthetic demands.[10] It is for precisely this reason that such works can still be enjoyed today, for the tensions within them work simultaneously on political and abstract planes.

Finally, all these insights help us see and explain the apparent "regression" in French music before the war—in the attempts to reconcile the two musical "poles." Hegemony—power—in the musical world had grown inseparable from political hegemony, so fused had these cultural areas become through the tactics ultimately born of the leagues. Well before the First World War, the turn to the "classic" had already begun, stimulated by the political mythology of those nationalists who now held power. There was thus no break between the cultural politics practiced before the war and the wartime turn to the neoclassical ideal as the "official" French style. By then the more conservative Republic had appropriated the musical rhetoric of the nationalist Right, one that had been developing in France since the period following the Dreyfus Affair. French music thus became integral to the forging of a national "memory" or myth, a sense of indigenous French values that helped define the nation's true "soul."[11] Hence, the concept of a national style and of the "classic" repertoire or canon originally stemmed from political contestation, and eventually from an attempt at a resolution. As we have seen, the technical, aesthetic, social, economic, and political dimensions of this process cannot be easily separated, so intricately were they intertwined. Politics did not "determine" musical direction, but it helped to shape it in various ways, and the political culture was, in turn, itself affected.

French Music and Political Culture

As Jean-François Sirinelli and Eric Vigne have aptly put it, political culture consists not of "pure ideas" but, rather, of what they term a complex "alchemy." It comprises "sieves" and "relays," or various means of transmission and circulation of a given ideology, which inherently modify what began as intellectual or conceptual. It is these carriers of political culture that have become new objects of historical study—these forms and networks of circulation of language, historical memories, and a conception of the world. As Sirinelli and Vigne convincingly argue in the context of the French Right, political "relays" consisted of such vehicles as journals, the publishing world, and the press. Equally central to this phenomenon were networks of "sociability," such as, in this period, salons, which brought together major figures in different cultural spheres. Thus political doctrine circulated through several fields, including, most prominently, literature and history, as well as the visual arts. This created zones of "contact" or "osmosis" between politics and culture, which came to share common values and beliefs, historical references, and canonic texts. The effect of this was profound; indeed, as Christophe Charle has shown, at the time of the Affair the involvement of French literary figures helped to recast the issues and realign factions.[12]

But, as we have seen, in this period these networks of sociability included musicians, who entered as engaged intellectuals or were later recruited in the aftermath of the Dreyfus Affair. Music thus also became a "carrier" or sieve for the political culture, charged, through its own symbolic means, with the representation of a political ideology. As part of the "complex alchemy" of the political culture, its role was distinct: it helped both to elevate and to vulgarize certain key concepts for a variety of political groups. It enlarged the terms and the territory of political debate in France, and it helped prepare for the dominant traditionalism and sense of national memory during World War I. In the course of the war, it would become a symbolic medium of political communication, a means to "imagine the community" and to reference in myth the political principles for which the war was being fought.[13] Music thus continued to be a key zone of contact or osmosis between politics and culture, affecting music as integrally as it did French political culture. This did not end with the war: the symbolic battle that we have traced during the seminal period under study here would continue throughout the interwar period. As we may conclude, the merger of artistic and political cultures is not just the characteristic of totalitarian or absolutist states— it can transpire through contestation in democracies.

Comparisons

In comparison with other countries that enlisted music for nationalistic purposes in this period or earlier, France was in the vanguard, for here the dynamics were changing. In nineteenth-century Germany, Italy, and central Europe, music was a symbol of national culture's contest against foreign political domination; in Russia and Britain, it was against foreign cultural domination. In France, however, with its political and cultural centralization, music became a symbol within an *internal* struggle over conflicting notions of identity and the legitimate state. Through a conscious ideological program carefully crafted by two nationalist leagues, music was pulled into the vortex of political-symbolic contestation within France. Here political values and meanings were associated with musical genres, forms, styles, and conflicting canons through a central institutional matrix. Composers either became politicized as professional and political boundaries disappeared or found their music construed politically on the basis of context and style.

Neither a comparable engagement of composers in internal politics nor the appropriation of existing music by factions was to occur elsewhere before the war and the political confrontation of the inter-war period. A political battle between tradition and innovation would appear in Weimar Germany as the state actively sought to reshape society, and to this end employed the arts.[14] Acquiescence or symbolic resistance would similarly become the choices for composers in Europe (and the Soviet Union) during the period of totalitarian domination. Composers, again, would either comply with the current stylistic meanings and codes, forged within the political discourse, or resist, either openly or more subtly. Many, too, like Richard Strauss, would find themselves courted and then victimized, seeing all too clearly that professional success carried an impossible political price.[15]

In France, political contestation through music would crest in the interwar period, although, as I shall show in a subsequent study, it would continue surreptitiously during the Vichy regime. Indeed, certain elements of the symbolic battle have visibly resurged in postwar France, most recently through the vociferous cultural initiatives of the Front National. Jean-Marie Le Pen's nationalist and racist movement, while focusing publicly on the blacklisting of books, has not neglected music, even holding its own "festivals" of French music. Like the two leagues at the turn of the century, it has contested political legitimacy through culture, using an argument rooted once more in the criterion of the "authentically French." Significantly, the government has again riposted; the first statement of purpose by the Minister of Culture in the Jospin government, Catherine Trautmann, was to "combat" the movement.

The lesson provided by the period we have studied is that political action through culture can be threatening to the symbolic legitimacy of a regime and, as such, cannot be ignored. The American Right and Left today have become all too aware of this fact, particularly in the case of conservative attacks on funding by the National Endowment for the Arts. In the domain of cultural tactics, then, nationalist leagues in France led the way, redrawing the country's cultural geography to make its politics and culture adjacent.

Lucien Febvre once remarked that his attempt to place French history in a larger social context stemmed from the need of French youth in his generation to recapture what they perceived as "reality." His goal was thus to avoid the "distortion" that resulted from the erection of artificial boundaries between areas or sectors of society on the basis of disciplinary divisions.[16] The goal of this study has been to show that the same is true of French music: if we are to explain its evolution in full, we must place it within the appropriate interacting contexts. In the period that we have examined, the musical and political worlds in France were not distinct, their boundaries as clearly demarcated as they appear to be today. To return to Huizinga's terms, it was on this distinctive historic terrain that the "forms" and "functions" of music and politics merged, redefining the French cultural landscape.[17]

NOTES

INTRODUCTION

1. On the conflicts emanating from the French Revolution, see Timothy Tackett, *Becoming a Revolutionary: The Deputies of the French National Assembly and the Emergence of a Revolutionary Culture (1789–1790)* (Princeton, N.J.: Princeton University Press, 1996), p. 313 ff. On the Dreyfus Affair and its impact, see Pierre Birnbaum, ed., *La France de l'Affaire Dreyfus* (Paris: Fayard, 1994); Jean-Denis Bredin, *The Affair: the Case of Alfred Dreyfus* (New York: G. Braziller, 1986); Robert Hoffman, *More Than a Trial: The Struggle for Captain Dreyfus* (New York: Free Press, 1980), and Douglas Johnson, *France and the Dreyfus Affair* (London: Blanford Press, 1966).

The Boulanger and the Panama scandals were essential in preparing the political realignment and oppositions that would crystalize in the course of the Affair and henceforth bifurcate French politics. The Boulanger crisis occurred in 1889, when the wily General Georges Boulanger, backed by the political Left, secretly sought the support of a new French Right. Although the general was exposed and disgraced, the incident did articulate the powerful rise of an urban Right that decisively appropriated the symbolic value of "patriotism" from the Jacobin Left. In addition, this new Right, as opposed to the more traditionalist Right of wealth and social authority, was not only chauvinistic but also authoritarian, demagogic, and violent. On this subject see Gordon Wright, *France in Modern Times* (New York: Rand McNally, 1974), p. 247.

Then came the Panama Scandal in 1892, when the supporters of Ferdinand de Lesseps attempted to raise a loan for the Panama Canal using bribes to politicians and journalists. When the scandal became public, the violently anti-Semitic journalist Alfred Drumont (author of *La France Juive,* 1886) attacked the Jewish agents involved. Despite Drumont's defamation, the so-called scandal ended abruptly in 1893 with an official whitewash, thus disillusioning the supporters of the Moderate government. The result of the scandal was not only further to articulae a political shift of forces but also to speed the development of a leftward trend in Third Republic politics. This was followed by the Dreyfus Affair, the force of which was so profound that the memory of it, and the passions it ignited, have endured almost to the present. On the Panama Scandal, see Wright, pp. 250–251.

2. The Ligue de la Patrie Française was born in January 1899; soon a group within it, seeking a firmer doctrinal foundation, seceded to join Charles Maurras, who founded the journal *Action française* the same year. (The Action Française technically became a league later, in 1905.)

As Serge Berstein observes, the nationalist "Right" in France now embraced those political groups that rejected not only parliamentary democracy but also laïcity and rationalism; henceforth nationalism in France was no longer associated with the Republican Left, as it had been until the Boulanger crisis and the Affair but was now repositioned on the political Right. A "Republican," from this point on, was a solid supporter of parliament and laïcity, a defender of the individual's rights, and distrustful of the army because of its degree of autonomy from the state. See Serge Berstein, "La Ligue," in Jean-François Sirinelli, ed., *Histoire des droites en France* Vol. 2 *Cultures* (Paris: Gallimard, 1992), pp. 64, 77. Most Republicans thus construed the Affair mythically as a contest, which they had triumphantly won, between the forces of righteousness and progress, as opposed to nationalist bigotry and obscurantism. See Gordon Wright, *France in Modern Times,* p. 254.

3. As Berstein points out in "La Ligue," pp. 65–69 and 81–84, the leagues were original political organizations in France, conceived with the appearance of a new populist Right which recruited primarily among French workers and "petits-bourgeois." Their antiparliamentary attitude is further explained by the fact that the parliament was the center of political power in the Third Republic (as in the Fourth).

4. Berstein, "La Ligue," p. 82.

5. Jean-François Sirinelli and Eric Vigne, "Introduction. Des cultures politiques," in Jean-François Sirinelli, ed., *Histoire des droites en France* Vol. 2, p. 7. It is important also to note that, as opposed to the more populist leagues, the membership of these two was largely bourgeois, as well as aristocratic, which had an impact on their substantial funding.

6. On the concept of new modes of political intervention and action in France at this time, see Christophe Charle, *Naissance des "intellectuels" 1880–1900* (Paris: Les Editions du Minuit, 1990), p. 230. On the recruitment of intellectuals in the Patrie Française, see Berstein, "La Ligue," p. 82. As he notes, its membership impressively included twenty-six members of the Académie Française, as well as prominent members of the Institut de France and the Collège de France. Both the Académie and the university had a significant number of members who, while not anti-Republican, remained faithful to a conservative conception of the Republic.

7. The Patrie Française included the leadership and sponsorship of prominent figures in the literary world, such as the poet François Coppée, the critic Jules Lemaître (who had an important column in the *Revue des deux mondes*), and the writer Fernand Brunetière. See Berstein, "La Ligue," p. 82.

8. See, for example, Eugen Weber's classic *Action Française: Royalism and Reaction in Twentieth-Century France* (Stanford, Calif.: Stanford University Press, 1962); Herman Lebovic's *True France. The Wars over Cultural Identity 1900–1945* (Ithaca, N.Y.: Cornell University Press, 1992); and Jean-François Sirinelli, "Littérature et politique: Le

cas Burdeau-Bouteille," *Revue historique* CCXXII (1985) Vol. I: 91–111, and Olivier Corpet, "La Revue," in Jean-François Sirinelli, ed., *Histoire des droites en France* Vol. 2, pp. 161–212.

9. David Carroll, *French Literary Fascism. Nationalism, Anti-Semitism, and the Ideology of Culture* (Princeton, N.J.: Princeton University Press, 1995), pp. 35, 73. Carroll explicitly draws the connection between nationalist and later fascist ideas concerning the fusion of artistic and political causes; see pp. 6–7.

10. Ibid., pp. 83, 72.

11. Ibid., pp. 40, 16. The politicizing of art and literature, of course, was not new to this period in France: after an attempt to depoliticize literature during the Second Empire, its repoliticization was again under way with the Third Republic and escalated in the 1880s (with writers like Zola on the Left and Bourget, Barrès, and Brunetière on the Right), culminating with the Dreyfus Affair. On this subject, see Christophe Charle, *Naissance des "intellectuels"* as well as his *La Crise littéraire à l'époque du naturalisme. Roman, théâtre, politique* (Paris: Presses de l'Ecole Normale Supérieure, 1979).

12. Jean-François Sirinelli and Eric Vigne, "Introduction. Des Cultures politiques," p. 3.

13. See especially Christopher Green, *Cubism and its Enemies. Modern Movements and Reaction in French Art, 1916–1928* (New Haven: Yale University Press, 1987), and Kenneth Silver, *Esprit de Corps. The Art of the Parisian Avant-Garde and the First World War* (Princeton, N.J.: Princeton University Press, 1989). Both books consider the prewar background as well as the war and its aftermath.

14. For treatment of various aspects of this phenomenon, see Charles B. Paul, "Rameau, d'Indy, and French Nationalism," *Musical Quarterly* Vol. LVIII/1 (Jan. 1972): 46–56; Jan Pasler, "Paris: Conflicting Notions of Progress," in Jim Samson, ed., *Music, Society, and the Late Romantic Era* (Englewood Cliffs, N.J.: Prentice Hall, 1991), pp. 389–416; and Michel Faure, *Musique et société du Second Empire aux années vingt* (Paris: Flammarion, 1985).

15. For a wide-ranging treatment of the effect of the politicization of music during the French Revolution, see Malcolm Boyd, ed., *Music and the French Revolution* (Cambridge: Cambridge University Press, 1992).

16. On the use of politically charged images at the time of the Dreyfus Affair and after, see Norman L. Kleeblatt, ed., *The Dreyfus Affair: Art, Truth, and Justice* (Berkeley: University of California Press, 1988).

17. The concept of bivocal forms comes from Abner Cohen, who uses it to describe "an ambiguous unity of cultural and political significance." On this and the anthropological use of Freudian "primary process thought," see Myron J. Aronoff, ed., *Political Anthropology* Vol. 2 *Culture and Political Change* (New Brunswick, N.J.: Transaction Books, 1983), p. 118 ff.

18. Pierre Bourdieu has discussed the concept of "symbolic domination" and "symbolic violence" in many of his books but most recently, and perhaps most relevantly here, in *Méditations pascaliennes* (Paris: Editions du Seuil, 1997). See especially pages 206–214.

19. As Gordon Wright points out, in *France in Modern Times,* p. 258, the coalition was "welded together" by the Dreyfus Affair. The "Gouvernement de Défense Républicaine" lasted from June 1899 to June 1902.

20. Such "essentialism" is characteristic of many, although not all, Marxist and neo-Marxist writers—those who deemphasize the historical aspect. This tendency has been particularly prevalent in studies of politics and music. On the more anthropological approach to the "construction of meaning" that is becoming prominent in historical writing today, see James McMillan, "Social History, 'New Cultural History,' and the Rediscovery of Politics: Some Recent Works on Modern France," *Journal of Modern History* 66 (Dec. 1994): 758.

21. This is one solution to the problem that Charles Rosen perceptively points out of the current opposite alternatives of "master narratives" (in the manner of Adorno) and deconstruction. See his review-article "Did Beethoven Have All the Luck?" *New York Review of Books* Nov. 14, 1996: 57–63.

22. I have taken this concept of an artistic culture from Priscilla Parkhurst Clark, *Literary France. The Making of a Culture* (Berkeley: University of California Press, 1987), pp. 8–12.

23. The role of both Saint-Saëns and Ravel in French cultural politics does become more central during the First World War, particularly that of Ravel in the inter-war period, as I shall show in a subsequent study.

24. On this development, see James McMillan, "Social History, 'New Cultural History,' and the Rediscovery of Politics," p. 757 ff.

25. This conception of the loss of professional autonomy within a field, or "champ," comes from Pierre Bourdieu, "The Market of Symbolic Goods," *Poetics* Vol. 14 (1985): 17.

26. See Johan Huizinga, *Men and Ideas: History, the Middle Ages and the Renaissance,* trans. James S. Holmes and Hans von Marle (New York: Harper and Row, 1959). Also see Pierre Bourdieu, Roger Chartier, and Robert Darnton, "Dialogue à propos de l'histoire culturelle," *Actes de la recherche en sciences sociales* 59 (Sept. 1985): 86–93.

CHAPTER 1

1. See Pierre Birnbaum, ed., *La France de l'Affaire Dreyfus* (Paris: Gallimard, 1994), especially Birnbaum's Introduction, pp. 7–15, and the article by Jean Estebe, "Un Théâtre politique renouvelé," pp. 19–55. On France immediately after the affair, see also Eugen Weber, *France: Fin-de-Siècle* (Cambridge, Mass.: Belknap Press, 1986) and Madeleine Rebérioux, *La République Radicale? 1898–1914* (Paris: Editions du Seuil, 1975). Concerning the political and social changes brought about by the affair, see also Christophe Charle, *La Naissance des "intellectuels" 1880–1900* (Paris: Les Editions du Minuit, 1990).

2. In 1899 the Radical Republicans replaced the more moderate "Opportunists," largely as a result of the Affair. See R. D. Anderson, *France 1870–1914* (London: Routledge and Kegan Paul, 1977), p. 5. On the Right and its incursion into the realm of French culture see Herman Lebovics, *True France. The Wars over Cultural Identity 1900–1945* (Ithaca, N.Y.: Cornell University Press, 1992).

3. Dreyfus himself had been "pardoned" in 1899 by the President, Emile Loubet, but was not to be formally acquitted until 1906. See Richard D. Mandell, *Paris 1900: The Great World's Fair* (Toronto: University of Toronto Press, 1967), p. 102.

4. On the origins of the leagues in the 1880s and their increasing prominence at the time of the affair, because of their ability to express political aspirations that traditional political channels could not, see Serge Berstein, *La France des années 30* (Paris: Armand Colin, 1988), p. 61. See also Jean-Pierre Rioux, *Nationalisme de conservatisme. La Ligue de la Patrie Française* (Paris: Beauchesne, 1977).

5. On the relation between the Ligue de la Patrie Française and the Ligue de l'Action Française see Jean-Pierre Rioux, *Nationalisme et conservatisme. La Ligue de la Patrie Française.*

6. On the intellectual impact of Wagner in Europe, including France, see David Large and William Weber, eds., *Wagnerism in European Culture and Politics* (Ithaca, N.Y.: Cornell University Press, 1984).

7. Christophe Charle, *La Naissance des "intellectuels," 1880–1900,* pp. 65, 107, 131.

8. See Frédérique Patureau, *Le Palais Garnier dans la société parisienne 1875–1914* (Liège: Margada, 1991), pp. 186, 274. She makes specific reference to the "groupe de la

musique," which included Xavier Leroux, Alfred Bruneau, Camille Erlanger, Gabriel Piérné, and Georges Huë.

9. I am greatly indebted to Christophe Charle, who brought these petitions to my attention and lent me his own photocopies of them.

10. I am most grateful to Sabina Ratner, who generously provided me with this material, which will appear in her forthcoming biography of Saint-Saëns, to be published by the Editions du Seuil, Paris. The remark of Colonne is contained in a letter of Sept. 3, 1898, to Castillon de Beauxhostes, as cited in Jacqueline Gachet's *Les Représentations lyriques aux arènes de Béziers de 1898 à 1911* (Université Paris IV, Thèse de Doctorat, 3e cycle, n.d.). The letter from Saint-Saëns concerning the chanson and the league is that of April 24, 1899, written from the Hotel de la Régence, in Algiers. It is contained on the catalogue of Saint-Saëns's autograph letters, of Dec. 1986, no. 298.

11. Rioux, *Nationalisme et conservatisme*, p. 11.

12. Alfred Bruneau, "Souvenirs inédits," *Revue international de musique française* Vol. 7 (Feb. 1989): 8; and Frédérique Patureau, *Le Palais Garnier dans la société parisienne*, p. 225. The Second Grand Prix de Rome did not confer the same "consecration" as the Premier Prix.

13. Alfred Bruneau, *A l'Ombre d'un grand coeur* (Paris: Charpentier, 1932), p. 10. This style he denounces as "le règne tyrannique de la cavatine, des couplets à vocalises, des formules commodément modifiable au gré des intreprétations virtuoses." Ironically, Vincent d'Indy, too, along with the group around César Franck, would also share these beliefs, although for different reasons and seeking a different solution.

14. Jean-Max Guieu, *Le Théâtre lyrique d'Emile Zola* (Paris: Fishbacher, 1983), p. 112. When Bruneau met Zola, the latter had already promised Bruneau's teacher, Massenet, the rights to *La Faute d'Abbé Mouret*.

15. Alfred Bruneau, *A L'Ombre d'un grand coeur*, p. 10.

16. Zola's political opinions were already well known in France, especially since the appearance of his article "Pour les Juifs," in *Le Figaro*, on May 16, 1896. But with the article "J'Accuse," he effectively "relaunched" the affair, making it a public and political issue. See Christophe Charle, *La Naissance des "intellectuels,"* p. 162. To demonstrate solidarity with Zola, Bruneau signed the "Protestation" in favor of Col. Picquart, of Nov. 28, 1898. On Bruneau's popularity to this point, see Marie-Christine Casale-Monsimet, "L'Affaire Dreyfus et la critique musicale," *Revue internationale de musique française* Vol. 28 (Feb. 1982): 63–65. Bruneau discusses the demonstrations against the operas in *A l'Ombre d'un grand coeur*. On this subject also see Adolphe Boschot, *La Vie et les oeuvres d'Alfred Bruneau* (Paris: Fasquelles, 1937), pp. 19–20.

17. On the anti-Dreyfusard belief in "Tradition," as established by "ancestors," see Jean-Pierre Rioux, *Nationalisme et conservatisme*, p. 36.

18. Casale-Monsimet, "L'Affaire Dreyfus et la critique musicale," p. 62.

19. See Robert Hoffmann, *More Than a Trial: The Struggle over Captain Dreyfus* (New York: Free Press, 1963), pp. 149, 162.

20. On the French nobility and anti-Dreyfusism, see Rioux, *Nationalisme et conservatisme*, p. 46.

21. Léon Vallas, *Vincent d'Indy* 2 Vols. (Paris: Albin Michel, 1950), p. 18.

22. Rioux, pp. 45, 114–115. On utopian socialism and its relation to music in France, see Jane F. Fulcher, "Music and the Communal Order: The Vision of Utopian Socialism in France," *Current Musicology* (Summer 1979): 27–35.

23. Joseph Canteloube, *Vincent d'Indy* (Paris: Henri Laurens, 1951), p. 11, and Léon Vallas, *Vincent d'Indy*, p. 22.

24. Vallas, pp. 28, 56.

25. Ibid., pp. 56, 72.

26. Canteloube, *Vincent d'Indy*, pp. 17, 20.

27. Vallas, pp. 13, 87–92.

28. Ibid., p. 13.

29. Canteloube, pp. 22–23.

30. On the impact of the Franco-Prussian war on French music, see Martin Cooper, *French Music from the Death of Berlioz to the Death of Fauré* (London: Oxford University Press, 1951).

31. Canteloube, p. 26. Michael Strasser is currently completing a detailed study of the founding and history of the Société Nationale de Musique Française as a dissertation at the University of Illinois at Champaign-Urbana.

32. Canteloube, pp. 29, 32.

33. Ibid., pp. 35–40. This is also the period when d'Indy appears in Fantin-Latour's portrait of the major French Wagnerian composers and critics, including Chabrier, Adolphe Jullien, and Camille Benoit.

34. Vallas, pp. 20 and 26. On the "Ralliement," see Edward Tannenbaum, *The Action Française: Die-hard Reactionaries in Twentieth-Century France* (New York: Wiley, 1962), p. 15, and R. D. Anderson, *France 1870–1914*, p. 5.

35. Vallas, p. 26.

36. Vallas, pp. 26–27, and Vincent d'Indy, *La Schola Cantorum en 1925* (Paris: Bloud et Gay, 1927), p. 48.

37. On Wagner and his perception of the revolution in Dresden, see Carl E. Schorske, "Wagner and Morris: The Quest for the Grail," in *The Critical Spirit; Essays in Honor of Herbert Marcuse* ed. by Kurt H. Wolff and Barrington Moore (Boston: Beacon Press, 1967). On the role of Right-wing "intellectuals" and aristocrats in the Affair, see Christophe Charle, *Naissance des "intellectuels,"* pp. 184 and 224.

38. D'Indy, *La Schola Cantorum en 1925*, p. 48.

39. Ibid., p. 128. On the background of religious music in nineteenth-century France, see Danièle Pistone, *La Musique en France de la Révolution à 1900* (Paris: Honoré Champion, 1979), pp. 131–132, 142. As Debussy wittily recounted in *Gil Blas*, on Feb. 2, 1903, Bordes originally organized a series of concerts for Holy Week to perform Renaissance choral music, at this point not often heard in France; given the poverty of contemporary religious music, the concerts were such a success that the ranking clergy condemned them for having "distracted the faithful." See François Lesure, ed., *Debussy on Music* (New York: Knopf, 1977), p. 110.

40. See Gail Hilson Woldu, *Gabriel Fauré as Director of the Conservatoire National de Musique et de Declamation, 1902–1920*, Ph.D. Dissertation, Yale University, 1983, pp. 43–45.

41. See Lynn Hunt, *Politics, Culture, and Class in the French Revolution* (Berkeley: University of California Press, 1989), p. 56.

42. Georges Favre, *Compositeurs français méconnus. Ernest Guiraud et ses amis: Emile Paladilhe et Théodore Dubois* (Paris: La Pensée Universelle, 1983), p. 101.

43. Ibid., p. 114.

44. Gail Hilson Woldu, *Gabriel Fauré as Director of the Conservatoire National*, p. 84.

45. On the Conservatoire, see Gail Hilson Woldu, "Gabriel Fauré, directeur du Conservatoire: les reformes de 1905," *Revue de musicologie* Vol. 70/2 (1984): 119–228. On the Société des Concerts du Conservatoire and the performance of the "classic" repertoire in France, see William Weber, *Music and the Middle Class: The Social Structure of Concert Life in London, Paris, and Vienna* (London: Crooms Helm, 1975), pp. 69–73.

46. Myriam Chimènes, "Le Budget de la musique sous la IIIe République," in *La*

Musique. Du théorique au politique eds. Hugues Dufourt and Joel-Marie Fauquet (Paris: Aux Amateurs de Livres, 1991), p. 279.

47. Rioux, pp. 28–29, and Pascal Ory, "Le Salon," in Jean-François Sirinelli, ed., *Histoire des droites en France* Vol. 2 *Cultures* (Paris: Gallimard, 1992), pp. 124–125.

48. Ibid., pp. 56–60. Also see Marc Martin, "Les Journalistes et l'Affaire Dreyfus," in *L'Affaire Dreyfus et le tournant du siècle (1894–1910)*, pp. 110–115, eds. Laurent Gervereau and Christophe Prochasson (Paris: Musée d'Histoire Contemporaine-BDIC, 1994).

49. See Gabriel Aubray, "Les Ecrivains et la Nation," *Annales de la Patrie Française* Vol. 1 (May 1, 1900): 19–20. On Barrès's view, see David Carroll, *French Literary Fascism. Nationalism, Anti-Semitism, and the Ideology of Culture* (Princeton, N.J.: Princeton University Press, 1995).

50. Rioux, pp. 52–55.

51. See d'Indy's letters to the league of June 13, 1899, and October 20, 1902, *Lettres Autographes*, Bibliothèque Nationale, Département de la Musique. And see Serge Berstein, "La Ligue," in Jean-François Sirinelli, ed., *Histoire des droites en France* Vol. 2, pp. 81, 83.

52. Brian Hart, The Symphony in Theory and Practice in France 1900–1914, Ph.D. Dissertation, Indiana University, 1994, pp. 78–81.

53. Vincent d'Indy, "Une Ecole d'art répondant aux besoins modernes," *La Tribune de Saint-Gervais* Nov. 1900, p. 311.

54. Paul Bertrand, *Le Monde de la musique* (Genève: La Palatine, 1947), p. 75, and François Lesure, ed., *Debussy on Music,* p. 111.

55. See Christophe Charle, "Noblesses et élites en France au début du XXe siècle," in *Noblesses Européens au XIXe siècle* (Paris: Collection de l'Ecole Française de Rome 107, 1988), p. 410.

56. Marcel Proust, *Le Côté des Guermantes* I (Paris: Gallimard, 1954), pp. 38, 129.

57. D'Indy, "Une Ecole d'art," p. 311, and Brian Hart, *The Symphony in Theory and Practice in France,* p. 81.

58. Hart, pp. 82–89.

59. D'Indy, *Lettres Autographes,* Département de la Musique, Bibliothèque Nationale. This letter was very kindly brought to the attention of Brian Hart by Michael Strasser, and Dr. Hart generously shared it with me.

60. Hart, p. 82. And see d'Indy's *Cours de composition musicale* 2 Vols. (Paris: Durand et Fils); Vol. I, published in 1903, is based on d'Indy's lectures of 1897–98 and covers the first year of "Art"; Vol. II, Book I, published in 1909, is based on his lectures of 1899–1900 and covers the second year of "Art"; Vol. II, Book II, published in 1933, is based on the lectures of 1901–1902 and covers the third year of "Art." All the volumes are based on the notes of d'Indy's student, Auguste Seriéyx, most of which d'Indy himself later supervised; Guy de Lioncourt edited the final volume in 1950, which covers years four and five. Again, I am indebted to Brian Hart for this clarification.

61. Rioux, p. 40. Here it is important to note that d'Indy diverged with the Ligue de la Patrie Française, which was, in fact, attempting to discourage the anti-Semitism so prominent in Catholic circles.

62. See d'Indy, "Une Ecole d'art," p. 311. It is significant to note that this was a moment of great popularity for Meyerbeer: in 1898, for example, *Le Prophète* was the most financially successful opera produced at the Paris Opera. See Frédérique Patureau, *Le Palais Garnier dans la société parisienne 1875–1914* (Liège: Margada, 1991), p. 283.

63. Robert Orledge, "D'Indy, Vincent," in *The New Grove Dictionary of Music and Musicians,* vol. 9, pp. 221–222. Edited by Stanley Sadie (London: Macmillan, 1980).

64. Canteloube, p. 29.

65. Zeev Sternhell, *Maurice Barrès et le nationalisme français* (Paris: Armand Colin,

1972), p. 23. As Sternhell points out, Barrès's ideas on Wagner may be found in his *Du Sang, de la volupté, et de la mort*. See also Claude Digeon, *La Crise Allemand de la pensée française 1870–1914* (Paris: Presses Universitaires de France, 1959), p. 413.

66. Romain Rolland, *Musiciens d'aujourd'hui* (Paris: Hachette, 1912), p. 273, Sternhell, *Maurice Barrès*, p. 4, and David Carroll, *French Literary Fascism*, p. 21.

67. On the "mobilizing" themes of the league, see Rioux, pp. 37, 48–49, and 62.

68. D'Indy, "Une Ecole d'art," pp. 303–305.

69. Ibid., p. 312, and Vallas, *Vincent d'Indy*, p. 58.

70. Rioux, p. 76; Eugen Weber, *Action Française: Royalism and Reaction in Twentieth-Century France* (Stanford, Calif.: Stanford University Press, 1962), p. 18, and Jack Roth, *The Cult of Violence: Sorel and the Sorelians* (Berkeley: University of California Press, 1980), p. 19.

71. This point is discussed at length by Brian Hart in "*La Mer* and the Meaning of the Symphony in Twentieth-Century France." Paper delivered at the annual meeting of the American Musicological Society, Pittsburgh, 1983.

72. D'Indy, "Une Ecole d'art," p. 305.

73. Ibid., pp. 310–311.

74. Ibid., p. 311.

75. Vincent d'Indy, *Lettres Autographes*, Bibliothèque Nationale, Département de la Musique. This was the same month that d'Indy's inaugural lecture for the Schola's new building, "Une Ecole d'art . . . ," was published in *La Tribune de Saint-Gervais*.

76. Vincent d'Indy, *Lettres Autographes*, Bibliothèque Nationale, Département de la Musique.

77. David James Fisher, "Romain Rolland the Ideology and Aesthetics of the French People's Theater," *Theater Quarterly* Vol. 9/33 (Spring 1979), p. 95. This is as opposed to the view of Antoine Compagnon that the Third Republic had a sense of the strict limitations of its cultural competence, particularly in the field of art. See his article, "Utopie d'une République athénienne," *Le Debat* Vol. 70 (May–Aug. 1992): 42.

78. Richard Mandell, *Paris 1900: The Great World's Fair* (Toronto: University of Toronto Press), p. 92, and Eugen Weber, *France: Fin-de-Siècle*, pp. 124, 238. On the ideological goals of the previous exposition, in 1889, see Lebovics, *True France*, p. 53.

79. Robert Hoffman, *More Than a Trial*, p. 152; Eugen Weber, *France: Fin-de-Siècle*, p. 124; Mandel, *Paris 1900*, pp. 90–91; and René Rémond, *Les Droits en France* (Paris: Aubier Montaigne, 1982), p. 148.

80. See Christophe Charle, "La Science et les savants: le debut de l'age d'or?" in *L'Affaire Dreyfus et le tournant du siècle*, pp. 66–71.

81. Madeleine Rebérioux, *La République Radical?*, p. 37. As Frédérique Patureau points out in *Le Palais Garnier dans la société parisienne*, p. 390, the attempt on the part of the Republic to make art available to the lower social classes in the 1880s, seemed to be a logical outgrowth of the principles of the French Revolution.

82. Eugen Weber, *Action Française*, p. 18, and Mandell, *Paris 1900*, p. 103.

83. Julian Jackson, *The Popular Front in France: Defending Democracy 1934–38* (Cambridge: Cambridge University Press, 1988), p. 2.

84. Anderson, *France*, p. 89.

85. Jean Touchard, *La Gauche en France depuis 1900* (Paris: Editions du Seuil, 1968), p. 28, and Anderson, p. 3.

86. Elaine Brody, *Paris: The Musical Kaleidoscope 1870–1925* (New York: George Braziller, 1987), p. 94.

87. Patureau, p. 274. This activism might well have been stimulated by earlier Republican initiatives, for in 1877 the government sponsored two provincial concert soci-

eties devoted to the propagation on French music, in addition to a subvention for the Société Nationale.

88. Patureau, pp. 433–435. In a letter to his friend Marcel Labey, d'Indy expresses his
opinion that the concerts were "serious" and should not be dismissed; he then gives Labey
advice as to whom to contact concerning a performance of his work. See the letter of July
21, 1895, from d'Indy to Labey, *Lettres Autographes,* Bibliothèque Nationale, Département
de la Musique. An impetus for the Opera Concerts may have been Edouard Colonne's series of "national" and historical concerts in the 1870s and '80s, as Jan Pasler discusses in
"Building a Public for Orchestral Music: Les Concerts Colonne," paper read at the conference "Concert et Public: Mutation de la Vie Musicale en Europe de 1780 à 1914," Göttin-
gen, Germany, Max-Planck-Institut für Geschichte, June 27–29, 1996. But it is important
to realize that here, in the context of firmly establishing "patriotism" and the Republic, in
the 1870s and early '80s, the political implications were entirely different, and the dialogic
element was not yet present.

It is important to note that, even before this, the state had the means of actively promoting new French musical works without resorting to official commissions: one way was
through such prizes as that of the Fondation Cressent, the jury of which included major
academic figures. The other, as we shall see, was to make the subventioning of concert societies dependent on the performance of new French works. See Chimènes, "Le Budget de
la musique," pp. 53–55. Hence, despite the fact that music was bureaucratically tied to the
academic as opposed to the "officiel" system, the latter continually interacted with the former, and thus exerted an indirect influence on the definition of aesthetic legitimacy.

89. Patureau, p. 275.

90. Ibid., pp. 433–435.

91. Leon Gastinel, *Influence des Expositions Universelles et Internationales sur l'art musical français autre-fois, au-jourd'hui, demain* (Paris: Imprimerie de la Poste, n.d.), p. 50.

92. Ibid., p. 11, and Elaine Brody, *Paris: The Musical Kaleidoscope,* p. 93.

93. This is as opposed to the Second Empire, when the arts were placed under the
Ministry of the Interior. See Marie-Claude Gênet-Delacroix, "Esthétique officiel et art national sous la Troisième République," *Le Mouvement social* Vol. 131 (April–June 1985):
111–114.

94. Ibid. Also see Marie-Claude Gênet-Delacroix, *Art et Etat sous la IIIe République. Le
Systeme des Beaux-arts 1870–1940* (Paris: Publications de la Sorbonne, 1992).

95. To quote the official legislation of 1896, concerning the conservation of artistic
monuments: "L'histoire des origines d'un pays, de sa civilization, de son génie, . . . est
écrite dans ses monuments. . . . La préoccupation de conserver les objets d'art, temoins
du temps passé, repond donc a un sentiment national." Gênet-Delacroix, "Esthétique officiel," p. 111.

96. The names are as listed in the review of Bruneau's report, in the *Revue d'histoire
et de critique musicale* (March 1901), by "X," "Ancien membre de la commission,"
pp. 110–111. And see Pierre Lalo in *Le Temps* (June 12, 1900).

97. For the remainder of the voting, see the review of Bruneau's "report" by "X,"
pp. 111–112.

98. The letter of d'Indy to Paul-Marie Masson, of March 30, 1900, is in the *Lettres Autographes,* Bibliothèque Nationale, Département de la Musique. As Brian Hart points out,
in *The Symphony in Theory and Practice,* pp. 278–282, several critics, including Pierre Lalo
in *Le Temps* (June 12, 1900), complained of the lack of symphonic music in the programs.

99. On the concept of master fictions, see Sean Wilentz, ed., *Rites of Power: Symbolism, Ritual, and Politics Since the Middle Ages* (Philadelphia: University of Pennsylvania
Press, 1985), p. 3.

100. Alfred Bruneau, *La Musique française*. Rapport sur la musique en France du XIIIe siècle au XXe siècle. La Musique à Paris en 1900 au théâtre, au concert, à l'Exposition. (Paris: Bibliothèque Charpentier, 1901), pp. 1–7. He does, however, acknowledge a precedent: in 1879 the Commission des Grandes Auditions attempted, in the course of ten concerts (conducted by Eduard Colonne), to sum up and characterize the development of the "French School" in music since 1830.

101. Ibid., p. 11.

102. Ibid., p. 13.

103. Ibid., p. 73.

104. Ibid., pp. 20–24.

105. Ibid., pp. 147–148.

106. Ibid., p. 154.

107. Ibid., p. 50.

108. Ibid., p. 242.

109. It appeared in March 1901.

110. Review of the "Rapport" by "X," *Revue d'histoire et de critique musicale* (March 1901), p. 110.

111. Ibid., p. 112.

112. Ibid., p. 114.

113. Ibid., p. 115. Here he goes on to point out that Bruneau then proceeds to make matters even worse by leaping across other important periods in order to arrive at Lully and Gluck.

114. Ibid., p. 115.

115. Ibid., pp. 115–116.

116. Ibid., p. 118.

117. Ibid., pp. 117–118.

118. Vallas, *D'Indy*, p. 20. D'Indy presided over competitions between Orphéon groups in the 1880s.

119. Review of Bruneau's "Rapport" by "X," p. 118.

120. "Willy" [Henri Gaulthier-Villars], "Qu'est ce que la musique française?" *Revue d'histoire et de critique musicale* (March 1903): 123–127.

121. François Caradec, *Feu Willy* (Paris: J. J. Pauvet, 1984), pp. 5, 107.

122. Willy, "Qu'est ce que la musique française?" p. 123.

123. Ibid., p. 124.

124. Vallas, p. 50. And see Olivier Corpet, "La revue," in Jean-François Sirinelly, ed., *Histoire des droites en France* Vol. 2, p. 166.

125. Maurice Denis, *Nouvelles théories sur l'art moderne: sur l'art sacrée 1914–1921* (Paris: Rouart et Watelin, 1921), p. 239. On the Context for Denis's conservative artistic views, see Michael Marlais, *Conservative Echoes in Fin-de-Siècle Parisian Art Criticism* (University Park, Pa.: Pennsylvania State University Press, 1992).

126. See Jane F. Fulcher, "D'Indy's 'Drame anti-Juif' and Its Meaning in Paris, 1920," *Cambridge Opera Journal* Vol. II/2: 295–319. On Jews in Paris and their association with the "oriental," see Paula Hyman, *From Dreyfus to Vichy: The Remaking of French Jewry, 1906–1939* (New York: Columbia University Press, 1979), pp. 63–64, 66, and 68. Also see David Carroll, *French Literary Fascism*, pp. 32, 75.

127. Lionel de la Laurencie, "Un Musicien de chez nous," *L'Occident* 1904: 1–10.

128. Ibid., p. 3.

129. Ibid., p. 7.

130. Ibid., p. 10.

131. Vallas, p. 56. The "Motu proprio" is reporduced in the appendix to Nicolas Slominsky's *Music Since 1900* (New York: Schirmer, 1994).

132. Vallas, p. 42, and Lionel de la Laurencie, "L'Oeuvre de Vincent d'Indy," *Durendel. Revue Catholique d'art et de littérature* (April 1902): 204–215.

133. La Laurencie, "L'Oeuvre de Vincent d'Indy," p. 205.

134. Ibid., p. 206.

135. Ibid., pp. 214–315.

136. Lionel de la Laurencie, "Le d'Indysme," *L'Art moderne* (Feb. 5, 1903), p. 49.

137. Ibid., pp. 50–51.

138. On the disillusionment of former Dreyfusards and the decline of the "Republican mystique," see Antoine Compagnon, *La Troisième République des lettres. De Flaubert à Proust* (Paris: Editions du Seuil, 1983), p. 121.

139. Mauclair was a signer of the Dreyfusard Manifest des Intellectuels. On his earlier anarchist period, see Eugen Weber, *France: Fin-de-Siècle,* p. 119.

140. Camille Mauclair, "La Schola Cantorum et l'education morale des musiciens," *La Revue* (Aug. 1901): 245, 253–54, 256.

141. See *Le Libertaire* (Feb. 8–15, 1896).

142. Mauclair, "La Schola Cantorum . . . ," p. 256.

143. Ibid., pp. 246, 256.

144. Ibid., pp. 242, 247–248.

145. Ibid., p. 251.

146. Ibid., p. 250.

147. Ibid., p. 251.

148. Ibid., p. 252.

149. Jean Marnold, "Le Conservatoire et la Schola," *Mercure de France* (1902): 105–115.

150. Ibid., pp. 105–106. Other examples of rarely performed repertoire that he cites include the works of the "clavecinistes" and organists of the seventeenth and eighteenth centuries, the works of Carissimi, the lieder of Schubert and Schumann, the organ chorales of Bach and Franck, and Mozart's *Requiem.*

151. Ibid., pp. 107–108.

152. Ibid., p. 111. In order to expand on Dubois's purported intolerance, Marnold recounts the reputed incident that occurred while Dubois was still teaching a class in harmony, when one of the students brought a score of *Parsifal* into the room. It caused such a commotion among the students that Dubois is said to have forbade the student to ever bring it into the institution again.

153. On the "liberal Right," see René Rémond, *Les Droites en France* (Paris: Aubier Montaigne, 1982).

154. Marnold, "Le Conservatoire et la Schola," p. 112.

155. Lionel de la Laurencie, "Le Mouvement musicographique," *Le Mercure musical* (June 1907): 659.

156. Her books include *Les Concerts en France sous l'ancien regime* (1900), and *La Musique de la Sainte-Chapelle du Palais* (1910).

157. See Michel Brênet, "La Musicologie," in *Rapport sur la musique française contemporaine,* pp. 18–19, ed. by Paul-Marie Masson (Rome: Armam et Stein, 1913).

158. It was Jules Combarieu who organized the "Congress" on music history, held in conjunction with the 1900 Universal Exposition. Another scholar, who specialized in education, Lionel Dauriac, was given "cours libres" to teach at the Sorbonne.

159. David James Fisher, "Romain Rolland and the Ideology and Aesthetics of the

French People's Theater," p. 87, and see Romain Rolland's *Théâtre de la Revolution* (Paris: Albin Michel, 1972).

160. Fisher, "Romain Rolland . . . ," pp. 84, 87.

161. Ibid., pp. 85–86, 97.

162. Ibid., p. 97. As Fisher points out, after 1904 Rolland enlarged his conceptions further by studying Rousseau's writings on festivals and David's on revolutionary theater and pantomime. He would be further influenced by his own personal experience of modern spectacles on Lausanne, Switzerland.

163. Romain Rolland, *La Vie de Beethoven* Vol. I (Paris: Hachette, 1903), pp. 98–99. D'Indy's perspective on Beethoven is discussed in chapter 4.

164. Romain Rolland, *Haendel* (Paris: Felix Alcan, 1911), pp. 17, 140.

165. Ibid., p. 142.

166. Christophe Prochasson, "Sur l'environnement intellectuel de Georges Sorel: L'Ecole des Hautes Etudes Sociales (1899–1911)," Cahiers *Georges Sorel* 3 (1985): 17. She was the sister of the historian Georges Weill.

167. Ibid. The College Libre des Sciences Sociales was directed successively by Théodore Franck-Brentano; the doctor Eugene Dalbert; and the "progressiste" deputy of the Seine-et-Marne Paul Deschanel. As Prochasson points out, it was based on the principle of theoretical plurality and offered lectures in economics, sociology, philosophy, and history.

168. Ibid., pp. 17–20. The institution received a subvention of 12,000 francs, as voted by Parliament in 1900–01. When it opened in November 1900, its president was Emile Boutroux, its director Emile Duclaux, and its three "administrators" were (the editor) Felix Alcan, Charles Gueryesi, and Georges Sorel. Its Comité de direction was composed of fifty-five members, half of whom were university figures. They included the historians Alphonse Aulard and Ernest Lavisse, the sociologist Gabriel de Tarde, and the "Directeur de Travail," Arthur Fontaine. Prochasson, "Sur l'environnement intellectuel de Georges Sorel," pp. 21–25.

169. Ibid., pp. 26–28, and David James Fisher, *Romain Rolland and the Politics of Intellectual Engagement* (Berkeley: University of California Press, 1988), p. 93.

170. Prochasson, pp. 28–29.

171. See Marie-Claude Gênet-Delacroix, "Esthétique officiel et art national sous la Troisième Republique," as well as *Art et Etat sous la IIIe Republique.*

172. On Sorel, see Prochasson, pp. 30–33. Sorel gave only two lectures at the institution—one in 1901, on "Valeur morale de l'art," and one, in 1903, on Marx.

173. Romain Rolland, "Musique," in *L'Ecole des Haues Etudes Sociales 1900–1910* (Paris: Felix Alcan, 1911), pp. 69–70.

174. Ibid. As Rolland points out, there were regular courses that ran from year to year as well as isolated lectures on various subjects.

175. Ibid., pp. 71–74. Julien Tiersot lectured on the "Chanson populaire"; Maurice Emmanuel (who was associated with the Conservatoire) spoke on "Musique tonale classique: fugue, sonate, symphonie"; and Hellouin lectured on "Les Nationalités musicales" and "La Critique musicale."

176. On the "salon," see Prochasson, pp. 26–28.

177. Rolland, in *L'Ecole des Hautes Etudes Sociales,* pp. 75–76. Lists of the works presented in the concerts are given on p. 77–78.

CHAPTER 2

1. See Brian Hart, *The Symphony in Theory and Practice in France 1900–1914,* Ph.D. Dissertation, Indiana University, 1994, pp. 82–103, 433–434.

2. Ibid.

3. Ibid.

4. René de Castera, "La Symphonie en si bemol de M. Vincent d'Indy," *L'Occident* (March 1904): 174–175.

5. Letter of Sept. 17, 1903, from d'Indy to Pierre de Bréville, as cited by Vallas, *Vincent d'Indy* 2 vols. (Paris: Albin Michel, 1950), Vol. II, p. 327. Vallas, who provides much of the information on this period of d'Indy's life, was a close friend of the composer from 1900 on. In 1902 he helped to found a branch of the Schola Cantorum in Lyon, together with Georges Wittokowski. See Christian Goubault, *La Critique musicale dans la presse française de 1870 à 1914* (Genève-Paris: Editions Slatkine, 1984), p. 78.

6. Adolphe Boschot, *Chez les musiciens* (Paris: Plon, 1922), p. 208. Massenet also used it in *Thaïs;* in literature, it was used by such figures as Flaubert and Anatole France.

7. Alain Boureau, *La Légende dorée: Le system narratif de Jacques de Voragine* (Paris, 1984), pp. 7–14. Theodore de Wyzewa was one of the editors of the *Revue Wagnérienne.*

8. Vallas, *Vincent d'Indy,* p. 326. The score was published by Rouart, Lerolle, et Cie. in 1918.

9. My synopsis is based on the French translation of the *Legende Aurea* published by Editions Rombaldi in Paris, 1942.

10. Vallas, p. 327.

11. This idea is developed by Reinhard Strohm in "Dramatic Time and Operatic Form in Wagner's *Tannhäuser,*" *Proceedings of the Royal Musical Association* 1977: 1–10.

12. As we shall see, the reference here is to Conservatoire students who supported Debussy.

13. See Reinhard Strohm, "Dramatic Time and Operatic Form in Wagner's *Tannhäuser.*"

14. René Dumesnil, *La Musique en France entre deux guerres 1919–1939* (Genève: Editions du Milieu du Monde, 1946), p. 86. For such scholarly research on the mystery play, see Gustave Cohen, *Histoire de la mise en scène dans le théâtre réligieux français du moyen age* (Paris: Honoré Champion, 1926).

15. Vallas, p. 328. However, d'Indy, in his *Cours de composition musical* Vol. I (Paris: Durand et Fils, 1903), p. 202, points out that *Fervaal* is in three acts, each with three scenes, and instead of interpreting this structure nationalistically, he describes its plan here as a "vaste lied."

16. See d'Indy's later *Richard Wagner et son influence sur l'art musical aujourd'hui* (Paris: Librairie Delagrave, 1930), p. 48. Vallas discusses tonal structure and d'Indy's symbolic use of keys in great detail (p. 326 ff.), noting the larger movement from B minor to B major, as well as the use of G for "gold." He lays out d'Indy's own diagram of the tonal plan, as does Fernand Biron, in *Le Chant gregorien dans l'enseignement et les oeuvres musicales de Vincent d'Indy* (Ottawa: Les Editions de l'Université d'Ottawa, 1941), p. 166.

17. These borrowings are analyzed and discussed in detail by Vallas (pp. 336–338) and Biron (pp. 171–172). Gregorian themes are used to symbolize the Cross (through a chant that makes reference to it) as well as "Prière," "l'Oracle," and "la Mort Chrétienne."

18. As Vallas, among others, notes (p. 335), d'Indy makes musical reference to Bach's Passions and to Beethoven's Mass; he also posits the influence of Debussy's *Le Martyr de Saint Sebastien* (premiered as d'Indy was nearing the completion of the score) on d'Indy's conception of a "modern" spiritualistic style (p. 341).

19. Where Wagner used the tritone judiciously for its "devilish" connotations, d'Indy employs it repeatedly, together with consecutive perfect fourths.

20. Vallas, pp. 335–336.

21. See Jean-Pierre Rioux, *Nationalisme et conservatisme. La Ligue de la Patrie Française* (Paris: Beauchesne, 1977), pp. 109, 114–115.

22. In an undated letter to the league, d'Indy reports that he has recruited Ernest Chausson and Pierre de Bréville. Also see his letter to the league of June 13, 1899, in d'Indy, *Lettres Autographes,* Bibliothèque National, Département de la Musique. And see the letters of October 20, 1902 and October 30, 1903, as well as other letters dated 1903.

23. Rioux, *Nationalisme et conservatisme,* pp. 107–108.

24. See, for example, the letters of March 12, 1909, and November 24, 1912, *Lettres Autographes,* Bibliothèque Nationale, Département de la Musique.

25. Gaston Carraud, *La Vie, l'oeuvre, et la mort d'Alberic Magnard* (Paris: Rouart, Lerolle, et Cie., 1921), pp. 24–48, 100, 113, 118.

26. Ibid., pp. 89–91.

27. As cited by Fréderic Malmazet in his notes to the cassette recording of Magnard's *Hymne à la Justice;* and see Carraud, pp. 82–83, 125.

28. On performative context, see Richard Bauman, *Verbal Art as performance* (Rowley, Mass.: Newbury House, 1977).

29. Martin Cooper refers to it as a "cross between the middle class 'comédie larmoyante' of the eighteenth century and a sentimental defense of free love, set against a pretentious mythical background," in *French Music from the Death of Berlioz to the Death of Fauré* (London: Oxford University Press, 1951), p. 111. Another indication of how misunderstood this work has been in the English-speaking world is that from the time of the first English edition, its subtitle, "Roman musical," has been incorrectly translated as "a musical romance," which reflects the misconstrual of its content. There have, however, been composers outside France who immediately appreciated the work, among them Richard Strauss. On his praise of the opera, see Edward Lockspeiser, *Debussy: His Life and Mind* (London: Cassell and Comp., Ltd., 1965), p. 90. Another composer who appreciated and even emulated it was Leoš Janáček; on his attraction to and use of the work, see Jaroslav Vogel, *Leos Janáček* (Kassel: Alkor-Edition, 1958). As Vogel points out, it was after Charpentier's example that Janáček wrote a libretto originally called "Fragments of a Novel from Life" and called the first version an "opera novel." He also observes that the choice of the story as well as the first part of *The Excursions of Mr. Broucek* could also have been inspired by *Louise.* Janáček had seen Charpentier's opera at the national theater in 1903.

30. I am greatly indebted to Carl E. Schorske for this observation.

31. Tzvetan Todorov, *Mikhail Bakhtine. Le Principe dialogique* (Paris: Editions du Seuil, 1981), pp. 95, 103–104; and Julia Kristeva, *Desire in Language: A Semiotic Approach to Literature and Art* (New York: Columbia University Press, 1980), p. 73.

32. Again, see Richard Bauman, *Verbal Art as Performance,* as well as his *Story, Performance, and Event. Contextual Studies of Oral Narrative* (New York: Cambridge University Press, 1986).

33. Tourcoing was (and is) an industrial center, closely connected to the textile trade. See Basil Dean, *Albert Roussel* (London: Barrie and Rockliff, 1961), p. 1; and see *Gustave Charpentier: Lettres inédits à ses parents,* ed. by Françoise Andrieux (Paris: Presses Universitaires de France, 1984), pp. 11–13. On the history of the "Orphéons," see Jane Fulcher, "The Orphéon Societies: 'Music for the Workers' in Second-Empire France," *International Review of the Aesthetics and Sociology of Music* Vol. 10 (1979): 47–56.

34. Charpentier, *Lettres,* p. 13. His first courses in composition were not rigorous enough to help him win the Prix de Rome, but he was exposed to Wagner.

35. Charpentier, pp. 65–67.

36. "J'y puise dans la lecture des chefs d'oeuvres des maîtres un stock de formules qui me serviront quand je me mettrai à la composition." Ibid., p. 54.

37. Ibid., p. 73.

38. Ibid., p. 86; and Jean Touchard, *La Gauche en France depuis 1900* (Paris: Editions

du Seuil, 1968), p. 28; René Remond, *Les Droites en France* (Paris: Aubier Montaigne, 1982), pp. 150–153; and Edward R. Tannenbaum, *The Action Française: Die-hard Reactionaries in Twentieth-Century France* (New York: Wiley, 1962), p. 8.

39. See Manfred Kelkel, *Naturalisme, vérisme, et réalisme dans l'opéra de 1890 à 1930* (Paris: Librairie Philosophique J. Vrin, 1984), pp. 20, 180–190. As Kelkel points out, the years when *Louise* was composed (c. 1889–92) coincided with the heated debates over Anarchism. This was the period of the Anarchist laws and the press campaign of the Socialists against them, for fear that they would help the government to silence opposition in the press. Like Kelkel, but in more detail, Steven Huebner identifies several Anarchist chansons in *Louise* in his paper read at the National meeting of the American Musicological Society in Minneapolis, 1994, "Between Anarchism and the Box Office: Gustave Charpentier's *Louise.*"

40. Richard Sonn, *Anarchism and Cultural Politics in Fin-de-Siècle France* (Lincoln: University of Nebraska Press, 1989), p. 4.

41. Ibid., pp. 5–7. Sonn also notes the significance of the location of the Anarchist press in both the Latin Quarter and Montmartre, which further facilitated this exchange.

42. Joseph Halpern, "Decadent Narrative: *A Rebours,*" *Stanford French Review* Vol. II/1 (Spring 1978): 91.

43. Zola had never passed his Baccalauréat, and Charpentier had only a primary education. On the hostility of the Academy to Naturalism, see Christophe Charle, *La Crise littéraire a l'époque du Naturalisme: Roman, théâtre, et politique* (Paris: Presses de l'Ecole Normale Superieur, 1979). There are, of course, symbolic elements in *Louise,* as in late Zola, but it is clearly Naturalism that supplies the generic model.

44. See Richard Taruskin, *Opera and Drama in Russia as Preached and Practiced in the 1860s* (Ann Arbor, Mich.: U.M.I. Research Press, 1981).

45. On Wagner's use of dramatic condensation through scenic contrast, see Reinhad Strohm, "Dramatic Time and Operatic Form in Wagner's *Tannhäuser.*" See also Jean-Max Guieu, *Le Théâtre lyrique d'Emile Zola* (Paris: Fishbacher, 1983), p. 156. As Guieu points out (p. 157), Zola was raised in Aix, a region quite marked by the "légende dorée" and the cult of saints, which was highly developed. Bruneau expands on his own theories of lyric drama in his *Musiques d'hier et de demain* (Paris: Charpentier, 1900). And in *Le Figaro,* on February 7, 1900, Bruneau wrote of *Louise,* "Ah! quelle joie j'éprouve à annoncer cette éclatante victoire de la musique, de notre musique!" as cited in Johann Trillig, *Untersuchung zur Rezeption Claude Debussys in der zeitgenössischen Musikkritik* (Tutzing: Hans Schneider, 1983), p. 62.

46. See, for example, the *Revue Wagnérienne,* as well as Léon Guichard, *La Musique et les lettres en France au temps du Wagnérisme* (Paris: Presses Universitaires de France, 1963). Also see Jane F. Fulcher, "Wagner as Democrat and Realist in France," *Stanford French Review* Spring 1981.

47. Kelkel, *Naturalisme, vérisme, et réalisme,* p. 179.

48. Ibid., p. 176.

49. On the Republican "fête," see Charles Rearick, *Pleasures of the Belle Epoque: Entertainment and Festivity in Turn-of-the-Century France* (New Haven: Yale University Press, 1985).

50. The score was published in Paris by M. Delanchy, and sold for the benefit of the charitable "L'Oeuvre des Muses."

51. Naomi Ritter, *Art as Spectacle: Images of the Entertainer since Romanticism* (Columbia: University of Missouri Press, 1989), p. 202.

52. See Strohm, "Dramatic Time and Operatic Form."

53. On the special prestige and desirability of having a work premiere in connection

with the Universal Exposition, see Frédérique Patureau, *Le Palais Garnier dans la société parisienne 1875–1914* (Liège: Margada, 1991), p. 189.

54. Maurice Emmanuel, "La Vie réele en musique," *Revue de Paris* (June 15, 1900): 841–883. Emmanuel was a student at the Paris Conservatoire at the same time as Debussy and went on to become a professor of music history there in 1909, after having written a thesis on ancient Greek drama and served as Maître de Chapelle at Sainte Clotilde. See Maurice Emmanuel, "Lettres inédites," *Revue internationale de musique française* Vol. 11 (June 1983): 8.

55. Constant Pierre's book was published in Paris by the Imprimerie Nationale in 1899.

56. Emmanuel, "La Vie réele an musique," pp. 863, 882.

57. *Germinal,* January 15, 1900.

58. J. E. Flower, *Literature and the Left in France. Society, Politics, and the Novel Since the Late Nineteenth Century* (Totowa, N.J.: Barnes and Noble, 1983), p. 5.

59. Camille Mauclair, "L'Artiste moderne et son attitude sociologique," *La Grande revue* April 1902. In his "Mémoires," located in the manuscript material on Charpentier at the Bibliothèque Nationale, Département de la Musique, Charpentier recalls his friend Mauclair on April 27, 1952, as follows: "Qui n'a pas son Violon d'Ingres. Mon ami, C. Mauclair en eu de tout façons, j'ai de lui un pastel admirable. . . . Vincent d'Indy: Schola Cantorum."

60. Mauclair, "L'Artiste moderne et son attitude sociologique," p. 141.

61. As cited in Edward Lockspeiser, *Debussy,* pp. 67–68. Charpentier recalls Debussy's behavior toward him in his "Mémoires" (cited in note 59), on April 24, 1952: "Debussy dans reunion d'artistes, hommages sur le front, confidences affectueuses—le tout bien different de ce que ses lettres, hélas, si peu genereuses, si injustes, proclament. (Le lecture de certaines lettres privées, écrites après 1900, l'année de *Louise,* ne sauraient l'effacer de mon souvenir.) Nulle jalousie m'y apparêt."

62. Interview with Charpentier by Eugene Allard and Louis Vauxcelle in *Le Figaro* (Oct. 23, 1900). For many, the comparison was naturally with Wagner. The critic for the *Revue bleue,* for example, on February 10, 1900, p. 188, praised Charpentier for not having attempted "à faire un Wotan." As cited in Trillig, *Untersuchung zur rezeption Claude Debussys,* p. 627.

63. Paul Gerbod, "La Scene lyrique parisienne en 1900," *Revue internationale de musique française* Vol. 12 (Nov. 1983): 17.

64. Claude Debussy, *Debussy on Music,* eds. Françoise Lesure and Richard L. Smith (New York: Knopf, 1977), p. 183.

65. On the receipts gained by *Le Couronnement de la muse,* see Kelkel, *Naturalisme, vérisme, réalisme,* p. 200.

66. This letter is contained in Charpentier's manuscripts, *Souvenirs. Lettres. Poésies,* at the Bibliothèque Nationale, Departement de la Musique.

67. Letter to Guy Ropartz of November 20, 1900, in d'Indy, *Lettres Autographes,* Bibliothèque Nationale, Departement de la Musique.

68. David James Fisher, "Romain Rolland and the Ideology and Aesthetics of French People's Theater," *Theater Quarterly* Vol. 9/23 (Spring 1979), p. 83.

69. See Pierre Nora's article in the collection he edited, *Les Lieux du mémoire. Vol. II, La Nation* (Paris: Gallimard, 1986), p. 327, and Madeleine Rebérioux, *La République Radicale? 1898–1914* (Paris: Editions du Seuil, 1975), p. 37.

70. Lucien Mercier, *Les Universités populaires 1899–1914: Education populaire et mouvement ouvrier au debut du siècle* (Paris: Les Edition Ouvrières, 1986), p. 15, and Charpentier, *Lettres inédits,* p. 13.

71. As Frederick Brown points out in *Theater and Revolution: the Culture of the French Stage* (New York: Viking, 1981), p. 179, these efforts were the projects of "cultural missionaries" such as Louis Lumet and Henri Dugel. They included the Théâre du Cirque, the Théâtre du Peuple, the Théâtre Populaire de Belleville, the Théâtre de la rue de Tocqueville, and the Théâtre d'Avant-Garde de Ménilmontant.

72. For earlier attempts to found a "popular opera," see Jane F. Fulcher, *The Nation's Image: French Grand Opera as Politics and Politicized Art* (New York: Cambridge University Press, 1987, pp. 113–119.

73. Gerbod, "La Scène lyrique parisienne en 1900," pp. 16–23.

74. F 21 4669, letter from Gailhard to the Ministre de l'Instruction Publique," July 14, 1905. Paris, Archives Nationales.

75. As cited in Kelkel, p. 50. Responses to Charpentier during the war will be treated in my forthcoming study, "Music and Political Culture in France from the First to the Second World Wars."

76. F 21 4552 #2, letter from the Oeuvre de la Chanson Française, of May 20, 1926, requesting an official subvention. Paris, Archives Nationales.

77. By the mid-1920s, the President d'Honneur was Paul Léon, Director of the Beaux-Arts. Its statutes are articulated in a pamphlet entitled "L'Art Pour Tous," in F 21 455 #3. Paris, Archives Nationales.

78. A. Mangeot, "L'Oeuvre de Mimi Pinson," *Le Monde musical* (1902): 317. The combination of pragmatism and idealism was indeed characteristic of Charpentier's personality, as one of his contemporaries, Paul Bertrand, recalled: "Animé d'un esprit précis, clairvoyante, réaliste, fouillant avec une instinctive méfiance l'interlocuteur, de son regard d'acier, ordonne avec minutie attentif à ses comptes en liaison constant avec son conseil. Il veillait à ce qu'on n'oubliât de l'appeler 'Maître,' et cela non par vanité, mais parce qu'il n'avait pas le droit de negliger les avantages tangible qui impliquait ce titre." Paul Bertrand, *Le Monde de la musique* (Genève: La Palatine, 1947), p. 57. As Kelkel points out (p. 200), Charpentier brought the same qualities to his social projects, particularly as co-founder and Président d'Honneur of the Syndicat des Artistes Musiciens.

79. Myriam Chimènes, "Le Budget de la musique sous la IIIe République," in *La Musique du théorique au politique,* eds. Hugues Dufourt and Joël-Marie Fauquet (Paris: Aux Amateurs de Livres, 1987), p. 270.

80. During the war it would be completed by "L'Ouvroir (Lady's Working Party) de Mimi Pinson," "Les Infermières de Mimi Pinson," and "La Cocarde de Mimi Pinson." The latter was subventioned by the Conseil Municipal, Le Conseil Général, and Le Ministre de l'Instruction Publique et des Beaux-Arts and had branches in different towns throughout France. See Charpentier, *Souvenirs. Lettres. Poesies.*

81. Ibid.

82. Debussy, *Debussy on Music,* p. 129.

83. Patureau, *Le Palais Garnier dans la société parisienne,* p. 186. As she points out, presenting French operas of the past was not at first specified in the Cahier des Charges but had become standard practice. She also observes that the number of new works required by the Cahier was a direct result of opinions expressed in the Chamber of Deputies and in the musical world, particularly by the Société des Auteurs, Editeurs, et Compositeurs de Musique. Concerning the proposal of specific works, she points out (p. 182) that ministers, deputies, or senators could and did act as advocates for particular composers; the final decision, however, generally lay with the Director of the Opera (apart from those works of Prix de Rome composers, which he was required to perform) (p. 178). All works to be presented at the Opéra had then to be studied and approved, if unofficially, by the Ministre des Beaux-Arts. By 1896, there was clearly a concern that a score belong to "la tradition classique française" (p. 68).

84. Ibid., p. 254.

85. Ibid., p. 167.

86. Again, as Patureau points out (p. 404), it was ultimately the director who chose the works to be performed; but we have seen how sensitive Gailhard was to the Third Republic's priorities. Paladilhe's *Patrie!* had been given in 1898 and Méhul's *Joseph* in 1899; Bruneau's *Le Rêve* was presented at a free performance in 1899, and Rossini's *Guillaume Tell* in 1906. On the role of the Protestants in France during the Affair, see André Encrevé, "La Petite musique huguenote," pp. 451–504, in *La France de l'Affaire Dreyfus,* ed. Pierre Birnbaum (Paris: Gallimard, 1994).

87. Patureau, p. 208. She notes, as well, that the French composers most frequently performed at the Opéra were those appointed to all the major commissions and who were generally members of the Institut and the Légion d'Honneur. Most had studied at the Conservatoire and had won the Prix de Rome: performance at the Opéra was thus the ultimate consecration. She also points out that bargains were frequently struck. For example, in 1899, the Ministre des Beaux-Arts, upon the advice of one of his commissioners (A. Bernheim), agreed to count the revival of Berlioz's *Le Prise de Troie* as a new work if the director of the Opera would revive Massenet's *Le Cid* and Paladilhe's *Patrie!* before December 31, 1900. The director accepted this offer. Ibid., pp. 162, 229, 231.

88. Ibid., p. 244.

89. Miriam Chimènes, "La Princesse Edmond de Polignac et la création musicale," in *La Musique et le pouvoir,* eds. Hugues Dufourt and Joël-Marie Fauquet (Paris: Aux Amateurs de Livres, 1987), p. 135. These included symphonies, orchestral suites, symphonic poems—even those with soloists and chorus. It continued until 1932.

90. Ibid., p. 136. The winners were generally Prix de Rome recipients and students in the classes of the members of the jury.

91. Ibid., and see Brian Hart, *The Symphony in Theory and Practice in France,* pp. 299–312.

92. See Christophe Charle, *Naissance des "intellectuels" 1880–1900* (Paris: Minuit, 1990).

93. Morland's "Enquête" appeared in the *Mercure de France* in November and December 1902, and January 1903. Also see Claude Digeon, *La Crise Allemande de la pensée française 1870–1914* (Paris: Presses Universitaires de France, 1959), pp. 463–464.

94. In Morland's "Enquête," Bruneau praised German influence and said he believed French composers would continue to be nurtured by the work of the old German masters. According to Debussy, German influence was harmful only on those "esprits susceptibles d'être domestiqués." D'Indy opined: "Je vois rien de repréhensible à cela et ce libre échange internationale. . . ." He continued that if French composers used foreign procedures, the results would necessarily be "French." But in the survey, all agreed on the need to move away from German influence—to return to the "sources" of the "French Tradition."

95. Paul Landormy, "L'Etat actuel de la musique Française," *Revue bleue* (Jan.–June 1904): 394–397; 421–426.

96. This view is opposed to that of J. Peter Burkholder, presented in a number of articles but perhaps most specifically in "Museum Pieces: the Historicist Mainstream in Music of the Last Hundred Years," *Journal of Musicology* Vol. 2 (Spring 1983): 115–134. Burkholder sees the relation of composers to the "canon" as highly personal or professional, essentially devoid of sociopolitical resonance. This was clearly not the case in France.

97. Landormy, "L'Etat actuel de la musique française," p. 425.

98. Ibid., p. 394.

99. Ibid., pp. 394–395.

100. Ibid., p. 396. On the Liberal Right in France, see René Remond, *Les Droites en France* (Paris: Aubier Montaigne, 1982).

101. Landormy, "L'Etat actuel," p. 396.

102. Ibid., p. 424.

103. On the political ramifications of the separation of Church and State in France, see Eugen Weber, *Action Française: Royalism and Reaction in Twentieth-Century France* (Stanford, Calif.: Stanford University Press, 1962).

104. The *Mercure musical,* of which Laloy was an editor, was closely associated with the *Mercure de France*. His articles were published on May 1, July 1, and August 1, 1905.

105. Christian Goubault, *La Critique musicale dans la presse française de 1870 à 1914,* p. 106.

106. In its opening statement, the editors of the *Mercure musical* professed to wish to do for music what the *Mercure de France,* which was equally socially conservative but aesthetically liberal (approximating the position of the Liberal Right) had done for literature. See Johann Trillig, *Untersuchung zur Rezeption Claude Debussys in der zeitgenössischen Musikkritik* (Tutzing: Hans Schneider, 1983), p. 123.

107. Louis Laloy, "Le Drame musical moderne," *Le Mercure de France* (1905): 84.

108. Roland Barthes, *Le Dégre zero de l'écriture* (Paris: Editions du Seuil, 1953), p. 24.

109. Laloy, p. 175.

110. Goubault, *La Critique musicale,* p. 109. Mauclair had denounced the reaction against social art in an article in *La Revue* on March 15, 1906, on Alfred Bruneau.

111. It appeared on January 15, 1905: 151–174.

112. On this distinction, see Raoul Girardet, *Le Nationalism français 1871–1914* (Paris: Armand Colin, 1966), pp. 8–11.

113. Camille Mauclair, "La Réaction Nationaliste en art et l'ignorance de l'homme de lettres," *La Revue mondiale* (Jan. 15, 1905): 151–152.

114. Ibid., p. 155.

115. Ibid., pp. 157–158.

116. Ibid., p. 160.

117. Ibid., p. 161; and see Camille Mauclair, "Le Classicisme et l'academisme," *La Revue bleue* (March 15, 1903): 340.

118. Mauclair, "La Réaction Nationaliste," p. 162.

119. Ibid., p. 163.

120. Ibid., pp. 155–156.

121. Ibid., p. 156.

CHAPTER 3

1. On the attempt of the Right to renew the terms of political debate, see Eugen Weber, *Action Française: Royalism and Reaction in Twentieth-Century France* (Stanford, Calif.: Stanford University Press, 1962) and Eugen Weber and Hans Roger, eds., *The European Right: A Historical Profile* (Los Angeles: University of California Press, 1965). On the concept of a "true" as opposed to a merely "legal" France, see Herman Lebovics, *True France. The Wars over Cultural Identity* (Ithaca, N.Y.: Cornell University Press, 1992), esp. pp. 138 ff. Also see Gordon Wright, *France in Modern Times* (New York: Rand McNally, 1974), pp. 267–268, and Jean-François Sirinelli and Eric Vigne, "Introduction. Des cultures politiques," in Jean-François Sirinelli, ed., *Histoire des droites en France* Vol. 2 *Cultures* (Paris: Gallimard, 1992), pp. 7–8.

2. Ibid., p. 10. And see Victor Nguyen, *Aux origines de l'Action Française. Intelligence et politique à l'aube de XXe siècle* (Paris: Fayard, 1991).

3. Joel Blatt, "Relatives and Rivals: The Response of the Action Française to Italian Fascism," *European Studies Review* Vol. II/3 (July 1981): 266–267.

4. Eugen Weber, *Action Française,* p. 9.

5. Ibid., pp. 10–11; Lebovics, *True France,* p. 10; and Jack Roth, *The Cult of Violence: Sorel and the Sorelians* (Berkeley: University of California Press, 1980), p. 126.

6. See Eugen Weber, *Action Française,* pp. 36 ff. and Edward Tannenbau, *The Action Française: Die-hard Reactionaries in Twentieth-Century France* (New York: Wiley, 1962). See also Pascal Fouché, "L'Edition 1914–1992," in Sirinelli, ed., *Histoire des droites en France* Vol. 2, pp. 260–261, and Olivier Corpet, "La revue," ibid., p. 168.

7. Tannenbaum, *The Action Française,* p. 88. Lasserre was also to contribute articles on literary criticism and the arts to the daily *Action Française.* Ibid., p. 93.

8. Antoine Compagnon, *La Troisième République des lettres. De Flaubert à Proust* (Paris: Editions du Seuil, 1983), p. 19. Portions of Lasserre's book had already appeared in the *Revue de l'action française,* which he edited. He became the literary critic for the daily *l'Action française* in 1908.

9. Pierre Lasserre, *Le Romantisme français* (Paris: Société du Mercure de France, 1908), pp. VIII–XII, 515–543. Maurras had emphasized the weak, "feminine" quality of Romanticism in his *L'Avenir de l'intelligence* (1905).

10. On the concept of symbols and how they are generated, see Garth Gillian, *From Sign to Symbol* (New York: Harvester Press, 1982), esp. p. 29 ff.

11. Pierre Lasserre, *Des Romantiques à nous* (Paris: La Nouvelle Revue Critique, 1927). Although he had left the Action Française by this point, his ideas had not essentially changed.

12. Ibid., p. 193.

13. Pierre Lasserre, *L'Esprit de la musique française* (Paris: Payot, 1917), p. 236.

14. Lasserre, *Des Romantiques à nous,* pp. 143–144, 154, and 193. And see Charles Maurras, *La Musique intérieur* (Paris: Bernard Grasset, 1925).

15. See, for example, the praise of the paper *Action française* for d'Indy's efforts on the part of the French musical past, in Sept. 1908, pp. 257 ff. Also see the *Revue critique des idées et des livres* July–Sept. 1908, on d'Indy's *Cours de composition musicale.* In noting the Action Française's reserve for certain aspects of d'Indy's teaching, I differ from the position presented by Charles B. Paul in his article "Rameau, d'Indy, and French Nationalism," *Musical Quarterly* Vol. 58/1 (Jan. 1972): 46–56.

16. See Léon Daudet, *Salons et journaux. Souvenirs des milieux littéraires, politiques, artistiques, et médicaux de 1880 à 1908* (Paris: Nouvelle Librairie Nationale, 1917), pp. 307–308.

17. Louis Bourgault-Ducoudray, "L'Enseignement du chant dans les lycées," *Revue musicale* 1903: 723–727.

18. Ibid., p. 723.

19. Ibid., p. 727.

20. This letter, contained in the *Lettres Autographes,* Bibliothèque Nationale, Département de la Musique, was generously brought to my attention by Michael Strasser.

21. Ibid. The Schola d'Action Française was active in the early 1920s.

22. Christian Goubault, *La Critique musicale dans la presse française de 1870 à 1914* (Genève-Paris: Editions Slatkine, 1984), p. 51.

23. On the political evolution of the Republic in these years, see Madeleine Rebérioux, *La République radicale? 1898–1914* (Paris: Editions du Seuil, 1975). Also see Gordon Wright, *France in Modern Times,* pp. 264–265.

24. Eugene Mittler, *Des Rapports entre le Socialisme, le Syndicalisme, et la Franc-Maçonnerie* (Paris: Imprimerie Industrielle, 1911), pp. 13–24.

25. See Madeleine Rebérioux's "Présentation" to the issue on "Critique littéraire et socialisme," *Le Mouvement social* Vol. 59 (April–June 1967): 3–28. See also Lebovics, *True France,* p. 139.

26. J. E. Flower, *Writers and Politics in Modern France 1909–1961* (London: Hodder and Stoughton, 1977), p. 9.

27. *Le Courrier musical* was among the musical journals for which he wrote. See Goubault, *La Critique musicale,* pp. 56–58.

28. Ibid.

29. *L'Effort* (June 1, 1910), p. 2. See Gordon Wright, *France in Modern Times,* p. 265.

30. Ibid., p. 4.

31. *L'Effort* (June 15, 1910), pp. 3–4. And see Wright, *France in Modern Times,* p. 293.

32. Ibid. *L'Effort* welcomed the contribution of syndicalists such as Gustave Hervé, who, like Sorel, was gradually embracing a "national" conception of socialism. See Hervé's "Reflections sur l'art," in the issue of Sept. 1912.

33. "Les Nécessités actuelles de l'art," *L'Effort* (Jan. 11, 1910), p. 50.

34. *L'Effort* (Nov. 10, 1910), p. 38. Indeed, the issue of Sept. 12, 1912, includes an excerpt from Rolland's novel *Jean Christophe.*

35. "De l'Utilité en art: Pour en finir avec l'art pour l'art," *L'Effort* (March 1912).

36. *L'Humanité* (Jan. 16, 1913). Louis Laloy undoubtedly had a role in these concerts, since he was assisting Rouché at the theater at the time and orchestrated the Fauré piece.

37. See Lebovics, *True France.*

38. *L'Humanité* (Jan. 12, 1913).

39. See Jane F. Fulcher, *The Nation's Image: French Grand Opera as Politics and Politicized Art* (New York: Camnbridge University Press, 1987), pp. 141–144.

40. Jean Marguerite, *Les Fêtes du peuple: l'Oeuvre, les moyens, le but* (Paris: Les Fêtes du Peuple, 1921). One could enroll in the organization at the Bourse de Travail.

41. Ibid., pp. 32–33. The Fêtes du Peuple in Lyon was led by another Conservatoire student, Cesar Geoffroy. Ibid., p. 53. On Albert Doyen, see Christophe Prochasson and Anne Rasmussen, *Au nom de la Patrie: Les intellectuels et la première guerre mondiale (1910–1919)* (Paris: Editions de la Découverte, 1996), pp. 51–52, 149, 234, and 278. Prochasson places Doyen within the "milieu de Créteil" before the war, together with socialists, "vitalistes," and revolutionary syndicalists.

42. Ibid., p. 47.

43. Gustave Charpentier, *Rapport. Ville de Paris. Concours musical de 1910–12,* p. 3. He notes that Bruneau was the "rapporteur" for the competition in 1900.

44. Ibid.

45. Marguérite, *Les Fêtes du peuple,* pp. 46–48. On the original Republican model of the "fête," see Mona Ozouf, *Festivals of the French Revolution* (Cambridge, Mass.: Harvard University Press, 1988). On the more conservative, nationalistic model of the outdoor "fête," particularly the ideas proposed in the 1880s by Déroulède, see Elinor Olin, "Festivals de plein-air: Cultural Nationalism in fin-de-diècle France," paper delivered at the annual meeting of the American Musicological Society, Minneapolis, 1994.

46. See my article "Cultural Politics and Musical Aesthetics in France on the Eve of the Second World War," in *Journal of Musicology* Vol. 8 no. 4 (Fall 1995): 425–453.

47. Marguérite, p. 4.

48. Ibid., p. 8, and Flower, *Writers and Politics,* p. 7.

49. Pierre Andrieu, "Fascism 1913," *Combat* 1936: 25. As Andrieu points out, on April 4, 1910, *Action Française* published another article by Sorel, "Le réveil de la charité de Jeanne d'Arc de Peguy." It hence referred to Sorel as "le plus pénétrant des sociologues

français." And see Jack Roth, *The Cult of Violence: Sorel and the Sorelians* (Berkeley: University of California Press, 1980), p. 90.

50. Zeev Sternhell, *Ni Droite ni Gauche. L'Idéologie fasciste en France* (Paris: Editions du Seuil, 1983), p. 7.

51. Roth, *The Cult of Violence*, p. 117.

52. Andrieu, "Fascism 1913," p. 25. As Andrieu points out, this led to the subsequent formation of the "cercle d'études" and the eventual development of the *Cahiers du Cercle Proudhon* by Henri Lagrange, Georges Valois, and Gilbert Maire, among others. Also see Eugen Weber, *Action Française*, p. 74. Sorel left *l'Indépendance* in 1913, and the journal disappeared soon after. See Olivier Corpet, "La revue," in Jean-François Sirinelli, ed., *Histoire des droites en France* Vol. 2, pp. 167–168.

53. See James Joll, *The Anarchists* (Cambridge, Mass.: Harvard University Press, 1980).

54. Roth, pp. 108–109.

55. Ibid.

56. Review of Sorel's *La Valeur social de l'art* in the *Cahiers du Cercle Proudhon* 1912.

57. The lectures had been delivered at Saint-Jean de Lez on October 13, 1910, and published in the *Tablettes de la Schola* in the issue of Oct.–Nov. 1910.

58. *L'Indépendance* (March 15, 1911), p. 12.

59. The issue of the ethical dimension of lyric expression, or its ability pragmatically to "affect" its audience was suggested to me by Steven Winspur's paper, "The Pragmatic Force of Lyric," delivered at the Conference on "Mallarmé": Music, Art, and Letters," Indiana University, 1994.

60. *L'Independance* (March 15, 1911), pp. 37–41.

61. Romain Rolland in *L'Ecole des Hautes Etudes Sociales 1900–1910* (no editor given) (Paris: Felix Alcan, 1911). While Hellouin's book is discussed in Johann Trillig's *Untersuchung zur Rezeption Claude Debussys in der zeitgenössischen Musikkritik* (Tutzing: Hans Schneider, 1983), pp. 100–102, it is completely apart from its intellectual context. In addition, Calvocoressi gave lectures on music criticism at the Ecole, which were published in the *Courrier musical* on Nov. 1, 1910.

62. Frédéric Hellouin, *Essai de critique de la critique musicale* (Paris: A. Joanin et Cie., 1906), pp. 144–149.

63. Ibid., pp. 159–160, 214.

64. Goubault, *La Critique musicale dans la presse française,* p. 109.

65. Ibid., p. 39.

66. See Madeleine Rebérioux, "1913: L'Art et la reflection sur l'art," *Annales E.S.C.* Vol. 29/4 (July–Aug. 1974): 913–924. (Also see note 69.)

67. Goubault, *La Critique musicale dans la presse française,* pp. 106–109.

68. Ibid., pp. 79–80.

69. On the *Mercure de France* (as well as the art criticism in other journals, including the *Gazette des Beaux-Arts*), see Liliane Brion-Guerry, ed., *L'Année 1913. Les Formes esthétiques de l'ouvre d'art à la veille de la première guerre mondiale* (Paris: Klincksieck, 1971), pp. 2076–2080, 1094.

70. As we shall see, in the context of Fauré's education, the Ecole Niedermeyer, although founded in the Second Empire with state funds, was the immediate predecessor of, and in some ways the model for, the later Schola Cantorum. Begun by the Swiss Louis Niedermeyer, it was called an "Ecole de Musique Religieuse et Classique," like the Schola, propagating both the religious and "classic" German repertory.

71. "La Musique et l'Etat," *Revue musicale* (1910): 536–537.

72. Lionel de la Laurencie, *Le Goût musical en France* (Genève: Slatkine Reprints,

1970). In 1907 André Pirro, who had also been associated with the Schola, published his *L'Esthétique de Jean-Sebastien Bach* (Paris: Fishbacher).

73. La Laurencie, *Le Goût musical,* pp. 303–306.

74. Ibid., p. 353.

75. Ibid., pp. 353–354.

76. Ibid., pp. 354–355.

77. Antoine Compagnon, *La Troisième République des lettres. De Flaubert à Proust* (Paris: Editions du Seuil, 1983), pp. 119, 142. Henri Massis was to become an influential proponent of Maurras, but in the prewar period he was also partially linked to Barrèsian ideology. See Jean-François Sirinelli, ed., *Histoire des droites en France* Vol. II, p. 4.

78. Ibid.

79. Ibid., pp. 136–137, and Robert Wohl, *The Generation of 1914* (Cambridge, Mass.: Harvard University Press, 1979), p. 6.

80. Agathon [Henri Massis and Gabriel de Tarde], *L'Esprit de la nouvelle Sorbonne. La Crise de la culture classique. La Crise du français* (Paris: Mercure de France, 1911), pp. 8–11.

81. Ibid., pp. 17–18.

82. Ibid., pp. 21–24.

83. As cited in Zakone, "Les ennemis de la Schola," *Revue musicale* (1905): 83.

84. Jean-Pierre Rioux, *Nationalisme et conservatisme. La Ligue de la Patrie Française* (Paris: Beauchesne, 1977), pp. 109–110, and Jean Desaché, *De L'Intervention administrative dans l'art musical* (Paris: Librairie de la Société de Recueil Sirey, 1910), p. 16.

85. Gail Hilson Woldu, *Gabriel Fauré as Director of the Conservatoire National de Musique et de Déclamation, 1905–1920,* Ph.D. Dissertation, Yale University, 1983, p. 4.

86. Ibid., p. 1. See also Gail Hilson Woldu, "Gabriel Fauré, directeur du Conservatoire: Les reformes de 1905," *Revue de musicologie* Vol. 70/1 (1984): 119–128.

87. Paul Léon, *Du Palais-Royal au Palais-Bourbon* (Paris: Albin-Michel, 1947), pp. 83–97.

88. Woldu, *Gabriel Fauré as Director of the Conservatoire,* pp. 58–59.

89. Ibid., pp. 69–70, and André Coeuroy, *La Musique française moderne* (Paris: Librairie Delagrave, 1924), p. 24; see also Charles Koechlin, *Gabriel Fauré* (Paris: Felix Alcan, 1927), p. 5.

90. Woldu (in her dissertation) discusses Niedermeyer's school as itself a successor to Charon's pioneering but abortive Ecole de Musique Classique et Religieuse, after the revolutionary period (pp. 18–20).

91. Ibid., pp. 17–18. Woldu also notes the impact of Fauré's training on his style (pp. 21–22), especially on his modal tendencies.

92. Jean-Michel Nectoux, "Gabriel Fauré," in *The New Grove Dictionary of Music and Musicians,* ed. Stanley Sadie, Vol. 6 (London: Macmillan, 1980), pp. 418–419. See also Fiamme Nicolodi, "Alfredo Casella et l'avant-garde parisienne au début du XXe siècle," *Revue internationale de musique française* Vol. 78 (Nov. 1985), p. 87. For further information on Fauré and Parisian salons, see Nectoux's introduction to *Gabriel Fauré, Correspondence,* ed. Jean-Michel Nectoux (Paris: Flammarion, 1980), pp. 194–200.

93. Michel Faure, *Musique et société du Second Empire aux années vingt* (Paris: Flammarion, 1985), p. 69. See also Coeuroy, *La Musique française moderne,* p. 24.

94. Gabriel Fauré, *Correspondence,* p. 253; and see *Revue d'histoire et de critique musicale* (July 1905). Fauré had been appointed director in June.

95. Woldu, *Gabriel Fauré,* p. 11.

96. Paul Léon, *Du Palais Royal . . . ,* pp. 97–99.

97. Woldu, pp. 59, 84.

98. Ibid., p. 59.

99. See Brion-Guerry, ed., *Année 1913,* pp. 15–17, and Brian Hart, *The Symphony in Theory and Practice in France 1900–1914,* Ph.D. Dissertation, Indiana University, 1994, pp. 95–98.

100. Hart, *The Symphony,* pp. 82–89.

101. See ibid., pp. 68–78, 113–125.

102. See ibid., 135–140.

103. Jules Combarieu, "L'Enseignement musicale du Conservatoire," *Revue musicale* (1910): 498.

104. According to Charles Koechlin, as of 1913 the Conservatoire still taught counterpoint according to Cherubini's treatise. See Paul-Marie Masson, ed., *Rapport sur la musique française contemporaine* (Rome: Armam et Stein, 1913), p. 141.

105. Combarieu, "L'Enseignement musicale . . . ,": 498–501.

106. Rollo Meyers, *Modern French Music* (Oxford: Blackwell Press, 1971), p. 140; and Christophe Charle, "Le Collège de France" in *Les Lieux du mémoire II. La Nation,* ed. Pierre Nora (Paris: Gallimard, 1986), pp. 389–390, 398.

107. Goubault, *La Critique musicale,* p. 82. In his youth, Vuillermoz was in a coterie of young musicians known as "Les Apaches," which also included Maurice Ravel.

108. Emile Vuillermoz, "Le Dictionnaire," *Le Mecure musical* (March 1, 1906): 549.

109. Ibid., pp. 551, 553.

110. Emile Vuillermoz, "La Schola et le Conservatoire," *Mercure de France* (1909): 235.

111. Ibid., p. 236.

112. Ibid., p. 241.

113. Ibid., pp. 237–238. He refers specifically to the *Anthologie des primitifs religieux,* published by the Schola, as a collection of motets "d'une platitude inégalable et d'une morne laideur."

114. Ibid., pp. 239–240.

115. Ibid., pp. 240–241.

116. Louis Combes, "La Schola et le Conservatoire," *Le Monde musical* (Oct. 15, 1909): 276. Two other articles in the same issue argue for a fusion of the "Schools" of harmony and counterpoint in the future, one by Alfred Casella anbd the other by L. Lambinet.

117. Louis Laloy, "Les Parties musicaux en France," *La Grande Revue* (Dec. 25, 1907): 792.

118. Ibid., pp. 794–795. Satie's rhetoric concerning the Schola was strikingly similar in this period, as we shall see in chapter 4.

119. Revue of the second volume of d'Indy's *Cours de composition musicale* in the *Revue musicale* 1910, pp. 184–185.

120. Later, from 1914 to 1929, d'Indy would also teach a class on conducting at the Conservatoire.

121. In the *Rapport sur la musique française,* p. 146.

122. Brênet in the *Rapport,* pp. 18–19.

123. Louis Laloy, *Rameau* (Paris: Felix Alcan, 1919), p. 110.

124. AJ 16 4751—Procès Verbaux, Faculté des Lettres, 22/7/1910. I am very grateful to Christophe Charle for generously supplying me with this information.

125. These lectures were published in the *Revue musicale* in 1906 and 1907.

126. Jules Combarieu, "L'Organisation des etudes d'histoire musicale en France dans la second moitié du XIXe siècle," *Revue musicale* (1906): 502.

127. Jules Combarieu, "Comment la musique s'est-elle formée?" *Revue musicale* (1910): 488–496.

128. Pierre Lasserre, *Les Chapelles littéraire. Claudel, Jammes, Peguy* (Paris: Garnier Frères, 1920), pp. IX–XI.

129. See especially, *La Foire sur la place,* and Léon Vallas, *Claude Debussy et son temps* (Paris: Felix Alcan, 1932), p. 152.

130. Ibid., pp. 148–150, and Camille Mauclair, "La Debussyste," *Le Courrier musical* (Sept. 15, 1905): 501–502.

131. Ibid., p. 503.

132. Michel de Cossart, *The Food of Love: Princesse Edmond de Polignac and Her Salon (1865–1943)* (London: Hamish Hamilton, 1978), p. 59.

133. Jean Lorrain, *Pelléastres: Le poison de la littérature* (Paris: A. Merceant, 1909), pp. 25–26.

134. Later, Laloy did not deny having been a so-called Debussyste, and he spoke of having banded together with Emile Vuillermoz and Jean Marnold, the latter having "converted" from "Scholisme" to "Debussysme." See Louis Laloy, *La Musique retrouvée 1902–1927* (Paris: Plon, 1928), p. 129, and Vallas, *Debussy,* p. 182.

135. Louis Laloy, "Les Parties musicaux en France," pp. 795–796.

136. See Brian Hart, *The Symphony in Theory and Practice,* pp. 167–180.

137. Ibid., pp. 180–184. Also see G. Jean-Aubry, *La Musique française aujourd'hui* (Paris: Librairie Académique Perrin et Cie., 1916), which contains a preface by Claude Debussy, describing his conception of "the French tradition."

138. Hart, pp. 176–187. Laloy reflects the Debussyste perspective on the symphony in "Les Parties musicaux."

139. See Charles Koechlin, "Les Tendences de la musique moderne française," in *Encyclopédie de la musique et dictionnaire du Conservatoire* eds. Albert Lavignac and Lionel de la Laurencie, Pt. 2 Vol. I, "Tendances de la musique; Technique générale" (Paris: Delagrave, 1925), p. 122.

140. As cited (and translated) in Hart, p. 186. For the full discussion, see Emile Vuillermoz, "La Symphonie," in *Cinquante ans de musique française (1874–1925)* 2 Vols. ed. Ladislas Rohozinski (Paris: Les Editions Musicales de la Librairie de France, 1925), I: 323–388.

141. On the "poles" in French music, see Jean Chantavoine in the *Courrier musical* (May 15, 1908): 313–314, and Goubault, *La Critique musicale,* p. 101.

142. Alfred Casella, "Musiques horizontales et musiques verticales," *Le Monde musical* (Oct. 30, 1909).

143. C. Caillard and Jose de Bérys, *Le Cas Debussy* (Paris: Bibliothèque du Temps Present, 1910), pp. 1–2.

144. Raphael Cor, "M. Claude Debussy et le snobisme contemporain," in *Le Cas Debussy,* pp. 24–25.

145. The article had appeared on February 19 and 21, 1908, and the survey in 1909.

146. Robert Wohl, *The Generation of 1914* (Cambridge, Mass.: Harvard University Press, 1979), p. 39.

147. Ibid., p. 9.

148. Caillard and de Bérys, pp. 55, 67.

149. Ibid., pp. 88–90, 96.

150. Ibid., p. 104.

151. Charles Koechlin, "Souvenirs sur Debussy, la Schola, et la S.M.I.," *Revue musicale* (Nov. 1934): 244–247; and Teresa Davidian, "Debussy, d'Indy, and the Société Nationale," *Journal of Musicological Research* Vol. 11/4 (Sept. 1991): 293; also see Michel

Duchesneau, "Maurice Ravel et la Société Musicale Independente: 'Projet mirifique de concerts scandaleux,'" *Revue de Musicologie* Vol. 80/2 (1994): 251–281.

152. See *Rapport sur la musique française,* pp. 63, 147. Huré went on to found the short-lived prewar Ecole Normale de Musique. Huré was a composer and organist at St. Séverin.

153. Gabriel Fauré, "Preface" to Jean Huré's *Dogmes musicaux (1904–1907)* (Paris: Editions du Monde Musical, 1909), p. 5.

154. Ibid., pp. 5–6.

155. Huré, *Dogmes musicaux,* pp. 1, 138, 111.

156. Ibid., pp. 53–54.

157. Ibid., p. 58.

158. Ibid., and p. 381. On the views of the young Debussy, see Maurice Emmanuel, *Pelléas et Melisande de Debussy* (Paris: Editions Mallote, 1950).

159. Huré, p. 339. Undoubtedly with *Pelléas* in mind, Huré argues (p. 288) that a composer should be free to present "une fresque théâtrale dénuée d'action, de mouvement même."

160. Ibid., p. 31.

161. Ibid., pp. 61, 65, 66.

162. Ibid., pp. 11–18. Concerning this issue, Huré cites his own article (pp. 61–62), his "Lettre sur l'education musicale," which appeared in *Angers artiste* in February 1900.

163. Ibid.

164. Ibid., p. 25.

165. Ibid., pp. 65–67.

166. Ibid., pp. 141, 165, 173, 177.

167. Ibid., pp. 67, 46, 41.

168. See Christian Goubault, "Les Chapelles musicales françaises ou la querelle des 'gros-boutiens' et des 'petits-boutiens,'" *Revue internationale de musique française* Vol. 5 (June 1981): 99–100, and *Rapport sur la musique française,* p. 145.

169. Déodat de Séverac, "La Centralization et les petites chapelles musicales," *Le Courrier musical* (Jan. 1908): 41.

170. Ibid., pp. 37–38.

171. Ibid., p. 58.

172. Ibid., pp. 38–39. Another such analytic study of the functioning of the French musical world by a partisan, if not student, of the Schola is M. Daubresse'e *Le Musicien dans la société moderne* (Paris: Le Monde Musical, 1914). Originally a series of lectures given for L'Action Sociale de la Femme, in 1911, its language and conceptions are Scholiste, and it includes an encomium to the Schola. Specifically, it praises the equality of the treatment of the sexes at the Schola, where men and women of equal rank in the orchestra receive identical remuneration (pp. 84–85).

173. Michel de Cossart, *The Food of Love,* p. 68. Also see Christophe Charle, "Noblesses et élites en France au début du XXe siècle," *Noblesses européens au XIXe siècle* (Paris: Collection de l'Ecole Française de Rome 107), p. 422. Charle notes the tendency of some aristocrats to return to the "State" as the Republic stabilized. The Princesse de Polignac, although "aristocratic," was no great supporter of the Schola and became an early supporter of the S.M.I.

174. Myriam Chimènes, "La Princesse Edmond de Polignac et la création musicale," in *La Musique et le pouvoir,* eds. Hugues Dugourt and Joel-Marie Fauquet (Paris: Aux Amateurs de Livres, 1987), p. 139.

175. Séverac, "La Centralizaion et les petites chapelles," p. 37.

CHAPTER 4

1. Gabriel Pierné, Paul Vidal, Henry Prunières, Maurice Emmanuael, and Henri de Régnier, *La Jeunesse de Claude Debussy* (Paris: Editions de la Nouvelle Revue Française, 1926), p. 14.

2. See Claude Debussy, *Debussy on Music*, eds. François Lesure and Richard L. Smith (New York: Knopf, 1977), p. 257, and Michel Faure, *Musique et société, due Second Empire aux années vingt* (Paris: Flammarion), pp. 36, 75.

3. Faure, *Musique et société*, p. 36.

4. Julia d'Almendra, "Debussy et le mouvement modal dans la musique du XXe siècle," in *Debussy et l'évolution de la musique au XXe siècle*, ed. Edith Weber (Paris: Editions du Centre Nationale de la Recherche Scientifique, 1965), pp. 110–111, and *La Jeunesse de Claude Debussy*, p. 11.

5. *La Jeunesse de Claude Debussy*, p. 10, and Faure, *Musique et société*, p. 20.

6. *La Jeunesse de Claude Debussy*, p. 11, and René Dumesnil, *Portraits de musiciens française* (Paris: Plon, 1938), p. 36.

7. *La Jeunesse de Claude Debussy*, pp. 32–33.

8. Leon Vallas, *Claude Debussy et son temps* (Paris: Felix Alcan, 1932), p. 89, and *La Jeunesse de Claude Debussy*, p. 47. See also Teresa Davidian, "Debussy, d'Indy, and the Société Nationale," *Journal of Musicological Research* Vol. 11/4 (Sept. 1991), p. 285, on the *Fantaisie* for piano.

9. Davidian, "Debussy, d'Indy, and the Société Nationale," pp. 292–293.

10. Dumesnil, *Portraits,* pp. 34–35.

11. *La Jeunesse de Claude Debussy*, p. 50; Vallas, *Debussy,* pp. 74–76; and Jacques Durand, *Quelques souvenirs d'un editeur de musique* Vol. 2 (Paris: Durand et Fils, 1925), p. 125.

12. It was in 1892 that Debussy orchestrated Satie's *Gymnopédies*. See Edward Lockspeiser, *Debussy* (London: J. M. Dent and Sons, Ltd., 1980), p. 64.

13. Faure, *Musique et société,* p. 77.

14. His friends included Arthur Fontaine, who held a high position in the "Direction du Travail" under Millerand and was among the group for whom Debussy read *Pelléas* at the piano. See Faure, p. 33.

15. Robert Orledge, on the other hand, argues for Debussy's "intense left-wing ideals in the years between the composition and performance of *Pelléas.*" See Robert Orledge, *Debussy and the Theater* (Cambridge: Cambridge University Press, 1982), p. 238. According to Lockspeiser, however, at the time of the Affair, Debussy, along with most of his friends, "instinctively sided with the nationalists." Lockspeiser, *Debussy,* p. 73.

16. Lockspeiser, p. 73; Vallas, *Debussy,* p. 152; and Jacques Durand, *Quelques souvenirs,* p. 125.

17. Myriam Chimènes, "La Princesse Edmond de Polignac et la création musicale," in *La Musique et le pouvoir,* eds. Hugues Dufourt and Joël-Marie Fauquet (Paris: Aux Amateurs de Livres, 1987), p. 139. It was in Chausson's Salon that he played fragments from *Pelléas.*

18. Lockspeiser, p. 77.

19. On Debussy's style in the *Prélude à l'après-midi d'une faune,* see William Austin, *Music in the Twentieth century* (New York: Norton, 1966), pp. 14–18.

20. On the collaboration with Peter on the play, see *Debussy on Music,* p. 7, and Orledge, *Debussy and the Theater,* p. 241. As Orledge points out (p. 242), René Peter published excerpts from the first version of the play, which dated from c. 1897, and was approached by a

theater director concerning its production. But Debussy did not want to make his debut in the theater with a nonmusical work before *Pelléas*, so they postponed the project. A later version, the so-called Meyer manuscript, which probably dates from around 1903, contains revisions that suggest it was written after Debussy decided to leave his wife, Lilly Texier, for Emma Bardac. No more of the play was to be published. I tried repeatedly throughout the research and writing of this book (between 1987 and 1995) to see the manuscript of *Frères en art* that is listed in the holdings of the Bibliothèque Nationale, Département de la Musique. I received the repeated firm reply each time that it was at the bindery and upon further inquiries was told that no microfilm had been made of it. Let us hope that this valuable manuscript will eventually return to the library's collection and be made accessible to scholars.

As opposed to the theory that the play contains ambiguous references to Anarchism, we find the statement in *Debussy on Music* (p. 9) that Debussy's writings here were "the first major outpouring of anarchist ideas in music." But we also find the significant point (pp. 7–8) that, while associated with the *Revue Blanche*, Debussy came into contact with Felix Fenéon, who was known for his Anarchist beliefs and who was tried and acquitted as an Anarchist.

21. Some have seen a reference to the pre-Raphaelite "brotherhood," which received much attention in France in the 1890s, while others perceive reference to Anarchist unions. See *Debussy on Music*, p. 8, and Orledge, pp. 241–243.

22. Orledge, p. 242. Also see *Debussy on Music*, p. 9.

23. Orledge, p. 243.

24. Ibid., p. 242.

25. On the response of Anarchists to academic and other cultural conventions, see Richard Sonn, *Anarchism and Cultural Politics in Fin-de-Siècle France* (Lincoln: University of Nebraska Press, 1989), pp. 3–4. On the relation of painters to Anarchist politics, see Theda Shapiro, *Painters and Politics. The European Avant-Garde and Society 1900–1925* (New York: Elsevier, 1976). Despite his initial attraction to Anarchist theories of culture, Debussy's ultimate realization of the contradictions inherent in Anarchism for artists may explain the conundrum of his leaving the *Revue Blanche*, for which he gave the simple excuse of "nervous strain." See *Debussy on Music*, p. 11.

26. Lockspeiser, *Debussy*, pp. 53–57.

27. On Debussy's initial attraction to the play, as well as his compositional process, see David Grayson, *The Genesis of Debussy's Pelléas et Mélisande* (Ann Arbor, Mich.: U.M.I. Research Press, 1986).

28. See Orledge's discussion of the opera in *Debussy and the Theater*, as well as Maurice Emmanuel, *Pelléas et Mélisande de Debussy* (Paris: Editions Malotte, 1950).

29. Joseph Kerman discusses this aspect of the opera extensively in *Opera as Drama* (New York: Vintage, 1959).

30. On Debussy's treatment of the motives in *Pelléas*, see Emmanuel, as well as Louis Laloy, *Debussy* (Paris: Dorbon, 1909), p. 24 ff.; Robin Holloway, *Debussy and Wagner* (London: E. Eulenburg, 1979); and Donald J. Grout, *A Short History of Opera* (New York: Columbia University Press, 1965), p. 449.

31. This is as opposed to the viewpoint presented by Jan Pasler in "*Pelléas* and Power: Forces behind the Reception of Debussy's Opera," *19-Century Music* Vol. 10/3 (Spring 1987): 243–264.

32. As the reader will recall, Carré had taken a clear stance during the Affair by signing the petition against Dreyfus circulated by the Ligue de la Patrie Française.

33. See Pasler, "Pelléas and Power," as well as the discussion of responses to the opera in Vallas, *Claude Debussy*, Lockspeiser, *Debussy*, and René Peter, *Claude Debussy* (Paris: Gallimard, 1944).

34. Again, on Anarchist theories of culture, see Richard Sonn, *Anarchism and Cultural Politics*.

35. Raymond Bouyer, "Le Debussysme et l'évolution musical (1901–1902)," *La Revue musicale* (Oct. 1902): 422.

36. Bouyer published his article in *La Nouvelle revue* on September 15, 1902: 278–280. And see Christian Goubault, "Les Chapelles musicales françaises ou la querelle des 'gros-boutiens' et des 'petits-boutiens,'" *Revue internationale de musique française* Vol. 5 (June 1981): 100.

37. See Emmanuel, pp. 6, 61 ff., 216.

38. *La Revue Musicale* (1902): 422–423, 427–429.

39. See Johann Trillig, *Untersuchung zur Rezeption Claude Debussys in der zeitgenössischen Musikkritik* (Tutzing: Hans Schneider, 1983), p. 324.

40. Vallas, p. 130.

41. Jacques Durand, *Quelques souvenirs,* p. 121.

42. Vallas, p. 137.

43. *Debussy on Music,* pp. 84–85.

44. See Christian Goubault, "Colette et Debussy: Compagnons de chaine en *Gil Blas* en 1903," *Revue internationale de musique française* Vol. 17 (June 1985): 77. Debussy was already apparently friendly with Pierre de Bréville by 1900, as indicated by a series of letters to Bréville that address him as "cher ami." *Lettres Autographes,* Bibliothèque Nationale, Département de la Musique.

45. In a letter of September 5, 1908, to Francisco de Lacerda, Debussy makes ironic reference to the "parfum de sacristie" and the "discipline" at the Schola. Claude Debussy, *Letters,* eds. François Lesure and Roger Nichols (Boston: Faber, 1987), pp. 77, 83.

46. *Debussy on Music,* p. 89.

47. Davidian, "Debussy, d'Indy, and the Société Nationale," p. 289.

48. Charles Koechlin, "Souvenirs sur Debussy, la Schola, et la S.M.I.," *La Revue musicale* (Nov. 1934): 241–242.

49. *Debussy on Music,* pp. 124–125.

50. See *Debussy on Music,* p. 129, which reprints the article that appeared in *Gil Blas* on March 2, 1903.

51. *Debussy on Music,* p. 130.

52. Ibid., p. 131. Here Debussy praises Claudel's translation of *Agamemnon.* If some of these ideas resemble those of Romain Rolland, it may very well be because of Louis Laloy. Now close to Debussy and Rolland, he was particularly influential in the shaping of Debussy's ideas and readings from this point on. François Lesure and Richard L. Smith also perceive the impact of Rolland's ideas concerning popular spectacle on Debussy and point out, as well, that in a later edition of *Le Théâtre de peuple,* Rolland included Debussy's articles on the subject in *Gil Blas* in the bibliography. See *Debussy on Music,* pp. 71–72.

53. Ibid., p. 132.

54. On early Barrès, see Jerrold Siegel, *Bohemian Paris: Culture, Politics, and the Boundaries of Bourgeois Life 1830–1930* (New York: Viking, 1986), p. 283. In his early period, Barrès collaborated with Mauclair on *Le Cocard,* which presented "the idea of continuity" as "the principle obstacle to a sane society" and posited instead the "autonomy of each generation." See Zeev Sternhell, *Maurice Barrès et le nationalisme français* (Paris: Armand Colin, 1972), pp. 43–44, 183. On Barrès's idea of the "self," see David Carroll, *French Literary Fascism* (Princeton, N.J.: Princeton University Press, 1995), p. 24.

55. In *Gil Blas,* on June 28, 1903, Debussy refers to the destructive force of "traditions cosmopolites."

56. Vallas, p. 159. As Jacques Durand recalls, in *Quelques souvenirs* (p. 126), on the hundredth performance of *Pelléas*, Albert Carré, the director of the Opéra Comique, organized a banquet. When the moment for official toasts arrived, a representative of the government was obliged to speak. He celebrated not only the work and its author but the eclectic artistic tastes of the Ministry, since it had just given the "rosette" to d'Indy and Charles Leloq.

57. Claude Debussy, *Letters*, pp. 141–142 (letter from Debussy to Laloy of August 8, 1904). See also the letter to Laloy of April 3, 1904 (p. 131).

58. Brian Hart, "*La Mer* and the Meaning of the Symphony in Early 20th-Century France," paper delivered at the national meeting of the American Musicological Society, Pittsburgh, 1992, pp. 1–3, 15–16.

59. Ibid.

60. For a more complete analysis, see David Cox, *Debussy. Orchestral Music* (London: British Broadcasting Corporation, 1974), as well as Brian Hart, *The Symphony in Theory and Practice in France 1900–1914*, Ph.D. Dissertation, Indiana University, 1994, pp. 366–378.

61. Emmanuel, p. 63.

62. Hart, *The Symphony in Theory and Practice*, pp. 367–368, and Louis Laloy, "La Nouvelle manière de Claude Debussy," *La Grande revue* (Feb. 10, 1908): 533.

63. Laloy, "La Nouvelle manière," pp. 530–531.

64. Ibid., p. 533.

65. Christian Goubault, "Les Chapelles musicales françaises," p. 106. As he notes, Debussy dedicated the second piece of the second collection of the *Images* for piano, "Et la lune descend sur le temple qui fut," to Laloy, who was an expert in sinology.

66. *Debussy on Music*, p. 242.

67. Debussy, *Letters*, p. 148.

68. Ibid., p. 146 (see letter of Feb. 24, 1906).

69. Vallas, p. 220, and Orledge, *Debussy and the Theater,* p. 252. This was also the period of the *Children's Corner Suite* (1908). Many historians have pointed out the playful or ironic references to Wagner in "The Golliwog's Cakewalk."

70. Letter to Louis Laloy, of September 10, 1906, in Debussy, *Letters,* p. 154.

71. *Debussy on Music,* p. 255. It is significant to note that Debussy had already been drawn to eighteenth-century forms in his *Suite Bergamasque* of 1890 and in *Pour le piano* of 1901. He was, in addition, attracted to the style of the entire school of French "calvecinistes," who had similarly reconciled the demands of programmatic suggestion and musical structure. Their clarity and delicacy, their attention to and structural use of sonority, as well as their finesse in both rhythm and ornamentation similarly inspired his work. The "Hommage à Rameau" is perhaps the most personal statement of his identification with this tradition, evincing his emotional commitment to it, and particularly to Rameau's harmonic sensibility, through the plangent chromatic harmony it incorporates.

72. Vallas, p. 183.

73. The best discussion of Debussy's so-called ancient style may be found in Arthur Wenk's *Claude Debussy and the Poets* (Berkeley: University of California Press, 1976), p. 102 ff.

74. "Gigues" was composed in 1900–2, "Ibéria," 1905–8, and "Rondes de printemps," 1905–10. A review of the work by Lalo, which made Debussy extremely unhappy, appeared in *Le Temps* on August 18, 1909. See his letter to Caplet of August 25, 1909, in Debussy, *Letters,* p. 186.

75. Letter to Jacques Durand of March 1908, Debussy, *Letters,* p. 169.

76. Cox, *Debussy. Orchestral Music,* p. 38.

77. Ibid., p. 43.

78. Vallas, p. 202.

79. Ibid., p. 198. Also see Trillig, *Untersuchung zur Rezeption Claude Debussys,* p. 324.

80. Vallas, p. 199.

81. Ibid., p. 190.

82. The interview appeared in *Harper's Weekly.* See *Debussy on Music,* p. 238.

83. See Hart, *The Symphony in Theory and Practice,* pp. 337–338.

84. Debussy, *Letters,* p. 185. (Letter to Andre Caplet of August 25, 1909.)

85. Vallas, p. 213.

86. Ibid., p. 223.

87. *Debussy on Music,* p. 247.

88. *Revue critique des idées et des livres* Vol. 13 (1911): 624.

89. Vallas, p. 232.

90. Ibid., p. 223.

91. Ibid., pp. 229–230.

92. *Debussy on Music,* p. 222 (from the interview with *Harper's Weekly*).

93. Christian Goubault, *La Critique musicale dans la presse française de 1870 à 1914* (Genève-Paris: Slatkine, 1984), p. 161.

94. Letter to René Lenormand of July 25, 1912, in Debussy, *Letters,* p. 237, and Vallas, p. 203.

95. On the concept of the "author" and his "oeuvre," see Michel Foucault, *L'Ordre du discours* (Paris: Gallimard, 1971). I am grateful to Roger Chartier for this insight.

96. See Hart, *The Symphony in Theory and Practice,* p. 178 ff., as well as Séverac's characterization of the "Debussyste" camp in "La Centralization et les petites chapelles musicales," *Le Courrier musical* (Jan. 1908): 1–6, 37–43, 142–144.

97. Debussy letter to Stravinsky of November 5, 1912 in Debussy, *Letters,* p. 233.

98. In a letter to Robert Godet of January 4, 1913, Debussy expressed the opinion that Stravinsky was using him to "climb the ladder" from the top of which to "explode his grenades." Ibid., p. 269. In addition, Debussy was unhappy about the influence of the eurhythmics of Jacques Dalcroze on Nijinsky, considering Dalcroze as "an enemy of music." See Vallas, p. 234, the letter to Robert Godet of June 9, 1913 in Debussy, *Letters,* pp. 238–239, and Arthur Gold and Robert Fizdale, *Misia: the Life of Misia Sert* (New York: Knopf, 1980), p. 143.

99. See Vallas, p. 237, as well as Cox, *Debussy. Orchestral Music.*

100. Vallas, pp. 241–242.

101. Debussy's letters to Paul Dukas of May 8, 1907, and to Jacques Durand of March 24, 1908, in Debussy, *Letters,* pp. 155, 170.

102. Debussy letter to Vittorio Gui of February 25, 1912, ibid., p. 223.

103. *Revue musicale S.I.M.* (1913): 50.

104. Debussy's attitudes within the musical and political culture of the First World War will be treated in my next study, "Music and Political Culture in France from the First to the Second World War."

105. My approach here is in contrast to the interpretation of Satie's musical semiology in most other studies, perhaps the most recent of which is Alan M. Gillmor's *Erik Satie* (Boston: Twayne, 1988), p. 158 ff.

106. Pierre-Daniel Templier, *Erik Satie* (Paris: Rieder, 1932), pp. 4–5, and Anne Rey, *Erik Satie* (Bourges: Tardy Quercy Auvergne, 1974), p. 13.

107. Templier, *Satie,* pp. 5–6, and Rey, *Satie,* p. 11.

108. Templier, pp. 7, 10.

109. Ibid., pp. 9–10.

110. Rey, p. 14, and William Austin, *Music in the Twentieth Century,* p. 162.

111. Rey, pp. 22–23, and see Jerrold Siegel, *Bohemian Paris,* p. 328.

112. Templier, pp. 10–13, 15.

113. Ibid., p. 15, and Rey, p. 36.

114. See Nancy Perloff, *Art and the Everyday. Popular Entertainment and the Circle of Erik Satie* (Oxford: Clarendon Press, 1991), pp. 81–83. As she points out, waiters at the Chat Noir, for example, wore the costumes of Academicians until the Institut forbade it in 1892.

115. Templier, p. 19.

116. In 1895, Willy accused Satie in the journal *Chat Noir* of being "affamée de réclame." Satie finally found the opportunity to confront him in 1904, at the Concerts Lamoureux, where he physically attacked the critic. Willy responded in kind, and Satie was promptly expelled by municipal guards. See François Caradec, *Feu Willy* (Paris: J. J. Pauvet, 1984), pp. 44–49.

117. Templier, p. 20, and Rey, p. 44.

118. Rey, pp. 45–48.

119. Templier, p. 22, and Ornella Volta, "Le Rideau se lève sur un os," *Revue internationale de musique française* Vol. 23 (June 1987): 63, Jean Cocteau, *Professional Secrets. An Autobiography of Jean Cocteau,* ed. Robert Phelps (New York: Farrar, Straus, and Giroux, 1979), p. 81. Jean Wiéner described Satie's dress in these years as that of "un professeur de physique au lycée de Troyes." See Rey, p. 7.

120. Templier, p. 25.

121. Volta, "Le Rideau se lève," pp. 16, 23, 25. The work was one of those found by Milhaud in Satie's room after his death. It was first performed in 1926, at the Théâtre des Champs-Elysées, as part of a festival organized as an homage to his memory, by the Count Etienne de Beaumont. Satie's sense of competition with Debussy was to increase with the completion of *Pelléas,* when he was moved to remark, "Ou je trouve autre chose, ou je suis perdu."

122. Ibid., p. 24.

123. Ibid., pp. 21, 23. Allan Gillmor sees the work as coming out of the cabaret milieu. See Gillmor, *Satie,* p. 151.

124. See Julia Kristeva, *Desire in Language: A Semiotic Approach to Literature and Art* (New York: Columbia University Press, 1980), pp. 80–81, 84–85.

125. Gillmor, *Satie,* p. 151. He also notes that figures such as Vincent Hyspa, Satie's collaborator, made reference to composers like Offenbach and Massenet. Satie was not the only "serious" composer to write for the Chat Noir: in 1889, Camille Saint-Saëns published his "Les Cloches de soir," written for the cabaret.

126. See, for example, G. Fregerolla's "La Marche à l'etoile," of 1889.

127. Debussy tried to convince him that it was too late in life for such a radical change—although he himself was undergoing one. See Paul Landormy, *La Musique française de Franck à Debussy* (Paris: Gallimard, 1948), p. 57.

128. Albert Roussel, *Lettres et écrits,* ed. Nicole Labelle (Paris: Flammarion, 1987), p. 208.

129. Erik Satie, *Ecrits,* ed. Ornella Volta (Paris: Champ Libre, 1981), p. 80.

130. Rey, p. 67.

131. Debussy letter to Francisco de Lacerda, September 5, 1908 in Debussy, *Letters,* p. 174.

132. Rey, p. 78.

133. Ibid., p. 70.

134. Ornella Volta, *Erik Satie* (Paris: Seghers, 1979), p. 109.

135. Jean Touchard, *La Gauche en France depuis 1900* (Paris: Editions du Seuil, 1968), pp. 42–43.

136. R. D. Anderson, *France 1870–1914. Politics and Society* (London: Routledge and Kegan Paul, 1977), p. 16, and Edward Tannenbaum, *The Action Française: Die-hard Reactionaries in Twentieth-Century France* (New York: Wiley, 1962), p. 11.

137. Daniel Mayeur, *Pour une histoire de la Gauche* (Paris: Plon, 1969), p. 26.

138. Ibid.

139. Templier, p. 28.

140. Templier, pp. 30–31. This recalls the efforts of programs such as "L'Art Pour Tous."

141. Satie, *Ecrits,* p. 164. This passage appears to be a parody of the opening of d'Indy's *Cours de composition musicale.*

142. Gillmor, p. 144.

143. Rey, pp. 70–71.

144. Gillmor, p. 59.

145. Ibid., p. 183.

146. Rey, p. 71.

147. Liliane Brion-Guerry, ed., *L'Année 1913. Les formes esthétiques de l'oeuvre d'art à la veille de la première guerre modiale* (Paris: Klincksieck, 1971), p. 1105. And see Olivier Corpet, "La revue," in Jean-François Sirinelli, ed., *Histoire des droites en France* Vol. 2 *Cultures* (Paris: Gallimard, 1992), p. 170.

148. Ibid., p. 1106.

149. Ibid., p. 1109. In issue #4 it published a composition of Florent Schmitt, and in #9–10 one by Albert Roussel.

150. Ibid., pp. 1110–1111. And see John E. Toews, "Intellectual History after the Linguistic Turn: The Autonomy of Meaning and the Irreducibility of Experience," *American Historical Review* Vol. 92/4 (Oct. 1987): 150. Also see Olivier Corpet, "La revue," p. 171.

151. See Robert Orledge, *Satie the Composer* (New York: Cambridge University Press, 1990).

152. See Avner Ben-Amos, "La Panthéonization de Jean Jaurès," *Terrain* Vol. 15 (Oct. 1990): 49–64.

153. The complete scenario is described in Adolphe Boschot, *Chez les musiciens* (Paris: Plon, 1922), pp. 178–179.

154. *Julien: ou la vie du poète.* Poème lyrique en un prologue, quatre actes, et huit tableaux. Poème et musique de Gustave Charpentier. (Paris: Max Esching, Editeur, 1913). The score is dedicated to "J. Paul-Boncoeur, en fermeté et reconnaissante affection." And see Manfred Kelkel, *Naturalisme, vérisme, et réalisme dans l'opéra de 1890 à 1930* (Paris: Librairie Philosophique J. Vrin, 1984), pp. 203, 208, 240.

155. Letter from d'Indy to Guy Ropartz of August 7, 1907. *Lettres Autographes,* Bibliothèque Nationale, Département de la Musique.

156. Letter from d'Indy to the Ligue de la Patrie Française, of November 29, 1912. On the fate of the league, see Jean-Pierre Rioux, *Nationalisme et Conservatisme. La Ligue de la Patrie Française* (Paris: Beauchesne, 1977), p. 109.

157. Ironically, as cited by Bernard Champigneulle, *Les Plus beaux écrits des grands musiciens* (Paris: La Colombe, 1946), p. 393.

158. See Danièlle Pistone, "Beethoven et Paris. Repères historiques et évocations contemporaines," *Revue internationale de musique française* Vol. 12 (Feb. 1987): 22. Also see Leo Schrade, *Beethoven in France* (New Haven: Yale University Press, 1942).

159. Vincent d'Indy, *Beethoven* (Paris: Henri Laurens, 1913), p. 137.

160. Gaston Carraud, *La Vie, l'oeuvre, et la mort d'Albéric Magnard* (Paris: Rouart, Lerolle, et Cie., 1921), pp. 68 and 83.

161. *La Revue française politique et littéraire* (Jan. 14, 1912), p. 445.

162. Letter from Ravel to Jean Marnold of February 7, 1906 in *A Ravel Reader: Correspondence, Articles, Interviews* trans. and ed., Arbie Orenstein (New York: Columbia University Press, 1990), p. 80.

163. The article appeared in February 1912. As cited in Marcel Marnat, *Maurice Ravel* (Paris: Fayard, 1986), pp. 364–375.

164. Brian Hart, "*La Mer* and the Meaning of the Symphony in Early Twentieth-Century France," and Hart, *The Symphony in Theory and Practice*, pp. 184–186.

165. Marnat, *Ravel*, pp. 351–352.

166. Debussy, *Letters*, p. 157.

167. Maurice Ravel, "A Propos des *Images* de Claude Debussy," *Les Cahiers d'aujourd'hui* (1913): 135–136.

168. Ibid., p. 137. It is perhaps significant that this issue of the journal also contains a highly critical review of "Agathon's" *Les Jeunes gens d'aujourd'hui*. It is also significant that Ravel had long felt animosity toward Gaston Carraud, the great supporter of Scholisme.

169. Hart, "*La Mer* and the Meaning of the Symphony," p. 5.

170. D'Indy, letter to Guy Ropartz of October 10, 1902. *Lettres Autographes*, Bibliothèque Nationale, Département de la Musique.

171. D'Indy, letter to Guy Ropartz of August 2, 1901. Ibid.

172. Hart, *The Symphony*, pp. 225–242.

173. Ibid., pp. 228–229.

174. The review appeared on February 10, 1907. As cited by Hart, "*La Mer* and the Meaning of the Symphony."

175. See Déodat de Séverac, "La Centralisation et les petites chapelles musicales," *Le Courrier musical* (Jan. 1908): 1–6, 37–43, 142–144.

176. Basil Dean, *Albert Roussel* (London: Barrie and Rockliff, 1961), p. 1.

177. Ibid., pp. 3–8. Roussel was thus part of the first "graduating class" at the Schola, together with August Sérieyx and Déodat de Séverac.

178. Ibid., pp. 8–9, 12–13. As we have noted, Roussel was a teacher of Erik Satie, who grew to admire him greatly. While at the Schola, he also taught Roland-Manuel and Edgar Varèse.

179. See my "Musical Style, Meaning, and Politics in France in the 1930s," *The Journal of Musicology* Vol. 8 #4 (Fall 1995): 425–453.

180. Eugen Weber, *The Nationalist Revival in France 1905–1914* (Berkeley: University of California Press, 1959), pp. 126, 154.

181. Paul-Marie Masson, ed., *Rapport sur la musique française contemporaine* (Rome: Armam et Stein, 1913), pp. 7–8. As this collection makes clear, in general, French musicians had difficulty coming to terms with post-1870 German composers, but with exceptions, one case being Richard Strauss, seen by some as influenced by Berlioz. Musicians, like Debussy, however, appreciated neither.

182. Ibid., p. 10.

183. Ibid., p. 13.

184. On the large concert societies, or "grand concerts," see Hart, *The Symphony in Theory and Practice*, pp. 282–289.

185. Ibid.

186. See Myriam Chimènes, "Le Budget de la musique sous la IIIe République," in *La Musique du théorique au politique*, eds. Hugues Dufourt and Joël-Marie Fauquet (Paris: Aux Amateurs de Livres, 1991), p. 289.

187. Ibid., pp. 294–295.

188. The sums received were often modest, but they did confer recognition and status: the "Concerts de l'Art Pour Tous" received eighteen hundred francs, the "Oeuvre de la Chanson Française" three hundred francs, and the "Oeuvre de Mimi Pinson" one thousand francs. And as Frédérique Patureau notes in *Le Palais Garnier dans la société parisienne 1875–1914* (Liège: Margada, 1991), p. 435, the Chamber of Deputies, through the Minister of Fine Arts, imposed a more vigorous politics of reduced-price performances at the Opera.

189. Fiamme Nicoldi, "Alfredo Casella et l'avant-garde parisienne au debut du XXe siècle," *Revue internationale de musique française* Vol. 78 (Nov. 1985): 85.

190. Patureau, *Le Palais Garnier,* pp. 185, 434.

191. For example, Gluck's *Armide* was performed in 1905, and Rameau's *Hippolyte et Aricie* in 1908.

192. Patureau, p. 434. Also see Jan Pasler, "Paris: Conflicting Notions of Progress," in *Music, Society, and the Late Romantic Era,* ed. Jim Samson (Englewood Cliffs, N.J.: Prentice Hall, 1991), p. 394.

193. See Modris Eksteins, *Rites of Spring. The Great War and the Birth of the Modern Age* (Toronto: Lester and Orpen Dinnys, 1989), p. 49. As Eksteins points out, both *Tristan* and *The Ring* were performed at this time.

194. Auric made this observation in *Les Nouvelles littéraires* on January 6, 1923, as cited in Jean Wiéner, *Allegro appassionato* (Paris: Pierre Belfond, 1978), p. 273. On the riot at the premiere of the work, see Robert Siohan, *Stravinsky,* trans. Eric Walter White (New York: Grossman, 1970), p. 45.

195. See François Lesure, ed., *Dossiers de press* Tome I. *Igor Stravinsky. Le Sacre du printemps* (Genève: Minkoff, 1980).

196. As cited in Christian Goubault, *La Critique musicale dans la presse française,* p. 426; and see *Dossiers de presse,* pp. 27–30.

197. Arthur Gold and Robert Fizdale, *Misia: the Life of Misia Sert,* p. 151.

198. Jacques Durand, *Quelques souvenirs,* pp. 48–49.

199. See René Remond, *Les Droites en France* (Paris: Aubier Montaigne, 1982), and Herman Lebovics, *True France. The Wars over Cultural Identity 1900–1945* (Ithaca, N.Y.: Cornell University Press, 1992), p. 10.

200. On the specific works that they supported, see Patureau, p. 340, and Chimènes, "La Princesse Edmond de Polignac et la création musicale," in *La Musique et le pouvoir,* eds. Hugues Dufourt and Joël-Marie Fauquet (Paris: Aux Amateurs de Livres, 1987), p. 140.

201. Marnat, *Ravel,* p. 539. Significantly, this was the year that Ravel completed his *Mélodies hébraïques;* unlike Debussy, Ravel had no tolerance for anti-Semitism, a stance that would become even more accentuated in the years after the war.

202. See the *Mercure de France* October 1, 1913. On Marnold's response, see Trillig, p. 133. For Vuillermoz's response, see the *Dossiers de presse,* pp. 35–38.

203. *Dossiers de presse,* pp. 23–24.

204. Louis Laloy, "Cabarets et music halls," *Revue musicale S.I.M.* (1913): 53–56.

205. See the *Dossiers de presse,* pp. 51–52.

206. Cannudo frequently gave receptions in association with the journal, which were attended by a motley international group. See René Chalupt, *Ravel au miroir de ses lettres* (Paris: Robert Lafont, 1956), p. 68.

207. *Dossiers de presse,* pp. 13–15. On the motivations of both Stravinsky and Diaghilev, see Eksteins, *Rites of Spring,* pp. 3–40. Also see Brion-Guerry, *L'Année 1913,* p. 1107.

208. *Dossiers de presse,* p. 39.

209. Georges Auric, in *Les Nouvelles littéraires* January 6, 1923, as cited in Wiéner, *Allegro appassionato,* p. 72.

210. This is as opposed to the view presented by Jan Pasler in "Paris: Conflicting Notions of Progress," p. 406.

CONCLUSION

1. This metaphor and concept has been developed extensively as well as suggestively by Edward Said in his *Musical Elaborations* (New York: Columbia University Press, 1991).

2. The "Querelle des Bouffons," or the ideologically charged "war" between traditional French (Baroque) and "modern" (early Classical) Italian music in the mid-eighteenth century, has been treated in myriad sources. For a summary and perspective on the issues involved, see Jane F. Fulcher, "Melody and Morality: Rousseau's Influence on French Music Criticism," *International Review of the Aesthetics and Sociology of Music* Vol. 11:1 (1980): 45–57.

3. See Howard Erskin-Hill, *The Augustan Idea in English Literature* (London: Edward Arnold, 1983). On the politicization of the musical canon in eighteenth-century England, see William Weber, *The Rise of Musical Classics in Eighteenth-Century England: A Study in Canon, Ritual, and Ideology* (Oxford: Clarendon Press, 1992).

4. This is as opposed to the perspective presented by Antoine Compagnon in "L'Utopie d'une république athénienne," *Le Debat* Vol. 70 (May–August 1992): 42–48.

5. On the concept of the "scholastic" realm, as opposed to the "practical," see Pierre Bourdieu, *Méditations pascaliennes* (Paris: Le Seuil, 1997), especially pp. 22–23.

The perspective on canon formation here is different from what Philip Bohlman sees today; for him, politics is synonymous with academic politics. See Catherine Bergeron and Philip Bohlman, eds., *Disciplining Music: Musicology and Its Canons* (Chicago: University of Chicago Press, 1992), pp. 203–204. It is also opposed to the phenomenon that Katherine Ellis perceives in *Music Criticism in Nineteenth-Century France* (Cambridge: Cambridge University Press, 1995), pp. 3–6, concerning the canon and the criteria of autonomy and moral values, as well as the network that defined canonicity. As I have argued in this study, the 'incipient' canon that arose in the first half of the nineteenth century was not institutionalized in the Conservatoire and was performed only for a very limited audience. The gradual politicization of the "classics," as the concept developed in nineteenth-century France and thus the contestation over their interpretation, was perceptively traced by Leo Schrade in *Beethoven in Paris* (New Haven: Yale University Press, 1942). Significantly, it was a German emigré scholar in wartime who was so attuned to this phenomenon.

6. I am grateful to William Cohen for bringing Blum's case to my attention and for the reference to Joel Colton, *Léon Blum, Humanist in Politics* (New York: Knopf, 1966).

7. On the idea of great art serving social truth through isolation, see Theodor W. Adorno, *Philosophy of Modern Music,* trans. Anne G. Mitchell and Wesley V. Bloomster (London: Sheed and Ward, 1973, p. 21 ff.

8. See Linda Nochlin, "Degas and the Dreyfus Affair: Portrait of the Artist as Anti-Semite," in Norman L. Kleeblatt, ed., *The Dreyfus Affair. Art, Truth, and Justice* (Berkeley: University of California Press, 1987), pp. 96–116.

9. See Harold Bloom, *The Anxiety of Influence* (New York: Oxford University Press, 1973).

10. The issue of the relationship between artistic excellence and political engagement is developed by Robert von Hallberg in his Introduction to the issue "Politics and Poetic Value," *Critical Inquiry* Vol. 13/3 (Spring 1987): 415–420.

11. On neo-classicism and its role during the First World War, see Kenneth Silver,

Esprit de Corps. The Art of the Parisian Avant-Garde and the First World War (Princeton, N.J.: Princeton University Press, 1989). The concept of "national memory" has been developed extensively in the series edited by Pierre Nora, *Les Lieux de mémoire.* See especially Vol. 2 *La Nation* (Paris: Gallimard, 1986).

12. Jean-François Sirinelli and Eric Vigne, "Introduction. Des cultures politiques," in Jean-François Sirinelli, ed., *Histoire des droites en France* Vol. 2 *Cultures* (Paris: Gallimard, 1992), pp. 1–3, 9–10. On the role of writers in the Dreyfus Affair see Christophe Charle, *Naissance des "intellectuels" (1880–1900)* (Paris: Editions du Minuit, 1990), and his *La Crise littéraire à l'époque du naturalisme. Roman, théâtre, politique* (Paris: Presses de l'Ecole Normale Supérieure, 1979).

13. On the concept of "imagining" a national community, see Benedict Anderson, *Imagined Communities: Reflections on the Origin and Spread of Nationalism* (New York: Verso, 1983). And on referencing the war in myth, see Modris Eksteins, *Rites of Spring. The Great War and the Birth of the Modern Age* (Toronto: Lester and Orpen Dinnys, 1989).

14. This is not to ignore the politicized war between tradition and innovation, or between the "music of the past" and the "music of the future" in mid-nineteenth-century Germany and Austria; but it is important to note that its political dynamics were different— it was transnational and did not involve centralized state institutions to the same extent, or the overt backing of specific political groups. On the new situation in Weimar Germany, see Peter Fritzsche, "Did Weimar Fail?" *Journal of Modern History* Vol. 68 (Sept. 1996): 629–656. On music during the Weimar Republic, see Bryan Gilliam, ed., *Music and Performance during the Weimar Republic* (Cambridge: Cambridge University Press, 1994). See also Michael H. Kater, "The Revenge of the Fathers: The Demise of Modern Music at the End of the Weimar Republic," *German Studies Review* 15 (1992): 295–315. On the interwar period in France, see Jane F. Fulcher, "Musical Style, Meaning, and Politics in France on the Eve of the Second World War," *Journal of Musicology* Vol. 13 (Fall 1995): 425–453, as well as Jane F. Fulcher, "The Preparation for Vichy: Anti-Semitism in French Musical Culture between the Two World Wars," *Musical Quarterly* Vol. 71 (Fall 1995): 458–475.

15. See Leon Botstein, "The Enigmas of Richard Strauss: A Revisionist View," in Bryan Gilliam, ed., *Richard Strauss and His World* (Princeton, N.J.: Princeton University Press, 1992), pp. 3–32.

16. Jane F. Fulcher, "Current Perspectives on Culture and the Meaning of Cultural History Today," *Stanford French Review* (Spring 1985): 91–104.

17. See Johan Huizinga, *Men and Ideas: History, the Middle Ages, and the Renaissance* trans. James S. Holmes and Hans von Marle (New York: Harper and Row, 1959).

Bibliography

ARCHIVAL SERIES AND MANUSCRIPT SOURCES

AJ 13—Archives of the Paris Opera.	The complete inventory is available in the *Archives du Théâtre Nationale de l'Opera. AJ 13 1 à 1466. Inventaire.* Compiled by Brigitte Labot-Pussin, Conservateur. Paris: Archives Nationales: diffusé par la Documentation Française, 1977.
AJ 16 4747–4758.	Registres de délibérations de la faculté des lettres de Paris 1881–1940). Paris: Archives Nationales.
F 21-Beaux Arts.	Paris: Archives Nationales.
F 7-Police Archives.	Paris: Archives Nationales.
Bibliothèque de l'Opéra-Fonds Rouché.	
Bibliothèque Nationale.	Département de la Musique. Gustave Charpentier. *Souvenirs, Lettres, Poesies.*
Bibliothèque Nationale.	Erik Satie. *Manuscrits.*
Bibliothèque Nationale.	Claude Debussy; Vincent d'Indy. *Lettres Autographes.*

BOOKS AND ARTICLES

Abbate, Carolyn. "Tristan in the Composition of Pelléas." *19th-Century Music* Vol. 5/2 (Fall 1981): 117–141.

Adamson, Walter. *Avant-garde Florence: From Modernism to Fascism.* Cambridge: Harvard University Press, 1993.

————. *Hegemony and Revolution: A Study of Antonio Gramsci's Political and Cultural Theory*. Berkeley: University of California Press, 1980.

———— "The Language of Opposition in Early Twentieth-century Italy: Rhetorical Continuities between Pre-War Florentine Avant-gardism and Mussolini's Fascism." *Journal of Modern History* Vol. 64/1 (March 1992): 22–51.

Agathon [Henri Massis and Gabriel de Tarde]. *L'Esprit de la nouvelle Sorbonne. La Crise de la culture classique. La Crise du français.* Paris: Mercure de France, 1911.

Agulhon, Maurice. "Conflits et contradictions dans la France d'aujourd'hui." *Annales E.S.C.* Vol. 42/3 (May–June 1987): 595–610.

————. *The French Republic: 1879–1992.* Cambridge, Mass.: Blackwell, 1993.

————. *Marianne au combat: L'Imagerie et la symbolisme républicaine de 1789 à 1880.* Paris: Flammarion, 1979.

————. *Marianne au pouvoir: L'Imagerie et la symbolisme républicaine de 1880 à 1940.* Paris: Flammarion, 1989.

————. "La Place des symboles dans l'histoire d'après l'exemple de la République Française." *Bulletin de la Société d'Histoire Moderne* Vol. 3 (1980): 9–15.

————. "Politics and Images in Post-Revolutionary France." In *Rites of Power: Symbolism, Ritual, and Politics since the Middle Ages*, pp. 177–205. Ed. Sean Wilentz. Philadelphia: University of Pennsylvania Press, 1985.

Allard, Eugene, and Louis Vauxelles. "Gustave Charpentier." *Le Figaro*, 23 Oct. 1900.

Almendra, Julia d'. "Debussy et le mouvement modal dans la musique du XXe siècle." In *Debussy et l'évolution de la musique au XXe siècle*, pp. 104–129. Ed. Edith Weber. Paris: Editions du Centre Nationale de la Recherche Scientifique, 1965.

Althusser, Louis. *Politics and History: Montesquieu, Rousseau, Hegel, and Marx*. London: NLB, 1972.

Amacher, Richard E., and Victor Large, eds. *New Perspectives in German Literary Criticism*. Princeton, N.J.: Princeton University Press, 1979.

Anderson, Benedict. *Imagined Communities: Reflections on the Origin and Spread of Nationalism*. New York: Verso, 1983.

Anderson, R. D. *France 1870–1914. Politics and Society.* London: Routledge and Kegan Paul, 1977.

Antiff, Mark. *Inventing Bergson: Cultural Politics and the Parisian Avant-garde*. Princeton, N.J.: Princeton University Press, 1993.

Appleby, Joyce, Lynn Hunt, and Margaret Jacobs, eds. *Telling the Truth about History*. New York: Norton, 1994.

Aronoff, Myron J., ed. *Political Anthropology*. Vol. 2. *Culture and Political Change*. New Brunswick, N.J.: Transaction Books, 1983.

Atkin, Nicholas, and Frank Tallatt, eds. *Religion, Society, and Politics in France since 1789*. London: Hambledon Press, 1991.

Attali, Jacques. *Bruits: Essai sur l'economie politique de la musique*. Paris: Presses Universitaires de France, 1977.

Austin, William. "Debussy, Wagner, and Some Others." *19th-Century Music* Vol. 6/1 (Summer 1982): 82–91.

————. *Music in the Twentieth Century*. New York: Norton, 1966.

Bach-Sisley, J. M. Boucher, H. Focillon, et al. *Pour la musique française. Douze causeries*. Zurich: Editions Cres, 1917.

Badie, Bertrand, and Pierre Birnbaum. *Sociologie de l'Etat*. Paris: Berard Grasset, 1978.

Bakhtine, Mikhail. *Le Marxisme et la philosophie du langgage*. Paris: Les Editions du Minuit, 1977.

————. *La Poétique de Dostoievsky*. Paris: Editions du Seuil, 1970.

Balandier, Georges. *Anthropologie politique*. Paris: Presses Universitaires de France, 1976.

Barrès, Maurice. *Les Déracinés*. Paris: Felix Juvien, n.d.

———. *Un Homme libre*. Paris: Imprimerie Nationale, 1988.

———. *Le Jardin de Berénice*. Paris: Perrin, 1891.

Barrows, Susanna. *Distorting Mirrors: Visions of the Crowd in Late Nineteenth-century France*. New Haven, Conn.: Yale University Press, 1981.

Barthes, Roland. *Le Degre zéro de l'écriture*. Paris: Editions du Seuil, 1953.

———. *Le Grain de la voix: Entretiens 1962–1980*. Paris: Editions du Seuil, 1981.

Bauman, Richard. *Story, Performance, and Event: Contextual Studies of Oral Narrative*. New York: Cambridge University Press, 1986.

———. *Verbal Art as Performance*. Rowley, Mass.: Newbury House, 1977.

Beaufils, Marcel. *Wagner et le Wagnérisme*. Paris: Aubier, 1946.

Bédier, Joseph. *Le Roman de Tristan*. Paris: L'Edition d'art, 1946.

Bellaigue, Camille. *Portraits and Silhouettes of Musicians*. Trans. Ellen Orr. New York: Dodd, Mead, 1898.

———. *Notes brèves*. Paris: Librairie Ch. Delagrave, 1914.

———. *Souvenirs de musique et de musiciens*. Paris: Nouvelle Librairie Nationale, 1921.

Bellanger, Claude. *Histoire générale de la presse française*. 2 Vols. Paris: Presses Universitaires de France, 1969.

Ben-Amos, Avner. "La Panthéonisation de Jean Jaurès." *Terrain* Vol. 15 (Oct. 1990): 49–64.

Benedict, Ruth. *Patterns of Culture*. New York: Houghton Mifflin, 1934.

Benoist, Luc. *Signes, symboles, et mythes*. Paris: Presses Universitaires de France, 1975.

de Bercy, Anne, and Armand Ziwès. *A Montmartre le soir*. Paris: Editions du Seuil, 1975.

Bergeron, Catherine, and Philip Bolman, eds. *Disciplining Music: Musicology and Its Canons*. Chicago: University of Chicago Press, 1992.

Bernard, Elisabeth. "La Musique symphonique." *Revue internationale de musique française* Vol. 12 (Nov. 1983): 39–48.

Berr, Henri. *Peut-on réfaire l'unité morale de la France?* Paris: Armand Colin, 1901.

Berstein, Serge, and Pierre Milza. *Histoire de la France au XXe siècle*. Brussels: Editions Complexe, 1994.

Berstein, Serge. *Histoire du Parti Radical*. Paris: Presses de la Fondation Nationale des Sciences Politiques, 1980.

Bertrand, Paul. *Le Monde de la musique*. Geneva: Le Palatine, 1947.

Birnbaum, Pierre. *La Logique de l'Etat*. Paris: Fayrad, 1982.

———, ed. *La France de l'Affaire Dreyfus*. Paris: Gallimard, 1994.

———. *Un mythe politique: "La République juive"*. Paris: Fayard, 1988.

———. "States, Ideologies, and Collective Action in Western Europe." *International Social Science Journal* Vol. 32/4 (1980): 671–686.

Biron, Fernand. *Le Chant gregorien dans l'enseignement et les oeuvres musicales de Vincent d'Indy*. Ottawa: Les Editions de l'Universite d'Ottawa, 1941.

Blatt, Joel. "Relatives and Rivals: The Response of the Action Française to Italian Fascism." *European Studies Review* Vol. 2/3 (July 1981): 263–292.

Bloom, Harold. *The Anxiety of Influence*. New York: Oxford University Press, 1973.

Bonnet, Jean-Claude, and Philippe Roger, eds. *La Légende de la Révolution Française au XXe siècle*. Paris: Flammarion, 1988.

Boschot, Adolphe. *Chez les musiciens*. Paris: Plon, 1922.

———. *La Vie et les oeuvres d'Alfred Bruneau*. Paris: Fasquelle Editeurs, 1937.

Bossuet, Pierre. *Histoire administrative des rapports des théâtres et de l'Etat*. Paris: Imprimerie Henri Jouve, 1909.

Botstein, Leon. "Listening through Reading: Musical Literacy and the Concert Audience." *19th-Century Music* Vol. 16/2 (Fall 1992): 129–145.

Bourdieu, Pierre. *Ce que parler veut dire. L'Economie des échanges linguistiques.* Paris: Fayard, 1982.

———. "Champ du pouvoir, champ intellectuel, et habitus de class." *Scolies* Vol. 1 (1971): 7–26.

———. "Champ intellectuel et projet créateur." *Les Temps modernes* Vol. 22/246 (1966): 865–906.

———. "Le Champ littéraire." *Actes de la recherche en sciences sociales* Vol. 89 (Sept. 1991): 3–46.

———. *Choses dites.* Paris: Les Editions de Minuit, 1987.

———. *Distinction. A Social Critique of the Judgment of Taste.* Cambridge: Harvard University Press, 1984.

———. "Flaubert's Point of View." *Critical Inquiry* Vol. 14/3 (Spring 1988): 539–562.

———. "The Market of Symbolic Goods." *Poetics* Vol. 14 (1985): 13–44.

———. *Méditations pascaliennes.* Paris: Editions du Seuil, 1997.

———. "Penser la politique." *Actes de la recherche en sciences sociales* Vols. 71–72 (March 1988): 2–3.

———. *Les Règles de l'art.* Paris: Editions du Seuil, 1992.

Bourdieu, Pierre, Roger Chartier, and Robert Darnton. "Dialogue à propos de l'histoire culturelle." *Actes de la recherche en sciences sociales* Vol. 59 (Sept. 1985): 86–93.

Bourdieu, Pierre, and Jean-Claude Passeron. *Reproduction in Education, Society, and Culture.* Trans. Richard Nice. Beverly Hills, Calif.: Sage, 1970.

Boussel, Patrice. *L'Affaire Dreyfus et la presse.* Paris: Armand Colin, 1960.

Bouyer, Raymond. "Le Debussysme et l'évolution musicale (1901–1902)." *La Revue musicale* (Oct. 1902): 421–429.

Boyd, Malcolm, ed. *Music and the French Revolution.* Cambridge: Cambridge University Press, 1992.

Bredin, Jean-Denis. *The Affair: The Case of Alfred Dreyfus.* New York: Braziller, 1986.

Bres, Sophie. "Le Scandal Ravel des 1905." *Revue internationale de musique française* Vol. 14 (June 1984): 41–50.

Brion-Guerry, Liliane, ed. *L'Année 1913. Les formes esthétiques de l'oeuvre d'art à la veille de la première guerre mondiale.* Paris: Klincksieck, 1971.

Briscoe, James. "The Compositions of Debussy's Formative Years." Ph.D. Dissertation. University of North Carolina at Chapel Hill, 1979.

Brody, Elaine. *Paris: The Musical Kaleidoscope 1870–1925.* New York: Braziller, 1987.

Brombert, Victor. *The Intellectual Hero: Studies in the French Novel 1880–1955.* New York: Lippincott, 1960.

Brown, Frederick. *Theater and Revolution: The Culture of the French Stage.* New York: Viking, 1981.

Bruneau, Alfred. *A l'Ombre d'un grand coeur.* Paris: Bibliothèque Charpentier, 1932.

———. *La Musique française.* Rapport sur la musique en France au XIIIe au XXe siècle. La Musique à Paris en 1900 au théâtre, au concert, à l'Exposition. Paris: Bibliothèque Charpentier, 1901.

———. *Musiques d'hier et de demain.* Paris: Bibliothèque Charpentier, 1900.

Bruneau, Alfred. "Souvenirs inédits." *Revue internationale de musique française* Vol. 7 (Feb. 1982): 8–82.

Brunet, Nathalie. "Musique germanique et modernisme musicale en France à l'aube du XXe siècle." *Revue internationale de musique française* Vol. 18 (Nov. 1985): 47–57.

Buell, Lawrence. *New England Literary Culture: From Revolution through Renaissance*. New York: Cambridge University Press, 1986.

Cahut, Alberic. *La Liberté du théâtre*. Paris: Dujarrir, 1902.

Callaird, C., and José de Bérys. *Le Cas Debussy*. Paris: Bibliothèque du Temps Present, 1910.

Calvocoressi, M. D. *L'Etranger (de V. d'Indy)*. Paris: Editions du Courrier Musical, n.d.

Canteloube, Joseph. *Vincent d'Indy*. Paris: Henri Laurens, 1951.

Caradec, François. *Feu Willy*. Paris: J. J. Pauvet, 1984.

Carlson, Marvin. *The French Stage in the Nineteenth Century*. Metuchen, N.J.: Scarecrow Press, 1972.

———. *Theories of the Theater: A Historical and Critical Survey from the Greeks to the Present*. Ithaca, N.Y.: Cornell University Press, 1984.

Carraud, Gaston. *La Vie, l'oeuvre, et la mort d'Albéric Magnard*. Paris: Rouart, Lerolle, 1921.

Carroll, David. *French Literary Fascsim. Nationalism, Anti-Semitism, and the Ideology of Culture*. Princeton, N.J.: Princeton University Press, 1995.

Carter, Lawson A. *Zola and the Theater*. New Haven, Conn.: Yale University Press, 1963.

Casale-Monsimet, Marie-Christine. "L'Affaire Dreyfus et la critique musicale." *Revue internationale de musique française* Vol. 28 (Feb. 1989): 57–69.

Casella, Alfred. "Musiques horizentales et musiques verticales." *Le Monde musical* Vol. 30 (Oct. 1909): 291–292.

Castera, René de. "La Symphonie en si bémol de M. Vincent d'Indy." *L'Occident* (March 1904): 172–178.

Chaitin, Gilbert. "The Politics of the Contingent." Unpublished manuscript.

Chalupt, René. *Ravel au mirroir de ses lettres*. Paris: Robert Lafont, 1956.

Champigneulle, Bernard. *Les Plus beaux écrits des grands musiciens*. Paris: La Colombe, 1946.

Charette, Jacqueline. *Claude Debussy through his Letters*. New York: Vintage, 1990.

Charle, Christophe. "Champ littéraire et champ du pouvoir: les écrivains et l'Affaire Dreyfus." *Annales E.S.C.* Vol. 32/6 (March–April 1977): 240–264.

———. *La Crise littéraire à l'époque du Naturalisme. Roman, théâtre, et politique*. Paris: Presses de l'Ecole Normale Superieur, 1979.

———. *Les Elites de la République 1800–1900*. Paris: Fayard, 1987.

———. *Naissance des "intellectuels" 1880–1900*. Paris: Les Editions du Minuit, 1990.

———. "Noblesses et elites en France au début du XXe siècle." In *Noblesses européens au XIXe siècle*, pp. 407–433. Paris: Collection de l'Ecole Française de Rome 107, 1988.

———. *La République des universitaires 1870–1940*. Paris: Editions du Seuil, 1994.

Charpentier, Gustave. *Lettres inédites à ses parents*. Ed. Françoise Andrieux. Paris: Presses Universitaires de France, 1984.

———. *Rapport. Ville de Paris. Concours musical de 1910–1912*. Paris: Imprimerie Paul Dupont, 1914.

Chartier, Roger. "Le Monde comme representation." *Annales E.S.C.* Vol. 44/6 (Nov.-Dec. 1989): 1505–1520.

Chimènes, Myriam. "Le Budget de la musique sous la IIIe République." In *La Musique du théorique au politique*, pp. 261–312. Ed. Hugues Dufourt and Joël-Marie Fauquet. Paris: Aux Amateurs de Livres, 1991.

———. "La Princesse Edmond de Polignac et la creation musicale." In *La Musique et le pouvoir*, pp. 125–145. Paris: Aux Amateurs de Livres, 1987.

Clark, Priscilla Parkhurst. *Literary France: The Making of a Culture*. Berkeley: University of California Press, 1987.

Clark, Terry N. *Prophets and Patrons: The French University and the Emergence of the Social Sciences.* Cambridge: Harvard University Press, 1973.

Cocteau, Jean. *Professional Secrets: An Autobiography of Jean Cocteau.* Ed. Robert Phelps. New York: Farrar, Straus, and Giroux, 1979.

Coeuroy, André. *Appels d'Orphée.* Paris: Editions de la Nouvelle Revue Critique, 1926.

———. *La Musique française moderne.* Paris: Librairie Delagrave, 1924.

Cohen, Gustave. *Histoire de la mise en scène dans le théâtre religieux français du moyen age.* Paris: Honoré Champion, 1926.

Cohen, William. "Symbols and Power: Statues in Nineteenth-century Provincial France." *Comparative Studies in Society and History* Vol. 31/3 (July 1989): 491–513.

Cole, David. *The Theatrical Event.* Middleton, Conn.: Wesleyan University Press, 1975.

Collaer, Paul. *A History of Modern Music.* New York: World, 1955.

Colton, Joel. *Léon Blum, Humanist in Politics.* New York: Knopf, 1966.

Combarieu, Jules. "L'Enseignement musical au Conservatoire et la pédagogie moderne." *Revue musicale* (1910): 498–501.

Combes, Louis. "La Schola et le Conservatoire." *Le Monde musical* Vol. 15 (Oct. 1909): 276–278.

Compagnon, Antoine. *La Troisième République des lettres: De Flaubert à Proust.* Paris: Editions du Seuil, 1983.

———. "L'Utopie d'une republique athénienne." *Le Debat* Vol. 70 (May–Aug. 1992): 42–48.

Cooper, Martin. *French Music from the Death of Berlioz to the Death of Fauré.* London: Oxford University Press, 1951.

Cossart, Michel de. *The Food of Love: Princesse Edmond de Polignac and Her Salon (1865–1943).* London: Hamish Hamilton, 1978.

Cot, Jean-Pierre, and Jean-Pierre Mounier. *Pour une sociologie politique.* 2 Vols. Paris: Editions du Seuil, 1974.

Cox, David. *Debussy. Orchestral Music.* London: British Broadcasting Corp., 1974.

Craft, Robert. "Jews and Geniuses." *New York Review of Books* (Feb. 16, 1989): 35–37.

Crubellier, Maurice. *Histoire culturelle de la France XIX-XXe siècles.* Paris: Armand Colin, 1974.

Curzon, Henri de. *L'Oeuvre de Richard Wagner à Paris et ses interprètes 1850–1914.* Paris: Maurice Senart, 1920.

Dahlhaus, Carl. *Between Romanticism and Modernism.* Berkeley: University of California Press, 1980.

———. *Richard Wagner's Music Dramas.* Trans. Mary Whittall. Cambridge: Cambridge University Press, 1979.

Darnton, Robert. *The Great Cat Massacre and Other Episodes in French Cultural History.* New York: Basic Books, 1984.

———. "The Symbolic Element in History." *Journal of Modern History* Vol. 58/1 (March 1986): 218–234.

Daubresse, M. *Le Musicien dans le société moderne.* Paris: Le Monde Musical, 1914.

Daudet, Léon. *Ecrivians et artistes.* Vol. 7. Paris: Editions du Capitole, 1929.

———. *Salons et journaux.* Souvenirs des milieux littéraires, politiques, artistiques, et médicaux de 1880 à 1908. Paris: Nouvelle Librairie Nationale, 1917.

Davidian, Teresa. "Debussy, d'Indy, and the Société Nationale." *Journal of Musicological Research* Vol. 11/4 (Sept. 1991): 285–301.

Dean, Basil. *Albert Roussel.* London: Barrie and Rockliff, 1961.

Debussy, Claude. *Debussy on Music.* Ed. François Lesure and Richard L. Smith. New York: Knopf, 1977.

————. "Du Goût." *Revue musical S.I.M.* (1913): 47–49.

————. *Letters.* Ed. François Lesure and Roger Nichols. Boston: Faber, 1987.

————. *M. Croche Anti-dilettante.* Paris: Gallimard, 1926.

Decaunes, Luc, and M. L. Cavalier. *Réformes et projects de réforme de l'enseignement français de la Révolution à nos jours.* Paris: Publication de l'Institut Pedagogique Nationale, 1962.

Delmas, Marc. *Gustave Charpentier et le lyrisme français.* Paris: Delagrave, 1931.

Desaché, Jean. *De L'Intervention administrative dans l'art musical.* Paris-Librairie de la Société de Recueil Sirey, 1910.

Demuth, Norman. *Cesar Franck.* London: Dennis Dobson, 1949.

————. *Ravel.* London: J. M. Dent, 1947.

————. *Vincent d'Indy, 1851–1931: A Champion of Classicism.* London: Rockliff, 1951.

Dietschy, Marcel. "The Family and Childhood of Claude Debussy." *Musical Quarterly* Vol. 46 (1960): 301–314.

Digeon, Claude. *La Crise allemande de la pensée française.* Paris: Presses Universitaires de France, 1959.

Donard, Véronique. "La Musique réligieuse d'inspiration Catholique à Paris en 1900." *Revue internationale de musique française* Vol. 12 (Nov. 1983): 79–86.

Douglass, Mary. *How Institutions Think.* Syracuse, N.Y.: Syracuse University Press, 1986.

Dreyfus, Alfred. *Souvenirs et correspondence.* Publiées par son fils. Paris: Grasset, 1936.

Duchesneau, Michel. "Maurice Ravel et la Société Musicale Indépendente: Projet mirifique de concerts scandaleux." *Revue de musicologie* Vol. 80/20 (1994): 251–281.

Duclert, Vincet. "L'Affaire Dreyfus et le tournant critique." *Annales: Histoire, Sciences Sociales* Vol. 50/3 (May–June 1995): 563–578.

Dufourcq, Norbert. *La Musique française.* Paris: Editions A. et J. Picard, 1970.

Dufourt, Hugues, and Joël-Marie Fauquet, eds. *La Musique. Du Théorique au politique.* Paris: Aux Amateurs du Livre, 1991.

Dumésnil, René. *La Musique contemporaine en France.* 2 Vols. Paris: Armand Colin, 1949.

————. *La Musique en France entre deux guerres 1919–1939.* Genève: Editions du Milieu du Monde, 1946.

————. *Portraits des musiciens français.* Paris: Plon, 1938.

Dunsby, Jonathan. "Music and Semiotics: The Nattiez Phase." *Musical Quarterly* Vol. 49/1 (Winter 1983): 27–43.

Durand, Jacques. *Quelques souvenirs d'un editeur de musique.* 2e serie (1910–1924). Paris: A. Durand et Fils, 1925.

Durkheim, Emile. *Le Socialisme.* Paris: Presses Universitaires de France, 1971.

Eckhardt-Bäker, Ursula von. *Frankreichs Musik zwischen Romantik und Moderne.* Vol. 2. *Studien zur Musikgeschichte des 19. Jahrhunderts.* Regensburg: Gustave Bosse, 1965.

L'Ecole des Hautes Etudes Sociales 1900–1910 (No author or editor given). Paris: Felix Alcan, 1911.

Edelman, Murray. *From Art to Politics: How Artistic Creations Shape Political Conceptions.* Chicago: University of Chicago Press, 1995.

Egbert, Donald. *Social Radicalism and the Arts.* New York: Knopf, 1970.

Eksteins, Modris. *Rites of Spring: The Great War and the Birth of the Modern Age.* Toronto: Lester and Orpen Dinnys, 1989.

Ellis, Katherine. *Music Criticism in Nineteenth-century France.* Cambridge: Cambridge University Press, 1995.

Elwitt, Sanford. *The Making of the Third Republic: Class and Politics in France 1869–1884.* Baton Rouge: Louisiana State University Press, 1975.

Emmanuel, Maurice. "Lettres inédites." *Revue internationale de musique française* Vol. 11 (June 1983): 79–92.

————. *Pelléas et Mélisande de Debussy*. Paris: Editions Mallote, 1950.

————. "La Vie réelle en musique." *Revue de Paris* Vol. 15 (June 1900): 841–883.

Encyclopédie de la musique et dictionnaire du Conservatoire. Vol. 2, *Pedagogie, écoles, concerts-théâtres*. Paris: Delagrave, 1931.

Ermath, Michael. "Intellectual History as Philosophical Anthropology: Bernard Groethusysen's Transformation of Traditional 'Geistesgeschichte'." *Journal of Modern History* Vol. 65/4 (Dec. 1993): 673–705.

Erskin-Hill, Howard. *The Augustan Idea in English Literature*. London: Edward Arnold, 1983.

Fauré, Gabriel. *Correspondence*. Ed. Jean-Michel Nectoux. Paris: Flammarion, 1980.

————. *Opinions musicales*. Paris: Les Editions Rieder, 1930.

Faure, Michel. *Musique et société du Second Empire aux années vingt*. Paris: Flammarion, 1985.

Favre, Georges. *Compositeurs français méconnus. Ernest Guiraud et ses amis: Emile Paladilhe et Théodore Dubois*. Paris: Le Pensée Universelle, 1983.

————. *Musique et naturalisme: Alfred Bruneau et Emile Zola*. Paris: Le Pensée Universelle, 1982.

Fernandez, James. "The Mission of Metaphor in Expressive Culture." *Current Anthropology* Vol. 15/2 (June 1974): 119–145.

Fisher, David James. "The Origins of the French Popular Theater." *Journal of Contemporary History* Vol. 12 (1977): 461–497.

————. "Romain Rolland and the Ideology and Aesthetics of the French People's Theater." *Theater Quarterly* Vol. 9/33 (Spring 1979).

————. *Romain Rolland and the Politics of Intellectual Engagement*. Berkeley: University of California Press, 1988.

Flower, J. E. *Literature and the Left in France: Society, Politics, and the Novel since the Late Nineteenth Century*. Totowa, N.J.: Barnes and Noble, 1983.

————. *Writers and Politics in Modern France 1909–1961*. London: Hodder and Stoughton, 1977.

Foucault, Michel. *L'Ordre du discours*. Paris: Gallimard, 1971.

Fox, Daniel M. "Artists in the Modern State: The Nineteenth-century Background." *Journal of Aesthetics and Art Criticism* Vol. 22/2 (Winter 1963): 135–140, 143–148.

Franck, Joseph. "The Voices of Mikhail Bakhtin." *New York Review of Books* (Oct. 23, 1986): 56–60.

Fritzsche, Peter. "Did Weimar Fail?" *Journal of Modern History* Vol. 68 (Sept. 1996): 629–656.

Fulcher, Jane F. "Musical Style, Meaning, and Politics in France on the Eve of the Second World War." *Journal of Musicology* Vol. 13 (Fall 1995): 425–453.

————. *The Nation's Image: French Grand Opera as Politics and Politicized Art*. New York: Cambridge University Press, 1987.

————. "The Preparation for Vichy: Anti-Semitism in French Musical Culture between the Two World Wars." *Musical Quarterly* Vol. 71 (Fall 1995): 458–475.

Gamboni, Dario. "Odilon Redon et ses critiques: Une lutte pour la production de la valeur." *Actes de la recherche en sciences sociales* Vols. 66–67 (March 1987): 25–34.

Gastinel, Leon. *Influence des Expositions Universelles et Internationales sur l'art musical français autrefois, aujourd'hui, demain*. Paris: Imprimerie de la Poste, n.d.

Gauthier-Villars, Henri. "Qu'est ce que la musique française?" *Revue d'histoire et de critique musicale* (March 1903): 123–127.

————. *La Ronde des blanches*. Paris: Librairie Molière, 1901.

Geertz, Clifford. "Art as a Cultural System." *Modern Language Notes* Vol. 91 (1976): 1473–1499.

———. *The Interpretation of Cultures.* New York: Basic Books, 1973.

Gênet-Delacroix, Marie-Claude. *Art et Etat sous la IIIe République: Le Système des Beaux-Arts 1870–1940.* Paris: Publications de la Sorbonne, 1992.

———. "Esthetique officiel et art national sous la Troisième Republique." *Le Mouvement social* Vol. 131 (April–June 1985): 105–210.

Gervereau, Laurent, and Christophe Prochasson, eds. *L'Affaire Dreyfus et le tournant du siècle (1894–1910).* Paris: Musée d'Histoire Contemporaine-BDIC, 1994.

Gildea, Robert. *The Past in French History.* New Haven, Conn.: Yale University Press, 1994.

Gillian, Garth. *From Sign to Symbol.* Harvester Press, 1982.

Gillmor, Alan M. *Erik Satie.* Boston: Twayne, 1988.

———. "Erik Satie and the Concept of the Avant-Garde." *Musical Quarterly* Vol. 49/1 (Winter 1983): 104–119.

Girardet, Raoul, ed. *Le Nationalism français 1871–1914.* Paris: Armand Colin, 1966.

Goguel, François. *La Politique des parties sous la IIIe République.* Paris: Editions du Seuil, 1946.

Gold, Arthur, and Robert Fizdale. *Misia: the Life of Misia Sert.* New York: Knopf, 1980.

Goléa, Antoine. *Georges Auric.* Paris: Ventadour, n.d.

Goss, Madeleine. *Bolero: The Life of Maurice Ravel.* Trans. Margaret Crosland. New York: Grove, 1959.

Gossett, Philip. "Up from Beethoven." *New York Review of Books* (Oct. 26, 1989): 21–26.

Goubault, Christian. "Les Chapelles musicales françaises ou la querelle des 'gros-boutiens' et des 'petits-boutiens'." *Revue internationale de musique française* Vol. 5 (June 1981): 99–112.

———. *Claude Debussy.* Paris: H. Champion, 1986.

———. "Colette et Debussy: Compagnons de chaine en *Gil Blas* en 1903." *Revue internationale de musique française* Vol. 17 (June 1985): 75–86.

———. *La Critique musicale dans la presse française de 1870 à 1914.* Geneva: Editions Slatkine, 1984.

Gourret, Jean. *Ces Hommes qui ont fait l'Opéra 1669–1984.* Paris: Albatros, 1984.

Grayson, David. *The Genesis of Debussy's Pelléas et Mélisande.* Ann Arbor, Mich.: UMI Research Press, 1986.

Green, Christopher. *Cubism and Its Enemies. Modern Movements and Reaction in French Art, 1916–1928.* New Haven, Conn.: Yale University Press, 1987.

Green, Nancy L. *The Pletzl of Paris: Jewish Immigrant Workers in the Belle Epoque.* New York: Holmes and Meuer, 1986.

Griffiths, Richard. *Révolution à rebours: Le renouveau catholique et la littérature en France de 1870 à 1914.* Paris: Desclie de Brawer, 1971.

———. *The Uses of Abuse: Polemical Language in the Dreyfus Affair.* New York: Berg, 1991.

Grout, Donald. *A Short History of Opera.* New York: Columbia University Press, 1965.

Guichard, Léon. *La Musique et les lettres en France au temps dy Wagnérisme.* Paris: Presses Universitaires de France, 1963.

Guieu, Jean-Max. *Le Théâtre lyrique d'Emile Zola.* Paris: Fishbacher, 1983.

Hahn, Reynaldo. *Thèmes variés.* Paris: J. B. Janin, 1946.

Hallberg, Robert von. "Introduction" to the issue on "Politics and Poetic Value." *Critical Inquiry* Vol. 13/3 (Spring 1987): 415–420.

Halperin, Joan U. *Félix Fenéon and the Language of Art Criticism.* Ann Arbor, Mich.: UMI Research Press, 1980.

Hamilton, Alastair. *The Appeal of Fascism: A Study of Intellectuals and Fascsim 1919–1945*. New York: Avon, 1973.

Harding, James. *Erik Satie*. New York: Praeger, 1975.

Hart, Brian. "The Symphony in Theory and Practice in France, 1900–1914". Ph.D. Dissertation. Indiana University, 1994.

Haskell, Francis. "Thanks for the Memory." *New York Review of Books* (Dec. 8, 1988): 48–51.

Hellouin, Frédéric. *Essai de critique de la critique musicale*. Paris: A. Joanin, 1906.

Hemmings, F. W. J. *Culture and Society in France 1848–1898*. London: B. T. Balsford, 1971.

Herbert, Eugenia W. *The Artist and Social Reform in France and Belgium 1885–1898*. New Haven, Conn.: Yale University Press, 1961.

Hervey, Arthur. *French Music in the 19th Century*. London: Grant Richards, 1903.

Hill, Edward B. *Modern French Music*. Cambridge, Mass.: Riverside Press, 1924.

Himonet, André. *Louise de G. Charpentier*. Paris: Paul Mellotée, 1992.

Hirsbrunner, Theo. *Debussy und seine Zeit*. Bern: Laaber, 1981.

———. *Die Musik in Frankreich im 20. Jahrhundert*. Bern: Laaber, 1995.

———. *Igor Stravinsky in Paris*. Bern: Laaber, 1982.

———. "Richard Wagner's Influence on French Opera: Towards an Invisible Theater." *IMS Congress Report*. Berkeley, 1977.

Hobsbawm, Eric. *Nations and Nationalism since 1780: Programme, Myth, Reality*. Cambridge: Cambridge University Press, 1992.

Hobsbawm, Eric, and Terrence Ranger, eds. *The Invention of Tradition*. Cambridge: Cambridge University Press, 1983.

Hoffman, Robert. *More Than a Trial: The Struggle over Captain Dreyfus*. New York: Free Press, 1980.

Hoffmann, Stanley, ed. *In Search of France*. Cambridge: Harvard University Press, 1963.

Holloway, Robin. *Debussy and Wagner*. London: E. Eulenburg, 1979.

Huebner, Steven. "Between Anarchism and the Box Office: Gustave Charpentier's *Louise*." Paper read at the national meeting of the American Musicological Society, Minneapolis, 1994.

Huizinga, Johan. *Men and Ideas: History, the Middle Ages, and the Renaissance*. Trans. James S. Holmes and Hans von Marle. New York: Harper and Row, 1959.

Hunt, Lynn. *Politics, Culture, and Class in the French Revolution*. Berkeley: University of California Press, 1984.

Hunt, Lynn, ed. *The New Cultural History*. Berkeley: University of California Press, 1989.

Huré, Jean. *Dogmes musicaux (1904–1907)*. Paris: Editions du Monde Musical, 1909.

Hyman, Paula. *From Dreyfus to Vichy: The Remaking of French Jewry, 1906–1939*. New York: Columbia University Press, 1979.

———. "The Dreyfus Affair: The Visual and the Historical." *Journal of Modern History* Vol. 61/1 (March 1989): 88–109.

d'Indy, Jacques. *Visage inconnu de Vincent d'Indy*. Marseille: Fondation Paul Richard, n.d.

d'Indy, Vincent. *Beethoven*. Paris: Henri Laurens, 1913.

———. *Cesar Franck*. Trans. Rosa Newmarch. New York: Dover, 1965.

———. *Cours de composition musicale*. Vols. 1 and 2. Paris: A. Durand et Fils, 1903 and 1909.

———. "Une Ecole d'art répondant aux besoins modernes." *La Tribune de Saint-Gervais* (Nov. 1900): 303–314.

———. *Emmanuel Chabrier et Paul Dukas*. Paris: Heugel, 1920.

———. *Richard Wagner et son influence sur l'art musical aujourd'hui*. Paris: Librairie Delagrave, 1930.

————. "La Schola Cantorum." In *Encyclopédie de la musique et dictionnaire du Conservatoire*. Ed. Albert Lavignac and Lionel de la Laurencie. Part 2, Vol. 6, *Pédagogie, écoles, concerts, théâtres,* pp. 3622–25. Paris: Delagrave, 1931.

————. *La Schola Cantorum en 1925.* Paris: Bloud et Gay, 1927.

Iser, Wolfgang. *The Implied Reader*. Baltimore: John Hopkins University Press, 1974.

Irvine, William D. *The Boulanger Affair Reconsidered: Royalism, Boulangism, and the Origins of the Radical Right in France*. New York: Oxford University Press, 1989.

Jackson, A. B. *La Revue blanche (1889–1903)*. Paris: Lettres Modernes, 1960.

Jameson, Frederick. *The Political Unconscious: Narrative as a Socially Symbolic Act*. Ithaca, N.Y.: Cornell University Press, 1981.

Jarocinski, Stefan. *Debussy: Impressionism and Symbolism*. Trans. Rollo Meyers. London: Eulenburg, 1976.

Jaurès, Jean. *La Classe Ouvrière*. Ed. Madeleine Rébérioux. Paris: Maspero, 1976.

Jelavich, Peter. *Munich and Theatrical Modernism: Politics, Play-writing, and Performance 1890–1914*. Cambridge: Harvard University Press, 1985.

Johnson, Douglas. *France and the Dreyfus Affair*. London: Blanford Press, 1966.

Joll, James. *The Anarchists*. Cambridge: Harvard University Press, 1980.

————. "Klingsor's Apprentices." *New York Review of Books* (April 27, 1989): 53–56.

Julliard, Jacques. *Fernand Pelloutier et les origines su syndicalisme d'action directe*. Paris: Editions du Seuil, 1971.

Kaes, René. *Images de la culture chez les ouvriers français*. Paris: Editions Cujas, n.d.

Kahane, Martine, and Nicole Wilde, eds. *Wagner et la France*. Paris: Bibliothèque Nationale, Editions Herscher, 1983.

Katz, Jacob. *From Prejudice to Destruction: Anti-Semitism 1700–1933*. Cambridge: Harvard University Press, 1980.

Kelkel, Manfred. *Naturalisme, vérisme, et réalisme dans l'opéra de 1890 à 1930*. Paris: Librairie Philosophique J. Vrin, 1984.

————. "Oeuvres du répertoire et créations chorégraphiques à Paris en 1900." *Revue internationale de musique française* Vol. 12 (Nov. 1983): 27–37.

Kendall, Alan. *The Tender Tyrant. Nadia Boulanger. A Life Devoted to Music*. London: Macdould and Jane's, 1976.

Kerman, Joseph. *Opera as Drama*. New York: Vintage, 1959.

————. "Wagner and Wagnerism." *New York Review of Books* (Dec. 22, 1983): 27–37.

Kleeblatt, Norman L., ed. *The Dreyfus Affair: Art, Truth, and Justice*. Berkeley: University of California Press, 1988.

Knights, L. C. *Public Voices: Literature and Politics with Special Reference to the Seventeenth Century*. London: Chatto and Windus, 1971.

Koechlin, Charles. *Gabriel Fauré*. Paris: Felix Alcan, 1927.

————. "Souvenirs sur Debussy, la Schola, et la S.M.I." *La Revue musicale* (Nov. 1934): 241–251.

Kristeva, Julia. *Desire in Language: A Semiotic Approach to Literature and Art*. New York: Columbia University Press, 1980.

La Capra, Dominick. *Rethinking Intellectual History: Texts, Contexts, Language*. Ithaca, N.Y.: Cornell University Press, 1983.

LaClau, Ernesto. "Universalism, Particularism, and the Question of Identity." *October* Vol. 61 (1992): 83–90.

Laitin, David. *Politics, Language, and Thought: The Somali Experience*. Chicago: University of Chicago Press, 1977.

La Laurencie, Lionel de. "Le d'Indysme." *L'Art moderne* Vol. 5 (Feb. 1903): 49–52.

————. *Le Goût musical en France*. Geneva: Slatkine Reprints, 1970. (First edition, 1905.)

————. "Le Mouvement musicographique." *Le Mercure musical* (June 1907): 657–661.

————. "Un musicien de chez nous." *L'Occident* 1904.

————. "L'Oeuvre de Vincent d'Indy." *Durendal: Revue Catholique d'art et de littérature* (April 1902): 204–215.

Lalo, Pierre. *La Musique 1898–1899.* Paris: Rouart, Lerolle, 1900.

Laloy, Louis. "Cabarets et Music-Hall." *Revue musical S.I.M.* (1913): 53–56.

————. *Debussy.* Paris: Dorbon, 1909.

————. "Le Drame musical moderne." *Le Mercure musical,* 1905.

————. *La Musique retrouvée 1902–1927.* Paris: Plon, 1928.

————. "Une Nouvelle école de musique: le cours de M. Vincent d'Indy." *Revue d'histoire et de critique musicale* (Nov. 1901): 393–398.

————. "La Nouvelle manière de Claude Debussy." *La Grande revue* Vol. 10 (Feb. 1908): 530–535.

————. "Les Parties musicaux en France." *La Grande revue* Vol. 25 (Dec. 1907): 790–799.

————. *Rameau.* Paris: Felix Alcan, 1919.

Landormy, Paul. "L'Etat actuel de la musique française." *Revue bleue* (Jan.–June 1904): 394–397; 421–426.

————. *La Musique française de Franck à Debussy.* Paris: Gallimard, 1948.

Lanson, Gustave. *Histoire de la littérature française.* Paris: Hachette, 1906.

Large, David, and William Weber, eds. *Wagnerism in European Culture and Politics.* Ithaca, N.Y.: Cornell University Press, 1984.

Lasserre, Pierre. *Les Chapelles littéraires. Claudel, Jammes, Péguy.* Paris: Garnier Frères, 1920.

————. *L'Esprit de la musique française.* Paris: Payot, 1917.

————. *Philosophie du goût musical.* Paris: Bernard Grasset, 1922.

————. *Le Romantisme français.* Paris: Société du Mercure de France, 1908.

————. *Des Romantiques à nous.* Paris: La Nouvelle Revue Critique, 1927.

Lavignac, Albert, ed. *Encyclopédie de la musique et dictionnaire du Conservatoire.* Paris: C. Delagrave, 1913–31.

————. *Notions scolaires de musique.* Paris: Henri Lemoine, 1908.

————. *Le Voyage artistique à Bayreuth.* Geneva: Minkoff Reprints, 1973. (First edition, 1897.)

Le Goff, Jacques, and Pierre Nora, eds. *Faire de l'histoire.* Paris: Gallimard, 1974.

Lebovics, Herman. *The Alliance of Iron and Wheat in the Third French Republic 1870–1914: Origins of the New Conservativism.* Baton Rouge: Louisiana State University Press, 1988.

————. *True France: The Wars over Cultural Identity 1900–1945.* Ithaca, N.Y.: Cornell University Press, 1992.

Lemaître, Jules. *L'Oeuvre de la Patrie Française.* Discours-programme du 13 Novembre, 1899. Paris: Editions L.P.F., 1899.

Léon, Paul. *Du Palais-Royal au Palais-Bourbon.* Paris: Albin-Michel, 1947.

Lepenies, Wolf. *Les Trois cultures: Entre science et littérature; l'avènement de la sociologie.* Paris: Editions de la Maison des Sciences de l'Homme, 1990.

Lequin, Yves, ed. *La Mosaïque, France: Histoire des étrangers et l'immigration.* Paris: Larousse, 1988.

Lesure, François, ed. *Claude Debussy. Lettres.* Paris: Hermann, 1980.

————. *Claude Debussy avant Pelléas, ou les années symbolistes.* Paris: Klinckieck, 1992.

————. *Debussy on Music.* New York: Knopf, 1977.

————. *Dossiers de presse.* Vol. 1. *Igor Stravinsky: Le Sacre du printemps.* Geneva: Minkoff, 1980.

Levin, Harry. *The Gates of Horn*. New York: Oxford University Press, 1963.

Lippman, Edward. *A History of Western Musical Aesthetics*. Lincoln: University of Nebraska Press, 1992.

Locke, Robert R. *French Legitimists and the Politics of Moral Order in the Early Third Republic*. Princeton, N.J.: Princeton University Press, 1974.

Lockspeiser, Edward. *Debussy*. London: J. M. Dent and Sons, 1980.

———. *Debussy: His Life and Mind*. London: Cassel, 1965.

———. *The Literary Clef: An Anthology of Letters and Writings by French Composers*. London: John Calder, 1958.

Lorrain, Jean. *Pelléastres: Le Poison de la littérature*. Paris: A. Merceant, 1909.

Mandell, Richard D. *Paris 1900: The Great World's Fair*. Toronto: University of Toronto Press, 1967.

Manevy, Raymond. *La Presse de la IIIe République*. Paris: J. Foret, 1955.

Mangeot, A. "L'Oeuvre de Mimi Pinson." *Le Monde musical* (1902): 317–318.

Marcuse, Herbert. *The Aesthetic Dimension: Toward a Critique of Marxist Aesthetics*. Boston: Beacon Press, 1977.

Margadant, Ted W. "Primary Schools and Youth Groups in Pre-War Paris: The Petit A's." *Journal of Contemporary History* Vol. 13/2 (April 1978): 323–336.

Marguérite, Jean. *Les Fêtes du Peuple: L'Oeuvre, les moyens, le but*. Paris: Les Fêtes du Peuple, 1921.

Marlais, Michael. *Conservative Echoes in Fin-de-Siècle Parisian Art Criticism*. University Park, Penn.: Pennsylvania State University Press, 1992.

Marnat, Marcel. *Maurice Ravel*. Paris: Fayard, 1986.

Marnold, Jean. "Le Conservatoire et la Schola." *Mercure de France* (1902): 105–115.

Massis, Henri. *Maurras et notre temps*. Paris: La Palatine, 1951.

Masson, Paul-Marie, ed. *Rapport sur la musique française contemporaine*. Rome: Armam et Stein, 1913.

Mauclair, Camille. "La Debussyste." *Le Courrier musical* Vol. 15 (Sept. 1905): 501–505.

———. "La Réaction Nationaliste en art et l'ignorance de l'homme de lettres." *La Revue mondiale* (Jan. 15, 1905): 151–174.

———. "La Schola Cantorum et l'éducation morale des musiciens." *La Revue* (Aug. 1901): 245–256.

———. *Servitude et grandeur littéraire*. Paris: Ollendorff, n.d.

Maurras, Charles. *La Musique intérieur*. Paris: Bernard Grasset, 1925.

Mayeur, Daniel. *Pour une histoire de la Gauche*. Paris: Plon, 1969.

Mayeur, Jean-Marie. *La Vie politique sous la Troisième République*. Paris: Editions du Seuil, 1984.

Mayeur, Jean-Marie, and Madeleine Rébérioux. *The Third Republic from its Origins to the Great War*. Trans. J. R. Foster. Cambridge: Cambridge University Press, 1984.

McGrath, William. *Dionysian Art and Populist Politics in Austria*. New Haven, Conn.: Yale University Press, 1974.

———. "'Volksseelenpolitik' and Psychological Rebirth: Mahler and Hofmannsthal." *Journal of Interdisciplinary History* Vol. 4 (Summer 1973): 53–71.

McMillan, James F. *From Dreyfus to DeGaulle: Politics in France 1898–1969*. London: Edward Arnold, 1985.

———. "Social History, 'New Cultural History,' and the Rediscovery of Politics: Some Recent Works on Modern France." *Journal of Modern History* 66 (Dec. 1994): 755–772.

———. *Twentieth-Century France: Politics and Society, 1898–1991*. New York: Routledge, Chapman, and Hall, 1992.

Mehlman, Jeffrey. *Legacies of Anti-Semitism in France.* Minneapolis: University of Minnesota Press, 1983.

Mellon, Stanley. *The Political Uses of History: A Study of Historians in the French Restoration.* Stanford, Calif.: Stanford University Press, 1958.

Menard, Louis. "Eliot and the Jews." *New York Review of Books* June 6, 1996: 34–41.

Mercanton, Jacques. *Poésie et religion dans l'oeuvre de Maurice Barrès.* Lausanne: F. Rouge, 1940.

Mercier, Lucien. *Les Universités populaires 1899–1914: Education populaire et movement ouvrier au début du siècle.* Paris: Les Editions Ouvrières, 1986.

Merriam, Alan. *The Anthropology of Music.* Chicago: Northwestern University Press, 1964.

Meyer, Leonard B. *Style and Music: Theory, History, and Ideology.* Philadelphia: University of Pennsylvania Press, 1989.

Meyers, Rollo. *Modern French Music.* Oxford: Blackwell Press, 1971.

Milza, Pierre. *Fascisme français: Passé et présent.* Paris: Flammerion, 1987.

Ministère de Commerce, de l'Industrie, et des Colonies. *Expositions Universelle de 1889 à Paris.* Direction General de l'Exploitation. Auditions musicales. Paris: Imprimerie Nationale, 1889.

Mittler, Eugene. *Des Rapports entre le Socialisme, le Syndicalisme, et la Franc-Maçonnerie.* Paris: Imprimerie Industrielle, 1911.

Monsaigneon, Bruno. *Mademoiselle. Conversations with Nadia Boulanger.* Trans. Robyn Marsack. Manchester, Eng.: Carcanet, 1985.

Mosse, George. *The Nationalization of the Masses: Political Symbolism and Mass Movements in Germany from the Napoleonic Wars through the Third Reich.* New York: Howard Fertig, 1975.

———. "The Political Culture of Italian Futurism: A General Perspective." *Journal of Contemporary History* Vol. 25 (1990): 253–68.

Nattiez, Jacques. *Music and Discourse: Toward a Semiology of Music.* Trans. Carolyn Abbate. Princeton, N.J.: Princeton University Press, 1990.

Nectoux, Jean-Michel. *Gabriel Fauré: A Musical Life.* Cambridge: Cambridge University Press, 1991.

Newcomb, Anthony. "The Birth of Music out of the Spirit of Drama: An Essay in Wagnerian Formal Analysis." *19th-Century Music* Vol. 5/1 (Summer 1981): 38–66.

Nguyen, Victor. *Aux origines de l'Action Française: Intelligence et politique à l'aube du XXe siècle.* Paris: Fayard, 1991.

Nichols, Roger. *Debussy.* London: Oxford University Press, 1973.

———. *Ravel.* London: J. M. Dent and Sons, 1977.

Nicolodi, Fiamme. "Alfredo Casella et l'avant-garde parisienne au début du XXe siècle." *Revue internationale de musique française* Vol. 78 (Nov. 1985): 83–92.

Niess, Robert J. *Julien Benda.* Ann Arbor: University of Michigan Press, 1956.

Nochlin, Linda. "Degas and the Dreyfus Affair: A Portrait of the Artist as Anti-Semite." In *The Dreyfus Affair: Art, Truth, and Justice,* pp. 96–116. Ed. Norman L. Kleeblatt. Berkeley: University of California Press, 1987.

Nora, Pierre, ed. *Les Lieux du mémoire.* Vol. 2. *La Nation.* Paris: Gallimard, 1986.

Norris, Christopher, ed. *Music and the Politics of Culture.* New York: St. Martin's, 1989.

Noske, Frits. *French Song from Berlioz to Duparc.* Trans. Rita Benton. New York: Dover, 1970.

Olin, Elinor. "Festivals de plein-air: Cultural Nationalism in fin-de-siècle France." Paper delivered at the annual meeting of the American Musicological Society, Minneapolis, 1994.

Olivera, Philippe. *La Librairie Valois (1928–1932).* Memoire presenté à l'Institut d'Etudes Politiques de Paris. Paris, 1989.

Orenstein, Arbie. *Ravel. Man and Musician.* New York: Columbia University Press, 1975.

Orledge, Robert. *Debussy and the Theater.* Cambridge: Cambridge University Press, 1982.

————. *Satie the Composer.* New York: Cambridge University Press, 1990.

————. *Satie Remembered.* Portland, Ore.: Amadeus Press, 1995.

Ory, Pascal. *Les Expositions Universelles de Paris.* Paris: Ramsay, 1982.

Ory, Pascal, and Jean-François Sirinelli. *Les intellectuels en France de l'Affaire Dreyfus à nos jours.* Paris: A. Colin, 1986.

Ozouf, Mona. *Festivals of the French Revolution.* Cambridge: Harvard University Press, 1988.

Parks, Richard. *The Music of Claude Debussy.* New Haven, Conn.: Yale University Press, 1989.

Pasler, Jan. "Paris: Conflicting Notions of Progress." In *Music, Society, and the Late Romantic Era,* pp. 389–416. Ed. Jim Samson. Englewood Cliffs, N.J.: Prentice Hall, 1991.

————. "Pelléas and Power: Forces behind the Reception of Debussy's Opera." *19th-Century Music* Vol. 10/3 (Spring 1987): 243–264.

Patureau, Frédérique. *Le Palais Garnier dans la société parisienne 1875–1914.* Liège: Margada, 1991.

Paul, Charles B. "Rameau, d'Indy, and French Nationalism." *Musical Quarterly* Vol. 58/1 (Jan. 1972): 46–56.

Paxton, Robert. "Radicals." *New York Review of Books* (June 23, 1994): 51–54.

Perloff, Nancy. *Art and the Everyday: Popular Entertainment and the Circle of Erik Satie.* Oxford: Clarendon, 1991.

Peter, Jean-Pierre. "Dimensions de l'Affaire Dreyfus." *Annales E.S.C.* Vol. 16/6 (Nov.–Dec. 1961): 1141–1167.

Peter, René. *Claude Debussy.* Paris: Gallimard, 1944.

————. *Le Théâtre et la vie sous la Troisième République.* Paris: Sanctandreana, 1945.

Philipps, Harvey. "Friend of the Working Girl." *Opera News* Vol. 6 (March 1971): 28–30.

Pierné, Gabriel, Paul Vidal, Henry Prunières, Maurice Emmanuel, and Henri de Régnier. *La Jeunesse de Claude Debussy.* Paris: Editions de Nouvelle Revue Française, 1926.

Pierre, Constant. "Le Conservatoire National de Musique." *La Revue musicale* Vol. 15 (July 1903): 313–324.

————. *Le Conservatoire Nationale de Musique et de Déclamation: Documents historiques et administratifs.* Paris: Imprimerie Nationale, 1900.

————. *B. Sarrette et les origines du Conservatoire Nationale de Musique et de Déclamation.* Paris: Delalaine Frères, 1895.

Pirro, André. *L'Esthétique de Jean-Sebastian Bach.* Paris: Fishbacher, 1907.

Pistone, Danielle. "Beethoven et Paris: Repères et évocations contemporaines." *Revue internationale de musique française* Vol. 12 (Feb. 1987): 7–31.

————. *La Musique en France de la Révolution à 1900.* Paris: Honoré Champion, 1979.

————. "Paris et la musique 1890–1900." *Revue internationale de musique française* Vol. 28 (Feb. 1989): 7–53.

————. "Wagner et Paris (1839–1900)." *Revue internationale de musique française* Vol. 1/1 (Feb. 1980): 7–84.

Pocock, J. G. A. *Politics, Language, and Time: Essays on Political Thought and History.* New York: Atheneum, 1971.

Poggioli, Renato. *The Theory of the Avant-Garde.* Trans. Gerald Fitzgerald. Cambridge, Mass.: Belknap Press, 1968.

Prado, Sharon S. "The Decadent Aesthetic in France 1880–1914: Musical Manifestations in the Works of Debussy and His Contemporaries." Ph.D. Dissertation. University of Cincinnati, 1994.

Prochasson, Christophe. *Les années électriques 1880–1910*. Paris: Editions de La Découverte, 1991.

———. *Les Intellectuels, le socialisme, et la guerre*. Paris: Editions du Seuil, 1992.

———. "Sur le cas Maurras: biographie et histoire des idées politiques." *Annales: Histoire, Sciences Sociales* Vol. 50/3 (May–June 1995): 579–587.

———. "Sur l'environment intellectuel de Georges Sorel: L'Ecole des Hautes Etudes Sociales (1899–1911)." *Cahiers Georges Sorel* Vol. 3 (1985): 16–38.

Prochasson, Christophe, and Anne Rasmussen. *Au nom de la patrie. Les intellectuels et la Première Guerre Mondiale (1910–1919)*. Paris: Editions de la Découverte, 1996.

Prod'homme, J.-G. *Richard Wagner et la France*. Paris: Maurice Senart, 1921.

Ravel, Maurice. "A Propos des *Images* de Claude Debussy." *Les Cahiers d'aujourd'hui* (1913): 133–138.

———. *A Ravel Reader: Correspondence, Articles, Interviews*. Trans., ed. Arbie Orenstein. New York: Columbia University Press, 1990.

Raymond, Marcel. *From Baudelaire to Surrealism*. London: Methuen, 1970.

Rearick, Charles. *Pleasures of the Belle Epoque: Entertainment and Festivity in Turn-of-the-Century France*. New Haven, Conn.: Yale University Press, 1985.

Rebérioux, Madeleine. "1913: L'Art et la réflection sur l'art." *Annales E.S.C.* Vol. 29/4 (July–Aug. 1974): 913–924.

———. "Histoire, historiens, et Dreyfusisme." *Revue historique* Vol. 518 (April–June 1976): 407–432.

———. "Presentation." [Issue on "Critique littéraire et socialisme."] *Le Mouvement sociale* Vol. 59 (April–June 1967): 3–28.

———. *La République radicale? 1898–1914*. Paris: Editions du Seuil, 1975.

Reddy, William. *Money and Liberty in Modern Europe: A Critique of Historical Understanding*. New York: Cambridge University Press, 1987.

Remond, René. *La Droite en France de 1815 à nos jours*. Paris: Aubier, 1954.

———. *Les Droites en France*. Paris: Aubier Montaigne, 1982.

———. *La Vie politique en France depuis 1789*. Paris: A. Colin, 1965.

Rey, Anne. *Erik Satie*. Bourges: Tardy Quercy Auvergne, 1974.

Ricoeur, Paul. *Interpretation Theory. Discourse and the Symbols of Meaning*. Forth Worth: Texas Christian University Press, 1976.

Riffaterre, Michael. "Decadent Features in Maeterlinck's Poetry." *Language and Style* Vol. 7/1 (Winter 1974): 3–16.

Ringer, Fritz. *Fields of Knowledge: French Academic Culture in Comparative Perspective, 1890–1920*. New York: Cambridge University Press, 1992.

Rioux, Jean-Pierre. *Nationalisme et conservatisme: La Ligue de la Patrie Française*. Paris: Beauchesne, 1977.

Rioux, Jean-Pierre, and Jean-François Sirinelli. *Pour une histoire culturelle*. Paris: Le Seuil, 1997.

Roche-Pézard, Fanette. "Création artistique et idéologie politique: futurisme et fascisme." *Cahiers d'histoire de l'art contemporaine* (May 1974): 4–11.

Rohoninski, L., ed. *Cinquante ans de musique française de 1874 à 1925*. Paris: Les Editions Musicales de la Librairie de France, 1925.

Roland-Manuel. *Ravel*. Paris: Editions de la Nouvelle Revue Critique, 1938.

Rolland, Romain. *Essays on Music*. New York: Allen, Towne, and Heath, 1948.

———. *Haendel*. Paris: Felix Alcan, 1911.

———. *Jean Christophe*. Paris: Albin Michel, 1931.

———. *Musiciens d'aujourd'hui*. Paris: Hachette, 1912.

———. *Théâtre de la Révolution*. Paris: Albin Michel, 1972.

————. *La Vie de Beethoven*. Paris: Hachette, 1903.

Rosen, Charles. "Did Beethoven Have All the Luck?" *New York Review of Books* November 14, 1996: 57–63.

Rosentiel, Léonie. *Nadia Boulanger: A Life in Music*. New York: Norton, 1982.

Rostand, Claude. *La Musique française contemporaine*. Paris: Presses Universitaires de France, 1952.

Roth, Jack. *The Cult of Violence: Sorel and the Sorelians*. Berkeley: University of California Press, 1980.

Roussel, Albert. *Lettres et écrits*. Ed. Nicole Labelle. Paris: Flammarion, 1987.

Rouvière, Balsan de la. "Le Conservatoire." *Revue musicale* (1911): 403–407.

Said, Edward W. *Musical Elaborations*. New York: Columbia University Press, 1991.

———— "Opponents, Audiences, Constituencies, and Commentary." *Critical Inquiry* Vol. 9/1 (Sept. 1982).

Saint-Saëns, Camille. *Outspoken Essays on Music*. Trans. Fred Rothwell. London: Kegan Paul, Trench, Trubner, 1922.

Saint-Saëns-Fauré. *Correspondence*. Ed. Jean-Michel Nectoux. Paris: Association des Amis de Gabriel Fauré, 1971.

Samazeuilh, Gustave. *Musiciens de mon temps: Chroniques et souvenirs*. Paris: Marcel Daubin, 1947.

Sapir, David J., and Christopher J. Crocker, eds. *The Social Use of Metaphor: Essays on the Anthropology of Rhetoric*. Philadelphia: University of Pennsylvania Press, 1977.

Sapir, Edward. *Anthropologie*. Vol. 1. *Culture et personalité*. Trans. Christian Baudelt and Pierre Clinquart. Paris: Minuit, 1967.

Satie, Erik. *Ecrits*. Ed. Ornella Volta. Paris: Champ Libre, 1981.

————. *Exposition organisée par la Bibliothèque Nationale*. Paris: Bibliothèque Nationale, 1966.

Schmitz, E. Robert. *The Piano Works of Claude Debussy*. New York: Dover, 1950.

Schorske, Carl E. *Fin-de-Siècle Vienna: Politics and Culture*. New York: Knopf, 1980.

Schorske, Carl E. "La Formation et l'évolution de Gustave Mahler." *Actes de la recherche en sciences sociales* Vol. 100 (Dec. 1993): 5–15.

————. "Revolt in Vienna." *New York Review of Books* Vol. 29 (May 1986): 24–28.

Schrade, Leo. *Beethoven in Paris*. New Haven, Conn.: Yale University Press, 1942.

Scott, John A. *Republican Ideas and the Liberal Tradition in France 1870–1914*. New York: Columbia University Press, 1951.

Sedgwick, Alexander. *The Ralliement in French Politics 1890–1898*. Cambridge: Harvard University Press, 1965.

Seigel, Jerrold. *Bohemian Paris: Culture, Politics, and the Boundaries of Bourgeois Life 1830–1930*. New York: Viking, 1986.

Selva, Blanche. *Quelque mots sur la sonate*. Paris: Paul Delaplane, 1914.

Séverac, Déodat de. "La Centralisation et les petites chapelles musicales." *Le Courrier musical* (Jan. 1908): 1–6; 37–43; 142–144.

Shapiro, Theda. *Painters and Politics: The European Avant-Garde and Society 1900–1925*. New York: Elsevier, 1976.

Shattuck, Roger. *The Banquet Years: The Origins of the Avant-Garde in France 1885 to World War I*. New York: Vintage, 1968.

————. "Catching Up with the Avant-Garde." *New York Review of Books* Dec. 18, 1986: 66–74.

————. *The Innocent Eye: On Modern Literature and the Arts*. New York: Washington Square Press, 1986.

Silver, Kenneth. *Esprit de Corps: The Art of the Parisian Avant-Garde and the First World War*. Princeton, N.J.: Princeton University Press, 1989.

Siohan, Robert. *Stravinsky*. Trans. Eric Walter White. New York: Grossman, 1970.

Sirinelli, Jean-François. *Intellectuels et passions françaises: Manifestes et petitions*. Paris: Fayard, 1990.

———. "Littérature et politique: Le Cas Burdeau-Bouteille." *Revue historique* Vol. 272/1 (1985): 91–111.

———, ed. *Histoire des droites*. Vol. 2. *Cultures*. Paris: Gallimard, 1992.

Slominsky, Nicolas. *Music since 1900*. New York: Schirmer, 1994.

Smith, Oivia. *The Politics of Language 1791–1819*. Oxford: Clarendon, 1984.

Société des Auteurs, Compositeurs, et Editeurs de Musique. *Maurice Ravel 1875–1975*. Paris: SACEM, 1975.

Sonn, Richard D. *Anarchism and Cultural Politics in Fin-de-Siècle France*. Lincoln: University of Nebraska Press, 1989.

Sorel, Georges. *La Révolution Dreyfusienne*. Paris: Librairie des Sciences Sociales, 1911.

Soucy, Robert. "Barrès and French Fascism." *French Historical Studies* Vol. 5/1 (Spring 1967): 67–97.

Speck, W. A. *Society and Literature in England 1700–1760*. London: Gill and Macmillan, 1983.

Spies, André. "French Opera during the Belle Epoque: A Study in the Social History of Ideas." Ph.D. Dissertation. University of North Carolina at Chapel Hill, 1986.

Starobinski, Jean. "La Littérature: La texte et l'interprete." In *Faire de l'histoire*, pp. 225–244. Ed. Jacques Le Goff and Pierre Nora. Paris: Gallimard, 1974.

Steegmuller, Francis. *Cocteau: A Biography*. Boston: Little, Brown, 1970.

Steinberg, Michael. *The Meaning of the Salzburg Festival: Austria as Theater and Ideology 1890–1938*. Ithaca, N.Y.: Cornell University Press, 1990.

Sternhell, Zeev. *The Birth of Fascist Ideology: From Cultural Rebellion to Political Revolution*. Trans. David Maisel. Princeton, N.J.: Princeton University Press, 1994.

———. *La Droite révolutionnaire*. Paris: Le Seuil, 1971.

———. *Maurice Barrès et le nationalisme français*. Paris: Armand Colin, 1972.

———. *Ni Droite ni Gauche: L'Idéologie fasciste en France*. Paris: Editions du Seuil, 1983.

Sterns, Peter N. *Revolutionary Syndicalism and French Labor: A Cause without Rebels*. New Brunswick, N.J.: Rutgers University Press, 1971.

Stone, Judith F. *Sons of the Revolution: Radical Democrats in France 1862–1914*. Baton Rouge: Louisiana State University Press, 1996.

Strohm, Rheinhard. "Dramatic Time and Operatic Form in Wagner's *Tannhäuser*." *Proceedings of the Royal Musical Association* (1977): 1–10.

Subotnik, Rose. "The Role of Ideology in the Study of Western Music." *Journal of Musicology* Vol. 2 (Winter 1983): 1–12.

Suleiman, Ezra N. *Politics, Power, and Bureaucracy in France: The Administrative Elite*. Princeton, N.J.: Princeton University Press, 1974.

Swart, Koenraad W. *The Sense of Decadence in Nineteenth-century France*. The Hague: Martins Nijhoff, 1964.

Tackett, Timothy. *Becoming a Revolutionary: The Deputies of the French National Assembly and the Emergence of a Revolutionary Culture (1789–1790)*. Princeton, N.J.: Princeton University Press, 1996.

Taine, Hippolyte. *The Ideal in Art*. New York: Holt and Williams, 1872.

———. *Philosophie de l'art*. Paris: Garmer Bailière, 1965.

Tannenbaum, Edward. *The Action Française: Die-hard Reactionaries in Twentieth-century France*. New York: Wiley, 1962.

Taruskin, Richard. "The Dark Side of Modern Music." *New Republic* (Sept. 5, 1988): 28–34.

Taylor, Una. *Maurice Maeterlinck: A Critical Study*. New York: Kennikat Press, 1968.

Templier, Pierre-Daniel. *Erik Satie*. Paris: Les Editions Rieder, 1932.

Thomson, Andrew. *The Life and Times of Charles-Marie Widor, 1844–1937*. New York: Oxford University Press, 1987.

———. *Vincent d'Indy and His World*. Oxford: Clarendon, 1997.

Tiersot, Julien. *Une Demi-siècle de musique française 1870–1914*. Paris: Felix Alcan, 1924.

Todorov, Tzventan. *Mikhail Bakhtine: Le Principe dialogique*. Paris: Editions du Seuil, 1981.

Toews, John E. "Intellectual History after the Linguistic Turn: The Autonomy of Meaning and the Irreducibility of Experience." *American Historical Review* Vol. 92/4 (Oct. 1987): 879–907.

Tosi, Guy. *Debussy et d'Annunzio: Correspondence inédite*. Paris: Denoel, 1948.

Touchard, Jean. *La Gauche en France depuis 1900*. Paris: Editions du Seuil, 1968.

Trillig, Johann. *Untersuchung zur Rezeption Claude Debussys in der zeitgenössischen Musikkritik*. Tutzing: Hans Schneider, 1983.

Vallas, Leon. *Claude Debussy et son temps*. Paris: Felix Alcan, 1932.

———. *Vincent d'Indy*. 2 Vols. Paris: Albin Michel, 1950.

Veeser, H. Aramm, ed. *The New Historicism*. New York: Routledge, 1989.

Vendler, Helen. "The Medley Is the Message." *New York Review of Books* (May 8, 1986): 44–50.

Vincens, Charles. "Wagner et Wagnérisme au point de vue français." In *Mémoires de l'Académie des Sciences, Lettres, et Beaux-Arts de Marseille*. Marseille: Barlatier, 1904.

Volta, Ornella. *Erik Satie*. Paris: Seghers, 1979.

———. *Erik Satie. Ecrits*. Paris: Editions Champ Libre, 1977.

———. "Le Rideau se lève sur un os." *Revue internationale de musique française* Vol. 23 (June 1987): 7–98.

Vuillermoz, Emile. *Claude Debussy*. Paris: Heugel, 1920.

———. "Le Dictionnaire." *Le Mercure musical* March 1, 1906 and June 15, 1906: 547–555.

———. *Musiques d'aujourd'hui*. Paris: G. Cres, 1923.

———. "La Schola et le Conservatoire." *Mercure de France* (1909): 234–243.

———. "Une Tasse de thé." *Le Mercure musicale* Vol. 15 (Nov. 1905): 505–510.

Weber, Edith, ed. *Debussy et l'évolution de la musique au XXe siècle*. Paris: Editions du Centre Nationale de la Recherche Scientifique, 1965.

Weber, Eugen. *Action Française: Royalism and Reaction in Twentieth-century France*. Stanford, Calif.: Stanford University Press, 1962.

———. *France: Fin-de-Siècle*. Cambridge, Mass.: Belknap Press, 1986.

———. *The Nationalist Revival in France 1905–1914*. Berkeley: University of California Press, 1959.

———. *Peasants into Frenchmen: The Modernization of Rural France 1870–1914*. Stanford, Calif: Stanford University Press, 1976.

Weber, Eugen, and Hans Rogger, eds. *The European Right: A Historical Profile*. Los Angeles: University of California Press, 1965.

Weber, William. *Music and the Middle Class: The Social Structure of Concert Life in London, Paris, and Vienna*. London: Crooms Helm, 1975.

———. *The Rise of Musical Classics in Eighteenth-century England: A Study in Canon, Ritual, and Ideology*. Oxford: Clarendon, 1992.

Weisz, George. *The Emergence of Modern Universities in France, 1863–1914*. Princeton, N.J.: Princeton University Press, 1983.

Wenk, Arthur. *Claude Debussy and the Poets*. Berkeley: University of California Press, 1976.

―――. *Claude Debussy and Twentieth-century Music.* Boston: Twayne, 1983.

Widor, Charles-Marie. *Fondations: Portraits de Massenet à Paladilhe.* Paris: J. Durand et fils, 1927.

Wilentz, Sean, ed. *Rites of Power: Symbolism, Ritual, and Politics since the Middle Ages.* Philadelphia: University of Pennsylvania Press, 1985.

Wilkins, Nigel, ed. and trans. *The Writings of Erik Satie.* London: Eulenburg Books, 1980.

Williams, Raymond. *Marxism and Literature.* Oxford: Oxford University Press, 1977.

Winock, Michel. *Edouard Drumont et Cie: Antisemitisme et fascism en France.* Paris: Le Seuil, 1982.

―――, ed. *Histoire de l'extreme droite en France.* Paris: Le Seuil, 1993.

Winspur, Steven. "The Pragmatic Force of Lyric." Paper delivered at the conference on "Mallarmé: Music, Art, and Letters." Indiana University, 1994.

Winzer, Dieter. *Claude Debussy und die französische musikalische Tradition.* Wiesbaden: Breitkopf und Härtel, 1981.

Wohl, Robert. *The Generation of 1914.* Cambridge: Harvard University Press, 1979.

Woldu, Gail Hilson. "Gabriel Fauré as Director of the Conservatoire National de Musique et de Déclamation, 1905–1920." Ph.D. Dissertation. Yale University, 1983.

―――. "Gabriel Fauré, directeur du Conservatoire: les réformes de 1905." *Revue de musicologie* Vol. 70/2 (1984): 119–228.

Wright, Gordon. *France in Modern Times.* New York: Rand McNally, 1974.

Wuthnow, Robert. *Communities of Discourses: Ideology and Social Structure in the Reformation, the Enlightenment, and European Socialism.* Cambridge: Harvard University Press, 1989.

Zakone, Constant. "Les Ennemies de la Schola." *Revue musicale* Vol. 1 (Feb. 1905): 83.

Zammito, John. "Are We Being Theoretical Yet? The New Historicism, the Philosophy of History, and Practicing Historians." *Journal of Modern History* Vol. 65/4 (Dec. 1993): 783–814.

Zeldin, Theodore. *France 1848–1945.* Oxford: Clarendon, 1973.

Zévaés, Alexandre. *L'Affaire Dreyfus.* Paris: Editions de la Nouvelle Revue Critique, 1931.

Zola, Emile. *Oeuvres completes.* No. 40. *La République en marche II. Chroniques parlementaires 19 septembre 1871-4 mai 1872.* Paris: Fasquelles, 1969.

―――. *La République et la littérature.* Paris: G. Charpentier, 1879.

―――. *Le Rêve.* Paris: Garnier-Flammarion, 1975.

―――. *Le Roman experimental.* Paris: Garnier-Flammarion, 1971.

―――. *La Vérité en marche.* Paris: Bibliothèque Charpentier, 1901.

Index